THE CRAFT OF
PUBLIC
ADMINISTRATION

Sixth Edition

GEORGE BERKLEY

University of Massachusetts

JOHN ROUSE

Ball State University

 Brown &
Benchmark
PUBLISHERS

Madison, Wisconsin • Dubuque, Iowa

Book Team

Executive Editor *Michael Lange*
Editor *Roger Wolkoff*
Developmental Editor *Steven Lehman*
Production Editor *Diane Clemens*
Visuals/Design Developmental Consultant *Marilyn A. Phelps*
Visuals/Design Freelance Specialist *Mary L. Christianson*
Marketing Manager *Steven Yetter*
Advertising Manager *Brett Apold*

Brown & Benchmark

A Division of Wm. C. Brown Communications, Inc.

Executive Vice President/General Manager *Thomas E. Doran*
Vice President/Editor in Chief *Edgar J. Laube*
Vice President/Sales and Marketing *Eric Ziegler*
Director of Production *Vickie Putman Caughron*
Director of Custom and Electronic Publishing *Chris Rogers*

Wm. C. Brown Communications, Inc.

President and Chief Executive Officer *G. Franklin Lewis*
Corporate Senior Vice President and Chief Financial Officer *Robert Chesterman*
Corporate Senior Vice President and President of Manufacturing *Roger Meyer*

Copyright © 1984, 1981, 1978, 1975 by Allyn & Bacon, Inc.

Copyright © 1988, 1991, 1994 by Wm. C. Brown Communications,
Inc. All rights reserved

A Times Mirror Company

Library of Congress Catalog Card Number: 93–71536

ISBN 0–697–12705–2

Printed in the United States of America by Wm. C. Brown Communications, Inc.,
2460 Kerper Boulevard, Dubuque, IA 52001

10 9 8 7 6 5 4 3 2 1

☆ ☆ ☆

CONTENTS

PREFACE

The Craft of Public Administration is not just a textbook; it is a pedagogical gathering of pertinent yet limited literature, assembled to inform and interest college students in the dynamics of the public, or government, sector in the United States. The literature is limited because we choose not to write a book that is "everything one wants to know about public administration but is afraid to ask." Local, state, regional, and federal governments are too overwhelming and far reaching to attempt a dictionary approach to the field.

In order to comprehend projected federal government spending of more than $1.5 trillion in 1996 (state and local government spending not included), the literature of public administration is divided into four pedagogical segments:

• *federalism* (craft of public administration, relationships to economic development, political and bureaucratic culture, the structure of politics, partisan, policy, and systems politics, equality, efficiency, synergy, formal organization, human relations). Chapters 1 through 4 focus upon the structure of American politics, or issues of U.S. federalism. Chapter 1 concerns *The Administrative Craft*; Chapter 2 deals with *The Ecology of the Administrative Craft*; Chapter 3 investigates *The Anatomy of Public Organization*; Chapter 4 studies *The Physiology of Organization*.

• *public personnel administration* (people, patronage, merit, equal opportunity, affirmative action, job classifications, labor relations, leadership, charisma, communication, technology). Chapters 5 through 8 address matters of public personnel administration. Chapter 5 explores *People and Personnel*; Chapter 6 reviews *Public Unionism*; Chapter 7 develops the role of *Leadership*; Chapter 8 relates the importance of *Communication* in government bureaucracies.

• *budgets* (taxing, appropriations, spending, productivity, efficiency, effectiveness, motivation, privatization of government functions, planning, program evaluation). Chapters 9 and 10 examine priorities of taxing, budgeting, spending, productivity, and program evaluation. Chapter 9 addresses *Taxing, Budgeting, and Spending* and points out how partisan, policy, and systems politics impact the likelihood of higher taxes but fewer government programs and services. Chapter 10 probes *The Productivity Challenge* and outlines the pressures for government employees to do more with less resources.

• *regulations* (administrative law, administrative controls, administrative law judges, ethics, discretion, rules, procedures, administrative responsibility, administrative state, clientele relations). Chapters 11 and 12 explain adminsitrative law, clientele relations, and government regulations. Chapter 11 outlines issues of *Administrative Law and Control* and describes the impact of administrative growth on democratic ideals, outlines traditional and contemporary cornerstones of American administrative law, notes the expanding role of administrative law judges, and probes how much law and control is enough. Chapter 12 develops the impacts of *Clientele Pressures and Regulatory Behaviors* and illustrates how economic, social, and subsidiary regulations are affected by administrative rules and rule-making.

The narrative and case studies are presented in such a way as to allow students to learn from analyzing the literature in conjunction with specific illustrations. Case studies force us to think about how the general (literature) affects the particular (case study) and how specific illustrations amend our perceptions of public administration literature. Examination of case study facts brings out the dynamic nature of the literature.

Public administration constitutes the "chemistry" of the United States. The two key principles that have come to embody the American ideal, equality and efficiency, are likewise the crucial determinants of how well the public, or government, sector functions in the United States. Democratic capitalism does not flourish if public infrastructures, such as schools, highways, institutions of public safety, and similar taxpayer funded government operations are devalued and rendered ineffective. Public sector functions, programs, and activities represent the "bottom line" expectations which society guarantees all citizens. The domestic and military spending priorities of the 1980s have forced public administration as a field to be more accountable, adjust to economic realities, and evolve in unforseen ways. The field is dynamic. The efficacy of *The Craft of Public Administration* depends upon people *effectively* relating to other people in the exchange of partisan, policy, and systems politics.

Professors Berkley and Rouse encourage feedback from professors and students on the effectiveness of *The Craft of Public Adminstration.* Your contributions will make future editions of this text reflect the dynamic "chemistry" of U.S. life as it is played out in everyday relations between the "equality" of government programs and services and the "efficiency" of private opportunities.

Acknowledgments

As principal author of the Sixth Edition of *The Craft of Public Administration*, I wish to express my thanks and appreciation to:
• George Berkley, author of the first four editions of this textbook, for the opportunity to co-author the Fifth Edition and this edition;
• Ed Laube, Roger Wolkoff, Steve Lehman, Tom Riley, and Diane Clemens of Brown & Benchmark Publishers, for their encouragement and feedback on the development and evaluation of various stages of the writing and production;
• Ray Scheele, Chairman and Professor, Department of Political Science, Ball State University, for his leadership in promoting a working environment conducive to integrating the tasks of teaching and research;
• Laurel Canan, Graduate Assistant in the Department of Political Science, Ball State University, for her proofreading and evaluation of the manuscript;
• faculty colleagues in the Department of Political Science, Ball State University, for creating an atmosphere where consensus is valued and productivity is recognized;
• Sharon Hinkley and Stephanie Thomas, administrative assistants to Chairman Scheele, who facilitated in many ways with telephone calls, faxes, and photo copying;
• employees of the more than 80,000 units of government in the United States, whose craft constitutes the challenges of federalism, personnel, budgets, and government regulations;
• thousands of Ball State University graduate and undergraduate students, past and present, who continually force me to think and rethink the dynamics of the public sector in the United States;
• Edward Baum, Professor of Political Science, Ohio University, for soliciting feedback from students in his public administration classes concerning likes, dislikes, and suggested changes for this edition;
• the generous taxpayers of the State of Indiana, my employer, for access to a professional career which bridges the worlds of partisan, policy, and systems politics with the rich and varied literature of public administration; and
• Barbara Maves, my wife and executive director of a government funded, not-for-profit East Central Indiana health care agency, which daily confronts the ever-present challenges of the craft of public administration.

These contributions in many ways enhanced my research and writing of this edition of *The Craft of Public Administration*.

John Rouse

1

☆ ☆ ☆

THE ADMINISTRATIVE CRAFT

The words *public administration* express a concept that at first glance may seem abstract and nondescript. However, a closer look at the phrase helps take away the ambiguity.

Public simply means the citizens of a given area—the people of a town, county, state or country. If an issue is considered in the public domain, information and discussion about that issue are open to, or shared by, the people, and can be generally known to all. The word *public* also refers to activities administered by the state in the name of the entire community. Public administrators serve the people.

Organized collectives of citizens constitute a variety of public communities in the United States. These publicly organized communities include national, state, and local governments. They include townships, state recreation areas and public utilities. They include school, sanitary, and water districts. There are also public libraries, public parks, public defenders (police, fire, legal), public roadways, and, of course, public servants.

In the event of war, citizens may be called upon to make the ultimate sacrifice to the national community—their lives. However, in peace time, Americans are required only to pay taxes and obey the laws. When April 15 rolls around, citizens have that one definitive economic opportunity to be patriotic by meeting their financial obligation to society. The one thing that all public programs have in common is the fact that they are financed by taxpayers, most of whom want a voice in how those dollars are spent.

The breakdown of government employees is 16 percent federal, 23.6 percent state, and 60.4 percent local. In 1992, there were 2,975,000 federal, 4,381,000 state, and 11,228,000 local government employees in the US, or a total of 18,584,000 government employees. Americans who want smaller government with fewer services numbers 42 percent while 43 percent call for larger government with more services.[1]

So, as we study *public administration*, the abstract, nondescript, colorless images of public bureaucracies will fade away. They will be replaced by more concrete concerns about the development, evaluation, and implementation of how we spend our tax dollars.

Such decisions are usually political decisions. A major function of politics is to allocate importance to numerous and often conflicting values in society. Public administration is the process of implementing those diverse values in our complex and ever-changing society and therefore plays a vital role in the daily lives of all citizens.

THE HEART OF THE MATTER

In a classic textbook, Herbert Simon, Donald Smithburg, and Victor Thompson define *administration* simply but graphically in this opening sentence: "When two men cooperate to roll a stone that neither could have moved alone, the rudiments of administration have appeared."[2] That illustrates much about what administration is and what it is not.

The first and foremost ingredient of administration is *people*. A stone by itself on a hill is not involved in any form of administration. If that stone rolls down the hill by some act of nature, administration is not involved. People have to be present before administration can take place.

The second ingredient of administration is *action*. Two people looking at the stone are not, in that act alone, involved in administration. They must take some action regarding the stone before administration can enter the picture. There is no such thing as inactive administration (although many who have dealt with administrative agencies sometimes believe otherwise).

The third ingredient is *interaction*. If one person moves the stone, administration does not occur. At least two must combine their efforts in some way to move the stone in order for the activity to involve administration. The essence of administration is *people relating to other people*.

People interacting with other people to accomplish tasks—this is what administration is about, although obviously not all activity involving human interaction can bear the label "administration." The line that separates administration from other types of human interaction often becomes blurred.

For example, a biology class lecture is not, in itself, a form of administration. The students are there to obtain a product and the professor is there to dispense that product. Consequently, the students, as learners, are no more engaged in an administrative relationship with their teacher than department store customers are with a sales clerk.

But if the professor and students undertake a joint project, such as investigating pollution levels in a nearby river and reporting the results to the state legislature, the relationship changes. Now they are *mutually* involved in an endeavor, and their joint activity is an essential part of all administration.

This joint activity need not be voluntary. A young man may be drafted against his will into the army. He may be sent, even more unwillingly, to a foreign base. Yet, in performing whatever role he is assigned, he is participating in administration. Like it or not, he is involved with others in the common effort to maintain the nation's security.

To sum up, administration is a process involving human beings jointly engaged in working toward common goals. Administration thus covers many, if not most, of the more exciting activities that take place in human society.

ART, SCIENCE, OR CRAFT?

The title of this book clearly proposes that administration is a craft. Why this classification instead of another? Why should we not consider administration a science or an art?

Science is characterized by precision and predictability. A scientific rule is one that works all the time. As a matter of fact, rules in science are so rigid and final that they are not called rules at all, but laws. Two parts of hydrogen combined with one part of oxygen will *always* give us water—or steam, or ice, depending on the temperature.

While it is true that some sciences, particularly the social sciences, do not achieve such a 100 percent predictability level, it is also true that any scientific theory must stand up to rigorous, repeated tests to be considered valid.

Administration uses scientific data, laws, and theories. An obvious example is the use of mathematics and computers to keep a public agency's financial records. But administration in itself is not a science.

Although administrators use scientific laws, techniques, and data, they do so in ways that allow free rein to individual imagination and temperament. Usually a variety of successful solutions exist for dealing with a particular administrative problem, and a creative administrator may even devise a new solution on the spot. Administrative problems are rarely identical and it is impossible to derive scientific equations that work the same way every time for such problems.

Administration shares traits with the arts as well as the sciences. Administrators often work in highly imaginative ways, employing a mix of methods, including intuition. Like painters and composers, administrators often find their own moods and personalities reflected in their work.

There is, however, a vital difference that keeps administration from being characterized as an art: Artists create works of aesthetics; administrators attempt to solve problems. The respective end products and the criteria for evaluating them differ as a result.

Since public administration shares traits with both science and art, categorizing the field as one or the other obviously paints an incomplete picture. There is, however, a category more suitable than these—or at least more comfortable and workable. That category is *craft*.

Let us assume a city is divided for the purpose of trash collection into two distinct and equal districts. One team of sanitation workers under an assistant sanitation commissioner is assigned to each section with the objective of keeping the streets clean. One of the assistant commissioners may choose to have his or her people work straight eight-hour shifts five days a week. The other may choose to bunch the efforts of his or her crew at key times in the week and work them for longer periods of time on fewer days. One may try to improve the conditions of work by conducting a promotional campaign designed to persuade the residents of his or her section to switch from garbage cans to plastic bags. The other may deem it more fruitful to ask the police to crack down on litter under the street litter law. One may offer his or her workers extra inducements if they do their jobs successfully, while the other may hold out to his or her crew the prospect of more time off for a job well done.

The way each team works may differ, depending on the personalities of the administrative leaders, the personalities of the workers, and a variety of other factors. In every case however, an objective standard exists for comparing the relative efficiency of each: Which team produces cleaner streets?

In the example above, and in most administrative situations, an objective standard lurks somewhere. This standard—however objective—is often shadowy, elusive, and hard to apply. At the same time, there is never a precise formula that will invariably work best in all situations. Not only do situations vary, but ideas for handling them are almost as infinite as the human mind. The objective standard, lack of precise formula, changing situations, and problem solving are all traits that best fall under the classification of craft.

Another example will further support the contention that administration may be more easily categorized as a craft rather than as an art or science.

As the New Deal was reaching its height, Harry Hopkins and Harold Ickes emerged as Franklin Roosevelt's most valued and trusted aides. Each man was given a substantial chunk of the federal public works and relief programs to administer. As they acquired power, however, they became increasingly suspicious and jealous of each other. Word of their growing rivalry and animosity soon leaked out, causing their respective partisans or opponents in the government, in the press, and in the public to leap to their attack or defense. Washington was abuzz with rumors of the feud, and the fact that so many people were choosing sides was producing disruption throughout the government.

The situation placed Roosevelt in a quandary. If he fired or encouraged the resignation of either man, he would not only lose a tried-and-tested aide but would also alienate and antagonize the aide's admirers and supporters. On the other hand, if Roosevelt issued a statement denying the feud, he would only succeed in acknowledging and giving credence to the rumors. Here was an administrator with a problem.

Roosevelt decided to solve his problem by embarking on one of his famous conservation tours and taking both Hopkins and Ickes with him. For nine days and nights the trio wound their way by train and automobile through the American countryside, inspecting dam sites, forestry projects, and other New Deal undertakings. At every opportunity, Roosevelt lavished public praise on his two associates and played up their importance in his administration. And every night he sat down with both of them for a poker game.

By the time the presidential party arrived back in Washington, the rumors of the feud were dissolving. The steady stream of news and pictures of the men standing shoulder to shoulder had worked. And, in fact, the two men appeared to have ended the junket on much better terms. One administrator had solved a pressing problem.

OUR LOVE-HATE RELATIONSHIP WITH GOVERNMENT

"Broadly speaking, President Clinton's nemesis is the modern welfare state. By welfare state, I mean something beyond the usual narrow concept: government as helper of the poor. The modern welfare state differs radically from that. It touches all of us, providing us with benefits of various types and claiming a huge part of our incomes. It creates a vast web of dependency on government that is the ultimate source of huge budget deficits and, quite perversely, distrust of government.

. . . we have no public philosophy by which to judge government. By public philosophy, I mean widely shared beliefs about what government should—and should not—do. . . . In an arithmetic sense, the budget deficits result from our over-optimistic economic assumptions and a loose concept of government . . . But in a larger sense, the deficits stem from an inadequate public philosophy. We lack the popular consensus that would enable the political process to cut some spending programs—because they're not deemed worthy of government support—and raise taxes to cover the rest. . . .

Sooner or later, we need to come to terms with the welfare state. We need more rigorous standards for judging whose welfare is being advanced, and why. As it is now, the welfare state is too big and intertwined in our social fabric for conservatives to dismantle. But it is too expensive and unpopular for liberals to expand endlessly. The irony is that the welfare state arose in the 1930s as an antidote to the insecurities of free markets. More than 50 years later, it has itself become a wellspring of anxiety and contention."

Source: Robert J. Samuelson, "Clinton's Nemesis," *Newsweek*, Vol. 121, No. 5 (February 1, 1993), page 51; "Our Love-Hate Relationship with Government," *The Washington Post*, January 27, 1993, page A19.

Roosevelt used a great deal of artistry and imagination in dealing with this situation. Yet he was not creating a work of art; he was resolving a difficult problem. He was not acting as a scientist because what he did would not lend itself to concrete formulation. His solution, although it might provide some ideas for other administrators in similar dilemmas, certainly does not provide an all-embracing equation.

Public administration, then, requires a mixture of artistic and scientific elements. It uses artistry but is not an art. It uses science but is not a science. It is more properly thought of as a craft, seeking to achieve goals and to meet standards, and in so doing, often demanding all the creativity and capability that its harried practitioners can muster. In the administrative state of the mid-1990s, the challenges of the craft of public administration are more demanding than ever before.

PARTISAN POLITICS, POLICY POLITICS, AND SYSTEM POLITICS

Three of the dynamic forces at work in our organized society are partisan politics, policy politics, and system politics.

Partisan politics is concerned with which political party wins office. Policy politics deals with deciding which policies to adopt. And system politics examines how administrative systems (decision structures) are set up.[3]

Public administration emphasizes two of the three forms of politics: policy and system politics. However, it originates from partisan politics.

Unemployment compensation and the Strategic Defense Initative (SDI) originated as Democratic and Republican partisan issues, respectively. Although unemployment compensation is a core Democratic Party issue, Republicans accept some version of compensation as a legitimate policy. Members of both parties argue over what particular unemployment policy may best be implemented by the Department of Labor. Although SDI is a core Republican party issue, Democrats accept the notion that the country needs a strong defense. Members of both parties argue over what particular defense policy may best be implemented by the Department of Defense. Therefore, unemployment and defense are partisan, policy, and system issues.

Meanwhile, Social Security is mainly a policy and system issue. Social Security is usually not hotly debated in an election campaign because most politicians from both political parties accept the necessity of Social Security. Social Security itself is not a partisan issue. But the policy and system issues that arise from social security do cause heated debates. Policy politics, which provides the means for carrying out the strategic utilization of resources to alleviate problems, is an integral part of public administration.

In a nutshell, the intertwining of partisan, policy, and system politics works like this: Citizens elect political partisans to public office; partisans establish regulatory, distributive, redistributive, and constituent policies; administrative systems implement policies adopted by partisans.

System politics is the core of public administration.

WHO'S IN CHARGE OF CENTRAL PARK?

Partisan, policy, and system politics are not separate, exclusive applications of the craft in practice. Politics to many is the "touchy, feely stuff" — the intangible relations among cronies, the ever-changing ways of doing the public's business. Things political may not mirror system accountability because in a public system everyone is accountable, and yet practically no one is.

Central Park in New York City is a public park. Located in the middle of Manhattan, the park runs from 59th Street to 110th Street, from 5th Avenue to 8th Avenue. In the midst of some of the most expensive private real estate in the world, the park somehow survives the marketplace values of New York City. Central Park affords the citizens of New York a wide variety of playgrounds, bicycle paths, wooded areas, jogging paths, swimming pools, picturesque lakes, and other natural scenery. The facilities of Central Park are offered to the public on a first come, first served basis.

But who's in charge of Central Park? Are the politicians in charge? Are the police in charge? Or are the bureaucrats from the parks department in charge? These kinds of questions demonstrate the subtleties of how politics shapes life in the public sector.

Similar analogies may be made to federal lands, state parks, and municipal buildings. So who is really responsible for the upkeep of the facilities of Central Park? In a general sense, the people of New York are responsible. In a more direct way, the New York parks department, the police, and the mayor are responsible since they are the custodians of this public interest.

Whereas the concept of political responsibility is often abstract, administrative aspects such as hierarchy, chain of command, unity of command, span of control, due process, regulations, rules, and even bureaucratic ineptness are more definitive and recognizable by citizens. Politics, in its varied definitions, may be vague to many citizens; on the other hand, citizens have concrete experiences with bureaucracies.

How is the study of public bureaucracy different from the study of elections, executives, legislatures, or the courts? The study of bureaucracy focuses upon obeying authority; the study of elections, executives, legislatures, or the courts relates to the institutionalizing of democratic values. The study of public administration tells us what actually happens to policies after enactment by legislatures and approval by executives. Decisions by government officials, representing departments and agencies, reflect the policy and system politics that occur in public bureaucracies. Such decisions are monitored by political partisans within the framework of majority rule and minority rights.

LEGALISM

On a visit to the United States in 1830, France's Count Alexis de Tocqueville was startled by the prominence of lawyers and the predominance of legal processes here. He noted with amazement how in the United States nearly every political issue of importance ends up in a courtroom.

This tendency has not abated, but instead has accelerated in the century and a half since de Tocqueville's visit. Today the country harbors two-thirds

ONE MILLION LAWYERS

The American Bar Association expects a 34 percent increase in attorneys in the decade of the 1990s, from 748,028 in 1990 to one million lawyers by the year 2000. The paralegal industry is also on the rise, with expected growth of 85 percent between 1990 and 2005.

Source: *The Wall Street Journal,* January 21, 1992, Section B, page 11.

of all the world's lawyers, while its courts have extended their reach into virtually all areas of political life. Judges now decide not only major policy disputes but also minor details of policy execution. The 1970s saw a federal judge in Boston determine how many basketballs a local high school may have, and another federal judge in Alabama determined the right temperature for hot water in a state mental hospital. In no other land do the bench and bar figure so formidably in the workings of everyday life.

The consequences of this state of affairs for public managers are both many and great. Public administration by its very nature enjoys, or suffers (depending on one's point of view), a close relationship with the law. Laws set up public agencies, prescribe and proscribe agency activities, and supply agencies with resources. Today, the relationship has become much closer. David Baselon notes that "as the constitutional right to due process of law expands, more and more administrators will find themselves locked into an involuntary partnership with the courts."[4]

For most administrators that time has already arrived.

For most of them the partnership is not only involuntary but unpleasant. Although at times they look to and depend on the courts to help them dispose of disruptive issues or to back them up on controversial matters, in most instances they view the court's role in their affairs from a quite different perspective. To the average administrator, the increasing legalization of the U.S. policy has meant harassment and hindrance in the fulfillment of administrative responsibilities.

One need not range very far or wide to find reasons for such sentiments. The hiring and firing of employees, the purchase of equipment, the adoption or even adjustment of a simple operational guideline have all produced costly and frustrating litigation. To activist administrators, the law and its practitioners often seem to exist merely to tie their hands.

Aggravating the problem for many public administrators is the fact that their craft is becoming increasingly result-oriented. This contrasts sharply with the legalistic approach, which stresses the correctness of procedure. To the legal mind, justice is not a product but a process.[5]

Public administrators rely on, and are vulnerable to, the law. Legalism in general, and laws in particular, tend to limit and influence the operation of a public institution much more than they do a private one. "This pervasive legal context is among the principal distinctions between public and private enterprise," note John M. Pfiffner and Robert Presthus. "In private management one is assured that he can do anything not specifically forbidden. In public administration, on the other hand, discretion is limited by a great number of laws, rules, and regulations."[6] To put it more succinctly, in private administration the law generally tells administrators only what they *cannot* do; in public administration, the law tells them what they *can* do.

This amplified preoccupation of public administration with the law is manifested in various ways. For example, a young campaign aide to a New England politician seeking high state office was horrified when he learned that the campaign committee had decided to make cash payments to local newspaper reporters in return for favorable publicity for the candidate. To the aide, this was rank corruption. However, there was nothing criminal in what was being done. The newspaper reporters were not working for a public institution but for a private one. It was up to the newspaper itself to determine whether or not it would allow its employees to accept fees from political candidates for "public relations services." What the reporters were doing may not have been ethical in terms of their profession, but neither they nor those who were paying them were committing an illegal act. However, similar behavior by public employees would, in most jurisdictions, violate a conflict-of-interest law, and disclosure could result in the employees not only being dismissed from their jobs but even prosecuted.[7]

Most newspaper reporters, of course, do not accept payoffs. But even so, their conduct often varies greatly from what we expect from public employees. News concerning socially prominent people receives much greater attention than the comings and goings of the less-well-off. While this can be justified to some extent in terms of reader interest, the discrepancy often far exceeds justifiable limits. Even the newspaper's book review editor could be heavily influenced by personal contacts and approaches in determining which of the 45,000 books published annually will be reviewed. Thus, a newspaper that is vigorous and sincere in ferreting out and denouncing corruption in government can be committing numerous acts every day that, if done by a public agency, would bring the wrath of the community upon itself and land its officials and employees in jail.

This discussion of the discrepancy between the way newspapers behave and the way public agencies are expected to behave is not intended to show the venality of the former but the vulnerability of the latter. A much more ethical and impartial pattern of behavior is expected and demanded from a public organization than from a private one. If the laws that govern the acts of public institutions were applied to private institutions, most of the management and staff of the latter would end up behind bars.

The legal limitations placed on public agencies contribute to or create many of the other differences between them and private enterprise. As we have already illustrated, government organizations must usually operate in a goldfish bowl, subject to scrutiny from politicians, the public, and the press. They must generally be ready to open their doors and their books to virtually any outsider, even though the outsider's interest in the agency may be prompted by no more than idle curiosity.

There are, of course, exceptions to this rule. The Central Intelligence Agency does not maintain an open-door policy for anyone who wishes to examine its records and find out what the agency is up to around the world. The Department of Defense rarely reveals the details of its troop deployments, particularly during a war. On the local scene, a police department may not choose to open its files on a current investigation, and a welfare agency may refuse to make public the names and circumstances of particular clients. Nevertheless, while many exceptions and qualifications exist, public agencies are expected to be much more open to public inspection and public investigation than are private ones.

The legal context within which the public sector functions also helps explain why its employees usually enjoy greater rights—and face greater obligations. Public employees benefit in many ways from the legal restrictions and restraints that are customarily imposed upon government operations. Their jobs are more secure, their pensions and perquisites are more certain, and their paths to promotion are more stable. Like most of the benefits of public administration, however, these are mixed blessings. If the risks faced by public employees are fewer, then so are their rewards. They often experience fewer opportunities for rapid advancement, rotation, and incentive for individual initiative than do their counterparts in the private sector.

What is true for the employees is likely to be true for the organization. Public agencies frequently possess less flexibility than private ones. They find it much harder to shift direction, change procedures, and revamp operations. Firmly entangled in a tight web of legality, public organizations must typically follow prescribed procedures and aim at traditional targets.

Underlying this state of affairs is the greater need of the public organization to hold itself accountable. Its obligations extend not just to a particular group of shareholders or sponsors but to the public at large. It is not allowed to do simply what it wants, how it wants. It is rather supposed to do what the public wants, in ways that the public or its elected representatives have decreed. Responsiveness and responsibility—these are held forth and hailed as the hallmarks of public administration in a democratic society.

One must not, of course, overlook the benefits that may, at least occasionally, result from the increasing legalization of the administrative process. Explosive issues often become defused when shifted to the legal system. Citizens are protected from abuses of authority. Politicians and administrators are constrained from acting rashly and without due regard for the rights of others. Still, those who would toil in the vineyards of the public sector must bear in mind that they labor under the scrutiny of more than just their superiors. What they do and, more important perhaps, how they do it, can easily get them ensnared in the coils of the law.

THE CRAFT AND THE AMERICAN POLITICAL SYSTEM

The craft of public administration is influenced by factors other than partisan, policy, and system politics and legalism. Our republican form of government, federalism, separation of powers, and constitutionalism—all of which will be discussed below—help put the craft into a larger perspective. Much is said pejoratively about public bureaucrats and their perceived power to operate without constraints in the American political system. However, a public administrator receives his or her authority for administrative decision making to certain constitutional principles. What are these constitutional principles?

C. Herman Pritchett cites four constitutional principles—embodied in the document signed September 17, 1787—which influence the lives of Americans every day.[8] First, the Constitution established a *republican* form of government. Many Americans hold on to their grade school conceptions of democracy in America, believing that we have a democratic form of government. We do, indeed, have a democratic philosophy of government; however, the structure of our government is republican. What *is* a republican form of government? Simply stated, we send representatives—legislators and executives to city hall, the general assembly, Congress, the governor's mansion, and the White House—since it would be impractical for all citizens to vote and decide public policy on every issue. Although Article IV of the Constitution guarantees "a republican form of government," the definition thereof was left open-ended for future generations of Americans. Democratic values characterize our system of periodic elections; however, once elected, politicians select administrative leaders, utilizing values of bureaucracy—like specialization, hierarchy, chain of command, authority, and so on—to get legislative mandates implemented by public and private organizations. Elected leaders, employing bureaucratic values, administer the collective will of a certain community of citizens, who may reside in a municipality, a state, or the nation.

The Constitution also created a *federal* system. The original U.S. government set up in 1776 was a confederation, or a mere league of states in which each state retained its sovereign powers. Under the auspices of the 1787 Constitutional Convention in Philadelphia, the delegates formed a stronger central government that was to receive its authority from the people. Powers not transferred to the new national government were to be retained by the states. As the cornerstone of the U.S. governmental system, federalism encompassed a two-level structure of government that divided power between the central government and state governments, allocating independent authority to respective levels. The federal concept contributed to the eventual organization of Congress. The larger states, represented by Virginia, Massachusetts, and Pennsylvania, saw an advantage to the new political system. The smaller states, led by New Jersey, fearing the political reorganization, sought protection of their interests. By a narrow vote, the Convention agreed to equal state representation in the U.S. Senate with senators to be elected by the state legislatures. The House of Representatives, on the other hand, would be elected directly by the people with its membership proportionate to the population of each state. The 17th Amendment, which was ratified in 1913, transferred the franchise for electing U.S. senators to the people of the respective states.

The condition of U.S. federalism has been altered by political conflicts and economic crises. The Civil War ended the political aspirations of those who had wanted a confederate political system, and the economic collapse of the 1930s brought down a dual form of federalism where states had been somewhat independent of the central government. Events culminating in the 1860s (Civil War) and 1930s (economic collapse) can be seen as signposts for a more centralized American political economy for the 1990s. The Civil War was a crisis in federalism, as its effects caused the influence of the states and political decentralization to decline. The Great Depression of the 1930s was also a crisis in federalism, as the effects of such an economic collapse resulted in the central government's intervention on behalf of the private economy.

Both the Civil War and the economic depression had centralizing effects upon federalism. The federal government's influence expanded, as did the expertise, skills, and knowledge of public administrators. Contrary to what the name implies, the United States are far from united on matters of politics and economics. A lack of consensus among Americans concerning political economy produces a corresponding lack of agreement on the development, implementation, and evaluation of public administration. Our political culture promotes diversity, not consensus. Federalism, then, is the structure of politics in the U.S.

The Constitution also advocates the *separation-of-powers* principle. Each branch of government is assigned a particular task: Congress makes the law, the executive branch administers the law, and the judicial system enforces and interprets the law. The separation-of-powers concept operates in tandem with the goal of limited government powers. Separation-of-powers doctrine restrains one branch from usurping the powers of the others; the limitation of government powers inhibits the national government from overpowering the rights of the states and restricts the intrusion of government into private lives. A system of checks and balances enables each branch to have some influence on the operation of the others. Congress regulates the kinds of cases to be heard by the Supreme Court and the Senate ratifies treaties and approves executive appointments. The president appoints federal judges and vetos laws, but the Senate must approve of his judicial appointments. The courts pass judgment on the validity of executive acts and interpret congressional statutes. With these checks and balances in place, abuse of power is less likely.

Finally, basic to the concepts of republicanism, federalism, and separation-of-powers is the idea of *constitutionalism* itself. Constitutionalism includes such ideas as rule of law, representative institutions, and guaranteed individual liberty. Two important elements of American constitutionalism are majority rule and minority rights. What happens when people disagree? The answer customarily given is "majority rule." It is here, however, that we must exercise caution. If 51 percent of the people voted to put the other 49 percent into concentration camps, we would hardly call this an exercise in democracy.

When we think therefore of constitutional democracy in American political culture, we must think not only of majority rule, but also of minority rights. This tenuous balance between the wishes of the majority and the rights of the few complicates democracy enormously, especially for public sector managers who must carry out the majority's mandate while simultaneously safeguarding basic minority interests. Public administration in a democratic society is a delicate and difficult task, requiring its practitioners to possess generous amounts of tolerance and tact. Those lacking such capacities may well do better in other fields.

President Clinton's proposed economic plans, for example, illustrate the roles of majority and minority. Numerically the Democrats have the votes in Congress. In the Senate, the leadership needs at least 3 GOP Senators to reach 60 in order to cut off debate. As the loyal opposition, the minority has responsibilities to offer amendments to the suggested programs of the majority.

As previously emphasized, public administration utilizes art and science, but is especially a craft. Considering public administration's grounding in constitutional principles incorporating both majority rule and minority rights, the use of the term *craft* to refer to public administration is both appropriate and realistic. With both the limitations and diversity of constitutional guidelines, public administrators need to be "crafty." In constitutional terms, then, public bureaucrats exercise power within the framework of a republican form of government, a federal system, the separation-of-powers principle, and constitutionalism itself.

Federalism is the basis of the American constitutional system and American public administration. A constitution is federal when two levels of government rule the same land and people. Each level must have at least one area of action in which it is autonomous. There is some guarantee of

---

POLLING AMERICAN PUBLIC OPINION

In a 1992 public opinion poll evaluating the American political process, five percent state that the process is working well as is, 41 percent say the process is working only OK and needs some changes; 38 percent insist that the process is not working well and needs major changes, and 16 percent conclude the process is not working at all and needs a complete overhaul.

The behavior of the voters in the 1992 presidential primaries has remained consistent with polls, focus groups and door-to-door interviews that showed they were worried about the economy, fearful about the future of the country, and frustrated with government performance. Recent surveys, however, conclude that Americans are alienated from politics, but are not apathetic about public affairs. They would also like to influence politics, but they feel that they cannot.

Sources: Peter D. Hart and Vince Breglio for NBC News-*Wall Street Journal* as cited in *National Journal*, Vol. 24, No. 24 (June 13, 1992) 1434; *The Washington Post*, March 8, 1992, Section A, page 1; *The Atlanta Constitution*, June 5, 1991, Section A, page 4.

---

each level's autonomy in its own sphere of influence. However, the character of federalism, or political power, has changed in the United States during recent times. What is this change, and how has it affected public policy and administration?

Americans commonly perceive that the federal government is quite powerful and that state and local jurisdictions have lesser influence and fewer responsibilities. The nation and states sometimes are seen as competitors, as they reflect diverse communities of citizens with a variety of economic, political, and cultural interests. As sovereign communities, states promote their own economic interests, seeking political advantage over each other; this sometimes results in a state public sector being able to offer a better quality of life to its citizens. For example, the "sun belt" states, with lower wages and "right-to-work" laws, may try to lure "rust belt" corporations to move south and west. All states seek foreign investments and, in this manner, they compete for such outside private investments as Japanese automobile companies. New investments boost the local economy, which provides more revenues for politicians to disperse as public services.

William S. Livingston illustrates three ways in which the changing pattern of modern day federalism has affected political bureaucracy.[9] First, he describes a cooperative federalism where the *centralization of power* is not accompanied by the *centralization of governmental function*. The central government makes policy, then delegates the function of implementing this policy to other levels of government. Since the New Deal era, the decentralization of governmental function has followed the centralization of governmental authority and power. According to this perspective, state and national governments supplement each other and jointly perform a variety of functions. The federal food stamp program illustrates centralization of power with decentralization of administrative function. Monies to finance the food stamp program are collected under the auspices of the federal purse and the 16th Amendment. Congress authorizes the Department of Agriculture to organize the food stamp program—to pen its varied regulations, and to monitor its progress—but depends upon the county welfare offices in the 50 states for administration. So the national government, with its enlarged powers, supplements rather than supplants the performance of functions by the states and local jurisdictions.

The American political party system is *highly decentralized*. Livingston concludes that the decentralization of power within the political parties enhances the decentralization of the political decision-making process and provides strength to federalism. The character of the parties lends support to federalism, and federalism, in turn, nourishes the decentralized character of the parties. According to Livingston, American political parties are decentralized in three ways: 1) As discrete units, local parties exist to pursue control over state and local governments. Political parties are free associations of citizens who wish to influence the expenditure of taxpayers' dollars. 2) Because local parties are organized at the "grass roots," national parties exercise only periodic and ineffective control over local parties. 3) Local parties exercise considerable control over national parties. National political conventions are organized by collectives of state and local political parties. Forces of the Religious Right, for example, have captured many GOP local party organizations and insisted that certain social issues, such as abortion, pornography, homosexuality, and prayers in public schools become priorities. The RNC (Republican National Committee) might think these concerns are divisive, but President Bush could not ignore the Right Wing's call for "family values." These priorities originated at the grass-roots of the GOP party structure. Political parties are private affairs; only public opinion constrains them.

The final feature that contributes to the increased vitality of modern day federalism is the diversity of *social values* in the United States. Livingston argues that the diverse people and values within a society determine the shape and character of political and governmental institutions. Federalism, as an arrangement of political power, responds to the changing values of society.

What are the social values of American society? Ways of behavior differ from state to state. Some states allow lotteries; others do not. Some states are very restrictive in alcohol sales; others are not. Some states maintain tough environmental standards; others do not. Some states have taken firm positions against racial and sexual discrimination; others back off from this enforcement.

These illustrations indicate that public bureaucrats will have considerable difficulty enforcing laws mandated by the U.S. Congress if support for such policies does not emerge from the "grass roots" throughout the nation.

From affirmative action to speed limits, public administrators have difficulty implementing laws that people do not support. Public bureaucrats have been described as timid and ineffectual, and at the same time power-seeking and dangerous. In reality, their influence depends upon the consensus of political support for government laws and programs. Cooperative federalism, the "grass roots" nature of the political party system, and the diverse social values of Americans require public bureaucrats to share power and responsibilities with federal, state, and local officials. Administrative federalism is the upshot of these political compromises.

THE CRAFT AND POLITICAL CULTURE

An understanding of culture is of great value to public administrators. To recognize the expectations and guidelines for professional behavior in one's culture is to promote understanding of the organization. The culture of an organization provides guidelines for both member behavior and performance. For example, the art of taking examinations can be mastered best by those students who understand that their academic setting is influenced by culture. Class size is one feature of academic culture. The number of students in class influences the kind and number of assignments professors may require. If the number of students in your class reaches into the hundreds, you may assume that your professor will emphasize short answer examinations instead of essays. However, the culture of small classes allows your professor to be more personable in his or her approach to teaching students and gives the professor more flexibility for evaluating your writing skills and critical thinking abilities. An understanding of this classroom culture can help you steer toward classes where you are likely to perform at your best.

For our purposes, "culture" is defined as "that complex whole which includes knowledge, belief, art, morals, law, custom, and any other capabilities and habits acquired by man as a member of society."[10] An awareness of culture is crucial for understanding the development, implementation, and evaluation of public administration.

The nature of our organized society and developments in public administration history underscore the importance of political and bureaucratic culture in the environment of public administration. Partisan, policy, and system politics occur within a larger framework of political culture.

Political culture, according to Daniel Elazar, is the particular pattern of orientation to political action in which each political system is embedded."[11]

Culture puts limits on individuals in organizational settings. An organization is a subculture within a larger culture. For example, your public administration class is a subculture of the Department of Political Science, which is a subculture of a larger academic unit—usually a college of humanities—which is a subculture of the university or college. An understanding of the concept of culture is vital because we must recognize that an organization's members or employees are not free agents in any society.

Any organization, whatever its limits or prospects, is part of a larger social system. At least indirectly, its employees are subject to a larger set of values. Certain cultural patterns of conduct and beliefs can be found in any organization. The culture of an organization reflects a general consensus of the particular values of that organization, but no organization can be isolated from its cultural environment.[12]

An understanding of culture can also allow for an advance indication of how people will act in a given situation. A keenly developed sensitivity to culture can also be a substitute for experience. If you expect to climb the ladder of managerial success, close attention to your organization's culture is important. Traditions, customs, and patterned modes of behavior run through all organizations. If you understand such structuring influences, you may even be able to facilitate changes in the organization.

The components of culture are both *material* and *nonmaterial*.

Physical layout and organizational techniques are illustrations of material culture. Both contribute to the environment of public administration by focusing upon the interaction between habitat and culture, and by emphasizing how and why certain actions occur. As students attend different classes in their academic experience, they move from one classroom culture to another. In chemistry, a chart showing the elements is part of the material culture. In biology, perhaps a skeleton hangs for the professor's demonstration to students. In architecture, drawing boards are a common indication of material culture.

Technology plays a key role in influencing material culture. Equipment and techniques affect the character of organizations. Personal computers are likely to be more helpful to you than typewriters when you are conducting research or writing a paper. The utilization of video cassette recorders in college classrooms allows an expanded teaching dimension. If technology becomes increasingly complicated, an organization may find more difficulty in entering a new field of endeavor.

Not all culture is observable in the same way as material culture. Nonmaterial culture includes beliefs, systems of communications, and modes of conduct. Rituals, taboos, and jargon are modes of conduct that influence important aspects of nonmaterial culture. All organizations follow these prescribed formulas where employees may act in ritualistic unison, observe a system of taboos, or speak in a peculiar jargon. One of the rituals of college classes is to arrive on time for example; cheating on examinations is taboo. Public administrators communicate in a jargon of "alphabet soup" of acronyms for departments, agencies, and programs.

Material and nonmaterial culture may conflict if organization members confuse patterns of conduct with changes occurring in the world outside the organization. In other words, your nonmaterial value system, or beliefs, may not be in line with the realities of the material world, which can result in *cultural lag.* Our organized society is constantly changing. Our values and preferences, however, tend to remain the same. The challenge is to respond appropriately to the changes in society without altering core values.

Material and nonmaterial bureaucratic cultures reflect a larger political culture. Political culture, as Elazar notes, includes perceptions held by the general public and politicians concerning the nature of politics and the perceived role of government in society. A statewide political culture provides a framework for what citizens expect from actors in government and how they perceive office holders, bureaucrats, and campaign workers. Political culture outlines boundaries and practices of citizens, politicians, and public officials with respect to the art of politics and government. Elazar carves out three types of political culture in the United States and describes the relation of bureaucracy to each type. The three types of political culture are *individualistic, moralistic,* and *traditionalistic.*

Individualistic — In this type of political culture, politics is viewed as dirty. Only professionals participate in politics. Parties dole out favors and responsibility. Party cohesiveness is strong. Competition arises between parties, not over issues. New programs are not to be initiated unless demanded by public opinion. Political competition focuses on winning office in order to reap tangible rewards. Government is viewed as a marketplace. Economic development is favored. The appropriate spheres of activity are largely economic. Bureaucracy is viewed ambivalently. The kind of merit system favored is one that is loosely implemented. Indiana, Nevada, New Jersey, and Pennsylvlania are examples of states reflecting the individualistic political culture.

Moralistic — In a moralistic political culture, the practice of politics is viewed as healthy and as every citizen's responsibility. Everyone can participate. Political parties are vehicles to attain goals believed to be in the public interest. Party cohesiveness is subordinate to principles and issues. Competition is over issues, not parties. Political orientation focuses upon winning office to implement policies. Government is viewed as a commonwealth, answering directly for the general welfare and common good of the people. Appropriate spheres of activity include any area that will enhance the community through nongovernmental action. New programs are initiated without public pressure if such are believed to be in the public interest. Bureaucracy is viewed positively, bringing desirable political neutrality. A strong merit system is favored. Colorado, Michigan, Minnesota, North Dakota, Oregon, Utah, Vermont, and Wisconsin reflect the moralistic political culture.

Traditionalistic—Politics is viewed as a privilege in which only those with legitimate claim to office should participate. Participation in politics is limited to the appropriate elite. Political parties serve as vehicles to recruit people for public offices not desired by established power holders. Party cohesiveness depends upon family and social ties and is highly personal. Competition is between the elite-dominated factions within a dominant party. The orientation to politics depends upon the political values of the elite. Government is viewed as a means of maintaining the existing order. Appropriate spheres of activity are those that maintain traditional patterns. New programs are initiated if the program serves in the interest of the governing elite. Bureaucracy is viewed negatively, as it depersonalizes government. Since it is thought that merit should be controlled by the political elite, no merit system is favored. Mississippi, South Carolina, Tennessee, and Virginia are states reflecting the traditionalistic political culture.

Some states fall into more than one type of political culture.

Those states that are mainly moralistic political cultures yet also have individualistic traits are California, Iowa, Kansas, Montana, New Hampshire, South Dakota, and Washington.

States that are mainly individualistic but have moralistic traits as well are Connecticut, Illinois, Massachusetts, Nebraska, New York, Ohio, and Rhode Island.

States that are individualistic yet traditional are Delaware, Hawaii, Maryland, and Missouri. Those that are traditionalistic, yet individualistic, are Alabama, Arkansas, Florida, Georgia, Kentucky, Louisiana, New Mexico, Oklahoma, Texas, and West Virgina. States that are traditionalistic, yet moralistic are Arizona and North Carolina.[13]

Political culture can then be said to encompass a state's orientation to political action. Culture includes knowledge, belief, art, morals, law, custom, capabilities, and habits institutionalized within an organization's environment. Material culture is observable, focuses upon relationships of people distributed in space, and includes tools and techniques for fulfilling organizational purposes. Nonmaterial culture is not so obvious since it incorporates belief systems and patterns of conduct. No organization can be isolated from its cultural environment. Therefore, the bureaucratic culture of government organizations in a particular state cannot be divorced from that state's political culture.

BEHAVIORS, INSTITUTIONS, PROCESSES, AND POLICIES

There is no homogeneous conception of bureaucracy, but all public bureaucracies operate in the administrative worlds of behaviors, institutions, processes, and policies.[14] These "worlds" significantly affect the professional lives of public administrators.

The administrator is engaged in a *behavioral* world—an incredibly complex amalgam of personal needs, interpersonal relations, and small and large social groupings. The deportment, habits, and tendencies of men and women shape the context, structure, and function of the organizations in which they toil. As college students, your behavior toward professors, administrators, and alumni will affect the functioning of your college. Interests and actions do influence the institution.

The administrator also functions in an *institutional* world. Your college environment reflects the institution in which you study, in which your professors teach, and in which administrators implement various academic programs. Educational policies and procedures are institutionalized into an academic format that provides opportunities for all students to achieve. The institution is a formally defined context in which administrators labor and to which a public organization's clientele respond. An institution's context shapes its policies and procedures for selecting, monitoring, and promoting its employees and delivering its services. Police, fire fighters, schools, libraries, and universities formalize and make routine their respective employee behaviors. As the contexts change, so will the specifics of institutions and functions. For example, the spread of AIDS in the 1980s changed the context, structure, and function of the Department of Health and Human Services; likewise, terrorism of recent years influenced the operation of the Department of Defense. Behavioral characteristics of bureaucrats depict *men and women without organizations*. The legal and formal features of institutions and functions portray *organizations without men and women*.

U.S. public administrators work in a world of major *processes* as well. Communicating with employees and clientele, coordinating people and programs, motivating employees, and controlling reporting and budgeting procedures are examples of major processes of public management. Computer and electronic data-processing techniques are common to public managerial processes. Processes are a series of changes leading to some result or a series of operations. As students, you experience processes in seeking a college degree. Penalties occur if you fail to register for classes on time, fail to pay your tuition on time, fail to arrive at class on time, fail to study effectively, or fail to meet prescribed academic deadlines. In many respects, the entire college experience is a process for organizing your goals and objectives.

Development, implementation, and evaluation of public *policies* constitute the fourth major world of the public administrator. Individuals, affiliated with small and large groups, can influence the policies and procedures of formal organizations, which, in turn, affect the major functions of agencies. Students, as clientele, may influence the policies adopted by their college or university. Administrators and professors respond to your individual and collective behaviors as consumers of education by changing policies, then processes, and, eventually, perhaps the institution itself. Successful administration includes the development, implementation, and evaluation of effective public policies.

SUMMARY

- *Administration* involves people, action, and interaction. It is a process in which human beings work toward common goals. Administration uses artistry but is not an art. It uses science but is not a science. It is more properly thought of as a craft.
- The breakdown of government employees is 16 percent federal, 23.6 percent state, and 60.4 percent local. By implication, the impacts of federal government budget cuts will be felt most acutely at state and local jurisdictions, not in Washington.
- Public administration involves elements of *policy and system politics* but originates from *partisan politics.*
- *Political culture* consists of the particular pattern of orientation to the political action of a political system. Any organization, whatever its limits or prospects, is part of a larger social system. At least indirectly, an organization's employees are subject to a larger social system. Its employees are also subject, at least indirectly, to a larger set of values. No organization can be isolated from its cultural environment.
- Public administrators rely on, and are vulnerable to, the law. *Legalism* tends to limit and influence the operations of public institutions much more than it limits private institutions. In private administration, laws generally tell administrators only what they *can't* do. In public administration, laws tell administrators what they *can and can't* do.
- The U.S. Constitution established a *republican form of government* and created a *federal* system. It also advocates the *separation-of-powers* concept and encourages rule of law, representative institutions, and individual liberty. *Centralization* of power in U.S. federalism is not accompanied by the *centralization of governmental function.* Federalism is also tempered by the diversity of social values in the United States.
- There is no homogeneous conception of government bureaucracy.
- Public opinion surveys indicate that the vast majority of public bureaucracy's clients in the United States are pleased with their bureaucratic encounters and transactions. The accusation that bureaucracy is dysfunctional cannot be substantiated. The stereotype of public bureaucracy as bungler is not a reality.
- The "worlds" of behaviors, institutions, processes, and policies significantly affect the professional lives of public administrators.
- In the next chapter, we will examine the environment in which public administrators practice their craft.

The following case study shows how behaviors, institutions, processes, and policies apply to the suburban-urban crisis after the Los Angeles riots. The case is analyzed in the framework of partisan, policy, and system politics and within contexts of "fend-for-yourself" federalism, legalism, and political culture.

CASE STUDY

America's Suburban-Urban Crisis and the Los Angeles Riots

Police power is the heart and soul of any society. The police are on the cutting edge of change. As economic, social, and cultural values change, the police are commissioned to enforce the evolving mores of modern society. Public school teachers, fire fighters, sanitation workers, street repair crews, and public bus drivers constitute the core of the public sector players, but the power of the police to interpret and enforce laws is pre-eminent among all local and state government functions.

This heart and soul is a reflection of its societal context, and in this country even police power must answer to democratic principles. The credibility of local police power rests on constitutional rule of law. Majority rule and minority rights form a tenuous balance in the application of police functions. The states delegate police powers to counties, municipalities, and other special districts for implementation. The police power is centralized in each state's executive, but state governments delegate police functions to local governments.

The dynamics leading up to the brutal beaing of African American Rodney King in the early hours of March 3, 1991 test the political consensus of the American federal system. Police power is carried out within the social values of each state, and no police action can be isolated from its cultural environment. Policital culture—the particular pattern of orientation to political action in which each state's political system is embedded—plays an important role in the use of police power. The Los Angeles Police Department (LAPD) operated within the greater framework of the political cultures of Los Angeles, southern California, and the United States. How did the political culture of southern California contribute to the outbreak?

Racism—for both whites and blacks—is among the most troubling and dysfunctional problems confronting U.S. society. The prelude to the Los Angeles riots and its aftermath illustrate the essential elements of the art, science, and craft of public administration. What role did federalism play? How did the awkward relationship between the national government, states, counties, and cities contribute to the crisis in Los Angeles? How were partisan, policy, and systems politics manifest? How did the laws, rules, and regulations of the U.S., California, and city of Los Angeles affect the outcome? How were republicanism and constitutionalism reflected in this crisis? What role did social values play? What behaviors, institutions, processes, and policies preceded the outbreak of the Los Angeles riots after the acquittal of the four police officers?

Brian Duffy captured the essence of the suburban-urban crisis in Los Angeles and the nation in the following perspective:

Changes in social attitudes during the past two decades, including faltering commitments to families and jobs, have had a doubly deleterious impact in many poor urban areas. No one, after all, forced individual rioters to loot—and most neighborhood residents refused to participate. In the years ahead, if demography is destiny, Los Angeles could be in for even more trouble. As in other big cities, demographic projections through the end of the decade sugggest that population growth will far outstrip job growth, further inflaming racial tensions. In the ghettos, "jobs, jobs, jobs" is more than a campaign slogan.[15]

Suburban-Urban Crisis: The Behaviors

The 1992 riots occurred in a historical context. The cultures of racism, policy brutality, white fears, high unemployment, widespread poverty, poor schools, drug peddlers, middle-class ambivalence, political indifference, and criminal mentality led to a hopelessness which erupted when LAPD officers Laurence Powell, Theodore Briseno, and Timothy Wind, supervised by Sgt. Stacey Koon, were found "not guilty" of beating citizen King.[16]

On that fateful night, motorist King was encircled by members of the LAPD after a high speed chase, forced out of his car, and beaten by LAPD officers. Unknown to the officers, their behavior was recorded by a white citizen as he witnessed the beating from his nearby apartment. The video captured 81 seconds in which King was kicked by the officers, jolted by a stun gun, and struck 56 times with nightsticks. This incident led to a trial of the four LAPD officers in predominantly white, prosperous, and suburban Ventura County. The jury acquitted the officers on April 30, 1992, finding that no excessive force had been used.

Riots erupted in the south central area of Los Angeles immediately after the surprise verdict. Before the violence abated, more than 50 persons had died, thousands were injured and arrested, and billions of dollars of private and public infrastructure damage resulted in the spectacular fires and uncontrolled looting. A communications breakdown and shortage of ammunition kept the first 2,000 National Guard troops in their barracks during the initial outbreak of violence. The police were likewise tardy in responding to the widespread outbreak of violence.[17]

The suburban policy agenda was illuminated in the glare of the urban Los Angeles fire storms as well. Although Los Angeles is just one of many municipal jurisdictions in the nation's largest state, the riots brought the issues of race, employment, fairness, opportunity and hope to the attention of all Americans. There appeared to be little consensus among Caucasians, African-Americans, and Asian-Americans regarding the causes or solutions to the crisis in Los Angeles or the widespread urban dilemmas it exemplified.

The King verdict and LA riots underscore the racial and ethnic divisiveness, economic stratification, and cultural decline confronting suburban and urban America. "The social consensus is breaking down in the 1990s," writes William Schneider. "Urban America is facing extreme economic pressure and the loss of political influence. The cities feel neglected, and with good reason: they are the declining sector of American life. Just as the Populists of the

1890s exalted the rural myth, urban leaders of the 1990s are trying to glorify the urban myth."[18] A move to suburbia has permitted citizens to choose "the private" over "the public," to afford their own government. The riots in urban Los Angeles interrupted the privacy of the suburbs.

Suburban-Urban Crisis: The Institutions

In the very best sense, the U.S. is a "welfare state." In other words, the government promotes the "welfare" of its citizens. The government—meaning governments at all levels—promotes the health, education, safety, opportunity, and hope for a better future of all Americans, regardless of sex, race, religion or national origin.[19]

The institutions or government bureaucracies involved *directly* in this suburban-urban dilemma were the county police and state court system. The federal Departments of Agriculture, Health and Human Services, Housing and Urban Development, Labor, and California and Los Angeles agencies administering federal programs were more *indirectly* involved in the delivery of economic opportunities to the citizens of South Central Los Angeles.

The LAPD and Ventura County court were *active* and *passive* institutional participants in the case of citizen King. As a private citizen, the law specified only what King could **not** do. He could not drive his car at an excessive speed nor could he operate his vehicle while intoxicated. As public administrators however, Los Angeles police officers are governed by rules and regulations grounded in laws enacted by the California state legislature and approved by its governor. The law prescribed to these officers precisely what they could do if they arrested citizen King.

The Ventura County court system's particpation in this public administration case could also be characterized as passive. The county court—a legal jurisdiction of the State of California—was a passive instrument in that no government official connected with Ventura County sought out the King-LAPD trial for its community of California citizens. The law permits such trials to be venued from the county in which the alleged violations occurred to a jurisdiction where the attorneys for the defendants believe their clients may receive a more receptive, if not fair, trial.[20]

The attorneys for the four LAPD officers convinced Judge Stanley Weisberg to move the controversial court proceeding to the dry hills of Simi Valley; an overwhelmingly white, middle-class community 35 miles northwest of downtown Los Angeles. In Ventura, the attorneys for the LAPD officers negotiated for a jury that was more understanding of their plight. The jury consisted of an even number men and women, ranged in age from 38 to 65, numbered ten whites, one Hispanic, and one Filipino (no blacks), and represented a political culture quite different from that of South Central Los Angeles.

South Central LA and the Simi Valley typify the urban-suburban divide. South Central LA is overwhelmed with poverty and criminality, gangs of youths gone astray if not mad, and a growing variety of ethnic cultures which live in tense proximity. There is certainly more fear than hope for economic renewal of this blighted urban community.

The Simi Valley—site of among other things, Ronald Reagan's Presidential Library—has a population of 100,000, 80 percent of which is white, 13 percent Hispanic, five percent Asian, and two percent African-American. The valley is a bedroom community for thousands of law enforcement officers where the average price of a home is $250,000. To no one's surprise, the citizens of Simi Valley vote overwhelmingly Republican, and consider their community a refuge from the gangs, crime, high housing prices, and minorities of Los Angeles.

As indirect institutional participants, the federal Departments of Agriculture (USDA), Health and Human Services (HHS), Housing and Urban Development (HUD), and Labor (DOL) implement policies which were enacted by the U.S. Congress over decades. State and local government agencies assisted these federal departments in implementing a variety of programs to benefit the citizens of South Central LA. USDA carries out the food stamp program. HHS implements Aid to Families with Dependent Children (AFDC) and Medicaid. AFDC is a cash-assistance program for the poor; Medicaid is a means-tested medical plan for the poor and disabled. HUD administers criteria for establishing urban enterprise zones, urban homesteading, and housing subsidies. DOL supervises employment and training prerogatives.

The "fend-for-yourself federalism" philosophy of the 1980s contributed to the political culture which resulted in police brutality as well as the LA riots. Competition, not cooperation, was the approach of "fend-for-yourself federalism." Diversity, competitiveness, and resiliency were to provide choices and stabilization by allowing state and local governments to fend for themselves. Were not local, state, and federal governmental institutions set up to work for the citizens of South Central LA?[21]

President Bush showed little interest in urban policy and said virtually nothing about racial injustice or the plight of the underclass. "They are not our issues," said a senior Republican strategist. After the riots, the citizens of South Central LA had to fend for themselves. Bush, who committed the U.S. to fight a war in the Middle East, did not commit the country to fight a war against poverty in South Central LA.

"Fend-for-yourself federalism" illustrates an institutional dilemma in federalism—the very structure of politics in our state and nation. Gridlock between Congress and President, no commitment by the richer states to assist the poorer ones, and lack of Presidential leadership concerning poverty, racial tension and economic blight shows how institutions of U.S. federalism impact the suburban-urban crisis.

Suburban-Urban Crisis: The Processes

The rule of law is based on process. Public or government organizations, grounded in law and funded by taxpayers, must find ways to hold themselves accountable. Governments attempt to respond to the public's demands for accountability through the processes instituted in law-based rules and regulations. Legal restrictions and restraints are placed upon all activities of the LAPD that give its activities credibility and accountability to the public. The urban agenda, however it is defined, is based upon the rule of law.

The various government programs are also grounded in process. USDA, HHS, HUD, and DOL implement laws enacted by the U.S. Congress. Government programs are developed based upon laws and federal appropriations for financing those programs. Processes like applying for food stamps (USDA), welfare (HHS), housing subsidies (HUD), and job training (DOL) create mechanisms for carrying out those laws and programs. In Los Angeles, looters were apprehended and prosecuted according to the criminal justice system established by the U.S. Department of Justice and Attorney General of California. When looters were caught, they were processed through the criminal justice system.

Rules and regulations abound in California's jury selection process. Only six African-Americans were present among 400 citizens in the array of likely candidates to serve on the King-LAPD trial jury. In the process for transferring the venue of the King case from Los Angeles to Ventura County, the attorneys for the defense realized the low likelihood of having African Americans on the jury in a county that was only two percent black. The prosecutor, defense attorneys, and judge were very concerned about violating processes, developed based on rules and regulations, grounded in laws passed by state and federal legislatures.

Government programs, if nothing else, are a maze of "dos and don'ts" based on process. The process is governed by rules and regulations guiding the implementation of government programs. The looter is told that he or she cannot steal. Stealing is against the law. In apprehending the looter, however, law enforcement officials are required to follow processes in accomplishing their assigned duties.

Suburban-Urban Crisis: The Policies

Public policies in the United States may be traced in a large part to their roots in the Great Depression and the New Deal of the 1930s.[22] Federal government activities in anti-poverty programs like the Social Security Act of 1935 date back to Franklin D. Roosevelt's New Deal. These programs still structure U.S. welfare policy today. The most controversial part of welfare policy came much later however. Aid to Families with Dependent Children (AFDC) was established in 1962 and has caused contention ever since.

AFDC is a joint national and state program. Depending on state poverty levels, the feds pay 50 percent of the administrative costs and up to 83 percent of the benefits. Cash benefits are paid to families where the parents are unemployed or disabled, or if the child is without a parent in the home. Problems arose in this case as the economy of Los Angeles and the nation changed in the 1980s, and government policies were not reformed to confront the changes in the family structure of the underclass.

President Lyndon Johnson responded to the urban crisis of the 1960s by recommending a policy, grounded in the Economic Opportunity Act of 1964, to develop a Job Corps program in which unemployed youths between 16 and 21 would move away from home to residential centers to learn job skills and gain work experience. Another program resulting from these policies is Head Start—a pilot program to help prepare poor children for school—was

Federally Funded Municipal Programs

GRS: General Revenue Sharing
(no funding after 1987)

CDBG: Community Development Block
Grant

UDAG: Urban Development Action Grant

EDA: Economic Development Administration

EPA: Wastewater Treatment

Housing: Low-income Housing Assistance

Jobs: Job Training CETA in 1980–82;
JTPA in 1983-onward

UMTA: Public Transit Assistance

H-less: McKinney Homeless Assistance
Program
(Began in 1988)

Total Spending on Municipal Programs

Billions of Current Dollars for Fiscal Year

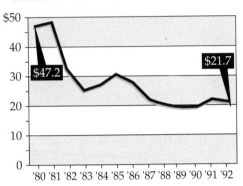

Component Spending

Billions of Dollars

	'80	'81	'82	'83	'84	'85	'86	'87	'88	'89	'90	'91	'92
GRS	4.6	4.6	4.6	4.6	4.6	4.6	4.6	0	0	0	0	0	0
CDBG	3.9	3.7	3.5	3.5	3.5	3.5	3	3	2.9	3	2.9	3.2	3.4
UDAG	0.7	0.7	0.4	0.4	0.4	0.4	0.3	0.2	0.2	0	0	0	0
EDA	1.1	0.5	0.2	0.2	0.3	0.2	0.2	0.2	0.2	0.2	0.2	0.2	0.2
EPA	3.4	1.6	2.4	2.4	2.3	2.4	1.8	1.2	2.3	2	1.9	2.1	2.4
Housing	22.7	26.7	15	8.7	9	12.2	12.2	11.6	8.3	7.9	7.8	9.5	7.8
Jobs	8.2	7.1	2.4	2.2	3.6	3.6	3.3	3.7	3.8	3.8	3.9	4.1	4.1
UMTA	2.2	3.5	3.5	3.5	3.6	3.5	3.1	3	2.9	2.8	2.7	3	3.4
H-less	0	0	0	0	0	0	0	0	0.4	0.4	0.4	0.4	0.4

FIGURE 1-1 Federal Spending for Cities.

Source: National League of Cities/*The Washington Post*, July 9, 1992, page A21.

formalized in 1965 and survived the massive cuts in federal spending for the
inner cities during the 1980s. (See Figure 1–1 depicting the downward spiral
of federal spending for cities.)

The Reagan administration argued that the Great Society programs of the
1960s were misguided at best. The taxpayers dollars were being wasted and
the poor were not lifting themselves out of poverty. Funding for many of
these programs was drastically cut or eliminated. The middle-class had little
patience with the lawless conditions existing in many poor neighborhoods
and hardly anyone objected when the poor had their food, health, housing,
and job creation subsidies curtailed or abolished. The middle-class taxpayer
had little interest in the need for a solution to the urban crisis in places such
as South Central LA until the looting began and the fires broke out.[23]

Jack Kemp, HUD Secretary under President George Bush, responded to the urban problems of the 1990s by shifting the direction of policy-making away from government intervention and toward solutions in the private sector. The Republicans favored tax incentives which encourage businesses to open or relocate in impoverished areas of the nation's cities. Kemp advocated the reestablishment of Urban Enterprise Zones.

President Bush, however, vetoed a $700 million demonstration plan to create 10 urban and rural enterprise zones because the Congressional Democrats failed to include a capital gains tax provision if or when a business was sold. Partisan gridlock between the President and Congress again contributed to the lack of political solution to the problems faced by those living in blighted areas of the nation's cities.

Suburban-Urban Crisis: Behaviors, Institutions, Processes, Policies, and Political Consensus in the 1990's

What do we learn about the practice and principles of public administration from the LA riots? With declining political leadership in meeting urban problems and in the face of federal and state budget cuts, local, state, and federal government officials (public administrators) must be "crafty" in the evaluation, development, and implementation of solutions for the suburban-urban crisis. Public administrators use science (technology) in order to understand better the challenges confronting the community. In the 1990s, however, public administration in the U.S. is primarily an art and craft.[24]

What role did federalism play in the Los Angeles riots? The theme of federalism in the 1980s was that governments must "fend-for-themselves" and not look to Washington for either financial assistance or political leadership. Among the powers of any executive, especially the Presidency, is the power to persuade. Racism is historical, and in the 1990s, the fallout from racism is dysfunctional to all Americans. Americans, like citizens of any nation, learn a great deal from their leaders. The President of the U.S. is perhaps our most visible teacher. If the President cannot deliver monetary rewards through government programs to poor neighborhoods, he can teach principles of justice and opportunity. Recent administrations, however, have considered the inequities of the inner cities "not our issues."[25] The power of the Presidency to promote justice and equality was not used to its potential.

How did the political culture of southern California affect the King case and subsequent riots? "Culture" is defined as "that complex whole which includes knowledge, belief, art, morals, law, custom, and any other capabilities and habits acquired by man as a member of society."[26] The political culture of southern California is very diverse, reflecting especially traditionalism and individualism, and less so moralism. In Los Angeles' cultural diversity of language, race, economics, every community, neighborhood, and citizen must "fend-for-themselves." The social values of the Los Angeles metropolitan region are as diverse as any region of the country. The people, character, languages, ethnicity, institutions, economics, and governments of metropolitan LA reflect this social diversity.

The police have the power, grounded in law, to restrain citizens whom they perceive are not acting according to prescribed laws and norms using whatever means deemed reasonable in a given situation. In all probability, the LAPD officers beat King not because they hated him or his race, but because they feared him and the culture he represented. The police were protecting themselves from the unpredictability associated with the culture of poverty. The officers, however, were victims of "cultural lag." A rather unique application of video technology brought the official accountability of the LAPD officers into stark relief.

How did the laws, rules, and regulations of the U.S., California, and city of Los Angeles affect the King case and the ensuing violence? The U.S. is divided into political jurisdictions, including states, counties, and cities. The law protects the rights of the accused, and permits a venue change for cases involving community bias against the accused. The attorneys for the LAPD officers argued that a jury in suburban Ventura County would be more receptive to their interests than one in Los Angeles County.

How were republicanism and constitutionalism reflected in this crisis? The U.S. is a republic, not a pure democracy. Politicians represent citizens of towns, cities, counties, states, and the nation indirectly, not directly. The idea of constitutionalism includes such notions as rule of law, representative institutions (republicanism), and guaranteed individual liberty. The awkward relationship between the national government, states, counties, and cities contributed to the fragmentation of government policies affecting the LA metropolitan area. The Los Angeles region is not governed by one political jurisdiction; it is governed by hundreds of towns, cities, counties, and the state of California.

William Bennett, former drug czar and education secretary, argued: "The broader issues raised by Los Angeles are the real substance of politics: justice, right and wrong, and how we should live together. The economy and jobs may be the engine of society, but what happened in L.A. is about its soul."[27] The King case and LA riots illustrate partisan, policy, and systems politics. The criminal justice system is a system governed by processes and grounded in policies enacted by elected political officials. The federal domestic institutions (USDA, HHS, HUD, DOL, DOJ) implement urban policies written into legislation by elected officials over many decades, but these laws alone will not result in citizens changing their behavior. Attitudes of citizens are influenced by partisan political leaders. Of these leaders, the President is in the best position to persuade citizens to be more responsible, realistic, and humane about justice, right and wrong, and how Americans should live together.

Scholars, ministers, human rights advocates, and residents of Los Angeles' arson-scarred and riot-torn neighborhoods almost unanimously agree that the violence sparked by the acquittal of four LAPD policemen in the beating of Rodney King has been simmering for 27 years. If social conditions fail to change for the better they say civil unrest will happen again.[28] Let's hope that the King-LAPD case and Los Angeles riots are not the "soul" of partisan, policy, and systems politics in the U.S. We cannot afford what historian Arthur Schlesinger Jr. calls "the disuniting of America."[29]

(Federalism, or the structure of American politics, allows for a dual court system. In a small federal courtroom in downtown Los Angeles in April, 1993, the jury found that Powell "did willfully strike . . . and kick and stomp Rodney Glen King," violating King's constitutional right "not to be deprived of liberty without due process of law, including the right to be . . . free from the intentional use of unreasonable force" by policemen. Briseno and Wind were found "not guilty" in the federal court. The federal jury found Koon, the officers' supervisor, "guilty" of willfully permitting the savage beating of King. *Source:* George J. Church, "Cries of Relief," *Time,* Vol. 141, No. 17 (April 26, 1993), 18–19.)

QUESTIONS AND INSTRUCTIONS

1. Why and how is police power or police bureaucracy the heart and soul of any society?
2. Why are social values important in the public administration of police powers?
3. In the Rodney King-LAPD case, how should we allocate responsibility for the crisis? How much is the individual (King) to blame for his behavior? How should we assign responsibility for these events to partisan, policy, and systems politics?
4. Federalism is the structure of politics in the U.S. How should this structure be modified to alleviate future crises of this magnitude? What roles should federal, state, and regional governments play?
5. In the 1990s, what role(s) should governments have in the public-private interface of citizens in society. What aspects of the "welfare state" should be retained in providing the basics of life—food, health, housing, work, protection, and justice?
6. Rank order and illustrate the significance of behaviors, institutions, processes, and policies for understanding why public officials and administrators responded to the violence in Los Angeles as they did?
7. What unique role did technology play in the prosecution of the LAPD officers? Why did the jury see events differently?
8. A crisis may be defined as both danger and opportunity. How do the crises of the King trial and riots reflect clear and present danger to U.S. society? In what ways is this crisis an opportunity for citizens and elected officials to learn from the past?
9. Is political consensus for providing food, health, housing, jobs, protection, and justice feasible in large metropolitan areas like Los Angeles?
10. Do political jurisdictions—towns, cities, counties, states, and nations—have souls?

ENDNOTES

1. *US News & World Report,* Vol. 113, No. 7, August 17, 1992, page 13. See also U.S. Department of Labor, Bureau of Labor Statistics, *Employment and Earnings,* Vol. 39, No. 7 (May 1992), page 81.

2. Herbert A. Simon, Donald W. Smithburg, and Victor A. Thompson, *Public Administration* (New York: Alfred A. Knopf, 1950), 3.

3. Aaron Wildavsky, *The Politics of the Budgetary Process* (Boston: Little, Brown, and Co., 1979), 191–193.

4. David Bazelon, "The Impact of the Courts on Public Administration," *Indiana Law Journal,* Vol. 52, No. 1 (Fall 1976), 101–110.

5. This view has been articulated by Alan M. Dershowitz in *The Best Defense* (New York: Random House, 1982). However, the same theme runs through many other statements and writings of legal authorities. Oliver Wendell Holmes, for example, once said that his job as justice of the U.S. Supreme Court did not require him to "do" justice but merely to see that the rules of the game were followed.

6. John M. Pfiffner and Robert Presthus, *Public Administration,* 5th Edition (New York: Ronald Press, 1967). In regard to the subsequent sentence in the text, Donald S. Vaughn, former Chair, Department of Political Science, University of Mississippi, points out that the law also tells the public administrator what he cannot do. Professor Vaughn cites the first eight amendments to the U.S. Constitution as a case in point.

7. The reader will no doubt understand the author's reluctance to provide additional details of this episode. However, the authors do vouch for its veracity.

8. C. Herman Pritchett, *The American Constitutional System* (New York: McGraw-Hill Book Co., 1981), 7–8.

9. William S. Livingston, "Federalism in Other Countries: Canada, Australia, and the United States," in *Federalism: Infinite Variety in Theory and Practice* (Itasca, IL: F. E. Peacock Publishers, Inc., 1968), 131–141.

10. Quotes from Tylor's *Primitive Culture* in Leslie A. White, "The Concept of Culture," *American Anthropologist,* Vol. 61, No. 227 (April 1959). White reports that there is great divergence of view among anthropologists as to a definition of culture.

11. Daniel J. Elazar, *American Federalism: A View from the States* (New York: Harper & Row, Pubishers, 1984), 109.

12. John M. Pfiffner and Frank P. Sherwood, *Administrative Organization* (Englewood Cliffs, NJ: Prentice-Hall, Inc., 1960), 249–272.

13. Elazar, *American Federalism,* 136.

14. Robert T. Golembiewski, Frank Gibson, and Geoffrey Y. Cornog, *Public Administration: Readings in Institutions, Processes, Behavior, Policy* (Chicago: Rand McNally College Publishing Co., 1976), 1–10.

15. Brian Duffy, "Days of Rage," *U.S. News & World Report,* Vol. 112, No. 18 (May 11, 1992), 21–26.

16. George J. Church, "The Fire This Time," *Time*, Vol. 139, No. 19 (May 11, 1992), 18–25; Richard Lacayo, "This Land is Your Land . . . This Land is My Land," *Time*, Vol. 139, No. 20 (May 18, 1992), 28–33; Harrison Rainie, "Requiem for the Cities?" *U.S. News & World Report*, Vol. 112, No. 19 (May 18, 1992), 20–26; and Rochelle L. Stanfield, "Black Frustration," *National Journal*, Vol. 24, No. 20 (May 16, 1992), 1162–1168.

17. David Ellis, "L. A. Lawless," *Time*, Vol. 139, No. 19 (May 11, 1992), 26–29.

18. William Schneider, "The Real Meaning of the 1992 Election: The Suburban Century Begins," *The Atlantic*, Vol. 270, No. 1 (July 1992), 34. See also: "It Takes a Crisis to Prompt a Remedy," *National Journal*, Vol. 24, No. 21 (May 23, 1992), 1270.

19. John Leo, "A New Deal for the Underclass," *U.S. News & World Report*, Vol. 112, No. 20 (May 25, 1992), 29.

20. Ted Gest with Constance Johnson, "The Justice System: Getting a Fair Trial," *U.S. News & World Report*, Vol. 112, No. 20 (May 25, 1992), 36, 38.

21. John Shannon, "The Faces of Fiscal Federalism," *Intergovernmental Perspective*, Vol. 14, No. 1 (Winter 1988), 15–17; See also: "The Return to Fend-for-Yourself Federalism: The Reagan Mark," *Intergovernmental Perspective*, Vol. 13, No. 3/4 (Summer/Fall 1987), 34–37.

22. Julie Rovner with Kitty Dumas, Susan Kellam, and Jill Zuckman, "Rhetoric, Not Radical Change, Likely Result of L.A. Riots," *Congressional Quarterly Weekly Report*, Vol. 50, No. 19 (May 9, 1992), 1247–1255.

23. Thomas Sancton, "How to Get America off the Dole," *Time*, Vol. 139, No. 21 (May 25, 1992), 44–47.

24. Walter Shapiro, "Lessons of Los Angeles," *Time*, Vol. 139, No. 20 (May 18, 1992), 38–39; and Mortimer B. Zuckerman, "The New Realism," *U.S. News & World Report*, Vol. 112, No. 20 (May 25, 1992), 92, 94.

25. Kenneth T. Walsh and Joseph P. Shapiro, "They Are Not our Issues," *U.S. News & World Report*, Vol. 112, No. 19 (May 18, 1992), 26.

26. Tylor/White, *op. cit.*

27. William J. Bennett, "The Moral Origins of the Urban Crisis," *The Wall Street Journal*, May 8, 1992, page A8.

28. Don Terry, "Decades of Rage Created Crucible of Violence," *The New York Times*, May 3, 1992, page 1.

29. Arthur Schlesinger Jr., *The Disuniting of America: Reflections on a Multicultural Society* (New York: W. W. Norton, 1992).

2

☆ ☆ ☆

THE ECOLOGY OF THE ADMINISTRATIVE CRAFT

CHAPTER HIGHLIGHTS

OUR ORGANIZED SOCIETY
EQUALITY AND EFFICIENCY
THE SYNERGISTIC ENVIRONMENT
EBBS AND FLOWS OF GOVERNMENT EXPANSION
AND CONSTRAINTS
THE GROWTH OF PUBLIC BUREAUCRACY
COMPARING PUBLIC AND PRIVATE ADMINISTRATION
NUANCES
INTEREST GROUPS AND PUBLIC BUREAUCRACY

A communications satellite peacefully orbits the Earth, silently catching and throwing radio signals. There are no winds or rains or hailstorms to buffet the satellite and affect its operation. Of course, the satellite may be affected by a meteor or the debris from the icy tail of a comet, but the odds against such occurrences are, well, astronomical. Generally, the satellite will operate unmolested in the vacuum of space.

Public administrators do not operate in a vacuum. There are countless environmental factors that buffet public administrators, making their tasks remarkably complex. Public administration cannot be separated from environmental factors as can the satellite.

Public administration occurs within the framework of the organized society. The principle barriers to the effective implementation of public programs are the conflicts between the political principles of democracy and the economic principles of capitalism.

Public administration is also carried out within the political cultures of states and communities. Culture, both tangible and intangible, affects the environment in which public administration takes place.

Ecology is the study of the relationships between organisms and their environments, and public administrators who are not acutely aware of how environmental factors influence administration are doomed to failure. This chapter unpacks the relationship between public administrators and the environment in which they work.

OUR ORGANIZED SOCIETY

A drive down Main Street, U.S.A., will take you past banks, dry cleaning establishments, cafes, and retail stores. Keep driving and you'll pass churches, shopping malls, fast food outlets, factories, gas stations, and schools.

All of the above are examples of organizations that affect our daily existence. All organizations must be managed or administered. We live in a complex society in which public organizations are needed if the smaller, private organizations are to thrive or operate at all. The alternative is anarchy.

Public organizations receive their lifeblood from legislative, executive, and judicial collectives in our organized society. Legislatures appropriate revenues for funding public programs. Presidents, governors, and mayors carry out the legislative will of the people. Courts adjudicate disputes between parties who are contesting, among other things, the delivery of government programs.

With its numerous organizations, modern America is the epitome of the organized society. The legislative, executive, and judicial branches of national and state governments are the basic units of public organization. For example, the president and Congress enacted the policy of social security for the elderly; the Social Security Administration implements the policy; and judges decide disputed claims.[1]

For all of our society's organization, questions still arise concerning the fairness and efficiency of public organizations—questions that contribute to these organizations' administrative entanglements.

EQUALITY AND EFFICIENCY

American society professes equal opportunities for all citizens. Professing equal opportunity does not, however, guarantee that citizens will achieve equal results for their efforts.

Your productive contribution in the competitive market depends on your skills, assets, and efforts and also on the supply of and demand for what you have to offer. As free speech does not guarantee an audience, free enterprise does not guarantee a demand for one's services. Effort does not guarantee excellence. Although a student studies long and hard for an exam, an "A" is not a foregone conclusion. It is easy to see that these factors, when applied to individuals in the marketplace, can result in unequal individual incomes.

Our organized society, therefore, exists in an environment of equal rights and unequal incomes. Conflicts between these two phenomena result in tensions between the *political principles of democracy* and the *economic principles of capitalism*.

The United States is a democratic society with a capitalistic economic system. In keeping with our democratic political philosophy, we hold elections. In keeping with our economic philosophy, we let supply and demand decide who achieves financial success. Arthur Okun describes contemporary U.S. society as "a split-level institutional structure" because of the combination of democracy and capitalism.[2] We have a "split-level institutional structure" because private institutions value efficiency, while public sector institutions favor equality. Efficiency gives the top-producers priority, and equality gives everyone priority.

So the services provided by public administrators reflect the concept of *equality*. The concept of *efficiency* comes from letting the marketplace decide what goods and services are produced and purchased. Services and programs produced by governments are afforded to all citizens. Police, fire, and sanitation (sewers) are almost always produced and provided by government. Electricity, water, gas, sanitation (garbage), and telephone services, although regulated by government, may be produced and provided for privately. Even though electricity, gas, and telephone utilities are produced privately, the government regulates their activities to assure "fairness" of delivery.

The rich and the poor have equal rights to travel on our network of interstate highways. Economic realities of the efficient marketplace may determine, however, that certain people not have cars to drive and that others are able to cruise along the turnpike in chauffeur-driven Mercedes.

The point to remember is the idea that a public program is not maintained for the very poor or the ultra rich, but for the masses of middle class citizens. In that respect, America's highway system serves as an example of an efficient economy—the more we drive, the more road and gasoline taxes we pay. The tax revenues provide funds for public administrators to implement highway maintenance policies and to have new highways built. Via interest group liberalism, citizens lobby elected officials to vote expenditures that will benefit their well-being. As the president and Congress attempt to cut federal spending, segments of the great middle-class will conflict on what programs should be cut.

The values of equality and efficiency are always in conflict. The pursuit of efficiency necessarily creates inequalities. Citizens make economic choices, like buying a car or riding a bus. If we all choose to commute only by car, bus drivers will be out of work—the victims of our equal freedom of choice and the workings of our efficient economy. It is often the role of the public administrator to step in if one of these values begins to supercede the other. This is where the public administrator's regulatory powers come into play. Through these powers, public administrators exercise great influence in determining the appropriate role of the marketplace. The public administrator does not, however, have unlimited regulatory power. As regulators of private interactions, public administrators are checked by limits on administrative power spelled out in laws such as the Administrative Procedure Act.[3]

In defending the state of affairs that leads to the conflict between equality and efficiency, Okun says, "the market needs a place, and the market needs to be kept in its place."[4] The market is kept in its place by the limited regulatory powers of public administrators.

So equality may be sacrificed for the sake of efficiency, and efficiency for the sake of equality. What provisions exist to protect the individual's equal rights in this market-driven economy?

American society promotes equality by maintaining social and political rights that are allocated equally and designed to be distanced from the marketplace of supply and demand. For example, due process is a constitutionally mandated guarantee that governments in the United States will act with fairness, justice, equity, and reasonableness—irrespective of economic considerations. Accused criminals seek fairness through due process in prosecution procedures. Equal opportunity is protected in a court of law by the constitutionally mandated accessibility of due process.

Due process is the legal cornerstone of the craft of public administration. There are two types of due process, *substantive* and *procedural*.

Substantive due process refers to the content or subject of a law. *Procedural due process,* the more commonly litigated of the two, refers to the procedures used in implementing a law or administrative practice. Deciding whether or not a law is constitutional is part of procedural due process.

The concept of equality is also demonstrated in the open admissions policies of many state universities. These policies require a university to accept students from all ethnic groups and income levels. The taxpayers subsidize public education to guarantee fairness, justice, equity, and reasonableness in the admission of students. The state university must pay careful attention to due process. On the other hand, a private college is not required to follow due process as stringently as a public university. A private college may, with some restrictions, select only those students who meet certain criteria that may not be used at a state institution. Such an adoption of standards of excellence embraces the value of efficiency.

The value of equality is embodied in guarantees grounded in basic citizen rights. The value of efficiency is embodied in productivity. Public administrators operate in this complex environment—an environment in which two fundamental values of our society often collide. The challenge of public administration must be to maximize efficiency without sacrificing equality—and vice versa.

THE SYNERGISTIC ENVIRONMENT

"Synergy" is the word used to describe the action two or more people carry out together to accomplish a task that cannot be accomplished by an individual working alone. According to the Roper Organization Inc., publisher of the Roper Public Opinion Poll, synergism is a dominant force shaping the public policy environment of the 1990s. This synergistic environment entails more cooperative action among government, business, and labor to deal with fundamental social and economic problems.

In a synergistic environment, issues of fairness become more significant. A crucial question for our democratic and capitalistic society is where and how the organized modern society establishes boundaries between the *domain of rights* (equality) and the *domain of the capitalistic marketplace* (efficiency). Conflicts between these domains are inevitable and pose dilemmas for our split-level, political economy.

Our democratic, capitalist society searches continuously for better ways to clearly establish boundaries between the domains. The marketplace needs equality to put some *humanity* into *efficiency;* our democracy needs efficiency to put some *rationality* into *equality*. Capitalistic and bureaucratic systems will be more effective if they are more humane. Equality will be more acceptable to those who value efficiency, and hence, less chaotic, if standards of consistency are applied to the diverse applications of this crucial democratic principle.[5]

Democracy is characterized by equality, due process, fairness, participation, suffrage, and electoral politics. Capitalism implies efficiency, productivity, hierarchy, competition, and entrepreneurship. Public administration finds its origins in democracy but owes much to the fundamental principles of capitalism.

The modern organized society can also be described as a *political economy.* Our society is political in that citizens have the opportunity to organize and express their priorities about what is important to them. The "economy" part of the phrase comes from the collective productivity of goods and services our society generates. The split-level structure of the political and economic systems affects public policy and administration. Communities cannot expect public services to be provided without an ample supply of *revenues,* which are raised by taxing citizens and businesses. Our organized society, therefore, depends upon the political system and the structure of the economic sector. The maintenance of the relationship between political power and economic structure is vital to the future of American democracy. Public administrators depend upon capitalism to generate economic growth in order to pay their salaries and to finance the delivery of their services to the American people.[6]

The thrust of democratic capitalism comes from the opposing values of political power and economic structure. Those middle-class citizens who do not possess the means of economic production agree to the private ownership of capital stock; meanwhile, wealthy citizens who own the instruments of economic production accept democratic political institutions that allow opposing interest groups to press claims for further allocation of material resources and the distribution of labor's output. The large middle class permits members of the economic elite to own capital and organize production (the economy). The economic elite allows the political prerogatives of the general population to affect the allocation of resources and the distribution of the material effects of economic production.[7]

For the first time since statistics in such things have been kept, employees of federal, state, and local governments outnumber factory workers. In 1991, the U.S. Bureau of Labor Statistics reported 18,410,000 government jobs throughout the U.S.; manufacturing jobs declined to 18,388,000 during the same period. Manufacturing jobs in the U.S. decreased from 19,391,000 in 1989 to 18,388,000 in 1992. Meanwhile, in the same time period, federal, state, and local government jobs increased from 17,574,000 to 18,410,000.[8]

The taxpayers, or our children through deficit federal spending, must raise revenues to pay salaries and benefits for all those government employees. The economic philosophy is that manufacturing jobs, not service sector jobs, are the core of any nation's political economy. We could argue that all those government employees have a vested interest in deficit federal spending. After all, the Reagan-Bush years have been devastating to public employees.

A decrease of 1,000 employees occurred in federal employment in the 1989–1992 period. However, the number of state and local employees increased by nearly one million, to 15.4 million. Since 1982, there has been a 20 percent growth in the work forces of state and local governments and an eight percent increase in the federal work force. The nation's industrial base is declining while demands for public services continue. The American economy is undergoing a fundamental restructuring. In 1980, the sector of the economy with the most jobs was manufacturing (20.3 million). In 1992, the sector with the most jobs was services (29 million).[9]

EBBS AND FLOWS OF GOVERNMENT EXPANSION AND CONSTRAINTS

Although the New Deal gave rise to the modern mix of federal, state, and local public bureaucracies, there have also been other milestones in America's history that can shed light on current problems and prospects for the administrative state of the 1990s. The retrenchment and decentralization efforts of recent years, authored by Richard Nixon and Ronald Reagan, were in response to measures initiated by Woodrow Wilson, Franklin Roosevelt, and Lyndon Johnson.

A review of the ebbs and flows of government expansion and constraints gives us a solid historical base for understanding why government is the way it is today. The dynamics behind growth of bureaucracy may be understood by looking at four crucial periods in the 20th century. These particular years signify eras of political economy in support of and in restraint of public bureaucracies. These eras, which have had a lasting impact upon American society, occurred around the years 1915, 1935, 1965, and 1985.

1915: NEW FREEDOM

The public sector achieved significance as an important player in American political and economic life during the Wilson administration (1913–1921). The excesses of the private laissez-faire political economy needed reform. Large corporations were dominating the American economy. Wilson's legislative reforms, known as the New Freedom, included a tariff revision that allowed foreign competition with U.S. corporate interests. Other reforms provided for the creation of a federal reserve system for administering our monetary system and adoption of a small income tax as authorized by the recently passed 16th Amendment. Antitrust legislation was approved, and the Federal Trade Commission was established to police business practices. This progressive era revitalized democracy by making officials more directly responsive to public opinion. Congress extended the power of federal and state governments to regulate big business, to halt the exploitation of children in the labor force, to initiate federal road-building plans, and to conserve natural resources. World War I marked the end of the progressive movement as a dynamic force in national affairs.[10]

How did the philosophy of the Progressive Era influence the conduct of public administration? A new realization that government could monitor the activities of the private sector emerged. Removal of protectionist tariff barriers, prohibition of child labor, passage of a federal income tax, establishment of a central banking system, and initial funding for highways bolstered the influence of the public sector in the national economy. As the progressive trend continued for another half-century, the power of public administrators also expanded.

1935: NEW DEAL

Under the New Deal umbrella, Roosevelt's emphasis (1933–1945) on relief, recovery, and reform called for more government intervention in the private lives of Americans. Temperamentally on the side of the underdog and an enemy of privilege and exploitation, FDR was guided by his personal experience rather than ideology or doctrine. The New Deal expanded the attitudes of the progressive era.

After the stock market crash of 1929 and depression of the 1930s, people were questioning Herbert Hoover's beliefs in private enterprise and "rugged individualism." FDR responded to the crises with legislation and more public administration initiatives.

How did the philosophy of the New Deal influence the character of public administration? Government became a legitimate means for attempting to solve matters once considered private in American society. Government entered the domains of banking, stocks, pensions, housing, employment, public works development, management of the economy, and, of course, deficit spending. Although its enemies described the New Deal as socialistic, FDR's central purpose was to preserve the capitalist system by bringing about recovery. Government assumed the societal responsibilities that private corporations could not.

The New Deal, in expanding the role of public administration, saw the establishment of numerous government agencies commissioned to revitalize the American private sector. The Federal Deposit Insurance Corporation, established in 1933, guaranteed bank deposits and fostered renewed confidence in the whole national banking system. The Securities and Exchange Commission (1935) regulated stock exchanges, hoping to prevent a repetition of the events of 1929.

The Social Security Administration (1935), which provides unemployment insurance, is an early illustration of intergovernmental attempts to share political, fiscal, and administrative responsibilities. The federal government collected the money; the states administered the legislation; and the private sector financed the program by payroll deduction. The expanded role of the public sector allowed considerable flexibility in experimenting with new plans for merging the talents of the public and private sectors to alleviate problems in society. One of the provisions authorizing payment of pensions to workers past the age of 65 applied to about half of the working population.

In 1934 Congress created the Federal Housing Administration, now part of the Department of Housing and Urban Development, to administer an amortized home mortgage program that resulted in the suburbanization of America. After obtaining low interest loans for repayment over 20–25 year periods, many Americans now achieved the reality of home ownership. The National Labor Relations Board was established in 1935 to supervise the right of workers to join unions and bargain collectively. By providing protection to farmers and wage-earners, the New Deal fostered the build-up of big agriculture and big labor as a check on big business. In establishing these agencies, the federal government had also assumed much larger responsibilities for regulating the movements of the economy, providing security, and protecting underprivileged groups.

Public investment became a permanent policy. Although revenues were appropriated in ways that enhanced the national wealth (low-cost housing, schools, hospitals, post offices, highways), budget deficits and a steady increase in the federal debt were viewed as a necessary evil. As the economy grew and revenues increased, the need for public administrators also expanded. The public sector had achieved parity, in some respects, with the private sphere. Public works projects generated an incalculable contribution to the quality of American life through the construction of roads, streets, schools, parks, swimming pools, and playgrounds. The administrative state of the 1990s owes its origins to the reforms of the 1930s.[11]

1965: GREAT SOCIETY

Lyndon Johnson (1963–1969) was a protégé of FDR. First elected to Congress in 1937, Johnson saw firsthand the positive role government could play in American life. He believed, as FDR had before him, that government could do good things for people. Among the key measures successfully championed by LBJ were voting rights for southern blacks, termination of racial discrimination in public accommodations, establishment of federal aid to education for the first time, and origination of the Medicare system to help America's hard-pressed senior citizens. Johnson's administration saw the establishment of the Office of Economic Opportunity (1964), Department of Housing and Urban Development (1965), Model Cities Program (1966), and Department of Transportation (1966). At the same time, millions of acres of new park land and wilderness were preserved. Johnson's celebrated "War on Poverty" focused national attention on the stubborn problem of hunger and want in the midst of plenty.

Johnson, recalling the potentialities of government action he had witnessed in the New Deal era, called for a Great Society. Under this umbrella, he advocated government support of equal employment, voting rights, air pollution control, highway safety, public broadcasting, food stamps, manpower training, fair housing, Social Security increases, and civil service pay raises. Federal deficits under Johnson ranged from $1.6 billion in 1965 to $25.1 billion in 1968. However, LBJ's last budget request provided a $3.2 billion surplus in 1969—we have not had a balanced budget or surplus since that year. Although Johnson is remembered for committing the country's resources to the unpopular Vietnam War, he was mostly a pragmatic president who responded to the needs of America's middle class.[12]

How did the philosophy of the Great Society influence the conduct of public administration? Although sincere in such efforts as eliminating poverty and racism, caring for the sick, and educating the masses, Johnson became caught up in a "credibility gap" of what government—domestically and internationally—could accomplish. Opponents charged that corruption and inefficiency were resulting from a laundry list of new federal government programs. As World War I had ended the progressive era and the New Freedom, and as World War II had concluded the New Deal, the Vietnam War proved to be the most disastrous and divisive armed conflict since the Civil War and a calamity for the Great Society.

Political tragedy occurred not only in foreign policy. Despite the Great Society's efforts to attend to the needs of the poor and downtrodden—especially blacks—the destructive ghetto riots of the middle and late 1960s led to widespread perceptions that government assistance was not working. Public bureaucracy and public administrators were despised and disparaged. The tendency to downgrade and malign institutions of public administration, regardless of their tasks, limits, and records, is a theme that was capitalized on by Ronald Reagan—the antithesis of Wilson, FDR, and LBJ.

1985: REAGAN REVOLUTION

The "body politic" of the United States is more pragmatic than ideological. Rarely have the citizens of this nation strayed from the middle of the political road. Wilson was pragmatic in responding to the causes of the progressive era. FDR was pragmatic in responding to the causes of the depression. And LBJ was pragmatic in responding to the human and environmental concerns of the 1960s. Then, in 1980, the public elected a president who championed the ideology of the conservative wing of the minority party.

Reagan (1981–1989) began by rejecting the moderate to liberal consensus that had come to dominate both Democratic and Republican administrations since the election of FDR in 1932. Reagan envisioned a better America, based on less government and more individual enterprise. Not since FDR has there been such a massive redirection of public goals. The essence of the "revolution" was Reagan's belief that our problems were caused mainly by high government spending and by government intervention in the private marketplace.

The perspective of recent presidents had been that if something was wrong, it was the responsibility of government to attempt to correct the malfunction. In contrast, Reagan planned a full-scale retreat from the march toward a welfare state for the masses. Although Reagan's rhetoric was *revolutionary in purpose*, but his actions were *evolutionary in practice*.[13] Reagan talked tough, sometimes in revolutionary tones, but governed pragmatically, or in evolutionary ways. Reagan, the person, was a "throw-back" to simpler times.

LBJ tried to be all things to all people. He governed in the charismatic shadows of FDR and John F. Kennedy. FDR, JFK, and Reagan all had at least one thing in common. They used rhetoric to raise their agendas for subsequent policy implementation by public administrators.

Under Reagan, tax cuts and the build-up of defense took precedence over balancing the budget. The budget deficits of the Reagan administration make a "fiscal conservative" out of George Bush and will do the same for President Clinton and the Legislature of the 90s. Reagan budget deficits ranged from a low of $127.9 billion in 1982 to a high of $220.7 billion in 1987. The implication of these figures for future commitment to public programs, domestic or foreign, is that the budgets of the public sector must be leaner at all government levels. Public administrators will continue to attempt to do more with less, and taxpayers will demand the same level of service delivery for similar costs.

Early in the 1980s, Reagan gave the fight against inflation precedence over the previous administration's attempts to moderate the recession then taking place. Tax cuts were made, but the corresponding domestic spending cuts were not. Despite the reduction in tax revenues, defense spending was increased, and the deficit grew larger while the recession worsened.

Reagan's income tax cuts reduced revenues for domestic benefits and services. The recession reduced the business profits that were usually taxed for public programs. Public administrators were affected by deep cuts in grants to state and local governments and for programs serving the poor. However, the chief sources of federal budget growth since the 1950s—Social Security, Medicare, government employee pensions, and other middle-class programs—were too politically sensitive for the Reagan administration to cut.

Another priority for the Reagan administration was economic growth—not economic fairness. Therefore, tax rates were framed to provide the greatest benefits to high-income families. Reagan focused on reducing the marginal tax rates that would enhance savings, investment, and the work ethic.

The Reagan administration's policy toward regulations valued productivity over concerns of health, safety, civil rights, and the environment. The growth of productivity in the 1970s had slowed, in part, due to environmental regulations. During the Reagan years, natural resource policy focused upon production of energy resources rather than conservation. Even public lands and wilderness areas were no longer sacred.

Ironically, deficits were a means of advancing the "Reagan Revolution." George Bush and now Bill Clinton will be pressured to curb federal spending and to restrain the growth of major federal entitlement programs. An increasing portion of the taxpayer's dollar will be devoted to paying for interest on the federal debt. Benefits and services will be curtailed. As federal programs are reduced, state and local jurisdictions will be forced to search for new ways of financing and implementing services no longer paid for by Washington. The shift of political power away from Washington and toward state and local governments reflects Republican political philosophies. The middle class will continue its revolt against taxes and therefore local services will be reduced or kept to a minimum. Due to their lack of political clout in the economic system, the poor will feel the effect more than the middle class and, certainly, more than the upper class.

Wilson, FDR, and LBJ advocated government intervention in order to provide a measure of equal opportunity in our democratic, capitalistic system. Reagan, instead of overthrowing cardinal elements of the New Freedom, New Deal, and Great Society, sought to redirect government's role in society toward efficiency and productivity. Federal spending certainly did not decrease under Reagan. Reagan, however, changed the agenda from *proportionally more* spending to *proportionally less* spending. The power of the federal government has furthermore been enhanced by two World Wars and conflicts in Korea and Vietnam. However, wars are important to the life of political bureaucracy because wars enhance federal budgets and tend to consolidate the centralization of federal power. During World War I, World War II, Korea, and Vietnam, national defense expenditures increased considerably and enhanced the dominance of the federal government.

The benchmarks—1915, 1935, 1965, and 1985—illustrate the ebb and flow of government response to the demands of citizens. The political, social, and economic environment of the day has tremendous influence on public administrators. We can see that presidents, in leading and marshalling support from public bureaucracies, generally respond pragmatically to the dynamics of their times.

THE GROWTH OF PUBLIC BUREAUCRACY

The organization of federal, state, and local jurisdictions is evidence of the fragmented nature of public administration in the United States. The concept of federalism, or the structure of politics in the U.S., implies a system of authority apportioned constitutionally between the national and state governments.

Frederick S. Lane points out the three principal dimensions of federalism: *political, fiscal,* and *administrative.* The political dimension accounts for the ways in which local, state, and national jurisdictions participate in the decision-making processes. The fiscal dimension indicates which jurisdictions pay what amount for services. The administrative dimension tells us which level will supervise the administration of various services. Lane concludes: "Federalism is a contradiction: it tries to marry diversity and central direction."[14]

In all, there are about 80,000 government bodies in the United States. There is one national or central government and 50 state commonwealths. The remaining jurisdictions are local governments, such as municipalities (cities), counties, townships, school districts, and special districts.

Counties (about 3,000)—Counties are jurisdictions that include both the nation's largest cities and its smallest villages. Counties possess powers and offer services that may vary considerably and are created explicitly to serve the interests of the local community.

Townships (about 17,000)—Townships are subdivisions of counties. Townships vary greatly in functions and governmental organization. They exist mainly in northeastern and north central states.

School districts (about 15,000)—School districts are separate governments established to administer public school systems.

Special districts (about 28,000)—Special districts are limited-purpose governments established to administer one or several public functions for a designated area.[15]

Change was the magic word in the 1992 presidential and congressional elections. George Bush and Bill Clinton focused on interpretations of change. Political debates concerning change centered on ways in which counties, townships, school districts, and special districts could be made to be more effective in delivering public services. The Ronald Reagan-led Republican Party of the 1980s sought to reduce the influence of federal agencies on the lives of citizens. The Reagan policies succeeded in reducing significantly the federal government's power and influence on state and local jurisdictions. As a result, some functions of public policy are now relegated to private groups and not-for-profit organizations.

The impacts of the political agenda raised by the Reagan and Bush administrations in the 1980s must be dealt with by the Presidential and Congressional wings of the national Democratic Party in the mid-1990s. The Democrats—in the White House and in Congress—are challenged to govern effectively by cutting federal spending programs and raising taxes, and thereby, stem the tide of red ink in federal deficits. The battles of partisan, policy, and system politics determine what government programs will be abolished and the ones to be retained, perhaps even bolstered. In one way or another, all 80,000 units of government in the U.S. will be affected.

Comparing Public and Private Administration Nuances

Since we now have a better idea of what administration is, let us proceed to describe and designate the different forms it may take. In some respects these forms are as numerous as the various fields that apply them. Within the fields of health administration, welfare administration, and university administration for example, each institution often has its own distinctive type of administration, which may differ considerably from that of another institution. In another sense, no essential differences exist from one institution to another because administration deals with the working relationship of human beings. This common denominator is often a stronger unifying bond than the disparateness of the numerators.

It is sometimes said that administration is everywhere the same, and to some degree this is true. Running a hospital or a factory presents similar problems that tend to crop up whenever human beings seek to work cooperatively. Be that as it may, it is helpful in furthering our understanding of administration to distinguish the two broad areas where it is utilized— the public and private sectors. Since this book focuses on the public sector, it is useful to spell out the ways in which public administration differs from private business administration.

Public and private administration exhibit two areas of comparison and conflict: *substantive* and *procedural*.

Substantive issues of public and private administration raise questions concerning the issues of politics versus profits, the measurement of objectives, and management versus administration. These are areas of potential conflict.

Procedural issues address management as a universal process. Issues for procedural deliberation include open versus closed systems, methods of evaluation, criteria for decision making, personnel systems, planning, and efficiency.[16]

Substantive issues refer to conceptual or abstract concerns such as goals, objectives, means, ends, values, results, and priorities. Nobel Prize winning author, Herbert Simon, argues that the means and ends of public administration differ significantly from those of private administration.[17] He maintains that the importance of an end or value should not be ignored and that the process, or means, of management is a value in itself and cannot be separated from other values.

The purpose of a college education, for example, is to seek learning, training, and knowledge about the significant values of life. The *end* is learning, training, and knowledge. Education is the substance and the institution is the procedure. The institution provides the procedural means for the attainment of specific substantive ends. The *means* are provided by the curricula of the respective disciplines. In other words, the *means* for achieving learning, training, and knowledge are to meet the requirements of your discipline's prescribed curricula by attending classes and successfully completing exams.

Justice and the implementation of justice, for example, are illustrations of *ends* and *means.* Justice, in the philosophical realm, is an *end* in itself, a commonly held value. Justice can only be found in the United States by a *means*—due process of law. Justice is an example of a substantive issue; the matters of the judicial process constitute processes, authorities, and institutions that enforce procedural concerns. By unpacking the distinctions between substantive and procedural issues in public administration, the differences between administration in the private and the public sector will become clear.

SUBSTANTIVE ISSUES

1. Politics versus Profits

One obvious distinction between public and private administration is that the goals of public administration are grounded in politics and decision making processes that may affect an entire community of citizens, whereas the goals of private management are founded on the maximization of profit. Decision making in public bureaucracies is achieved by meeting the objectives of compromise, consensus, and democratic participation.

These objectives are very different from the private sector's emphasis on the concepts of efficiency, rationality, and profit. Although the goals of both public administration and private administration respond to outside clientele pressures, their concepts of bottom line accountability differ: one's god is a consensus of citizens concerned about the issues confronting an entire community and the other's god is profit.

The private organization *also* suffers constraints, but these usually hinge on its need to make a profit. As long as it is advancing toward this goal, the private organization enjoys considerable latitude in the way it operates and in the specific goals it may set for itself. This profit motive accounts for another feature that many feel distinguishes the two types of administration—differences in their efficiency.

2. Measurement of Objectives

Objectives grounded in compromise, consensus, and democratic participation differ from objectives based on efficiency, rationality, and profit. The private sector ultimately makes rational decisions based upon clear, concise, and quantifiable statements found in the sales ledger. The public sector deals with social intangibles such as health, welfare, and common defense. The private sector places prime consideration on individual values and preferences, whereas the public sector allocates communal services, which are offered to all citizens.

For example, McDonald's produces hamburgers at a market price, responding to the public's hunger for hamburgers. And state universities produce college graduates, based upon their successfully meeting the requirements of the learning, training, and knowledge of a certain curriculum. You may immediately recognize if McDonald's has satisfied your demand for food. However, the success, or lack thereof, of your college professors in educating you may not be fully appreciated for a much longer period of time.

3. Management versus Administration

In the private sector, the term "management" commonly refers to those persons in line *positions*, whereas in the public sector, the term "administration" refers to those in line *functions*. (Line personnel command, have authority, and are generalists; staff personnel possess knowledge and skills, give advice, and are specialists. See chapter 3 for more explanation and illustration.)

A position implies *authority* for corporate action; a function implies *duty*, such as the function of the police to protect and assist the public. Modern technologies, rewards (profits) and penalties (defaults) enhance private sector productivity. Depending upon market trends, profits may be as likely in one year as defaults are in the following one.

However, the less systematic and less structured public sector produces intangible services that are difficult to measure. The term *management* is characterized by decision making in the corporate model of hierarchy. The term *administration* suggests decision making by the collegial model of consensus. One is led by a CEO; the other is guided by a committee.

PROCEDURAL ISSUES

1. Open versus Closed Systems

Procedural concerns, such as the accountability factor, reflect the *dilemma* of the open versus closed system, or the goldfish bowl of public administration versus the closed board room of private administration. The openness of the goldfish bowl image magnifies and broadcasts the activities of the public administrator and politician, while the closed board room image shows how those in the private sector can harbor corporate secrets to seek a competitive edge.

Government bureaucrats and politicians operate in the glare of the public's right to know about operations financed by taxpayers. The private corporation, meanwhile, escapes such scrutiny unless the firm breaks the law or defrauds the public, for example, by polluting the air or selling consumers harmful products. In such cases, an arm of government may demand more accountability. Failing these transgressions, private sector administration is a process to which the public is not invited.

2. Methods of Evaluation

Consensus, compromise, and democratic participation by citizens promote a natural diversity in the evaluation of government services. Community leaders seek consensus, agree to compromise, and advocate citizen participation in order to find support for policies. In contrast, efficiency, rationality, and concern for profit cause private sector entrepreneurs to view corporate evaluation quite differently. If a phase of an industry fails to produce profits, rationality dictates efficiency in cutting losses.

The public sector focuses on social good; the private sector emphasizes fiscal control. The two may, in some cases, be incompatible. For example, the social good of the Department of Defense may be to prevent war; however, if the privately-owned Boeing Corporation does not receive enough revenue from government business with DOD, the company may go out of business. Another illustration: If a university decides to toughen academic standards and slice the undergraduate enrollment by several thousand students, the resulting social good for the school may be a heightened academic reputation; however, private entrepreneurs operating bookstores, eateries, bars, and other businesses frequented by students may feel the pinch, lay off local employees, and even close their doors.

3. Public versus Private Decision-Making Criteria

Although the formal steps in decision making may be similar in both public and private management areas, the criteria managers use in making decisions are not. The definition of the goal or problem, the preferred consumer response, and the allocation of resources may apply similarly to both sectors: the logic, or mode of thinking, behind such decision making is distinct.

The public sector university's bookstore is, for example, under very different constraints from a privately run bookstore across the street. The public sector bookstore demands a higher standard in procedural process (the manner in which a function is carried out) and maintains certain expectations and guarantees in hiring, firing, promotions, and general conduct of bookstore business. The private sector bookstore can sell items based upon the supply and demand of the marketplace; the public sector bookstore must respond to every course, no matter how esoteric or obscure, and to every program offered by the state university.

4. Personnel Systems

Recruitment and socialization processes by both private management and public administration allow people to obtain and maintain employment and to be promoted under a system that evaluates skills, knowledge, and expertise. Unlike the private sector however, an applicant for a full-time civil service position governed by a merit system will go through a fixed process, monitored by law. Women and minorities may also receive some preference in the recruitment process for public sector jobs—a preference not always afforded them in the private sector.

The personnel systems in the public and private arenas reflect their essential differences. Public sector employees enjoy the privileges of administrative due process because laws prescribe guidelines for recruitment, selection, promotion, and retention of employees. Merit plans that evaluate skills, knowledge, and expertise are a hiring tool, but they may differ greatly from agency to agency. Private enterprise employees have no guarantees of due process; profit needs require flexibility as to the "when and how" of hiring and firing. In competitive work environments, skills dictate success.

5. Long-Term and Short-Term Planning

Planning may be considered part of the process of decision making. Some argue that planning is a means of controlling employees. The private sector manager does not need to seek consensus among employees before acting; the manager alone makes decisions, and the company's profit or loss ledger reflects success or failure. For the public sector employee, planning becomes hazardous if political leaders are continuously changing after elections regardless of their own success or failure. Public officials need program continuity and political stability in order to carry out their responsibilities consistently without turmoil and change. In the private sector, planning is easier because there are no demands of due process or legally prescribed guarantees concerning hiring, firing, and promotion. The public administrator may not have this luxury.

Stable political and economic conditions are essential for planning in both sectors. For example, America's Middle East policy should transcend political leaders and political parties. In other words, a new policy should not be adopted, changed significantly, or abandoned simply because a new political leader takes office. Foreign governments—allies and enemies—will not know how to respond if policy changes occur with every new president. Likewise, private entrepreneurs cannot plan or act decisively under economic conditions of stagnation or high interest rates and steep inflation. If the political and economic environments are unstable, entrepreneurs will shy away from new investments.

6. Efficiency

The need for efficiency is paramount in both the public and private sectors. Hierarchical control, coordination, planning, meritorious performance, and authority lines are emphasized in both public and private sectors. Stockbrokers and investors in private corporations demand efficiency and productivity for their dollars. Likewise, taxpayers demand that public administrators produce more services more effectively with fewer dollars. However, the bottom line, or profit concern, of the private sector allows managers to realize success or failure immediately; the circumstances of the public sector, with its less precise methods of evaluation, may take longer to reflect the value and efficiency of a public service.

BLURRING OR BIFURCATION?

On the substantive issues we have discussed (politics versus profits, measurement of objectives, and management versus administration), a comparison of the public and private sectors reveals more blurring than bifurcation into two separate arenas. A comparison of procedural issues (open versus closed systems, methods of evaluation, public versus private decision making criteria, personnel systems, planning and efficiency) reveals distinctions concerning the accountability factor, but similarities in developing participative personnel systems to evaluate the expertise, knowledge, and skills of employees.

The public sector is grounded in *political equality* with consideration for everyone's opinion, seeking consensus, compromise, and democratic participation. The private sector is based upon *economic efficiency*, seeking definitive results, rationality in decision making, and maximization of profit.

Public administration, then, differs in significant ways from private administration. These differences hinge largely on the greater legal accountability of the former compared to the flexibility of the latter. Determining which sector is the most efficient remains a complex question, subject not only to variances in products and procedures but also to differences in purposes and processes.

INTEREST GROUPS AND PUBLIC BUREAUCRACY

The corps of Washington lobbyists has grown steadily since the New Deal, but especially since the early 1970s. This growth parallels the growth in federal spending and the expansion of federal authority into new areas. Lobbyists compete vigorously to safeguard traditional spending in their areas of interest. During the Reagan administration, pressures to reduce federal spending intensified competition by interest groups for the dwindling supply of federal dollars.

Industries, labor unions, ethnic groups, religious groups, professional organizations, citizen groups, and even foreign business interests all periodically—and some continuously—seek to exert pressure on national and state legislatures in order to attain legislative goals. Pressure or interest groups usually have selfish aims: their members wish to assert rights, win privileges, or benefit financially. A group's power to influence legislation is often based less on its arguments than on the size of its membership, its financial resources, and the astuteness of its representatives.

If there were any doubt about the increasing presence of special interests in American politics, within the Capital Beltway, the interstate highway that circles Washington, D.C., there are 2,200 trade groups that employ more Washingtonians than any other organization except government or travel and tourism. See Table 2–1 depicting the top ten national associations in terms of members, budget and staff size, based on 1991 figures.

Expert articulation of particular citizen interests drives public bureaucracies in the United States. Legislatures write vague laws. Public administrators interpret those statutes with specificity in the *Federal Register*. The statutes are then codified in the *Code of Federal Regulations*. The public philosophy of the United States in the 20th century is no longer capitalism, but instead *interest group liberalism*, a concept developed by Theodore J. Lowi. Lowi claims that capitalism has declined as an ideology and is dead as a public philosophy. Capitalism, the old public philosophy, has become outmoded since World War II because the elite, such as lobbyists, no longer disagree about whether government should be involved in making policies for private citizens or for private sector businesses. Republicans and Democrats, as participants in interest group liberalism, fully agree that government should be a player in monitoring, if not directing, the relations among private citizens.[18]

As the great depression ended and World War II began, U.S. capitalism came to be called "conservatism," but Lowi argues that this description is a misnomer. He states that capitalism never became conservative, but declined because it became irrelevant and erroneous. Capitalist ideology according to Lowi, did not endure as the public philosophy because it could accept only one legitimate type of modern social control—competition.

TABLE 2–1   The Biggest Groups

The top ten national associations in terms of members, budget, and staff size, based on 1991 figures:		
Most Members		
	Members	Base
1. American Association of Retired Persons	32,000,000	Washington
2. American Automobile Association	31,000,000	Heathrow, Fla.
3. YMCA-USA	12,804,082	Chicago
4. National Geographic Society	10,500,000	Washington
5. International Association for Medical Assistance to Travellers	9,500,000	Lewiston, N.Y.
6. National Forensic League	7,420,000	Ripon, Wis.
7. National Wildlife Federation	6,200,000	Washington
8. National PTA Congress of Parents and Teachers	6,100,000	Chicago
9. National Council for Industrial Defense	6,000,000	Washington
Foundation for the Support of International Medical Training	6,000,000	Lewiston, N.Y.
10. Boy Scouts of America	5,363,593	Irving, Tex.
Most Money		
	1991 Budget	Base
1. YMCA-USA	$1,327,812,480	Chicago
2. American Red Cross	$1,105,389,000	Washington
3. United Nations Development Program	$800,000,000	New York City
4. Society of Women Engineers	$500,000,000	New York City
5. Planned Parenthood Federation of America	$331,000,000	New York City
6. CARE	$323,357,000	New York City
7. Electric Power Research Institute	$259,000,000	Palo Alto, Calif.

TABLE 2-1   The Biggest Groups, continued

The top ten national associations in terms of members, budget, and staff size, based on 1991 figures:		
Most Members		
	Members	Base
8. American Heart Association	$250,000,000	Dallas
9. United States Olympic Committee	$249,000,000	Colorado Springs
10. Catholic Relief Services	$246,000,000	Baltimore
Biggest Staffs		
	Staff Size	Base
1. Salvation Army	38,549	Verona, N.Y.
2. American Red Cross	25,394	Washington
3. YWCA-USA	21,000	New York City
4. CARE	8,800	New York City
5. YMCA-USA	8,710	Chicago
6. Farmland Industries	7,169	Kansas City, Mo.
7. PLAN International	6,000	East Greenwich, R.I.
8. Underwriters Laboratories	3,900	Northbrook, Ill.
9. Boy Scouts of America	3,850	Irving, Tex.
10. Save the Children Federation	3,045	Westport, Conn.

Source: Association Management and *The Washington Post*, April 30, 1992, page A21.

Lowi concludes that the old dialogue between liberalism and conservatism "passed into the graveyard of consensus," spelling the "decline of meaningful adversary political proceedings in favor of administrative, technical and logrolling politics. In a nutshell, politics became a question of equity rather than a question of morality. Adjustment comes first, rules of law come last, if at all."[19] As interest groups clash, the priority becomes equal opportunity for any group to put forth its unique version of how life should be conducted. The values of any particular organization are secondary. In interest group liberalism, diverse groups check the values, or perspectives, of opposing interests by arguing for their own set of values in the great American marketplace of ideas.

Republicans want government to rescue failing corporations. Democrats seek government intervention in labor concerns. The Rev. Jesse Jackson argues for government intervention on behalf of the poor, and the Rev. Jerry Falwell preaches for laws to control a woman's access to an abortion. Milk producers, tobacco growers, billboard advertisers, movie makers, bankers, physicians, broadcasters, cable TV operators, farmers, entrepreneurs, and energy interests are just a few of the more than 2,000 lobbyists who insist that their concerns should be written into law. Whether liberal or conservative, the elite want to utilize the power and funding of government for their personal ends. According to Lowi, the most significant difference between liberals and conservatives, Democrats and Republicans, can be found in the interest groups with which they identify. Accepted as legitimate, the values of organized interest groups guide Congressmen in their votes, presidents in their programs, and bureaucrats in their administrative discretion. The only necessary guidelines for the framing of laws depend upon the validity or legitimacy of interest group demands.[20]

The philosophy of interest group liberalism is pragmatic, with government playing the role of broker, and optimistic about government's role; that which is good for government is also good for society. The liberal process of private interaction with public officials is accessible to all organized interests and offers no value judgments concerning any particular claim or set of claims. Interest group liberalism defines the public interest as the amalgamation of claims of various interests. The principle of representation extends into public bureaucracy as administrators afford due process to all citizens.

In order to represent such diverse political, economic, and cultural interests, legislatures make open-ended, vague laws and issue broad delegations to public administrators to regulate interests in society. Says Lowi: "It (interest group liberalism) impairs legitimacy by converting government from a moralistic to a mechanistic institution. It impairs the potential of positive law to correct itself by allowing the law to become anything that eventually bargains itself out as acceptable to the bargainers . . . Interest group liberalism seeks pluralistic government in which there is no formal specification of means or of ends. In a pluralistic government there is, therefore, no substance. Neither is there procedure. There is only process.[21]

In other words, procedures and processes are vital, and substance and values are at the mercy of the strongest interests. For a listing of the most influential groups, see Table 2–2.

TABLE 2-2   Top 50 PACS (In Donations)

Political action committee donations to congressional candidates from Jan. 1, 1991, through March 31, 1992.

Rank, Name	Contributions	% Increase/decrease from 1/89 to 3/31/90
1. International Brotherhood of Teamsters	$1,366,720	55
2. Association of Trial Lawyers of America	937,550	20
3. American Federation of State, County & Municipal Employees	747,283	−0.4
4. Air Line Pilots Association	722,500	17
5. International Brotherhood of Electrical Workers	696,340	25
6. American Bankers Association	685,971	22
7. International Association of Machinists and Aerospace Workers	682,923	11
8. American Institute of Certified Public Accountants	681,051	31
9. American Medical Association	677,969	25
10. United Auto Workers	676,147	7
11. National Association of Realtors	660,373	−16
12. American Telephone & Telegraph Co.	638,770	−23
13. National Association of Home Builders	606,432	3
14. Laborers' International Union	595,250	38
15. American Federation of Teachers	556,150	29
16. District 2-Marine Engineers' Beneficial Association	535,850	51
17. National Association of Life Underwriters	529,700	−11
18. National Rifle Association	527,442	67
19. National Committee to Preserve Social Security and Medicare	526,550	n/a
20. Seafarers' International Union	518,250	92
21. American Postal Workers Union	505,390	20
22. National Automobile Dealers Association	503,140	51
23. Transporation Political Education Committee	486,215	45
24. American Dental Association	484,785	143
25. National Education Association	481,725	−22
26. Auto Dealers and Drivers for Free Trade	474,550	127
27. Federal Express Corp.	474,475	2
28. National Association of Retired Federal Employees	468,250	−9
29. United Food & Commercial Workers	463,293	29
30. UA Plumbing and Pipe Fitting Industry	454,500	50

TABLE 2-2 Top 50 PACS (In Donations), continued

Political action committee donations to congressional candidates from Jan. 1, 1991, through March 31, 1992.

Rank, Name	Contributions	% Increase/ decrease from 1/89 to 3/31/90
31. United Parcel Service	452,648	14
32. National Cable Television Association	431,400	43
33. RJR Nabisco Inc.	430,800	18
34. National Association of Letter Carriers	425,877	−52
35. National Beer Wholesalers	376,081	20
36. Phillip Morris Companies Inc.	368,317	28
37. General Electric Co.	363,875	n/a
38. Independent Insurance Agents of America	358,718	−10
39. United Brotherhood of Carpenters	350,954	−49
40. United Steelworkers of America	340,950	27
41. National PAC (pro-Israel)	331,000	23
42. Communication Workers of America	330,270	3
43. National Committee for an Effective Congress	323,700	70
44. Chicago Mercantile Exchange	322,600	31
45. GTE Corp.	320,250	86
46. National Rural Electric Cooperative Association	319,779	18
47. General Dynamics Corp.	311,491	59
48. Waste Management Inc.	308,439	23
49. Human Rights Campaign Fund	307,941	136
50. Aircraft Owners & Pilots Association	303,000	10

Highest percentage increases in political donations:

1. American Dental Association, up 143%
2. Human Rights Campaign Fund, up 136%
3. Auto Dealers, up 126%
4. Seafarers International Union, up 92%
5. National Committee for an Effective Congress, up 69%

Highest percentage decreases in political donations:

1. Letter Carriers, down 52%
2. United Carpenters, down 49%
3. AT&T, down 23%
4. National Education Association, down 22%
5. National Association of Realtors, down 16%

SOURCE: Federal Election Commission reports and *The Washington Post*, June 8, 1992, page A17.

SUMMARY

- The *ecology* of the administrative craft deals with the relationships between public administrators and their environments. Public administrators cannot operate in a vacuum.
- With its numerous organizations, modern America is the epitome of the *organized society*. Our organized society exists in an environment of equal rights and unequal incomes. Conflicts between these two phenomena result in tensions between the *political principles of democracy* and the *economic principles of capitalism*.
- The political economy of the U.S. is that of *democratic capitalism*. The thrust of this ideology comes from the opposing values of political power and economic structure.
- Democracy is characterized by equality, due process, fairness, participation, suffrage, and electoral politics. Capitalism implies efficiency, productivity, hierarchy, competition, and entrepreneurship. Public administration finds its origins in democracy but owes much to the fundamental principles of capitalism.
- The dimensions of U.S. federalism are *political, fiscal,* and *administrative.* Through federalism, Americans "structure" 50 sets of partisan politics. Counties, townships, school and special districts constitute the great majority of the 80,000 governments in the U.S.
- The ebbs and flows of government expansion and constraints may be understood by looking at four critical periods in the 20th century. These eras of political economy occurred around the years 1915, 1935, 1965, and 1985.
- In 1992, for the first time in American history, the number of federal, state, and local jobs outdistanced the number of manufacturing jobs.
- *Substantive issues* of public and private administration raise questions concerning issues of politics versus profits, measurement of objectives, and management versus administration. *Procedural issues* concern open versus closed systems, methods of evaluation, decision making criteria, personnel systems, planning, and efficiency.
- The public philosophy of the United States in the late 20th century is *interest group liberalism.* Whether liberal or conservative, the elite in society want to utilize the power and purse of government for their personal ends. The influence of organized interest groups extends to congressmen in their votes, presidents in their programs, and bureaucrats in their administrative discretion. The philosophy of interest group liberalism is pragmatic, with government exercising its role as broker. In pluralistic government, procedure and process may be as important as substance.

• The effectiveness of interest groups in the "Iron Triangle" of elected officials, consumers, and government bureaucrats depends, in large part, upon the group's number of members, size of its budget, and expertise of its Washington staff.

Now that we have explored the ecology of the craft, we are ready to move to another important subject public administrators must be aware of—the anatomy, or structure, of organizations.

The following case study shows how the private infrastructure of citizen interests affects the interplay of partisan, policy, and system politics. Are the political principles of democracy and economic principles of capitalism realized in the politics of building the Hubert H. Humphrey Metrodome?

CASE STUDY

Private Infrastructure: Public Influence[22]

A growing controversy in the life of today's city is the political economy of attracting and retaining professional sports teams. The cooperation between the public and private sectors in the building of the Hubert H. Humphrey Metrodome in Minneapolis illustrates the inner dynamic of civic planning and corporate entrepreneurship that contributes to economic growth, more revenues for public programs, and, indirectly, to a healthier community atmosphere with a better quality of life for everyone. In the ecology of democratic capitalism, where a growth economy is necessary, more vibrant economies can provide more tax dollars to support more public services. If a community's tax base is declining, the number and quality of public programs will decline as well.

Today the enclosed, multi-use stadium is not only a center of entertainment in the community but also a symbol of civic vitality that may be linked to sports, politics, and economics as well. In the 1990s, the dome stadium will be as much the center of civic activity as the public square with its gazebo was at the turn of the century. The dome stadium is often the center of the metropolis, if not in geographic terms, then certainly economically. Such a building opens up opportunities for varied entertainment and adds to convention and tourism prospects. Cities retain and seek major league professional franchises as dome tenants because of the perception that professional sports teams bring dollars and good publicity to the community.

The Politics of the Metrodome
This case study depicts the intricate weaving of political theory and practical politics. Personalities and individual efforts are set against the broader background of how issues are contested in Minnesota's public life. The study also illustrates how the public and private sectors can work together to produce an outcome acceptable to both forces, pointing out how business incentives and efficient market techniques may be incorporated into the workings of government.

Since the early 1960s, the Minnesota Twins and Minnesota Vikings played their games at Metropolitan Stadium in Bloomington, Minnesota, a Minneapolis suburb. The stadium, which had been built for the Minneapolis Millers minor league baseball team in the mid-1950s, was expanded for major league sports in 1961 and 1965. The Minnesota teams represent two diverse communities. When the Met was built in 1955, Bloomington was a "neutral" suburb, a rustic community with a population of about 10,000, a village that carried little, if any, political or economic clout in the state.

Within five years, Bloomington's population zoomed to 50,000. The "Bloomington strip," a string of hotels and restaurants, developed around the nearby stadium and airport. Minneapolis witnessed the exodus of city dwellers and city businesses to Bloomington and other surrounding suburbs. Minneapolis needed the economic development which a domed facility could generate with more jobs and a larger tax base, and the city certainly could use the national attention that professional sports teams bring.

At the Met, the sight lines for football were poor. The stadium was essentially a baseball stadium that accommodated football in the fall and winter. The seating capacity was 48,700, one of the smaller pro football stadiums, but certainly a suitable capacity for baseball. (There are only eight home professional football games yearly, whereas there are 81 baseball dates.)

The Vikings, therefore, needed a new home more than did the Twins. Besides the problem of viewing football from baseball angles, the field was an annual victim of Minnesota winters. Although some football purists claimed the Vikings had a psychological edge over opponents in the freezing weather, Viking management argued that stressful weather conditions kept fans away and created miserable weather conditions for those who chose to brave freezing temperatures. Regardless, the Vikings wanted out of the Met and threatened to leave Minnesota. As former Minnesota state senator, Steve Keefe, pointed out, "The Minnesota Vikings are not a Minnesota team. They're a company that plays football and happens to be located in Minnesota. They're here to make money. They're not here because they love us . . . no matter how much we love them."

Why did government get involved in the sports stadium business? William Donald Schaefer, former mayor of Baltimore, now governor of Maryland, comments: "You look at the prestige, you look at the jobs, you look at the things it generates in a city. You won't be able to replace them, and once they are gone, they are gone." Local government in Minnesota is characterized as a "strong council-weak mayor" urban arrangement of political power. The local political culture, therefore, dictated an active role for business in the stadium project. The mixture of business involvement made it improbable that a Minneapolis stadium could be constructed exclusively with public money. A conservative, Scandinavian community such as Minneapolis-St. Paul is likely to be frugal with the taxpayers' dollars, refusing to invest in such a public commitment.

Partisan, Policy, and System Politics in the Metrodome

Since Minneapolis is governed by a strong-council, weak-mayor plan, dominance by a political machine or party boss was unlikely. In recent years, neither the Democratic nor Republican parties, either in state or national politics, had been dominant for an extended length of time. Political power in Minneapolis is historically dispersed.

Minnesota state government is likewise characterized by a high degree of citizen participation. Despite such civic mindedness the citizens of Minnesota were never allowed an opportunity to express their preference in a direct vote on the stadium issue, since a tradition of citizens' referenda does not exist in Minnesota. Former governor Rudy Perpich, a populist Democrat, appointed a seven-member Stadium Commission whose functions and procedures were defined by the state legislature. Although members of the commission represented a broad base of interests in Minnesota, their decisions on the cost and location of the new stadium were by no means political in a partisan sense.

The extent of an interest group's influence depends on its resources. In this case, the resources were substantial. The Industry Square Development Company (ISDC), a private group of interested citizens, emerged as the "public service investment." John Cowles, Jr., owner of the Minneapolis Star and Tribune, committed $4 million in cash and $900,000 in land (the company owned 3/4ths of a block of the Industry Square area); the First National Bank and the Northwestern National Bank pledged $1 million each. The Vikings agreed to commit $972,500 until other businesses could be found to pay all or part of the remaining sum.

On November 15, 1978, Cowles announced that at least 42 business firms, including the Minnesota Vikings football team, had pledged $14,750,000 to pay the costs of the stadium land package. Of the total, $10.7 million had come from private investors who promised to buy common stock in ISDC if Minneapolis were chosen as the stadium site. The remaining $4 million had been given in the form of tax deductible, charitable contributions.

Other interests concerned with the stadium project were the Minneapolis Chamber of Commerce and the AFL-CIO. Ad hoc groups included the Committee to Let the People Decide, a group advocating more democracy in the stadium process; Citizens Opposed to the Stadium Tax (COST); and Minnesotans Against the Downtown Dome (MADD). COST's leader was Fred Primoli, a St. Paul bar owner, who opposed the extra two percent tax on every drink for a Minneapolis stadium that would benefit bar owners across the Mississippi River. Two neighborhoods near the proposed stadium site, Elliot Park and Cedar Riverside, combined forces to form MADD.

Members of the Stadium Commission had four policy options. They could decide: 1) to build a multipurpose, open-air stadium in Bloomington for football, baseball, and soccer at a cost estimate of $37.5 million; 2) to remodel the Met in Bloomington and build an open-air football and soccer stadium, Bloomington's Met, at a cost estimate of $42 million; 3) to construct a multipurpose, domed stadium in Minneapolis at a cost estimate of $55 million; 4) or to do nothing. The last option was never a popular alternative, since the Vikings had informed commission members that it would be "exceedingly difficult" for the team to sign a long-term lease for an open-air Bloomington stadium.

The commissioners' final decision was insulated from the control of democratic politics. They were accountable to no one—not the legislators, not the interest groups, not the public. [Throughout the 1970s, not one public opinion poll showed that either Minnesota, metropolitan, or Minneapolis residents favored a Minneapolis stadium over a Bloomington stadium, whether it be a new construction or a remodeled Met.] Since the Metropolitan Stadium Commission was created by the Minnesota legislature, the creation of the Stadium Commission was, in effect, the creation of another branch of government. According to researcher Amy Klobuchar, the transfer of authority from the legislative branch of the government to a bureaucratic one (the Commission) represents a phenomenon of American politics that commenced soon after the New Deal.

"There is a certain appeal of this 'apolitical' mode of decision-making," concludes Klobuchar. "Things seem cleaner, neater. Decisions are more comprehensive and prompt. In the hands of the commissioners, the stadium issue was no longer considered a legislative beachball to be tossed to and fro by the prevailing political winds." The Commission voted by a 4–3 margin to locate the new stadium in Minneapolis. "In choosing the Minneapolis alternative, I am simply making my best judgment based on what I perceive to be in the long-term, public interest," stated commission Chair, Dan J. Brutger.

The Minneapolis dome, while winning no high awards for architectural aesthetics, was built primarily with private funds, came in $8 million under the $55 million budget, and was completed on time. From a purely economic perspective, the project is quite successful.

The Metrodome provides important home field advantages for the Twins throughout the American League season in post-season championship competition, and during World Series games. In 1987 and 1991, the Minnesota Twins defeated the St. Louis Cardinals and Atlanta Braves, respectively, in the baseball World Series. During these World Series games, the noise levels created by overjoyed Minnesota fans broke all kinds of records, to the dismay of environmentalists. Baseball traditionalists, perhaps suffering from cultural lag, were not happy either; the World Series was played inside a building on a green rug for the first time in baseball history. During the season, the winning Twins provided entertainment for a record 2.2 million customers. Both the liquor and hotel-motel taxes, which had been levied to pay for the Metrodome, were lifted in 1984, so, with the exception of the indirect state subsidy in the form of the real estate tax exemptions, the dome is basically self-supporting.

With no professional teams, did Bloomington's plight worsen? The land upon which the old Met stood, which was appraised at $5 to $7 million, was sold for more than $18 million because of highly competitive bidding. Conflicts between Minneapolis and Bloomington, city and suburb, subsided when, in 1992, Mall of America (MOA), the nation's largest shopping and entertainment complex, opened on the old stadium site. Where the Vikings played those "ice bowl" NFL playoff games and Harmon Killebrew hit home runs, MOA employs 10,000 people in permanent jobs and is expecting 40 million customer visits annually by 1996.

MOA is expected to house 270 stores, about 30 eateries, 14 movie screens, 10 nightclubs, 12 sets of restrooms and a two-level 18-hole miniature golf course. A seven-acre "Camp Snoopy" theme park from Buena Park's Knott's Berry Farm is a drawing card. MOA enticed Nordstrom, Bloomingdale's, and Macy's—all big names in the shopping world—into their suburban Bloomington site. Mall operators expect 70 percent of sales to come from customers within a radius of 150 miles.

Controversies over public subsidies for private projects are part of America's social, political, and economic infrastructure. However, not everyone is pleased with Minneapolis' march into the future. "The park should be banned from baseball," stated the late Twins and Yankee manager, Billy Martin. Researcher Klobuchar, commenting on how economics has changed the sports of our youth, concludes: "The teams no longer play football or baseball, but domeball, a climate controlled, Orwellian version of sports."

What can we learn from the political economy of domeball?

- A complex, sensitive relationship between public and private spheres of influence has developed in every American community; a combination of public and private forces and priorities that is unique to every American community.
- Partisan, policy, and system politics blend together and are not separate modes of operation.
- The values of both democracy and bureaucracy are at work simultaneously. Citizens democratically elect their civic leaders every four years, having exercised their voting rights, the public does not, however, contribute directly to every public decision made in society during the interim. At this juncture, the principles of bureaucracy or public administration come to the front and center stage. In the Minnesota case, the corporate private bureaucracies, such as The Minneapolis Star and Tribune, the Mott Foundation, First National Bank, Northwestern National Bank, and of course, the Minnesota Twins and Vikings, emerged to influence public policy.
- The extent of an interest groups' influence depends on its financial and human resources.
- While public administrators need revenues for implementing a variety of publicly funded programs, business interests need to be creative by introducing new projects for achieving a more vibrant local economy. Businesses realize profits; profits are taxed; these revenues pay for qualified public personnel to provide government services. In democracy and capitalism, freedom to offer new ideas in the entrepreneurial spirit is essential for achieving human potential.

QUESTIONS AND INSTRUCTIONS

1. Was the public interest of Minnesotans served by the legislature's decision to create a Stadium Commission with the power to decide this issue? Was the decision to build a new stadium in the best interests of Minnesotans?
2. To whom, if anyone, was the Stadium Commission accountable for its decision?
3. What role did Minnesota's political culture play in stimulating local economic forces to build a new stadium?
4. In what ways are partisan, policy, and system politics evident in the building of the new stadium?
5. What interest groups influenced the partisan, policy, and system decision making processes to relocate the Twins and Vikings in downtown Minneapolis?
6. How are the political principles of democracy and the economic principles of capitalism manifest in this case?
7. Should professional sports franchises be permitted complete economic freedom to move to a more profitable economic setting without first compensating the community that supported them over the years? In other words, do the Minnesota Twins and Vikings owe compensation to the citizens of Bloomington?

ENDNOTES

1. Emmette S. Redford, *Democracy in the Administrative State* (New York: Oxford University Press, 1969), 3.
2. Arthur M. Okun, *Equality and Efficiency: The Big Tradeoff* (Washington, D.C.: The Brookings Institution, 1975), 4.
3. Henry T. Abraham, *Freedom and the Court: Civil Rights and Liberties in the United States* (New York: Oxford University Press, 1977), 110–129.
3. *Ibid.,* 119.
5. *Ibid.,* 120.
6. Lester M. Salamon and John J. Siegfried, "Economic Power and Political Influence: The Impact of Industry Structure on Public Policy," *American Political Science Review,* Vol. 71, No. 4 (December 1977), 1026–1043.
7. Adam Przeworski and Michael Wallerstein, "Democratic Capitalism at the Crossroads," *Democracy,* Vol. 2, No. 3 (July 1982), 52–68.
8. Barbara Vobejda, "In Job Strength, Manufacturing Eclipsed by Public Sector," *The Washington Post,* August 18, 1992, page A11.
9. *US News & World Report,* Vol. 113, No. 7, August 17, 1992, page 13. See also John Rouse, "Government-Dominated Workforce Creating Change," *The Muncie Star,* August 23, 1992, page 10A.

10. John D. Hicks, George E. Mowry, and Robert E. Burke, *A History of American Democracy* (Boston: Houghton Mifflin Co., 1966), 552–558; and Henry Bamford Parkes, *The United States of America: A History* (New York: Alfred A. Knopf, 1968), 560–564.

11. Hicks, Mowry, and Burke, *A History of American Democracy*, 670–691; and Parkes, *The United States of America*, 628–645.

12. See Doris Kerns, *Lyndon Johnson and the American Dream* (New York: Harper & Row, 1976), 210–250; Lyndon Baines Johnson, *The Vantage Point: Perspective of the Presidency, 1963–1969* (New York: Holt, Rinehart, and Winston, 1971); John E. Schwarz, *America's Hidden Success: A Reassessment of Public Policy from Kennedy to Reagan* (New York: W. W. Norton & Co., 1988).

13. See John L. Palmer and Isabel V. Sawhill, editors, *The Reagan Record* (Washington: The Ballinger Press, 1984); "The Reagan Record," *The Urban Institute Policy and Research Report*, Vol. 14, No. 1 (August 1984), 1–17; "Perspectives on the Reagan Years: Popular vs. Political Leadership," Vol. 17, No. 1 (April 1987), 1–3.

14. Frederick S. Lane, *Current Issues in Public Administration* (New York: St. Martin's Press, 1982), 156.

15. Lawrence J. O'Toole, Jr., *American Intergovernmental Relations, Foundations, Perspectives, and Issues* (Washington, D.C.: CQ Press, 1985), 2.

16. Michael A. Murray, "Comparing Public and Private Management: An Exploratory Essay," *Public Administration Review*, Vol. 35, No. 4 (July/August, 1975), 364–371.

17. Herbert A. Simon, *Administrative Behavior* (New York: Macmillan, 1957).

18. Theodore J. Lowi, *The End of Liberalism: The Second Republic of the United States* (New York: W. W. Norton & Co., 1969).

19. *Ibid.*, 43.

20. *Ibid.*, 51.

21. *Ibid.*, 63.

22. For an authoritative account of the politics of building the Hubert H. Humphrey Metrodome, see Amy Klobuchar, *Uncovering The Dome* (Prospect Heights, IL: Waveland Press, Inc., 1982). The Minnesota dome case study is based on Klobuchar's research. See also Gwen Ifill, "Meet Economic Development's New Designated Hitter—the Stadium," *The Washington Post*, National Weekly Edition, April 6, 1987, page 19; and Hal Lancaster, "Stadium Projects Are Proliferating Amid Debate Over Benefit to Cities," *The Wall Street Journal*, March 20, 1987, page 33; Rod S. Shilkrot, "Minnesota's Magnificent Mall of America," *Home & Away* (May/June 1992), 38–43; and Jennifer Lowe, "Oh Beautiful, for Spacious Mall . . . Is This America, or What? Retailers Wait for the Answer," *The Muncie Star*, August 16, 1992, page 9C.

3

☆ ☆ ☆

THE ANATOMY OF PUBLIC ORGANIZATION

CHAPTER HIGHLIGHTS

THE BASIS OF ORGANIZATION
POINTS ABOUT PYRAMIDS
LINE AND STAFF
CENTRALIZATION AND DECENTRALIZATION

Every public administrator works within an organizational framework. The successful public administrator must have a solid understanding of the principles of organization and must realize that the structure of an organization plays a vital role that cannot be overlooked.

This chapter provides an examination of the key organizational principles that have a major impact on how public administration operates. The public administrator who understands the broad implications of organization will be better prepared to meet the daily challenge of contributing to a public institution that most effectively serves its constituents.

The *anatomy* of public bureaucracy is its organizational framework or administrative structure.

THE BASIS OF ORGANIZATION

The structures of most public organizations are rather complex. These complexities can, however, be simplified by taking a look at the fundamental principles of organization outlined by Luther Gulick.

Gulick, a trailblazer in U.S. administrative theory, classified organizations into four different categories. These categories are based on an organization's *raison d'être*—the reason it was established. The categories are *purpose, process, place,* and *clientele*.[1] Gulick's categories should be viewed as a Navy captain views the terms "port" and "starboard"—terms that may seem so basic as to be unimportant, but are, nevertheless, essential elements of a more complex operation.

Purpose

Organizations established on the basis of *purpose* are oriented toward the accomplishment of specific tasks. Examples of organizations developed on the basis of purpose are school systems, fire departments, and the branches of the military. The activities that these organizations engage in are fundamentally purpose-specific, and seldom extend beyond that purpose.

Process

A *process* organization is oriented not so much toward accomplishing specific goals but toward performing certain functions. From our understanding of the law as process, we might guess that a good example of such an agency is a city legal department. Typically, at least in a large city, this department will consist of a group of lawyers who service other departments. One lawyer may represent the city's urban renewal authority in the use of eminent domain while another may defend the city's public works department in lawsuits. These kinds of organizations concern themselves almost completely in the procedural aspects of administration.

Place

Organizations under this heading serve particular locales. So far, only a few public agencies meet the strict classification standards for this category, but the idea is clear—these organizations are involved in the administration of a particular locale only. The neighborhood city halls that Boston and a few other cities have established are one example. These centers provide a variety of services to all the people who live in a particular neighborhood.

Clientele

Closely linked to *place* organizations, *clientele* organizations are not a common feature of our administrative landscape. These agencies serve particular groups of people. One notable example is the federal government's Bureau of Indian Affairs, which is designed to provide a variety of services to all Native Americans, regardless of the region in which they live. Another example is the federal government's Children's Bureau, which, from the time of its creation in 1912 to its dissolution in 1969, sought to furnish a variety of services to children, proudly claiming that it serviced the whole child.[2]

Overlap in the categories is obvious, but there is always a dominant organizational motif. Fire departments are not only established for the purpose of putting out fires but are also organized on the basis of the area (place) of their fire protection coverage; yet purpose, not place, is the main reason for establishing a fire department. Organizations are established not only on the basis of one of Gulick's categories, but also through a combination of purpose, process, place, and clientele, regardless of which factor dominates.

POINTS ABOUT PYRAMIDS

The organizational structure of most institutions is best thought of as a pyramid. The organization must delegate its work to a number of employees. In order to make sure that these employees do the work delegated to them and to see to it that their efforts are coordinated, the organization establishes supervisors. These supervisors may be so numerous that they, in turn, require supervisors. As a result, one or more levels of hierarchy tend to emerge in any sizeable organization, with the numbers of persons in each level dwindling until the tip of a pyramid is reached.

So pervasive is this pyramidal concept that it can even be seen in the operations of organized crime. In his book, *Theft of the Nation*, sociologist Donald Cressey points out that each of the twenty-four or more Mafia "families" in the United States is under the command of a boss, or *capo*. The capo and his immediate aides oversee a group of *caporegime*, or field managers, who act as chiefs of the families' operating units. These field managers, all of whom are supposed to be of equal status, supervise a varied number of subordinates. Frequently, these subunits spawn further subunits, comprising five or so "button men" under a section head.[3]

In many respects, the organization of a Mafia family is similar to an army infantry division, which comprises the smoothest and most orderly pyramidal pattern of organization found in the public sector. Soldiers are grouped into squads under the control of sergeants. Squads are formed into platoons under the leadership of lieutenants. Platoons are collected into companies under the command of captains. The progression continues up to the apex of the divisional triangle, which is headed by the division's commanding general. However—and this is a point that bears continued emphasis—nearly every organization is part of an even bigger organization, and so the infantry division and its general are answerable to still others above. The pyramidal structure continues into the higher levels of the Pentagon where the Secretary of the Army and the Secretaries of the Navy and the Air Force are accountable to the Secretary of Defense. The latter, meanwhile, occupies one of twelve seats in the Cabinet, a body presided over by the President of the United States.

Much less structurally rigid organizations than infantry divisions or Mafia families tend to assume, to a greater or lesser degree, a pyramidal structure. A large university, for example, will often contain many diverse types of subunits and a variety of levels of authority. Yet we generally find that the professors are under the administrative leadership of their department chairpersons, the chairpersons are responsible to their deans, the deans are answerable to their chancellors, provosts, or whatever the heads of their respective colleges and universities may be called, and the chancellors are accountable to the president of the entire university.

The pyramid model brings with it the concepts of *unity of command, chain of command*, and *span of control*.

Unity of command describes the exclusive relationship of those who follow orders to those who give orders. This principle is based on the idea that no one can serve two masters. This maxim generally has been true for work organizations, particularly those operating under the bureaucratic norms of delegation, specialization, and accountability, and accounts for much of their success.

Requiring an individual or a group to respond to the orders of two or more superiors may produce conflict, confusion, and even chaos. If unity of command does not exist, conflict and confusion will not only characterize those being commanded but those doing the commanding. In other words, multiple superiors will not only confuse their subordinates but also each other. One of the most ardent admirers of the unity of command principle was Alexander Hamilton. "That unit is conducive to energy will not be disputed," he wrote in his famous *Federalist Paper 70.* "Decision, activity, secrecy and dispatch will generally characterize the proceedings of one man in a much more eminent degree than the proceedings of any great number, and in proportion as the number is increased, these qualities will be diminished."[4]

An old-world contemporary of Hamilton, Napoleon Bonaparte, shared this view. The great French conqueror once said that when it came to fighting a war, he would rather have one bad general in charge than two good generals.

The unity of command principle may come into conflict with methods of boards and commissions. It is argued that such multiple–headed bodies are suitable only for organizations of a semijudicial nature (such as regulatory commissions) or for certain policy-making or advisory functions. If an organization is administering a program, if it is in fact *doing* things, then the reins of its authority should converge eventually into one pair of hands. Responsibility can then be pinpointed, and conflicting orders, internecine warfare, and a host of other organizational ills can be avoided.

Unity of command usually requires a *chain of command,* for in any large organization the person at the top cannot oversee all that is going on below. He or she needs others to help do this. Frequently, these helpers themselves cannot supervise all those beneath them. As a result, several echelons of command may emerge through which authority is presumed to proceed downward in a neat, orderly flow. Unity of command dictates that the captain of A Company does not give orders to the soldiers of B Company. With chain of command, the battalion major does not give orders directly to soldiers from either company, but works instead through their company commanders.

Even less structured organizations observe, at least to some degree, the same principle. The college dean, if he or she has reason to be disturbed by the behavior of a particular professor, will usually first contact the professor's department chairperson before taking any direct action against the troublesome faculty member. In this way the chain of command at the university streamlines the administrative process.

A third concept that is linked to a pyramidal structure, is *span of control.* Span of control refers to the number of units, be they individuals or groups, that any supervising unit, be it an individual or a group, must oversee. Unlike unity of command and chain of command, span of control does not in itself constitute a principle of organization. Instead, it serves as a frame of reference. Span of control is not something that organizations *ought* to have but something they *do* have. Usually, a government organization develops guidelines for span of control based on an organization's mission.

A challenge exists in making sure that the number of the subunits to be supervised is neither too many nor too few—or, to put it differently, to make sure that the supervisor's span of control is neither too great nor too

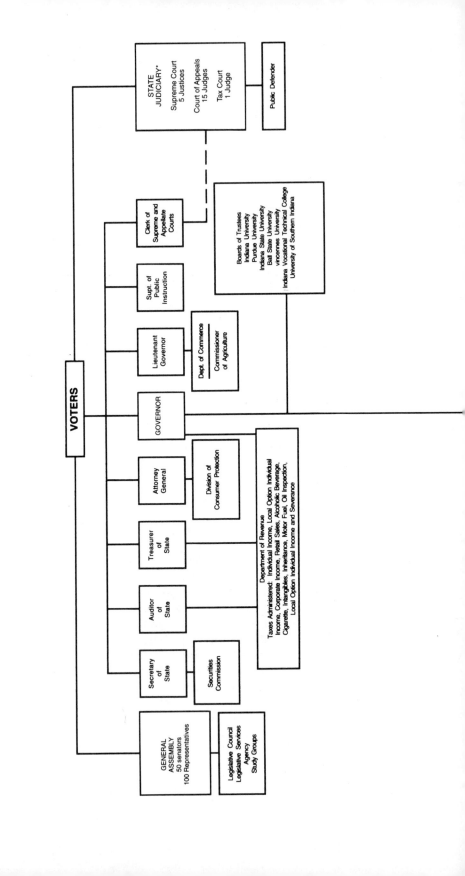

STATE BOARDS, DEPARTMENTS, COMMISSIONS AND OTHER AGENCIES*

Board of ACCOUNTS...ADJUTANT GENERAL...Department of ADMINISTRATION...ADMINISTRATIVE BUILDING COUNCIL...ADVOCACY SERVICES...AERONAUTICS DIVISION...AFFIRMATIVE ACTION OFFICE...AGING AND REHABILITATIVE SERVICES...Office of AGRICULTURE...AIR POLLUTION CONTROL BOARD...AIRPORT AUTHORITY...ALCOHOLIC BEVERAGE COMMISSION...Board of ANIMAL HEALTH...ARTS COMMISSION...BOXING COMMISSION...BUDGET AGENCY...CIVIL RIGHTS COMMISSION...COMMUNITY RESIDENTIAL FACILITIES COUNCIL...Department of CORRECTION...CRIMINAL JUSTICE INSTITUTE...Department of EDUCATION...EDUCATION COUNCIL...EDUCATION EMPLOYMENT RELATIONS BOARD...EDUCATIONAL SERVICES FOUNDATION...EGG BOARD...Bureau of ELEVATOR SAFETY...EMERGENCY MANAGEMENT AGENCY...Department of WORKFORCE DEVELOPMENT...Department of ENVIRONMENTAL MANAGEMENT...ETHICS COMMISSION...FAMILY AND SOCIAL SERVICES ADMINISTRATION...Department of FINANCIAL INSTITUTIONS...Department of FIRE AND BUILDING SERVICES...FIRE MARSHAL...Commission on FORENSIC SCIENCES...GOVERNOR'S VOLUNTARY ACTION COMMITTEE...GREAT LAKES COMMISSION...Department of HEALTH...HEALTH FACILITIES COUNCIL...HEALTH PROFESSIONS BUREAU...Commission for HIGHER EDUCATION...HISTORICAL BUREAU...HOSPITAL REGULATORY AND LICENSING COUNCIL...HOUSING FINANCE AUTHORITY...INDUSTRIAL BOARD...INSURANCE DEPARTMENT...KANKAKEE RIVER BASIN COMMISSION...Department of LABOR...LAW ENFORCEMENT TRAINING BOARD...LIBRARY SERVICES AUTHORITY...LITTLE CALUMET RIVER BASIN COMMISSION...MEDICAL ADVISORY COMMISSION ON DRIVER LICENSURE...MEDICAL AND NURSING GRANT FUND BOARD...MEDICAL EDUCATION BOARD...MENTAL HEALTH...MERIDIAN STREET PRESERVATION COMMISSION...Bureau of MINES AND MINING...Bureau of MOTOR VEHICLES...Department of NATURAL RESOURCES...OCCUPATIONAL SAFETY STANDARDS COMMISSION...OHIO RIVER VALLEY WATER SANITATION COMMISSION...PERSONNEL DEPARTMENT...PESTICIDE REVIEW BOARD...PORT COMMISSION...Commission for PROPRIETARY EDUCATION...PROFESSIONAL LICENSING AGENCY...PUBLIC EMPLOYEES' RETIREMENT FUND...RADIATION CONTROL ADVISORY COMMISSION...REDEVELOPMENT COMMISSION...REHABILITATION SERVICES AGENCY...Committee on SAFETY...Board of SAFETY REVIEW...SCHOOL PROPERTY TAX CONTROL BOARD...STANDARDBRED BOARD OF REGULATIONS...STATE EMPLOYEES' APPEAL COMMISSION...STATE FAIR BOARD...STATE LIBRARY...STATE OFFICE BUILDING COMMISSION...STATE PLANNING SERVICES AGENCY...STATE POLICE DEPARTMENT...STREAM POLLUTION CONTROL BOARD...STUDENT ASSISTANCE COMMISSION...Board of TAX COMMISSIONERS...TEACHERS' RETIREMENT FUND BOARD...TECHNOLOGY PREPARATION CURRICULUM DEVELOPMENT...Department of TRANSPORTATION...UTILITY CONSUMER COUNSELOR...UTILITY REGULATORY COMMISSION...Department of VETERANS' AFFAIRS...Commission on VOCATIONAL AND TECHNICAL EDUCATION...Council on VOCATIONAL EDUCATION...WAGE ADJUSTMENT BOARD...WAR MEMORIALS COMMISSION

BELOW: Semi-independent agencies largely ex officio in nature

CREAMERY EXAMINING BOARD...ELECTION BOARD...Board of FINANCE...JUDICIAL CONFERENCE...PROPERTY TAX REPLACEMENT FUND BOARD...PROSECUTING ATTORNEYS COUNCIL...Board for PUBLIC DEPOSITORIES...Commission on PUBLIC RECORDS...RECIPROCITY COMMISSION...SCHOOL BUS COMMITTEE...SURPLUS PROPERTY EVALUATION COMMISSION

*There are approximately 400 boards and agencies. Those listed above are only representative.

Chart by: INDIANA CHAMBER OF COMMERCE

FIGURE 3-1 Indiana State Government: A Simplified Organizational Chart.

Source: *Here Is Your Indiana Government* (Indianapolis, IN: Indiana Chamber of Commerce, 1991), page 47.

small. Unfortunately, the slippery world of public administration provides no hard and fast criteria for determining such things. As with so many other questions concerning this capricious craft, the only intelligent answer is the highly unsatisfactory, "It all depends." The proper span of control hinges on the type of work being done, the type of employees doing it, the degree of geographical dispersion of the employees, and a multitude of other factors that can often be deceptive. For example, it would appear that a foreman who is overseeing a group of laborers performing routine chores in a small work area would be able to supervise a greater number of people than could a senior scientist who is heading up a team of colleagues, each of whom is engaged separately in a unique task in various parts of a large laboratory complex. But this may not be the case. The scientists can work on their own and may even insist on doing so. The assembly line workers, on the other hand, may dislike their work and even each other. In this case the harried foreman's effective span of control may be less than that of the chief scientist.

Public administrators in America have generally functioned with relatively narrow spans of control. It is rare to find a manager overseeing more than twelve subordinates or subunits, and it is not rare to find managers overseeing as few as three. In some cases union contracts limit spans of control by requiring a fixed ratio of supervisors to those supervised. Police unions, for example, often insist on a sergeant for every eight, and sometimes every seven, police officers.

These narrow spans of control have led to a proliferation of supervisors. It has been estimated that the ratio of supervisory to rank-and-file personnel in most government agencies is at least 50 percent greater than in private industry. At one time people joked that the Spanish Army supposedly contained one officer for every three men. Today over half the men and women in the United States Army hold some kind of advanced rank.

For many years, however, the highest level of many governments often offered an exception to the narrow spans of control. Governors and big-city mayors frequently found themselves with an amazing array of agencies reporting to them and answering to them alone. During the 1960s and 1970s, several states and municipalities carried out far-ranging reorganizations, however, combining and consolidating agencies with the aim of making their governmental machinery more manageable. New York City, for instance, amalgamated over 100 independent departments, bureaus, and offices into ten "superagencies" under the mayor's direct control.

That such consolidations can create personnel problems as well as alleviate them became evident in 1970 when New York City's highly regarded commissioner of hospitals suddenly resigned. The real reason behind his resignation, it was felt, lay in the new and diminished status that the reorganization had brought to him and his department. Previously he had reported directly to the mayor. Since his department had become a subunit of one of the superagencies, the city's new Department of Health Services, he reported to the health commissioner. The consolidation had curtailed the hospital commissioner's access to the mayor and weakened his influence, causing his departure.

In reporting the resignation, *The New York Times* raised some questions. "Have these superagencies, designed to encourage rational planning in city government, merely added to the red tape and imposed another bureaucratic layer between the city officials and the mayor? Have they discouraged able men from taking commissionerships? Is Mayor Lindsay, in fact, less accessible to his commissioners than was Mayor Robert F. Wagner?"[5]

Some of the questions that critics and experts raised regarding New York City's reorganization had already been suggested by Herbert Simon nearly twenty-five years earlier. In a widely heralded article published in 1946, Simon challenged much of the conventional wisdom regarding span of control, noting that one of the "proverbs of administration" calls for limiting the number of subordinates and subordinate agencies that report directly to any one administrator. He pointed out that this proverb contradicted another proverb of administration, however; administrative efficiency will be increased "by keeping at a minimum the number of organizational levels through which a matter must pass before it is acted upon."[6]

The tighter the span of control, the more numerous are the intervening levels between top and bottom, increasing both paperwork and procrastination. A tight span of control also leads to decisions being made and policies being formulated too far from the scene of action itself. And it can lead, as the New York City example brings out, to difficulties in acquiring and retaining the services of top-notch people in vitally important, but no longer top-rated positions.

Simon's caveats and the New York City example may point out the difficulty of using span of control as a frame of reference, but they do not render it useless. As with so much in public administration, span of control becomes a question of finding a proper balance for each particular situation. In finding this balance, we must assess the specific circumstances involved, keeping in mind that a gain achieved by moving in one direction may be offset by some losses. These losses do not, however, necessarily cancel out the gain entirely. If an executive has 100 agencies under his or her tutelage, some consolidation is nearly always needed, even at the expense of creating more administrative levels. However, every consolidation carries a price tag that we must be willing to pay if we wish to reap the benefits.

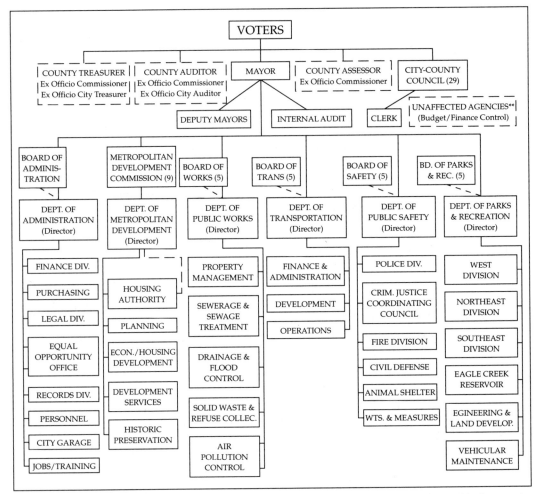

*Chart does not list certain county offices, such as sheriff, recorder, surveyor, coroner, clerk of Circuit Court or prosecuting attorney, which were not affected by consolidated city legislation.

**Council reviews budgets of municipal operating departments and corporations including otherwise unaffected bodies, such as Airport Authority and Health and Hospital Corporation.

FIGURE 3-2   Organization Chart: Consolidated Government for Indianapolis-Marion County.

Source: *Here Is Your Indiana Government* (Indianapolis, IN: Indiana Chamber of Commerce, 1991), page 81.

LINE AND STAFF

The individuals working in the pyramid examples discussed above—Mafia families, infantry divisions, and large universities—are called *line personnel*. There is another group of people to be considered—*staff personnel*.

Where *line personnel* are primarily concerned with implementing policy, *staff personnel* are all the working members of an organization who do not implement policy. Line agencies and employees are directly responsible for furthering an organization's goals. Staff responsibilities are primarily concerned with assisting senior administrators in the determination of policy and the effective operation of the agency.

Line people are generalists, occupy positions of authority in the organization, and command implementation of the organization's operations. The Departments of Agriculture, Commerce, Defense, Education, Energy, Health and Human Services, Housing and Urban Development, Interior, Justice, Labor, State, Transportation, Treasury, and Veterans Affairs constitute the major line agencies of the federal government. These organizations administer clientele programs and deal directly with the public.

The primary line officers are members of the President's Cabinet. In chronological order, these line and staff departments and agencies were established in the following order.

1789: State; War; Treasury and Attorney General;
1798: Navy;
1829: Postmaster General;
1849: Interior;
1870: Justice;
1889: Agriculture;
1903: Commerce and Labor;
1913: Commerce; Labor (split);
1939: Office of Management and Budget;
1947: Defense (took the place of Navy and War)
1953: Health, Education, and Welfare;
1965: Housing and Urban Development;
1966: Transportation;
(1971: Postmaster General removed from cabinet)
1974: Office of the U.S. Trade Representative;
1977: Energy;
1979: Health and Human Services; Education (HEW split into HHS and Education);

1989: Veterans Affairs;
1993: Environmental Protection Agency; United Nations Ambassador;
Note: The Office of Management and Budget and the Office of U.S. Trade Representative are part of the Executive Office of the President and are not executive departments.
Source: Barbara J. Saffir, "Evolution of Cabinet," *The Washington Post* (February 9, 1993), page A15.

The expansion of the President's Cabinet has occurred over time. The U.S. Constitution does not provide specifically for a Cabinet, but Article II, Section 2 stipulates that a president may seek advice from heads of the executive departments. Cabinet status for an agency puts the agency on stronger footing when dealing with the Office of Management and Budget on fiscal and policy matters. In 1993, President Clinton proposed that the Environmental Protection Agency receive Cabinet status. He also elevated the position of ambassador to the United Nations to Cabinet level.

Staff people, on the other hand, are specialists who provide skills, knowledge, and expertise to line personnel. For example, staff personnel draw up job classifications, program computers, or provide legal services. These are the employees who are most accurately referred to as the "staff."

Staff agencies aid the chief executive and line personnel in developing, evaluating, and implementing public policies. Within the Executive Office of the President of the United States, for example, the main staff agencies are the White House Office, Office of Management and Budget, Council of Economic Advisors, National Security Council, Office of Policy Development, Office of the U.S. Trade Representative, Council on Environmental Quality, and Office of Science and Technology Policy.

The essence of staff work is thought, fact-finding, and planning.[7]

Staff units are usually formed on the basis of process. An organization's computer center, for example, is typically comprised of people engaged in a process while serving a variety of purposes, places, and clientele within the context of the larger organization in which they operate. In a school system, the computer center prepares figures on attendance records for principals, correlates statistics on children with learning disabilities for the director of special education, and pinpoints certain cost trends for the budgeting department. The latter chore illustrates the fact that staff agencies may serve not only line departments but also other staff units.

The bureaucratic pyramid, in its pure form, makes no provision for staff units and their personnel. Traditionally, staff units have played only a small and shadowy role in the structure of work organizations. The place they occupied was usually at the hands or feet of the organization's leader, providing advice and assistance of various kinds. The boss of a Mafia family, to cite one traditionally structured organization, usually has a consiglieri or counselor. The consiglieri is most often a partially retired, older line official who advises the boss but who does not give orders to anyone.

In modern times, staff services and personnel have increased tremendously. They occupy an ever greater place in an organization's structure, play an ever–greater role in its activities, and consume an ever–greater chunk of its budget. In so doing, they provide the organization with new benefits and new problems.

The problems stem basically from the fact that the model pyramid makes no provision for staff units. It is difficult, at times almost impossible, to establish the correct niche for staff within an organization's hierarchy. Staff people tend to be specialists whose expertise does not lend itself to a graded ranking except, possibly, within their own ranks.

The authority of a line unit is fairly definite. Its personnel know which units are above them and which ones are below. The authority of staff units is, by contrast, much more nebulous and elusive. Such authority is determined by whatever need the line units have for the staff group at a particular time, the proficiency the staff can demonstrate in meeting this need, the administrative and political skill with which the staff handles its relationships with other units within the organization, and a variety of other factors.

Underlying the uncertainties of line–staff dilemmas is the basic principle that specialization tends to destroy hierarchy. The more the members of an organization are differentiated from each other in terms of specific and separate skills, the harder it becomes to position them on a ladder-like scale. As management expert Peter Drucker has pointed out, knowledge, in and of itself, knows no hierarchy. There are no higher or lower knowledges.

Thus, the ever–increasing presence of staff personnel is disturbing and disrupting bureaucracy and bureaucratic organizations as specialists begin to dominate generalists in making agency policies. Staff people are undermining the cherished bureaucratic principles of unity of command, chain of command, and span of control.

Once again, it was Herbert Simon who first called attention to this fact. In his 1946 classic *Public Administration Review* essay entitled the "Proverbs of Administration," he points out that to the extent that specialization comes in through the organizational door, unity of command goes out the window. Unity of command requires one channel of authority, but specialization creates several channels of authority. The specialists, in one form or another, start giving orders. The fact that these orders are not labeled as such and stem not from rank but from expertise does not fundamentally alter the situation. If the organization intends to use the energies and abilities of specialists, it must respond to what they say. And to the extent that the specialists' capabilities are utilized, the authority of line personnel, particularly those in a supervisory capacity, is undermined.

THE DEPARTMENT HEAD VS. YOUR P.A. PROFESSOR –
LINE VS. STAFF

A student of political science need go no further than his or her university bureaucracy to note the tensions inherent between staff and line personnel. Faculty members in the Department of Political Science are selected, retained, and promoted based upon their skills, knowledge and expertise in a sub-field or sub-fields of political science. Political science faculty are hired to teach a certain specialty, such as political theory, political parties, legislative studies, the presidency, constitutional law and jurisprudence, law and courts, federalism and intergovernmental relations, state politics, public policy, urban politics, comparative politics, foreign policy, and public administration. Faculty specialize in a certain sub-field or sub-fields of political science, developing skills and expertise in that area or areas of knowledge.

As experts in particular aspects of political science, faculty are "staff" advisors in your college or university community to the chairperson of the Department of Political Science, who is a "line" official. Line officials are in command; they have certain authority as specified in the university's administrative guidelines; and in the case of the political science chairperson, the department head is a generalist in the discipline of political science. The Dean, Provost, and President of your college or university are also line officials.

The tension between the chairperson, or department head, of the political science department and a certain faculty member who teaches a particular specialty in political science is almost a given. An individual political science professor might consider courses in public policy and administration to be most important in the department's academic curriculum. The department head must evaluate and balance the priorities of this and other recommendations of the political science professors under his or her supervision as he or she makes decisions as to what courses to offer students.

The faculty member, as specialist, promotes student interest in a certain sub-field or sub-fields of political science expertise. The department head, as generalist and the administrative authority in command of the political science administrative unit, has responsibility that all sub-fields of political science are given appropriate emphasis in course offerings. Department heads, implementing line functions, and faculty, carrying out staff teaching assignments, have different program priorities in the Department of Political Science. It is not difficult to imagine that they, as line and staff employees of your college or university, often come into interpersonal conflicts as each person seeks to do their jobs to the best of their respective abilities.

The contrasting assignments of line (generalist) and staff (specialist) personnel generate a good deal of conflict and tension in organizations. At times, line people will complain or become annoyed at the staff people for not sharing enough responsibility. More often, however, line personnel resent and repel the intrusions of staff people. To line employees, the activities of staff personnel frequently seem more subversive than supportive.

Felix A. Nigro and Lloyd G. Nigro point out that staff employees are often younger and better educated than line officials.[8] Both provide a fertile terrain for discord. When the line employees, who are often old-timers, see the new "whiz kids" moving into high-paying jobs and exercising authority over line employees' activities, tensions rise. Further aggravating the situation is the fact that the line personnel fear, often with some justification, that the staff people will discover and point up deficiencies in line work and behavior.

The Nigros point out, however, that staff personnel also have problems. The services they provide are indirect and often intangible. Their work is not only hard to evaluate but hard to credit. This often gives staff another disadvantage in contesting the more tangible prerogatives of line employees. Line personnel can and frequently do build a base of political support among elected officials or among the organization's clientele. The staff person remains largely excluded from such sources of organizational strength.

Line officials themselves are often keenly conscious of the subtleties of politics and, in some cases, they owe their positions to the development and use of political acumen. They frequently possess, or at least acquire, more dexterity in the handling of people inside and outside the organization. In many cases, their organizational gamesmanship more than compensates, in terms of power and position, for what they lack in specialized expertise. They may also be tougher and more ruthless than their staff peers. "You can always tell a staff man," sneers line business executive Robert Townsend, "by the number of people he has fired."[9]

To reduce the rivalry and rancor that may creep into line–staff relationships, organizations try to integrate the two as much as possible. They may make the staff people spend time familiarizing themselves with line functions and line personnel, sometimes to the point of requiring staff personnel to perform some line functions for specified periods of time. Or they may recruit their staff people from the ranks of the line personnel, giving them special training for their new positions. This is a practice that the Forest Service has used with some success. This practice does not, unfortunately, always provide the best trained or best qualified staff specialists. It also tends to make the organization inbred, a problem examined in Chapter 4.

As for handling the line personnel, organizations are supplying them with increasing doses of in-service training or encouraging them to take courses with outside educational institutions. One of the benefits of such educational programs is that line people acquire more awareness and appreciation for the competencies of the staffers and the complexities of their work. The liners frequently find that their teachers and many of their fellow students are staff personnel, and this helps build a base of understanding between the two groups.

The education of line personnel and the development of their capacities illustrates a more fundamental trend toward the gradual diminution of the gap between line and staff in modern administration. Both groups are actually becoming more alike. Staff employees are taking on quasi-line functions, while line employees are acquiring specializations more often associated with staff. In many a large metropolitan high school, for example, the social worker and the guidance counselor are participating to some degree in the instructional process. Teachers, meanwhile, by becoming more specialized, are developing some of the attitudes and ambivalences of the staff. The teacher of learning-disabled children may technically be a line employee, but he or she may feel, act, and relate to the organization in much the same way as a member of the staff.

Since there is no "correct" organizational arrangement of unity of command, chain of command, span of control, and line and staff, the alignment of these organizational principles varies from organization to organization and is generally based upon the most satisfactory way to serve the needs of clientele. Current organizational trends concerning the dynamics of centralization and decentralization are, as Simon foresaw, making orthodox applications of unity of command, chain of command, and span of control less and less useful. Modern organizations are paying diminishing deference to such bureaucratic and hierarchical rules. They are by no means obsolete, however. All organization members must become more adept at responding to diverse, and occasionally divergent, lines of authority. Specialists, in their expanding role, will exercise their skills in making their weight felt. Generalists in positions of authority must consider perspectives of specialists without undermining their own position.

New technologies and changing consumer attitudes affect the mix of decision making as well. The need for a minimum coordinating nexus, or link between individuals in the organization, will nevertheless remain. While span of control and chain of command may become more frequently disrupted as the role of specialists increases, these concepts still cannot be completely ignored. The need for some orderly flow of communication and authority within an organization remains. The modern administrator is challenged to retain the consistency provided by the pyramid structure while adapting to the requirements that an age of increasing specialization and innovation imposes.

CENTRALIZATION AND DECENTRALIZATION

One issue that has bewildered public managers since the beginning of public organization is centralization. In early times their concern focused largely on how to achieve it; for in those days, even the simplest communication between headquarters and the field often took weeks, months, or, in a few instances, years. Egyptian pharaohs, Roman emperors, and Chinese mandarins spent a good deal of time wondering and worrying about how to both control and utilize the energies and experimentation of subordinates in their distant subunits.

In more recent times the emphasis has shifted. Now the number one concern often centers on how much centralization should be achieved. Centralization is no longer viewed as an unmixed blessing: In fact its opposite, decentralization, has become the watchword, if not the battle cry, of many theorists and practitioners involved in the administrative craft.

In previous chapters we saw how decentralization has characterized our country's *political* system since its very inception. While such political decentralization may facilitate and foster *administrative* decentralization, it does not necessarily ensure it—at least not in all instances. Political decentralization calls for policies to be developed as much as possible at the lower levels (the "grass roots"). Administrative decentralization requires that those organizations charged with carrying out these policies allow their subunits a great deal of autonomy in interpreting and applying them. When a city institutes, say, its own health program, we can call this an example of political decentralization at work. If at the same time its health department refuses to set up neighborhood centers or insists that even the centers' most minor decisions must be made at headquarters, then we cannot say the program is administratively decentralized.

It should be evident that centralization and decentralization are relative terms. Virtually every organization of any size and scope must, to some extent, decentralize, for once it sets up subunits of any kind it must grant them some degree of discretion in carrying out their functions. The question, therefore, becomes one of deciding how far this independent discretion should go. Many argue that it should be pushed to the maximum limits.

Decentralization, or lack of thereof, is no abstract concept in public organizations. An organization's *tasks, values, and organizational structures* are related to unique political, administrative, and economic characteristics. Nor are the structural arrangements of an organization value neutral. The locations of decisions affect an administrator's objectives and values. The perspectives of federal employees located in Washington are different than those implementing services in Peoria. As Miles' Law states, "Where you stand depends upon where you sit."

The structure of an organization affects the delivery of services to its clientele. Public organizations must mobilize resources in order to perpetuate themselves and their values. Decisions cannot be imposed from the top down if actors in the subunits do not ascribe to the values and methods of implementing particular services. Administrators sometimes entertain *reorganization* plans in order to gain more control over the structure of the organization's policies and programs. Since any reorganization is implemented by the permanent bureaucracy, or the employees in the field accomplishing the everyday tasks of the organization, any decision to decentralize, or to recentralize, are of great consequence to the organization. These decisions should be made with sensitivity to the skills, knowledge, and expertise of field employees in order to operationalize the organization's values and purposes.[10]

The Reagan Administration saw centralization as the best way to put its values into action and to achieve its goals. From January, 1981, to January, 1989, the administration "devised a strategy for centralizing unprecedented decision-making power in the White House."[11] What the Reagan Administration did was centralize the budgetary process, the federal appointments process, decision making in the executive branch, and control of federal regulation. [12] A future president may take the opposite approach and opt for decentralization as a way of expressing a different set of values and achieving different goals. *There are two types of decentralization: political and administrative.*[13]

POLITICAL DECENTRALIZATION

Political decentralization describes the allocation of powers among territories, which, in this context, refers to states, provinces, counties, municipalities, and other local governments. According to this model, general purpose government officers residing in a specific territory coordinate public sector activities, since they are in closer contact with citizens and may alter programs according to particular territorial priorities. Political decentralization advances few real restrictions for guidelines and control, keeping them at a minimum to allow for local discretion. The territories, or sub-units, possess considerable power on their own, coordinating and reshaping resources coming into their geographic areas to meet local needs.

Manifestly parochial and unable to formulate and act on national goals, politically decentralized systems experience difficulty "vertically" integrating a diverse set of governmental activities. The transfer of political power from nation to state to community constitutes a vertical pass through of influence at each level. How is this vertical pass through frustrated in a decentralized system?

Issues such as equal opportunity, the environment, and occupational safety illustrate the barriers to vertical pass through posed by the parochialism of local jurisdictions. Congress may, for example, impose affirmative action criteria for implementing equal opportunity goals for every state in the union. If local groups of citizens are opposed to civil rights, however, any form of equal opportunity may be frustrated. Likewise, when administrative specialists in the Environmental Protection Agency interpret U.S. environmental statutes to mean that private industry must control its waste emissions, EPA field officials may be frustrated in their efforts to enforce these laws if a community values the economic status of that industry more than clean air or water. If occupational safety is a concern of federal officers but not of local government, industry, and labor leaders, then Congress and the Occupational Safety and Health Administration may be wasting their time attempting to convince local residents otherwise. Groups of citizens in every political jurisdiction must be committed to the goals of the organization, at least in some fashion, before procedures and processes are effective in implementing these goals.

ADMINISTRATIVE DECENTRALIZATION

Administrative decentralization occurs when a public organization delegates powers to subordinate levels within the same department or agency. The delegating authority may revise or retract such delegations at will. The central office in Washington transfers functions performed by the federal government to regional or state offices, for example. Where political decentralization pertains to powers allocated among geographic areas, administrative decentralization emphasizes functions, or specialties, and lines of authority for implementing agency functions. Functional and professional specialties of the central office bureaus and agencies are held in high regard in the field offices.

Politically decentralized jurisdictions grapple with "vertical" integration of governmental activities; administratively decentralized systems experience difficulties with "horizontal" integration of governmental activities. Instead of a city that relates to a vertical hierarch of state and federal governments for policy determination, as is the case in political decentralization, federal administrators—in administrative decentralization—horizontally coordinate the activities of several agencies within the same geographic area. In such operations, problems are often addressed in a fragmented manner with specialists (staff) dominating the narrowly focused programs and generalists (line) concerned for the whole project and guidelines emanating from the central office.

For example, the issue of civil rights concerns several federal departments and agencies; specific implementation policies need horizontal coordination at the grass roots level of actual citizen impact. Those departments challenged to coordinate civil rights regulations based upon administrative discretion of bureaucrats include the Departments of Commerce, Education, Health and Human Services, Housing and Urban Development, Justice, Labor, and Transportation. Independent agencies also involved include the Commission on Civil Rights, the Equal Employment Opportunity Commission, and the Small Business Administration. The line officials of all these departments and agencies could be in agreement on general purposes for implementing civil rights statutes; however, the more narrowly focused specialists within each bureaucracy may disagree on the specifics.

GOVERNMENTAL STRUCTURE AND AMERICAN VALUES

Decentralization has its proponents in every political camp; left, center, and right. Suspicion of the dangers inherent in a strong, centralized government dates back beyond the American Revolution. Participation, access, and responsiveness are characteristics of decentralized systems that in principle promote flexibility and democracy within federal organizations at the grass roots. By allowing flexibility within federal guidelines, political decentralization enhances the ability of state and city officials to meet the needs of their constituents. Rigid functional categories of administratively decentralized systems restrict options of leaders representing general purpose governments. Students of political decentralization argue that governors and mayors are more able to effectively allocate available resources according to local priorities than are non–elected bureaucrats.

There are cogent arguments against political decentralization as well. Local jurisdictions may be fragmented and ineffective; states sometimes refuse to grant sufficient resources for local bureaucracies to implement functions in a professional and effective manner. Accusations of unprofessional behavior and political graft undermine citizens' confidence in the legitimacy of local governments. Regional and national concerns may be overlooked, ignored, or unmanagable by smaller jurisdictions.

Essentially, conflicts between political and administrative decentralization models pit the values and priorities of geographic area (Peoria) against administrative function (Washington). Local partisans champion the political will of the former; national leaders insist upon the dominance of the latter. Some balance between the extremes usually results. The vertical and horizontal mixing of political and administrative decentralization illustrates that values, tasks, and organizational structure interrelate in an effective organization. Our discussion implies, furthermore, that structural arrangements selected for implementing a task affect the success administrators enjoy and whether or not their objectives and values will be achieved.

Decisions to centralize or decentralize public organizations cannot, therefore, be divorced from values, tasks, and organizational structure. An appropriate organizational design facilitates an administrator's values and objectives; an inappropriate organizational structure frustrates his or her purposes and accomplishes the opposite effects. A variety of political, administrative, and economic characteristics typify public program functions. As new values and technologies emerge, organizational objectives change; new technologies affect community values. Issues of governmental centralization and decentralization include political, administrative, economic, and technological factors that may point the agency in conflicting directions while attempting to integrate its values, tasks, and organizational structure into an effective organization. In a dynamic society espousing democracy and capitalism, we may ask: an effective organization for whom, what, when, where, and how?

SUMMARY

- The *anatomy* of public bureaucracy is its organizational framework or administrative structure.
- *Purpose, process, place,* and *clientele* explain why an organization was established.
- *Unity of command* shows the relationship between those who order and those who follow orders. Unity of command usually requires a *chain of command*, because in any large bureaucracy, the person at the top cannot oversee all that is going on below. *Span of control* refers to the number of units, be they individuals or groups, that any supervising unit must oversee.
- *Staff personnel* are specialists who provide skills, knowledge, and expertise to line personnel. The purpose of staff functions is to provide planning, fact-finding, and organizing support for line executives.
- Staff units in the Executive Office of the President include the Office of the Vice President, Council of Economic Advisers, Office of the United States Trade Representative, Office of Management and Budget, National Security Council, Office of National Drug Control Policy, Council on Environmental Quality, National Space Council, Office of Policy Development, and Office of Science and Technology Policy.

- *Line personnel* are primarily concerned with developing, implementing, and evaluating policy. Line administrators are generalists. They legitimize authority and are in command. Line employees are directly responsible for furthering an organization's goals. Staff and line employees sometimes come into conflict. This should come as no surprise, since their goals and functions are inherently different.
- Line departments in the federal government include Agriculture, Commerce, Defense, Education, Energy, Environmental Protection, Health and Human Services, Housing and Urban Development, Interior, Justice, Labor, State, Transportation, and Veterans Affairs.
- *Decentralization* occurs when an organization delegates powers to subordinate levels within the same department or agency. Political decentralization addresses the allocation of powers among states, counties, cities, and other local governments. Decisions to centralize or decentralize cannot be divorced from the values, tasks, and structure of an organization.
- The next step in understanding the craft of public administration is to examine some key theories about organizations. That is the focus of the next chapter.

This case study illustrates the potential conflicts that arise between administrative and political decentralization and ways in which these modes of operation affect the delivery of an agency's programs to its clientele. Assuming society's lack of consensus concerning matters of housing, race, and urban development, what action would you have taken if you had been HUD's Secretary?

CASE STUDY

HUD Goes to the Grass Roots[14]

The history of housing and urban development policies in the United States mixes politics and economics. It is the story of a federal department attempting to respond to the changing dynamics of housing, race, and urban development. Administrative decentralization by the Department of Housing and Urban Development in the early 1970s points out how functions, values, and organizational structure of a particular department runs up against political and economic realities. The HUD case reflects conflicts that occur when politicians who represent a geographic area disagree with the public administrators responsible for program functions in that same area.

How were HUD's functions, values, and organizational structure unique? What special economic, political, and administrative characteristics contributed to the administrative decentralization of HUD? HUD's ancestry is traced to the establishment of the Federal Housing Administration (FHA) by Franklin D. Roosevelt in 1934. FHA, responding to difficult economic times, came up with the concept of the amortized mortgage, whereby a pledge to pay for a family home is prorated over a fixed number of years. The Public Housing Administration (PHA) in 1937, Urban Renewal Administration (URA) in 1949, and Community Facilities Administration (CFA) in 1954, followed FHA as housing, home finance, and urban development bureaucracies.

The administrative umbrella for FHA, PHA, URA, and CFA was the Housing and Home Finance Administration (HHFA), established by Congress and President Truman in 1947 as the single agency responsible for the principal housing programs and functions of the Federal Government. HHFA was only an "umbrella" for supervision and coordination of such programs, not a Cabinet Department with presidential prestige. The mid–1960s, however, brought citizen pressure to resolve the nation's urban problems—especially those related to discrimination and race. As in 1934, housing administrators were challenged to respond to difficult economic times. In the early 1970s, those knocking on government's door were not poor whites; they were African Americans who wanted to realize the American dream of political and economic opportunities. In 1965, HHFA and its subordinate agencies—FHA, PHA, URA, and CFA—became the Department of Housing and Urban Development (HUD).

Centralization Before Decentralization

President Nixon's new leader in housing policy implementation, former Michigan governor George Romney, took the helm at HUD in 1969 with a burst of enthusiasm and elan. HUD was an agency with a most challenging and timely mission. Romney was eager to see what it, and he, could do. He immediately found himself confronted with the sticky administrative challenges of how best to organize HUD and to respond to diverse housing and urban development problems, including ways for integrating blacks into better housing. In a flurry of newly–mandated programs and emerging bureau power struggles, HUD was already bogged down in paperwork and procrastination. It was attempting to administer a potpourri of programs and was apparently not administering most of them effectively.

Romney looked to decentralization to supply part of the solution. As president of American Motors, he used this device to help bring the beleaguered automaker back to profitability. His subsequent experience as a very successful governor of a large state had persuaded him that the grass roots could and should play a greater role in governmental activity. His first move toward decentralization was to get control of HUD's far-flung operations by centralizing all power in his own office. This may seem a strange way to decentralize, but this sort of consolidation is generally recognized as a necessary first step in undertaking such a process. A person or an office must possess authority before it can be given away. Romney's first initiative, therefore, was to make sure his office possessed authority by restricting the authority exercised by the agency's ten regional offices and its functional units in Washington.

After consolidating HHFA operations in his Washington headquarters, Romney then delegated a goodly amount of this authority to some seventy-seven HUD local field offices. "HUD employees at the area offices," Romney insisted, "are more familiar with local conditions and are in better positions to make judgments on HUD's programs and to be most effective with these programs. The local employees work closely with the local government leadership and are able to involve local officials in the decision-making process. The local HUD employees are more informed with respect to local conditions."

About half of these field offices would handle only the department's FHA mortgage-insurance program. The other half would operate all the agency's other programs, such as urban renewal, public housing, community planning, and similar programs. Since these offices would, of necessity, be more thinly staffed than the ten, larger regional offices that had previously discharged such functions, they would not have the in-depth specialization that the latter had enjoyed. Area office employees would therefore have to be generalists, with both the authority and the responsibility to carry out or to oversee, as the case may be, a large and diverse number of activities in their locales. The decentralization scheme went into effect, and soon a network of local offices was handling most of HUD's ordinary business. In the process, these offices and their employees were making numerous decisions affecting the shape and fate of the department's programs in their respective areas.

How did HUD's decentralization affect the challenges confronting the nation? How did HUD's values, tasks, and organizational structure change? Political decentralization of housing prerogatives to the states and municipalities was not functioning properly, at least, for African Americans. State and local jurisdictions met neither the aspirations nor the needs of African Americans. Interestingly, the civil rights leaders of the late 1960s and early 1970s called for political centralization of public accommodations, housing, and other civil rights programs by the Federal Government. In other words, on issues of civil rights, political leaders from grass roots jurisdictions were insensitive to political and economic needs of leaders looked to the White House, Congress, and federal departments for solutions.

The consolidation of FHA, PHA, URA, and CFA functions, first under the umbrella of HHFA and subsequently under HUD's direction, represented changes in the organizational structure of the housing department, which likewise represented a change in political values. Changes in the structural arrangements of HUD were, by no means, value neutral. The locations of decision making do affect administrators' objectives and values. As Romney decentralized, he reached for some measure of programmatic control in reality, thereby recentralizing a bureaucracy represented by employees with quite differing values who were pulled in all directions by a diverse clientele.

Although the handling of many routine, often irksome, administrative matters, such as minor budget alterations, interpretation of grant-in-aid contracts, and the overseeing of basic procedures, all improved, problems touching on fundamental program issues increased. HUD's administrative decentralization resulted in a generalist, as opposed to a specialist, emphasis in the area offices. Under the old HHFA umbrella, the FHA area offices reflected specialist application of specific skills, knowledge, and expertise. Changes in HUD's structure, as a result of numerous decentralization directives, encouraged area office employees to be knowledgeable in all of HUD's programs, not only FHA mortgage inquiries. Teetering on the edge of becoming "a jack of all trades, yet master of none," employee program effectiveness in the field suffered.

Processes Versus Programs

How did administrative experimentation and adaptation fare in the HUD case? The most outstanding feature of the area office concept was administrative, not programmatic. The response of area office personnel to administrative matters, i.e., minor budget alterations, interpretation of grant-in-aid contracts, and general procedures for how dollars are used (as opposed to the substantive impact of dollars) was improved under decentralization. As "generalists" however, area office personnel lacked the necessary knowledge to deal with all the complexities contained in HUD's various programs. As one employee put it, "HUD is now operating like the post office. If you want a ten cent stamp, you go to one window. If you want a fifty cent stamp, you go to the same window. General Motors does not operate in this manner. Different programs appeal to different user groups."

Although area office personnel responded positively to minor budget alterations, interpretation of grant-in-aid regulations and the impact of actual utilization of dollars caused the economy of HUD operations to be very much in question. Some local officials expressed dismay over the additional cost that, in their view, decentralization entailed. More local offices consumed a greater share of HUD's budget. Paying the administrative expense involved in hiring new personnel and maintaining new and expanded offices proved expensive. This expansion made less money available for the programs themselves. One employee maintained that HUD's clients were "getting the shaft," while another labeled the scheme the "Romney Follies."

The reduction of administrative detail work at HUD's Washington headquarters did not materialize. In an ideal decentralized pattern, line and staff officials at headquarters are freed to concentrate on policy making. HUD's central office was so busy issuing directives, changing job descriptions, and monitoring the closing, combining, and establishing of field offices and the supervision of their staff professionals that the attention required for policy implementation increased instead of declining. HUD's private and public clientele were generally confused by all the constant reorganizations and changes in delegation responsibilities. The creation of better public relations for HUD was probably not Romney's most immediate concern. The control of HUD's diverse program functions was. The alteration of HUD's administrative structure in order to respond to an emerging set of values, the control of its permanent bureaucracy consisting of former FHA, PHA, URA, and CFA personnel, and the renewal of its diverse program tasks and functions appeared crucial for Romney's survival as an administrative leader. These were the Secretary's priorities.

With HUD's massive decentralization, it is not surprising to learn that there has been an absence of uniform policies and inconsistent application of housing programs at the grass roots. Area office personnel response to administrative matters appears to have been quite satisfactory under decentralization, but when these same employees were asked to resolve problems concerning program matters they usually found themselves at a loss and, more often than not, had to call senior officials in either the regional office or in the central office in Washington for consultation. HUD's administrators and clientele became confused and frustrated as national housing objectives tended to fuse the values of equality and efficiency, both promoting equal housing opportunity and responding to market demands.

The Absence of Consensus

We need to be aware that there is fragile, if any, consensus on housing, racial, and urban development policies in the U.S. There will be no neat solutions to the issues raised by decentralization. As the history of FHA, PHA, URA, CFA, HHFA, and HUD illustrates, some combination of administrative decentralization is desirable and feasible in practice, and, as some of the material to be covered later will make clear, it may even be a necessary goal. But decentralizing national programs should be approached with caution, care, and some measure of political consensus.

In conclusion, HUD, a multipurpose department, suffered from a lack of consensus on department goals.

1. By confusing generalist and specialist roles of former FHA, PHA, URA, and CFA employees, HUD's field objectives were confounded and misunderstood; the interaction and coordination of employees and production components needed to carry out program functions was often frustrated.
2. In political decentralization among jurisdictions representing nation, states, and municipalities, there is the need for vertical integration (up and down the political hierarchy) of governmental activities.
3. In administrative decentralization, there is the necessity for horizontal integration (across departments and agencies) of governmental activities within one or more geographic jurisdictions. The complexity of coordination necessary to perform HUD tasks required careful monitoring of vertical and horizontal integration of governmental activities; such emphasis was not forthcoming.
4. The priorities of local politicians often conflicted with HUD regulations implemented in area offices, typifying conflicts between geographic area and administrative function.

QUESTIONS AND INSTRUCTIONS

1. How are the categories of purpose, process, place, and clientele represented in HUD's attempts to respond to the changing dynamics of housing, race, and urban development?
2. How are the principles of unity of command, chain of command, and span of control manifest in HUD's decentralization of program functions?

3. How are HUD's tasks, values, and organizational structures reflective of unique political, administrative, and economic characteristics?
4. Why was it necessary for HUD's Secretary to centralize HUD's program functions before decentralizing them?
5. How did the structure of HUD affect the delivery of services to its clientele?
6. Why did HUD field employees become "generalists" rather than "specialists" in carrying out their tasks? Why did HUD's area office decentralization promote administrative, not programmatic, employee expertise?
7. In what ways do the premises of political decentralization by geographic area and administrative decentralization by program function come into conflict?
8. Why is there an absence of consensus on housing, race, and urban development policies in the United States?
9. Was HUD's administrative decentralization a success? Why or why not? If so, for whom? If not, for whom?

ENDNOTES

1. Luther Gulick and L. Urwick, *Papers on the Science of Administration* (New York: Institute of Public Administration, 1937), 15.
2. For a more detailed critique of the various bases of organization, see Scuyley C. Wallace, *Federal Decentralization* (New York: Columbia University press, n.d.), 91–146.
3. Donald R. Cressey, *Theft of the Nation* (New York: Harper & Row, 1969), Chapter 6.
4. Alexander Hamilton, John Jay, and James Madison, *The Federalist* (New York: Modern Library, n.d.), 455.
5. *New York Times,* 5 March 1970.
6. Herbert A. Simon, "The Proverbs of Administration," *Public Administration Review,* Vol. 6 (Winter, 1946), 53–67.
7. John M. Pfiffner and Frank P. Sherwood, *Administrative Organization* (Englewood Cliffs, NJ: Prentice-Hall, Inc., 1960), 170–188.
8. Felix A. Nigro and Lloyd G. Nigro, *Modern Public Administration*, 3rd edition (New York: Harper and Row, 1973), 122.
9. Robert Townsend, "Up the Organization," *Harper's Magazine,* Vol. 240, No. 1438 (March, 1970), 73–90.
10. David O. Porter and Eugene A. Olsen, "Some Critical Issues in Government Centralization and Decentralization," *Public Administration Review,* Vol. 36, No. 1 (January/February, 1976), 72–84.

11. Harold Seidman and Robert Gilmour, *Politics, Position, and Power: From the Positive to the Regulatory State,* 4th edition (New York: Oxford University Press, 1986), 127.

12. *Ibid.*

13. Herbert Kaufman, "Administrative Decentralization and Political Power," *Public Administration Review,* Vol. 29 (January/February, 1969), 3–15.

14. Material for this case study is drawn from John E. Rouse, Jr., "Administrative Decentralization as a Complement to Revenue Sharing: A Case Study of the HUD Programs" (Paper presented to the annual meeting of the American Political Science Association, Chicago, 1975). See also unpublished Ph.D. dissertation, *The Impact of Decentralizing Program Administration: The Department of Housing and Urban Development Case Study* (College Park, MD: 1974).

4
☆ ☆ ☆

THE PHYSIOLOGY OF ORGANIZATION

CHAPTER HIGHLIGHTS

DEMOCRACY IN BUREAUCRACY
BASELINE ORIGINALS IN ORGANIZATIONAL LIFE
NEO-CLASSICAL THEORIES
HUMAN RELATIONS THEORIES

A young man—we'll call him "Phil"—landed a job as an administrative assistant in his state's highway department. Although it was not a position of great authority, it was a chance to learn the ropes in one of the state's larger departments. Fresh out of college, Phil was fired up. He was ready to change "the system" to make it more effective, more responsive, more than what the citizens of his state had come to expect of the highway department. He was determined to serve the public in a positive, productive manner. He had good ideas on how to improve everything from snow removal to bridge inspections.

Phil was idealistic, but not naive. He had a political science degree framed on his wall and had worked in numerous local political campaigns both in his home county and in the county where he went to college. But once he started work in the highway department, Phil was astonished at what he found.

His immediate supervisor was a person who had owned a business but who had no prior experience or training in public administration. The supervisor was not the least bit interested in Phil's ideas on how to improve the highway department. Phil was never told as much in precise words, but the subtle message was clear: "Do as you're told and don't make waves."

As papers crossed Phil's desk, he learned more about the highly-detailed complexity of the day-to-day functioning of the department. He understood the issues and the policies, but the complex forces driving the bureaucracy overwhelmed him. Just getting simple things accomplished took a great deal of effort. The operation seemed to lumber along painfully instead of streaking along smoothly to meet the needs of the public. Surprise and shock came at the realization that one administrator seemed to make decisions based not on what was best for the citizens driving on state highways but on what was best for his poker buddies who just happened to get frequent state contracts.

Phil was not prepared for the intricate, informal, and occasionally unethical pressures involved in the daily operation of a real-life bureaucracy. Pressures mounted and he became confused and disheartened. The chain of command he was forced to follow seemed to arbitrarily stifle every chance for employees to improve the organization, to feel a part of the team. The way things really worked had little to do with his dreams of public service. He felt swept away by the bureaucratic current, as if he were trying to hold on to a slippery log floating swiftly down a raging river. In less than a year, he quit his job.

Phil would have been better prepared to deal with the inner workings of a bureaucracy if he had a more thorough background in the basic theories about how bureaucracies and other organizations work. If he understood what forces were sweeping him toward frustration, he would have seen "the big picture" and not felt so helpless.

Physiology is the study of life processes, activities, and functions. Just as a medical student must study physiology to understand how the human body works, students of public administration must be familiar with organizational theories so they will be better prepared than Phil when confronted by the realities of bureaucracy. This chapter provides a look at the most influential and helpful organizational theories and theorists.

DEMOCRACY IN BUREAUCRACY

Bureaucracy and democracy are the central pillars of the public and private organizations of our society. Bureaucratic hierarchy and democratic equality influence the functions and vital processes of all organizations. Despite the apparent paradox, bureaucracy and democracy are both antithetical and complementary.

In partisan politics, we periodically elect presidents, governors, and mayors. In such electoral processes, we take advantage of the fundamental principle of democracy. While in office, however, presidents, governors, and mayors depend upon principles of bureaucracy, where formalism, strict rule adherence, impersonality, chain of command, unity of command, span of control, and similar values contribute to the exercise of authority. Authority in a bureaucracy is checked by democratic voting procedures, but only on a periodic basis. As we consider the functions and vital processes of organizations therefore, an understanding of the philosophical differences between bureaucracy and democracy is crucial for understanding why public organizations exist.

The development of our organized society underscores the need for democracy in the administrative state. We, the voting public, come into contact with numerous public and private organizations each day. The functions of government are always expanding their influence on the public. Legislatures continuously allocate public functions to administrative structures. What input should employees and clientele have in internal decision-making within public organizations? Can there be democracy in bureaucracy? How democratic should life in organizations be?

If you are not already employed, in a matter of years, even months, you will probably enter the American work force. You may be employed by a business, labor, social, or public organization. You will be full of ideas and energy for expressing your solutions to your employer's challenges and problems, and you will want to be heard. How much democracy will exist in your bureaucratic workplace?

The authoritarian tenets of bureaucracy and the *egalitarian tenets of democracy* are major forces shaping life and the pursuit of happiness in the 20th century. These concepts interact with other organizational philosophies, such as capitalism, nationalism, industrialism, and socialism, which are historical antecedents to democracy and bureaucracy.

Defining democracy is not easy. We live in a democracy. In the classical sense, though, our system of *political economy*, or politics and economics, is not a democracy, but a republic. We have a democratic *kind* of government; however, we have a republican *form* of government. In our republic, elected officials represent us in our state and national legislatures. Other tenets of democracy call for "rule by the people." However, who are the "people?" How, and by what means, do they "rule?"

Democracy is not an economic, social, or ethical concept, but a political one. It points toward the realization of the values of liberty, equality, human worth, human dignity, and freedom by guaranteeing the right to secret voting by all citizens. Along with these values comes free expression of ideas, free association of persons, representation, legislatures, due process of law, and generally, the privilege of assuming our soap box and speaking our minds about almost anything.[1]

While democracy has a leveling, or *horizontal*, feature about its application, bureaucracy is *vertical* in implementation. Democracy implies equality and equal opportunity; however, bureaucracy also denotes hierarchy. Every four years American citizens vote for, or perhaps against, a presidential candidate because of the candidate's and the party's support of political principles as expressed in the party's platform. The party platform serves as the voters' guide to how its leaders should address the nation's challenges during the next term of office. Voting, which espouses equality, is a political right in a democratic society.

However, once a candidate becomes president, the direct democratic powers of voters are diluted; voters, as citizens, may encourage members of Congress to oppose the president's new programs, for example, but the rights of suffrage in our electoral democracy come only periodically. Except for those periodic elections, the premises of bureaucracy, or hierarchy, assume preeminence in our society. Public institutions—ranging from health to defense—develop, evaluate, and implement public policies.

The oft-used term, *bureaucracy*, has two meanings. In its most popular sense, the concept refers to any substantial public organization or group of organizations, as in "federal bureaucracy" or in "welfare bureaucracy." The other meaning is more specialized; it refers to a particular method or manner of administration. A bureaucracy in this sense is an organization or group of organizations that operates in a particular way.

What constitutes the bureaucratic way of doing things? The German sociologist Max Weber (1864–1920) was the first to define it. He saw bureaucracy as an impersonal system operating on the basis of "calculable rules" and staffed by full-time and professional (as opposed to political) employees. Bureaucracy presupposes hierarchy, but this hierarchy is based strictly on organizational rank, not on social status or other considerations.

The chief characteristic of a bureaucracy in Weber's sense of the word was its uniform, nonarbitrary and nonpersonal method of administering the public's affairs. "Bureaucracy," wrote Weber, "is like a modern judge who is a vending machine into which the pleadings are inserted along with the fee. The machine then disgorges the judgement based on reasons mechanically derived from the code."[2]

In Weber's view, bureaucracy is a bloodless mechanism devoid of all the capriciousness and color we associate with human activity. Yet the positive features of such an administrative approach—characterized by impersonality and professionalism—must not be overlooked. Impersonality implies impartiality, and professionalism opens the possibility for an employee selection system based less on social status than on personal skill.

The bureaucratic way of doing things has made great headway in Europe, especially in Germany. As such, it has brought more uniformity, predictability, and equality to public administration. Since bureaucratic systems rest upon a highly systematized administrative arrangement, they often show great resistance to change. The devotion to "calculable" rules often causes rule-conscious bureaucrats to "go by the book," regardless of the situation. Such persistence of routinized organizational behavior may, however, sometimes prove advantageous. France, with its long history of unrest and upheaval, has often been held together by its plodding, but enduring, bureaucracy.

Although the bureaucratic style has conquered the public sector in Western Europe, it has scored somewhat less decisively in this country. The dynamics of U.S. political bureaucracies, especially in state and local jurisdictions, are highly personal. It is often *who* one knows rather than *what* one knows that affects the administrative system. Just as personalities so often count for more than parties or principles in policy making, so personalities often outweigh "calculable rules" in policy execution. This is not always true, but it is verified often enough to differentiate U.S. administration from that of other economically developed democracies such as England, France, or West Germany.

Lessened concern for abiding by rules provides many rewards. Although U.S. administration has often been accused of stodginess, and rightly so, it is perhaps less guilty of such offenses than its Western European counterparts. In general, it is much easier to bend, if not break, the rules in the United States than elsewhere in the world of modern democratic capitalism. The U.S. administrative setup, reflecting vast differences in bureaucratic cultures, can more easily accommodate individual idiosyncrasies and initiatives.

Before breaking out into cheers, the anti-bureaucratic enthusiast should note some of the benefits that we thereby forego. A system more open to the influence of individual personality is open to caprice and whim as well. As "calculable rules" become more easily manipulated it is also more vulnerable to corruption. And if change can sometimes come more quickly, then such change may spring not just from public demand but from personal desire as well.

The distinctiveness of U.S. administration in this respect should not be overstated. The bureaucratic way of doing things is scarcely a stranger to our shores. The systems of other countries are certainly not incapable of capriciousness or change. Yet for both good and ill, bureaucracy in Weber's sense characterizes the U.S. public sector less than that of many other modern, developed nations.

INTERPRETATIONS OF "BUREAUCRACY"

According to Dwight Waldo, the term "bureaucracy" has two interpretations. The *popular-pejorative* interpretation is widely recognized in society: bureaucracy is bad because bureaucrats are timid, ineffectual, power-seeking, and dangerous.

A second interpretation of bureaucracy is *descriptive* and *analytical*. This interpretation says that bureaucracy fosters advanced legal and economic systems and therefore advances civilization. Descriptive and analytical terms used for this interpretation include form of government, formalism, rules, impersonality, hierarchy, expertise, records, large-scale, complex, efficiency, and effectiveness.

In reality, the concept of bureaucracy is neither good nor bad. Bureaucracy simply is; it exists. The concept of bureaucracy simply entails procedures for organizing people within a certain culture for the purpose of implementing a particular set of goals and objectives. *Bureaucracy exists for accomplishing tasks.* The tasks range from fighting dictators to fighting poverty.

How, then, are the societal values of democracy and bureaucracy antithetical, yet complementary?

According to Waldo, there are two problems in reconciling democracy and bureaucracy. One concern focuses upon the definition of the administrative "unit." Any organization able to respond to clientele is a unit. The function of a unit of bureaucracy may be defined by the manner in which the organization responds to its clientele. Academic departments, as administrative units at a college or university, are organized depending upon the demand from students for certain skills, knowledge and expertise.

For example, English and math may be the largest departments on campus since most college curriculums mandate that students take courses in these subjects. Meanwhile, the departments of philosophy, anthropology, and foreign languages may be smaller because the demand for courses taught by those departments is lower than for English and math courses.

Waldo's concern is the status and weight to be accorded to nondemocratic values. Liberty and equality are democratic values. Examples of nondemocratic values are national security, personal safety, productivity, and efficiency. If the chairperson of an academic department is elected by members of that unit, the values of democracy have predominated. However, if the department head is selected by the dean of the college, then the values of bureaucracy—efficiency and productivity—have taken precedence.

BASELINE ORIGINALS IN ORGANIZATIONAL LIFE

Max Weber, Frederick Winslow Taylor, Elton Mayo, and Chester Barnard form an intellectual baseline of early classical thinkers concerned with the anatomy and physiology of private and public organizations. Thinking of the organization as a "rational machine" provides a useful metaphor in understanding this approach to organizational behaviors.[3]

MAX WEBER

Weber's work on the nature of bureaucracy is considered by many the most important of its kind. He was trained in law, history, and economics. He viewed action as both individual and social. Weber postulates the "idealtype" of bureaucracy, not referring to goodness or "badness," but suggesting a standard or model for organizational environment. Characteristics of the ideal-type may be found in any organization.

Below, John M. Pfiffner and Frank P. Sherwood summarize components of Weber's ideal-type. These components contribute to our understanding of the functions and vital processes of organizations.

Emphasis on form. Bureaucracy's first, most cited, and most general feature according to Weber is its emphasis on form of organization. In a sense the rest are examples of this.

The Concept of Hierarchy. The organization follows the principle of hierarchy, with each lower office under the control and supervision of a higher one.

Specialization of task. Incumbents are chosen on the basis of merit and ability to perform specialized aspects of a total operation.

A specified sphere of competence. This flows from the previous point. It suggests that the relationships between the various specializations should be clearly known and observed in practice. In a sense, the use of job descriptions in many American organizations is a practical application of this requirement.

Established norms of conduct. There should be as little as possible in the organization that is unpredictable. Policies should be enunciated and the individual actors within the organization should see that these policies are implemented.

Records. Administrative acts, decisions, and rules should be recorded as a means of insuring predictability of performance within the bureaucracy.[4]

Weber emphasized the universality of bureaucracy by emphasizing its rationality. His observations on bureaucracy coincided with the industrial revolution in Germany at the turn of the century. In seeking rationality in human behavior, he concluded that the ideal-type is the best means for achieving rationality at the institutional level.

Weber also assumed freedom for bureaucrats. Far from promoting a master-slave relationship, he emphasized that man is a free agent, even within 19th century economic bureaucracies.

Finally, Weber forecast a general separation of policy-making and administration. Because the ideal-type organization is grounded in predictable, decision-making processes and is staffed by professionals, bureaucracies should not be subverted by nonprofessionals according to Weber. In this view, professionals organize and implement expertise. Nonprofessionals, armed only with opinions about expertise and goals, do not fit Weber's game plan. Neither the monarch ruling by divine right nor the elected American president would be part of Weber's ideal-type framework.[5]

FREDERICK TAYLOR

Frederick Taylor (1856–1915) is often called the father of scientific management. He recognized the importance of technology, work, and organization to understanding the functions and vital processes of bureaucracies. In the opening of his classic, *The Principles of Scientific Management,* Taylor wrote:

"The principal object of management should be to secure the maximum prosperity for the employer, coupled with the maximum prosperity for the employee.

"The words 'maximum prosperity' are used, in their broad sense, to mean not only large dividends for the company or owner, but the development of every branch of business to its highest state of excellence, so that prosperity may be permanent."[6]

According to Taylor, scientific management is both liberating and economically rational. Employees and employers are assumed to be rational. Through rationality in the work process, labor and management determine the proper way of completing a task.

Taylor, like Weber, assumes the importance of the individual. And like Weber, Taylor foresaw the shift of power from both the *bourgeoisie* (economic elites) and the *proletariat* (masses) to the *expert* (possessor of skills and knowledge).

Taylor emphasized cooperation in the workplace and spoke of making life better for the individual employee. He represented a pre-World War II spirit that there are principles and laws that order our knowledge of the world. In seeking the scientific method, the impersonality of organizations results.

ELTON MAYO

In 1932, Harvard Business School professor, Elton Mayo (1880–1949), and a team of researchers completed five years of study outside Chicago, Illinois, at the Hawthorne plant of the Western Electric Company. Later published as *The Human Problems of an Industrial Civilization*, Mayo's research found that many problems in worker/management relations are caused not by insufficient task specialization or inadequate wages, but by social and psychological forces. The "Hawthorne Experiments," as they were subsequently to be known, were the first systematic research to expose the *human factor* in work situations. The study marked a major turning point in the history of administrative theory and practice.[7]

The Hawthorne experiments encouraged management people to conceptualize an organization as a *social institution*.

According to Pfiffner and Sherwood, Mayo's Hawthorne findings contributed to the ideological revolution in organization and management in two ways: by challenging the physical or engineering approach to motivation and by becoming the first real assault on the purely structural, hierarchical approach to organization. In other words, there was no scientific or one best way to motivate employees to be productive. The "father knows best" authoritarian way of running an organization was seen as only one of several approaches available. The whims of scientific management were no longer accepted as gospel. The human relations movement was underway.[8]

CHESTER BARNARD

Chester Barnard (1886–1961) completes the baseline foursome. Intrigued by the experiments at the Hawthorne Works, Barnard formulated a theory of organizational life that focuses on *the organization as a system, formal and informal organizations, and the role of the executive*.

In *The Functions of the Executive*, Barnard distinguishes between *organizational purpose* and *individual motive*. He postulates that each person in the organization reflects a dual personality—one organizational and the other individual. As an individual leaves home and enters the workplace, he or she becomes the "organization man or woman."

An organization is a collection of actions focused toward a purpose; an equilibrium is necessary for an organization to sustain itself. A successful equilibrium must exist between the organization and its employees. The organization receives energies and productive capacities from employees, and employees receive compensation, benefits, and meaning from their work.[9]

Although the distinction between formal and informal organization is now commonplace, Barnard, in the late 1930s, introduced these concepts as new, analytic tools for examining organizational life. According to Barnard, *formal organization* is comprised of the consciously coordinated activities of people, while *informal organization* entails the unconscious group feelings, passions, and activities of the same individuals. Informal organization is essential to the maintenance of formal structures and relationships. The formal organization cannot exist without its informal counterpart. Because of the reality of informal organization, not all activity can be structured by a chain of command.

Finally, Barnard addresses *executive functions* of organizations. These functions are maintaining organization communication, securing essential services from individuals, and formulating the purpose and objectives of the organization. Barnard writes that the functions of the executive are "those of the nervous system, including the brain, in relation to the rest of the body. It exists to maintain the bodily system by directing those actions which are necessary more effectively to adjust to the environment. But it can hardly be said to manage the body, a large part of whose functions are independent of it and upon which it in turn depends."[10]

The writings of Weber, Taylor, Mayo, and Barnard form an axis around which the theory and practice of public organizations revolve. Focusing upon three early organizational themes—system, hierarchy, and structure, writers who follow these "classical" thinkers assume that understanding human rationality is central to theorizing about organizational physiology.

NEO-CLASSICAL THEORIES

The neo-classical perspective toward organizational theory is represented by the works of Luther Gulick and Herbert Simon. "Decision-set" organizational theory, as it is called, is characterized by several important themes, including: decision making as the heart and soul of administration; administrative capacity as measured by efficiency; organizational roles, not individual roles, are emphasized as they relate to decision making; and instrumental rationality as the center of operation.

LUTHER GULICK

In 1937, Gulick and Lyndall Urwick edited the *Papers on the Science of Administration,* a collection of 11 papers reflecting the predominant thinking concerning organizations in Europe and the United States prior to World War II. Divided into two general groups, the papers examined structural aspects and social and environmental aspects of organization.[11]

Gulick's "Notes on the Theory of Organization," in which he introduced the acronym POSDCORB, has influenced teaching and thinking about public administration for 50 years. Consequences of Gulick's POSDCORB concern the Wilsonian separation of politics from administration, the need for a division of work in order to reach organizational objectives, and the efficiency criterion for judging governmental activities. In POSDCORB, Gulick outlines the work of the chief executive in the following manner:

> *Planning,* that is working out in broad outline the things that need to be done and the methods for doing them to accomplish the purpose set for the enterprise;
>
> *Organizing,* that is the establishment of the formal structure of authority through which work subdivisions are arranged, defined, and coordinated for the defined objective;
>
> *Staffing,* that is the whole body of bringing in and training the staff and maintaining favorable conditions of work;
>
> *Directing,* that is the continuous task of making decisions and embodying them in specific and general orders and instructions and serving as the leaders of the enterprise;
>
> *Coordinating,* that is the all important duty of interrelating the various parts of the work;
>
> *Reporting,* that is keeping those to whom the executive is responsible informed as to what is going on, which thus includes keeping himself and his subordinates informed through records, research, and inspection;
>
> *Budgeting,* with all that goes with budgeting in the form of fiscal planning, accounting, and control.[12]

HERBERT SIMON

After World War II, in 1947, Simon illustrated the decision-set perspective in "The Proverbs of Administration," which was incorporated later into his classic, *Administrative Behavior.* He viewed the decision as the central act of organization, and instrumental rationality as the basis for decision making. By instrumental rationality, Simon meant that the individual is rational and responsible only within the environment of a particular organization. The organizational environment encompasses the purposes of rational behavior; autonomous individuals behave only within the confines of those organizational purposes.

In emphasizing the decision as the basis for administrative theory, Simon distinguished between value premises and factual premises of public administrators. He wrote: "The process of validating a factual proposition is quite distinct from the process of validating a value judgment. The former is validated by its agreement with the facts, the latter by human fiat."[13] In other words, the facts of any circumstance are validated by the given set of values in which those facts, or actions, occur.

Simon focuses upon the "means-end" sense of rationality as most significant. Since administrators weigh the means, ends, and consequences of acting, Simon suggests that decisions may prove "objectively" rational, "subjectively" rational, "deliberately" rational, "organizationally" rational, or "personally" rational.

Regardless of adverb, to be rational means consideration of **only** those choices present within a prescribed system of values. Government employees are not autonomous individuals. The organizational environment of the department or agency articulates the values that incorporate the determination of rational behavior.

In other words, an employee is rational and responsible only within the environment of a particular department or agency. A government employee acts rationally only within the framework of the department's pre-established goals and purposes.

Values, on the other hand, are arbitrary, regardless of their origins. Human decree, sanction or authority, validates a certain set of organizational values. Executives, legislatures, and judges decide by fiat that a set of values, encompassed in laws and implemented by bureaucrats, are of importance to organizations and to society. Citizens of public organizations, then, respond to the rules and regulations and the boundaries imposed upon them by these values.

All decisions in organizations only satisfy and suffice, that is, they "satisfice." Our focus on choices and decision making and acceptance of organizational premises brings us to the limits of administrative rationality. This final Simon theme, that of "satisficing," recognizes that rationality, or human reasoning, is bounded by administrative settings. After analyzing the problem and considering the complexities of the situation, administrators "satisfice," surveying their options and selecting the first one they find at least minimally satisfactory. With prospects for "satisficing" by employees, Simon concludes that rationality is bounded. In describing "bounded rationality," he concludes that an administrator's reasoning options are limited by unconscious habits and skills, values and conceptions of purpose, and degree of information and knowledge.[14]

MILES' LAW

Rufus E. Miles, Jr. proudly claims to have parented Miles' Law. The law states simply that, "Where you stand depends on where you sit." Miles says he discovered the law while serving as a Division Director of the former Bureau of the Budget. He noted that a budget examiner might be a constant critic of an agency whose budget he oversaw, yet if the examiner were to be later hired away by the agency, he would promptly do a 180 degree turn and become one of the agency's most adamant advocates. What position a bureaucrat takes depends on what position he is in, or, "Where you stand depends on where you sit."

Miles points out in illustration how John Gardner, as Chairman of President Johnson's Task Force on Education, authored a report strongly favoring the removal of Education from the Department of Health, Education, and Welfare. Shortly thereafter, Gardner was appointed secretary of HEW. When asked whether he now planned to push for Education's removal from HEW, he firmly and flatly rejected any such nonsensical idea.

HUMAN RELATIONS THEORIES

As we have seen in the above passages, Max Weber speaks in *bureaucratic* terms; Frederick Taylor writes in *productivity* terms; Chester Barnard thinks in *organizational* terms; and Herbert Simon stresses *decisional* terms. Writing histories of the increasing bureaucratization of society, each of these authors emphasizes *efficiency* in some form as a potent force in any organization, but also concludes that organizations embody social purposes. In other words, they believe that if there is conflict within the organization, individuals must subordinate their interests to those of the organization.

For example: If students are not learning, the professor is not at fault. Instead, the onus usually is placed upon the students to change their behavior or study habits to respond to the professor's demands. Likewise, if the college's basketball team is losing, the assumption is that the players are lousy, lazy, and generally do not respond to their coach's leadership. Student athletes must subordinate their ways of acting to those of the administrator in charge.

Human relations theories question such assumptions, placing responsibility on the professor to change his or her teaching methods and on the coach to change his or her leadership style and set up a new strategy for winning games. This shift in responsibility makes for several new ways of envisioning organizational structure and function.

MARY PARKER FOLLETT

An early prophet of human relations thinking was Mary Parker Follett (1868–1933). While the classical and neo-classical writers were attempting to construct a field of public administration along systematic and somewhat mechanical lines, Follett was marching to the beat of a different drummer. She had become impressed with the psychological factors she had seen at work in her active life as an organizer of evening schools, recreation agencies, and employment bureaus and as a member of statutory wage boards. Already the author of two books on political science, *The New State* and *Creative Experience*, she embarked on a series of speculations in the 1920s concerning the functions and vital processes of organizations. Her work signaled the advent of a new era in administrative theory.[15]

In various papers and articles, Follett depicted administration as essentially involved with reconciling the agendas of both individuals and social groups. An organization's principal problems, in her view, were not only determining what it wanted its employees to do, but guiding and controlling the employees' conduct in such a way as to get them to do it. This, she indicated, was a much more complex task than previous writers had suggested.

Follett not only anticipated what was to become the human relations school of administration, she also foreshadowed the humanistic school that was to grow out of it. She urged organizations to stop trying to suppress the differences that may arise within their boundaries, and rather seek to integrate those differences, thereby allowing them to contribute to the organization's growth and development. She advocated replacing the "law of authority" with the "law of the situation," admonishing organizations to exercise "power *with*" rather than "power *over*" their members.

While Follett's writings did not go unnoticed, they failed to score the impact that similar ideas would later achieve. This was perhaps due partly to the fact that she was a woman writing in a society not yet willing to taking women thinkers seriously. A more serious obstacle, however, may have been the fact that she was an iconoclast, challenging the sacred credos of her time. She died during the same year in which Elton Mayo wrote on the Hawthorne experiments. Mayo's work was the first systematic research to expose the "human factor" in work situations. Mayo's study, as we have seen, marked a major turning point in the history of administrative theory and practice.

MASLOW, MCGREGOR, AND LIKERT

Like Follett, organizational psychologists Abraham Maslow, Douglas McGregor, and Rensis Likert wrote from a progressive, humanistic viewpoint. They have profoundly influenced the teaching and practice of public administration concerning the role of democracy in bureaucracy, advocating expanded scope and encouragement for individual initiative and enterprise by allowing employees to make many of their own decisions on the job. These authors call, generally, for *less hierarchy and more humanity in organizational life,* and emphasize *the integration of individuals in organization.*

Writing in *Motivation and Personality* (1954), Maslow identifies a hierarchy of personal needs that the organization must contend with in order to successfully integrate the individual. He writes that food and shelter demands are the first needs humans meet. Then freedom from physical harm and deprivation is sought. Next, the desire for affectionate and supportive relationships with family, friends, and associates becomes a priority. Then comes recognition of worth by peers. Finally, there is the need to actualize one's inherent potential, to release one's creative abilities, to achieve everything that one hopes for in life.[16]

Like Maslow, McGregor's thinking is essentially optimistic concerning individuals' capacity for self-realization. McGregor examines possibilities for merging individual and organizational demands in ways that would prove satisfactory to both. In *The Human Side of Enterprise* (1960), McGregor outlines management's conventional view of harnessing human energy to organizational requirements which he calls "Theory X," and then boldly steps forward with a new theory of administration, which he calls "Theory Y."

Theory X is based on a few basic assumptions: The average person is by nature lazy. He or she will work as little as possible. Such an individual lacks ambition, dislikes responsibility, and prefers to be led. By nature resistant to change, he or she is gullible, not very bright, and the ready dupe of the charlatan and the demagogue. Such a person is furthermore inherently self-centered and indifferent to organizational needs.

Theory Y, or McGregor's new way of merging individual and organizational demands, takes a more humanistic approach:

- People are not naturally passive, lazy, and dumb. They are, on the contrary, generally eager for opportunities to show initiative and to bear responsibility.
- Work is a natural activity and people by nature want to perform it.
- People work best in an environment that treats them with respect and encourages them to develop and utilize their abilities.
- There is no inherent and intrinsic conflict between the goals of the organization and the goals of the individual member. Meeting the goals of the individual will only result in the organization becoming more productive.[17]

Rensis Likert, writing in *The Human Organization* (1967), develops four systems which positively or negatively influence the integration of individuals into organizations.

System 1 is *punitive authoritarian* and closely resembles Theory X mentioned previously. System 1 administrative leaders have no confidence or trust in subordinates.

System 2 is *benevolent authoritarian* and is more generous and humanitarian toward the employee. While System 1 takes everything from the individual and gives very little in return, System 2 rewards employee behavior only as prescribed employer directives are followed. If the employee does his or her tasks as so prescribed, he or she is dutifully rewarded. System 2 leaders are condescending in bestowing their confidence and trust, engaging in something resembling a master/servant relationship with subordinates.

System 3 is *consultative* and allows still more participation by employees. Administrative leaders in such an organization may be democratic, allowing free discussion regarding policy-making, but still assuming final responsibility for all decisions. System 3 illustrates substantial, but not complete confidence and trust in subordinates.

System 4 is a *participative group model* and closely resembles Theory Y mentioned previously. Senior bureaucrats promote complete confidence and trust in employees in all matters. Employees are utilized for guidance and for coordinated problem solving. Employees are not treated punitively.

According to Likert, administrative leaders adopting the participative style achieve from 10 to 40 percent greater productivity, experience much higher levels of employee satisfaction and much better employee health, enjoy much better labor relations, suffer less absence and less turnover, obtain better product quality, and, finally, record better customer satisfaction as a result of better products and services than managers operating with System 1, 2, or 3 styles.[18]

SUMMARY

- The *physiology* of organization deals with the functions and vital processes of public bureaucracies and their subunits. Bureaucracy and democracy are at the center of what occurs in the public and private organizations of our society.
- In a classical sense, our system of *political economy*, or politics and economics, is not a democracy but a republic. We have a democratic *kind* of government; however, we have a republican *form* of government.
- *Democracy implies equality while bureaucracy* implies hierarchy. Bureaucracy exists for accomplishing tasks ranging from fighting dictators to fighting poverty.

- Max Weber's "ideal-type" of bureaucratic organization entails an emphasis on form, hierarchy, specialization of tasks, specified spheres of competence, established norms of conduct, and record keeping.
- The advent of large scale bureaucracy has seen the shift of power from both the *bourgeoisie* (economic elites) and the *proletariat* (masses) to the *expert* (possessor of skills and knowledge).
- The acronym POSDCORB outlines the work of the chief executive in terms of planning, organizing, staffing, directing, coordinating, reporting, and budgeting.
- *Formal organization* is only part of the study of bureaucracy. Every organization has its informal counterpart—its unconscious group feelings, passions, and activities. *Informal organization* is essential to the maintenance of formal structures and relationships.
- Weber stresses *bureaucratic* terms, Taylor stresses productivity terms, Barnard organizational terms, and Simon decisional terms. All emphasize efficiency.
- The human relations theorists, Maslow, McGregor, and Likert, emphasize principles of *equality*. They call for less hierarchy and more humanity in organizational life.

While the study of theories related to the craft of a public administration is vital, it is also valuable to look at a concrete example. While you're reading the following case study, see if you can spot where previously discussed theories come into play in the real world of public administration.

CASE STUDY

An Authoritarian Approach to Management[19]

Richard Patton had grown up in a small town in a largely rural Midwestern state where the economy was based on agriculture. His parents were hardworking and devout, and had subjected their children to severe discipline. As a boy, Patton had done odd jobs to pay for his own clothes and school supplies. He was a typical product of a society that valued the work ethic: disciplined, conservative, industrious, and respectful of authority.

At the university, where he studied public administration, Patton was mainly interested in those aspects of courses that he considered down-to-earth. He found theoretical and philosophical propositions boring because he had difficulty in applying the abstract to practical matters.

Upon graduation Patton got his first job in his own state as an assistant to the director of the Social Welfare Department in Jefferson County, a rural county of about 40,000 people who were neither wealthy nor poor. Demand for social welfare services was not great, and the problems facing the department staff of ten were readily taken care of. Patton won the respect of his director and coworkers by his conscientious work and reliability. When the director moved on after a year, Patton succeeded him in the post.

A year later Patton accepted an offer to direct a department in a large county with more industry, a more varied economy, and a more diverse population than Jefferson County. Patton became head of a department with 40 staff members that was governed by the Polk County Board of Commissioners and the county Social Service Commission. Although the county had a mixed population that included Native Americans, Hispanics and African Americans, no members of these groups worked at the department.

It was a typical public-welfare agency, administered by the county, supervised by the state, and funded by the county, state, and federal governments. Its program included Aid for Families with Dependent Children (AFDC), Work Incentive (WIN), Supplemental Security Income (SSI), and Medicaid, all administered under guidelines set by the state and federal governments.

The staff members, Patton soon discovered, frequently failed to follow guidelines and even appeared unfamiliar with them, applied rules inconsistently, and were sometimes indifferent to their clients' needs. Employees often arrived late at the office, took time off without permission to take care of personal matters, left clients waiting while getting coffee or chatting with fellow employees, and, in general, were inefficient and lackadaisical. Patton found few of them had the education and training for their work and quickly discovered the reason: qualified people were hard to obtain because of the low pay scale—the minimum acceptable by state requirements. The county commissioners, all conservative politically and economically, held budgets to the lowest possible level. Salary levels in all county offices were not competitive with those in the private sector.

Patton's initial review of the agency revealed that three persons appeared potentially useful in establishing an organizational structure to replace the present slipshod operation. They were the assistant director and two other employees who had ill-defined supervisory powers.

The course of action necessary to reform the agency appeared clear to Patton. What was needed was a highly structured and disciplined organization. He envisioned himself as keeping close tabs on all the programs administered by the agency. Supervisors would be selected from within the organization. Authority would be delegated to the supervisors, and line workers would be classified according to a strict hierarchy. Jobs would be highly specialized and all employees would be trained to do their jobs in a prescribed manner. Weekly staff meetings would be used to review and modify work styles and to inculcate respect for authority.

In putting his plans into effect, Patton rejected suggestions of the workers. He felt that their ideas on pay, job design, and office procedures had no place in a well-run operation. "If they don't like the way the office is run, they can work some other place," he said. Despite Patton's authoritarian approach to management, some improvement began to be made. The office was brightened by fresh paint, and the furniture was rearranged so that counselors had more privacy in discussing problems with their clients. Responsibility for certain tasks was assigned to specific people, files were kept up-to-date, and clients were handled more quickly. Patton and his supervisors, carefully chosen from among the staff, seemed to receive proper respect from other employees.

Dissatisfaction and dissent soon boiled over, however. Line workers challenged Patton's edicts at staff meetings, complained about many of the imposed rules and regulations, wrangled over policies and goals, and threatened to appeal to the governing boards.

Patton's supervisors periodically approached him with suggestions for changes. He had been upset at first and had felt they were interfering with his prerogatives as an administrator, but he was now willing to listen to their opinions, especially since he was beginning to fear losing his job if the extent of the objections among the staff reached the agency's governing boards.

The supervisors explained to him that, although many improvements had been made in the department, they believed the administrative structure had to be made more responsive to staff personnel. They suggested that staff input in salary plans, office-procedural policies, and staff meetings be increased and that a program of upgrading jobs and pay be introduced. They thought that the administrative system was too strict. The department under the former director had not been tightly controlled but the work had gotten done and the public had seemed satisfied as to the level of service delivery.

It was hard for Patton to believe he had been wrong in thinking the welfare department needed the imposition of a more rigid system, but he now recognized that his reforms had failed and that there were aspects of management to which he had been blind.

QUESTIONS AND INSTRUCTIONS

1. Analyze Patton's conception of leadership.
2. If we grant that the Welfare Department needed to be made more efficient, what course could Patton have followed to make his reforms more acceptable to his staff?
3. What needed changes in the department did Patton overlook?
4. What courses of action would you recommend for Patton to correct his mistakes?
5. Would another organizational theory and management practice have been more appropriate for the welfare department than that followed by Patton? Explain.
6. What are some of the organizational factors that can impede change? What are some factors that can facilitate change? How can resistance to change be overcome?

ENDNOTES

1. Dwight Waldo, *The Enterprise of Public Administration* (Novato, CA: Chandler & Sharp Publishers, Inc., 1980), 33–47.

2. H. H. Gerth and C. Wright Mills, eds. *From Max Weber: Essays in Sociology* (New York: Oxford University Press, 1946), 197.

3. Michael M. Harmon and Richard T. Mayer outline the most important contributions to conceptual theories of public organizations. The authors create a general framework for examining the world confronting the public administrator. They describe six perspectives that bridge the theoretical with actual practice in public organizations. These perspectives, as analyzed by various authors, focus upon three organizational themes-system, hierarchy, and structure. See Harmon and Mayer, *Organization Theory for Public Administration* (Boston: Little, Brown, and Co., 1986).

4. John M. Pfiffner and Frank P. Sherwood, *Administrative Organization* (Englewood Cliffs, NJ: Prentice-Hall, Inc., 1960), 56–57.

5. *Ibid.*, 217.

6. Frederick Winslow Taylor, *The Principles of Scientific Management* (New York: W. W. Norton & Co., Inc., 1947 [1911]), 9.

7. Elton Mayo, *The Human Problems of an Industrial Civilization* (New York: Macmillan, 1933). Also see F. J. Roethisberger and William J. Dickson, *Management and the Worker* (Cambridge, MA: Harvard University Press, 1946).

8. Pfiffner and Sherwood, *Administrative Organization*, 102.

9. Chester Barnard, *Functions of the Executive* (Cambridge, MA: Harvard University Press, 1968 [1938]).

10. *Ibid.*, 217.

11. Luther Gulick and Lyndall Urwick, eds. *Papers on the Science of Administration* (New York: Institute of Public Administration, 1937).

12. Gulick, "Notes on the Theory of Organization," in Gulick and Urwick, *Ibid.*, 13.

13. Herbert A. Simon, "The Proverbs of Administration," *Public Administration Review*, Vol. 6 (Winter, 1946), 53–67.

14. Simon, *Administrative Behavior: A Study of Decision-Making Processes in Administrative Organization*, 3rd revised edition (New York: The Free Press, 1976).

15. Mary Parker Follett, *The New State: Group Organization—The Solution to Popular Government* (Longmans, Green: 1918); *Creative Experience* (Longmans, Green: 1924); and *Dynamic Administration*, Henry C. Metcalf and L. Urwick, eds.

16. Abraham Maslow, *Motivation and Personality* (New York: Harper and Brothers, 1954).

17. Douglas McGregor, *The Human Side of Enterprise* (New York: McGraw–Hill, 1960).

18. Rensis Likert, *The Human Organization: Its Management and Value* (New York: McGraw–Hill, 1967).

19. "An Authoritarian Approach to Management," in *Practicing Public Management: A Casebook*, by C. Kenneth Meyer and Charles H. Brown (New York: St. Martin's Press, 2nd edition, 1989), 90–92. Reprinted with permission of St. Martin's Press.

5

☆ ☆ ☆

PEOPLE AND PERSONNEL

CHAPTER HIGHLIGHTS

CONFLICTING DOCTRINES IN PUBLIC ADMINISTRATION
PROCEDURES AND POLICIES
RECRUITMENT
THE POSTRECRUITMENT PHASE
PROMOTION
THE CHALLENGES OF PUBLIC PERSONNEL
ADMINISTRATION
THE CHANGING DEMOGRAPHICS OF THE
FEDERAL WORKFORCE
EQUAL OPPORTUNITY AND AFFIRMATIVE ACTION
PERFORMANCE RATINGS
JOB CLASSIFICATIONS

"Let me control personnel," George Kennan has said, "and I will ultimately control policy. For the part of the machine that recruits and hires and fires and promotes people can soon control the entire shape of the institution."[1]

Few administrative theorists or practitioners would dispute this statement, and in the course of history, few able administrators have thought or acted otherwise. Their attitudes and approaches to the subject have, however, often differed.

Thomas Jefferson, for example, believed that civil servants should be provided with "drudgery and subsistence only" so that they would not want to stay too long in office.[2] This would enable the country to escape the establishment and growth of an administrative class, a development that Jefferson greatly feared. His fears were echoed by a U.S. business journal in the 1920s, which published an editorial stressing "the urgency of keeping this country's civil service ineffective lest it become dangerous."[3]

Most public administrators have taken a different tack, and through the years increasing effort has gone toward improving the capabilities and stature of those toiling in the public sector. Today, with the increased importance of the public sector in private lives, increased emphasis should be placed upon strengthening the competency of civil servants.

Conflicting Doctrines in Public Administration

Herbert Kaufman provided a foundation for describing conflicts in the doctrines of public administration—a foundation that remains solid in this last decade of the 20th century. He notes that different values are reflected in different periods in American history. The quests for representativeness, for neutral competence, and for executive leadership reflect norms of public personnel administration.[4]

The quest for *representativeness* has its roots in the colonial period. In our republican system, government bureaucrats are accountable to policies initiated by representatives of the voters.

The quest for *neutral competence* originated in the 1880s with abuses of legislative supremacy, the long ballot, and the spoils system. The goal of this quest was "taking administration out of politics."

The quest for *executive leadership* was an effort to deal with such governmental issues as budgeting, reorganization, fragmentation, and the size of the bureaucracy. The personnel function is an essential part of these issues.

In addition to these "quests," it is helpful to look at Donald E. Klingner's and John Nalbandian's description of factors affecting public personnel practices that may contribute to the conflicting values in public administration. These factors are:

- *Value Influences,* especially the rights of the individual, administrative efficiency, responsiveness, and social equity.
- *Mediating Activities,* including affirmative action, human resource planning, productivity, and labor relations.
- *Core Functions,* such as procurement, allocation, development, and sanction of human resources.[5]

PROCEDURES AND POLICIES

Public organizations in this country use essentially one of two different methods of establishing and operating personnel systems. One method stresses *political appointment and election* while the other emphasizes an *objective determination of merit.*

Political appointment and election has a long history in the United States. Units of the Revolutionary army frequently elected their own officers, and once the hostilities ended, states and their communities undertook to elect most of the administrators they would need. This practice has persisted in many places up to the present day. Many cities and towns, particularly older ones, follow the same practice. Some New England communities elect as many as 50 officials. Newer areas of the country, such as the Far West, disdain such practices, but even they maintain county organizations with many elective posts. No other major country in the world elects so many of its administrators as does the United States. Most state governments elect at least some officials whose tasks would be regarded in Europe or Canada as purely administrative.

Although election is supposed to give the people a deciding voice in determining who will administer their government, it can lead to abuses, such as confusing and misleading promises and campaign funding from special interests. Underlying all such problems is the fact that most of the electorate finds it impossible to know all the candidates for whom they must vote.

The political appointment of officials is a practice that also dates back to colonial times. Even John Adams, who considered himself something of a paragon of political propriety, felt constrained to provide his ne'er-do-well son-in-law with a government job. Such practices gained increased favor with the arrival of Andrew Jackson at the White House. Jackson strongly adhered to Jefferson's views on rotating public servants in office. At the same time, Jackson did not believe that this would entail any loss of public confidence. As he put it, "The duties of all public servants are, or at least admit of being made, so plain and simple that men of intelligence may readily qualify themselves for their performance."[6] Of course, Old Hickory's espousal of this philosophy was fortified by the fact that he had a virtual army of job seekers at his back who were clamoring loudly for the plums of patronage.

From Jackson's time on, U.S. presidents frequently found themselves besieged by persons seeking positions on the public payroll. One aggressive appointment seeker jumped into Abraham Lincoln's carriage to ask for a job while the president was riding through Washington. Lincoln started to listen to him but then drove him away, saying, more in despair than in anger, "No, I will not do business in the street."

When a disappointed job seeker assassinated President James Garfield in 1881, the nation's appetite for such administrative practices began to change. Political appointment continues to play a prominent role in U.S. administrative life however. Our presidents, for example, have nearly 100 times more appointments to fill than do British prime ministers.

The assassination of President Garfield did have its effect. It gave rise to an alternative method of recruitment, namely the *merit system*. Two years after the president's violent death, Congress passed the Pendleton Act, setting up a systematized procedure for hiring and employing vast numbers of federal civil servants in virtually every category. The merit system principle has continued to grow ever since. Today it not only encompasses over 90 percent of all positions in the federal government but includes increasing numbers of employees in state and local governments as well. About two-thirds of our states now have what are called comprehensive merit systems that cover the vast majority of their jobholders. Even those remaining states without comprehensive merit systems make some provisions for merit-style appointments. The federal government has helped prod states and municipalities to move in this direction, for federal grants-in-aid frequently require the recipient agency to operate a merit system of some sort.

The Pendleton Act itself, passed in 1883, provided the substance of modern merit principles. First, administrative reform focused upon nonpolitical appointments in attempting to neutralize the civil service. Such nonpartisanship in selecting, promoting, and regulating public bureaucrats was a reaction against the evils of the spoils system. Second, the Pendelton Act embraced egalitarianism, the most important legacy of Jacksonian democracy. Congress, in adopting civil service reform, refused to pattern the U.S. career system after the British. The American merit system would be open to all applicants of appropriate aptitude and skills. Theoretically, at least, all classes of citizens may contest for government employment. Third, competence, as determined by competitive examinations, constituted a theme of the Pendleton Act's provisions. The emphasis was the requirement that exams be practical, related to the duties to be performed and not grounded in theoretical or scholarly essays based on academic achievement.[7]

More recently, the Civic Service Reform Act of 1978 established the merit system principles that the government employs today. The act states, in addition to many other merit principles, that:

> *Recruitment should be from qualified individuals from appropriate sources in an endeavor to achieve a work force from all segments of society, and selection and advancement should be determined solely on the basis of relative ability, knowledge, and skills, after fair and open competition which assures that all receive equal opportunity.*

Another key part of the 1978 law states:

> *Employees should be retained on the basis of the adequacy of their performance, inadequate performance should be corrected, and employees should be separated who cannot or will not improve their performance to meet required standards.*

Despite the law, the merit system has its detractors who say such a system leads eventually to a triumph of mediocrity, with initiative and enterprise sacrificed to the pressures of security and the forces of stagnation. Even when a merit system encourages merit, the argument continues, it may lead only to a "meritocracy" that shuts out otherwise capable people who cannot pass its tests or meet its formal and sometimes fatuous requirements.

Although the merit system may have lost some of its luster through the years, it retains a good deal of support from both theorists and practitioners. If it leads to a "meritocracy" then, they say, this is still likely to be more egalitarian and democratic than a system built on political contacts and allegiances. When operated properly, it attracts the better people and encourages them to stay and develop their capabilities.

In a 1990 decision, the United States Supreme Court ruled that the U.S. Constitution prohibits partisan political considerations for hiring, promoting, or transferring most public employees. The ruling clearly prevents a mayor or local chief executive from reserving nonpolicymaking jobs like road equipment operations, prison security, highway repair, and parks department for the party faithful. Although the practical impacts of the ruling are difficult to assess, the Supreme Court, nevertheless, dealt a sharp blow to political patronage at all levels.

RECRUITMENT

If the merit principle has become the most widely accepted basis for personnel operation in U.S. administration, it nevertheless continues to catalyze controversies and pose problems. In terms of recruitment, there is first the task of making sure that the system truly rewards merit. Most civil service systems make extensive use of comparative examinations to bring this about. While such exams may more impartially weigh the merits of the various candidates than would a system built on favoritism, they offer difficulties of their own.

For one thing, the exams must be predictive. In other words, high scores on the examinations should correlate with high performance on the job and vice versa. This is not necessarily the case. The issue of the validity of tests (whether tests results are accurate or appropriate) and other recruitment criteria has come to the fore in recent years, thanks to the stepped-up efforts to recruit members of minority groups into government service. Civil rights supporters claim that many of these criteria serve to exclude blacks, Puerto Ricans, Chicanos, and others. In so doing, these tests fail to determine the true capability of a job applicant. A study in Chicago found that a black police recruit would perform as well as a white recruit who scored 10 percent higher on the entrance exam.[8] In other words, the entrance test failed to measure the true ability for police work of black applicants in comparison with white applicants.

The federal government has been moving to require test validation as a means of ensuring and expanding equal opportunity. The move to include more members of minority groups in public administration is part of a larger movement aimed at making government agencies more representative of the public they serve. This brings us to another issue in administration. Government agencies have at times become "captured" by one or more particular sectors of society. The "captive" agency—the term is Brian Chapman's—tend to recruit heavily from one particular ethnic, religious, social, or geographical group.

THE POSTRECRUITMENT PHASE

The personnel agency, once it has cleared a group of recruits, will then usually place their names on a list. Such a list usually runs in order of eligibility with the top scorers on the exam placing first and continuing down the line. Many other factors may also figure into the standings, however. One of these is veterans' preference. The federal government and most state and local civil service systems award some bonus points to those who have served in the armed forces. The federal government bestows five points for such service alone and five additional points if the applicant qualifies as a disabled veteran.

TABLE 5-1 December 31, 1991 Full-Time Permanent White-Collar College Graduate Federal Civilian Employment in the Executive Branch by Academic Discipline Group

Academic Discipline Group	Degree Holders	% of Total
Agriculture and Natural Resources	44,541	6.7%
Architecture and Environmental Design	4,581	0.7
Area Studies	1,581	0.3
Biological Sciences	29,492	4.4
Business and Management	139,696	20.9
Communications	8,074	1.2
Computer and Information Science	12,500	1.9
Education	40,487	6.0
Engineering	109,705	16.4
Fine and Applied Arts	6,224	0.9
Foreign Languages	5,130	0.8
Health Professions	45,668	6.8
Home Economics	3,964	0.6
Interdisciplinary Studies	13,385	2.0
Law	28,267	4.2
Letters	12,658	1.9
Library Science	2,533	0.4
Mathematics	14,186	2.1
Military Science	713	0.1
Physical Sciences	31,214	4.6
Psychology	17,984	2.7
Public Affairs and Services	19,270	2.9
Social Sciences	72,344	10.8
Theology	1,831	0.3
Unspecified Academic Discipline	2,354	0.4
Total	668,754	100.0

Data Source: Records for 1,582,384 Federal civilian employees in Executive Branch agencies with full-time work schedules, permanent tenure, and white-collar occupations were extracted from the Central Personnel Data File (CPDF).

Of the total (668,754) of full-time permanent white-collar college graduate Federal civilian employment in the Executive Branch by academic discipline group, 496,742, or 74.3%, held Bachelor's degrees, 141,947, or 21.2%, held Master's degrees, and 30,065, or 4.5%, held Ph.D. degrees. The 668,754 degree holders in white-collar Federal civilian employment represent 42.3% of the full-time work employees.

Agencies customarily take their recruits from the top of the list, but here again there are some exceptions. In some cases, particularly for higher-level positions, the rule of three may apply. This permits the appointing authorities to skip the top scorer or even the second scorer on the list of qualified applicants. The agencies can choose any of the top three. The advantages of permitting such discretion for certain positions are obvious. An applicant may score highest on a well-conceived exam for public relations officer, but if he exudes unpleasant breath and changes his shirt once every two weeks, he is not likely to perform the agency's public relations duties in the most effective manner.

In addition to these perfectly proper ways of relaxing their requirements to take recruits from the top of the list, agencies sometimes resort to more surreptitious strategies. They may hold off taking any recruits at all until they can be sure that enough people at the top of the list will have found other jobs or moved away so that some favored person or persons farther down the list can be reached. The lists themselves usually expire after one or two years, and an agency may wait until such a list expires in order to gain someone who will be on the new list. The appointing authority may also let the list expire and discourage attempts to set up a new one, choosing instead to fill positions on a temporary basis.

There is nothing inherently suspect about temporary appointments, and virtually all merit systems make some provisions for them. Usually such appointments can be made only for prescribed periods, such as 30 working days. Abuses have come when such appointments are indefinitely extended. The federal government and some state and local jurisdictions have taken steps to counteract this by prohibiting any temporary appointee from serving successive terms in any particular position. Many other jurisdictions are, however, more lenient—hence, the ability of Chicago mayors to name precinct captains to temporary positions lasting several years and even decades.

Assuming that the recruit has qualified for and received an appointment, he or she still has some hurdles to surmount before claiming full-fledged membership in the organization. One of these is the probationary period. During this time the recruit can be dismissed without the safeguards that protect those who have successfully completed such a phase. Probationary periods vary in length from six months to six years. The six month term is common in some state and local governments, while the federal government and some other subnational jurisdictions require one year of service. It is common to vary the time somewhat depending upon the nature of the position. While a fledgling sanitation person may acquire permanent status in six months, an officer on the police force may have to wait a full year. A teacher, on the other hand, may not be given tenure for three years. The largest waiting periods are usually found at colleges and

---

WHAT THE FEDS TAKE AWAY, THE STATES ASSUME

Despite huge federal deficits and inefficiency in the federal bureaucracy, in the last 20 years state employees' numbers have increased more than five times faster than the tally of federal workers. Now four million strong, the combined state-government work force exceeded the federal payroll, which numbers three million, since 1972.

Source: *The Wall Street Journal,* July 1, 1991, page A1.

---

universities where new faculty members may have to serve six years before becoming tenured. Some positions, such as political appointments to high-level posts, confer no privileges or permanency at all.

Another aspect of the postrecruitment phase is typically training. Some agencies do nearly all their own recruit training. These include police departments, fire departments, and the like. Other public bodies, such as school systems and public health agencies, expect the newcomer to have acquired the needed basic skills beforehand. Generally, the higher the professional level of the position, the more likely it is that the recruit for that position will have obtained the essential training prior to appointment.

Training of all kinds is receiving increasing attention in public administration today. It has become an accepted fact that a fast-moving and fast-changing society exhibits a high need for, and must place increasing emphasis on, wide-ranging and high-level skills. It was not so long ago that a typical police officer's training consisted of some on-the-job supervision. Today an officer is likely to receive many weeks or months of schooling at a police academy. The same holds true for many other public positions. Street cleaners are now apt to operate fairly complicated equipment where previously they may have pushed brooms, and so they, too, must receive a certain level of instruction to cope with their once simple tasks.

The fastest growing area of attention in recent years may be what is called in-service training. The upsurge of interest in this training method arises from the growing realization that in a modern society scarcely anyone is ever fully trained for the rest of his or her career. Not only must skills be continually upgraded, but new skills must frequently be acquired if the employee and the organization are to meet the shifting demands and the changing work patterns that are so characteristic of our present time. Administrators are progressively accepting the notion that education is a life-long process and that the organizations they manage must plan to provide training on a nearly nonstop basis throughout an employee's career.

PROMOTION

Once an employee has cleared all the hurdles and achieved full status as a member of the organization, the possibility of promotion arises. Advancement may come in the form of a simple pay increase, an increase in grade at the present level, or a move up to a new level, usually involving at least some new duties and responsibilities.

Merit systems customarily provide two basic criteria for promotion: *seniority* and *merit*. In the majority of instances, both factors enter into consideration. The question to be answered in evaluating this system is, "Which of these, seniority or merit, is the most conducive to effective administration?"

The answer at first seems obvious. Merit is normally deemed the best and most effective method for determining who shall rise and who shall not. Seniority presents obvious drawbacks. It rewards the incompetent along with the competent. It offers little inducement for the employee to upgrade skills or exert his or her best efforts. A seniority system may make it harder for an organization to attract the best and the brightest and may make it even more difficult for it to retain them once they find that moving upward is merely a matter of biding one's time.

For these reasons, seniority has often served as a whipping boy for civil service critics and the dominant role it has played in many merit systems has made them seem far from meritorious. Yet, seniority-based system does have its benefits. It is probably the only truly impartial system possible for conferring promotion. No merit measures can ever achieve the complete objectivity of the seniority principle; for though a dispute may arise as to whether employee A is better than employee B, no dispute is likely to spring up over the question of which of them joined the organization first.

As a completely neutral system for promotion, seniority may also temper discord among employees. There is little incentive to backbite or backstab when such activities are doomed to go unrewarded. Strange as it may seem, the fact that employees have little motivation to seek shortcuts to the top can, at least in some instances, induce them to concentrate more resolutely on their existing work.

Seniority can also—and the emphasis is on "can"—stimulate productivity by encouraging employee identification with the organization or by allowing those who have built up seniority to feel freer to point out ways to improve operations. A seniority system can also reduce turnover since an employee's investment in the job grows day by day.

Seniority has its blessings, and the wise administrator would do well to keep them in mind. It is particularly useful in deciding who gets first choice in such things as vacation time, desk location, and the like. And it probably does not deserve the blame that it so often is made to bear for the inefficiency of many public organizations.

The trend, however, is unanimously toward decreasing the emphasis on seniority in promotion. Civil service systems in this country are gradually reducing the preeminence that had previously been accorded this method of promotion. The federal government today makes little use of it as such, and many other jurisdictions are re-evaluating its role. Most administrators favor genuine merit systems, at least for major promotions, and most writers on administration agree with them.

Whether an organization relies on seniority or merit, and whether it measures merit by examination or performance, a further question arises: To what extent should an organization promote its own members at all?

This brings us to the issue of *lateral entry*. Organizations may fill upper-level positions from within or without. When they accept outsiders for posts other than those at the bottom level, they are using what is called lateral entry. It is an almost universal practice in the private sector, but it is far less common in the public one. Many public organizations, such as most police departments, fire departments, and sanitation departments, make no provision at all for lateral entry except for occasional highly specialized positions. Other organizations, such as school departments, may allow lateral entry only at the uppermost level. The school superintendent may, for instance, come in from outside the school system, but the assistant superintendents and the principals will all have to come up from the ranks.

Lateral entry is a distinctly two-edged sword. Its flagrant use can easily undermine an organization, for it seals off promotional opportunities and motivation from those who are already serving the organization. Employees who see the positions they prize go to outsiders become disheartened and discouraged, and the more able and aggressive employees will tend to leave the organization for greener pastures. At the same time, the caliber of those applying for its rank-and-file positions will tend to fall, since these entry positions will hold little chance for advancement. Carried to an extreme, lateral entry can lead to a caste system such as the one that characterized many European armies in bygone years, when no soldier could ever hope to advance to officer rank.

Lateral entry can also present other problems. The organization has obviously had far less chance to study the outsider than it has its own people, and it runs a greater risk in giving the outsider a position of responsibility. Furthermore, no matter how capable a person may be, there is no telling how long it will take the new employee to adjust to the way things work in that particular organization. In some instances, this adjustment may never take place.

Lateral entry thus seems like a dangerous device. Yet an administrator may find that excluding the possibility of lateral entry can pose even greater perils. Only through a lateral entry system can an organization take advantage of the vast range of talent and techniques that society has to offer. This involves not just specialized positions, although they are becoming more numerous and important all the time, but also more generalist posts. In an age when increasing numbers of young people are starting their careers after having acquired one or more college degrees, an organization must be able to offer them posts commensurate with their abilities if it hopes to stave off stagnation. Finally, the outsider brings fresh ideas and different perspectives. He or she often sees things that are wrong that insiders do not see and may suggest changes that otherwise would never have been considered.

With such factors as these in mind, public organizations are beginning to look more favorably on lateral entry. State governments are starting to follow the federal government in instituting management intern programs. Police departments are beginning, at last, to give extra pay and credit toward promotion for education achieved beforehand. It is not a question of entirely abandoning promotion from within. Such a step, for reasons that we have already seen, would in many cases prove disastrous. Rather, it is a question of striking a balance. And striking balances is what administration in general is all about.

THE CHALLENGES OF PUBLIC PERSONNEL ADMINISTRATION

There are 18,584,000 government employees. Of that number, 60.4 percent, or 11,228,000 jobs, were in local government; 23.6 percent, or 4,381,000, were in state government, and 16 percent, or 2,975,000 were federal employees. Almost all government employees are paid with tax dollars. Given the cost of managing them, the public has a very real interest in governments that are efficient, effective, and economical. To serve that interest, local, state, and federal governments must:

- Attract high-quality job applicants;
- Hire a reasonable share of the high-quality applicants;
- Train and develop employees;
- Motivate employees to perform at their best; and
- Retain good performers and remove poor ones.

TABLE 5-2 Full Time Employment With Permanent Appointments: 1988–1992

Cabinet Departments	1988	1992	Difference 1988–92
Agriculture	88,043	95,139	+ 7,096
Commerce	28,371	30,967	+ 2,596
Defense	946,961	901,756	− 45,205
Education	4,241	4,561	+ 320
Energy	15,569	18,863	+ 3,294
Health and Human Services	109,173	116,925	+ 7,752
Housing and Urban Development	12,278	13,507	+ 1,229
Interior	57,023	61,945	+ 4,922
Justice	66,522	87,804	+ 21,282
Labor	16,877	16,903	+ 26
State	22,982	23,776	+ 794
Transportation	59,734	67,111	+ 7,377
Treasury	147,415	160,415	+ 13,000
Veterans Affairs	193,698	200,556	+ 6,858
Agencies	**1988**	**1992**	**Difference 1988–92**
Environmental Protection Agency*	13,300	16,373	+ 3,073
Equal Employment Opportunity Commission	3,020	2,759	− 261
Federal Deposit Insurance Corporation	4,598	9,535	+ 4,937

*The Environmenta. Protection Agency has been renamed to be a Cabinet Department.

Source: U.S. Office of Personnel Management, Office of Workforce Management, *Employment and Trends: Federal Civilian Workforce Statistics* (Washington, DC). See Table 7: Total Employment and Full-Time Employment with Permanent Appointments by Selected Agency, May 1988 and 1992.

Continued

TABLE 5-2 Full Time Employment With Permanent Appointments: 1988–1992, continued

Cabinet Departments	1988	1992	Difference 1988–92
Federal Emergency Management Agency	2,154	2,517	+ 363
General Services Administration	18,758	19,613	+ 855
National Aeronautics and Space Administration	22,058	24,760	+ 2,702
National Archives and Records Administration	1,832	2,048	+ 216
National Labor Relations Board	2,195	2,052	− 143
Nuclear Regulatory Commission	3,135	3,267	+ 132
Office of Personnel Management	4,735	5,447	+ 712
Panama Canal Commission	7,386	7,153	− 233
Small Business Administration	3,789	4,037	+ 248
Smithsonian Institution	4,137	4,604	+ 467
Tennessee Valley Authority	24,112	18,301	− 5,811
U.S. Information Agency	8,180	7,542	− 638
U.S. International Development Cooperation Agency	4,417	4,288	− 129
U.S. Postal Service	638,755	640,013	+ 1,258
Executive Branch Totals	2,535,448	2,574,537	+39,089

PROFILE OF THE "TYPICAL" FEDERAL CIVILIAN NON-POSTAL EMPLOYEE SEPTEMBER 30, 1991

by Christine E. Steele

The **"typical Federal civilian employee"** is a topic of frequent interest for the news media, businesses, private citizens and organizations as well as the Congress, White House, and other Federal agencies. This factsheet lists the summary statistics often requested for speeches, letters and reports. **(Data are for total on-board employment unless otherwise indicated [i.e., all work schedules] and may differ from other releases due to coverage — e.g., agency, work schedule, tenure — and as-of dates.)**

Demographic Characteristics

Age .... 42.5 years average for full-time permanent employees

Length of Service .... 13.5 years average for full-time permanent employees

Retirement Eligibility .... 8% of full-time permanents covered under Civil Service Retirement (excluding hires since January 1984)

Education Level .... 35% have Bachelor's Degree or higher degree

Gender .... 56% men and 44% women

Race and National Origin .... 27.7% minority group members: 16.8% Black, 5.4% Hispanic, 3.6% Asian/Pacific Islander, 1.9% Native American

Handicapped Status .... 7% have handicaps

Veterans Preference .... 28% have veterans preference (15% are Vietnam Era veterans)

Retired Military .... 4.7% of total: 0.5% officers and 4.2% enlisted personnel

Job Characteristics

Annual Base Salary .... $34,100 average for full-time permanent employees; $42,515 in Wash., DC

Special Rates .... 10% paid higher rates for retention in shortage occupations

Grade .... 8.8 average General Schedule grade; 10.4 in Washington, DC, Metropolitan Area

Pay System .... 73% General Schedule, 17% wage systems, and 10% others

Work Schedule .... 93% full time, 4% part-time and 3% intermittent

Tenure .... 89% permanent appointments; 87% full-time permanent appointments

Occupation and PATCO .... 83.5% White-Collar (21.8% Professional, 24.5% Administrative, 18.1% Technical, 16.8% Clerical, 2.3% Other), 16.5% Blue-Collar

Supervisory Status .... 10.4% Supervisors and 2.0% Managers

Union Representation .... 74% eligible and 60% represented

Service (Position Occupied) ...... 80.4% Competitive, 19.2% Excepted, and 0.4% Senior Executive Service

Agency .... 44.5% Dept of Defense and 11.9% Dept of Veterans Affairs

Geographic Location .... 97% USA and 15% Washington, DC, Metropolitan Area

Retirement Plan .... 50.0% Civil Service Retirement (including 1.6% in special plan for law enforcement and firefighter personnel) 2.6% Civil Service Retirement *and* Social Security, 38.4% Federal Employees Retirement System *and* Social Security, 7.5% Social Security only, 0.7% Foreign Service Retirement or other system, 0.8% none.

Life Insurance .... 91.5% eligible for Federal Employees' Group Life Insurance: 15.2% waived, 26.5% have basic coverage and 49.8% have more than basic coverage

Employment Covered in This Profile

    2,199,486 Total; 1,882,249 Full-Time Permanent

Data Source: U.S. Office of Personnel Management's Central Personnel Data File covers Federal civilian employees except Members and employees of Congress, Architect of the Capitol, Botanic Garden, Library of Congress, Congressional Budget Office, Copyright Royalty Tribunal, Office of Technology Assessment, Judicial Branch, White House Office, Office of the Vice President, Federal Reserve Board, U.S. Postal Service, Postal Rate Commission, Tennessee Valley Authority, Defense Intelligence Agency, Central Intelligence Agency, National Security Agency, and foreign nationals employed overseas.

Any employing organization's ability to achieve these goals is closely linked to its personnel policies, systems, and procedures. For the Federal civil service, those policies, systems and procedures are inextricably bound to the concept of merit, which is defined through various laws and regulations. Today the U.S. civil service is experiencing a "quiet crisis" in its inability to meet the goals listed previously. There is a body of evidence suggesting that "the Government is not perceived as an 'employer of choice' by many graduates of the country's most highly rated academic institutions."[9] Ironically, "since the Federal Government employs relatively more managers, professionals, and technicians than other U.S. employers, the skills required of Federal workers are greater, on average, than those employees in the nation as a whole."[10] This attitude towards Federal employment is therefore quite damaging. Results of a 1989 survey said that less than half of senior-level federal managers and executives would work for the government again if they had a choice.[11]

THE CHANGING DEMOGRAPHICS OF THE FEDERAL WORKFORCE

Labor economists and other experts do not agree that labor shortages and skills gaps are likely to occur by the year 2000. Experts generally agree, however, that the demographic composition of the labor force has changed and will continue to change in the future. The Office of Personnel Management and U.S. Bureau of Labor Statistics data indicate that many workforce changes and conditions are more prevalent in the federal workforce than in the nonfederal sector of government employment. The nonfederal workforce includes both private sector employees and state and local government employees. Table 5-3 depicts race/national origin composition and change in the federal and nonfederal workforces between 1976 and 1990.

Adjusting to changes in the number of women, minorities, and older workers in the federal government can be accomplished through a variety of human resource policies and programs such as child care, flexible work schedules, diversity training, and reemployment incentives. Demographic differences in the federal workforce indicate that different policies and programs may be needed in different agencies and regions. Workforce planners should consider specific needs of the workforce and the organization.[12]

TABLE 5-3 Race/National Origin Composition and Change in the Federal and Nonfederal Workforces Differed Between 1976 and 1990

	Percentage of workforce					
	Federal			Nonfederal		
Race/national origin	1976	1990	Change	1976	1990	Change
White	78.9	73.0	−5.5	84.9	79.1	−5.8
Minority	21.5	27.0	+5.5	15.1	20.9	+5.8
Black	14.6	16.9	+2.3	9.4	10.4	+1.0
Hispanic	3.5	5.0	+1.5	4.2	7.5	+3.3
Asian/other	3.4	5.1	+1.7	1.5	3.0	+1.5
Total	100.0	100.0		100.0	100.0	

Source: *The Changing Workforce: Demographic Issues Facing the Federal Government* (Washington, DC: U.S. General Accounting Office, 1992), 45. Federal data are from OPM; nonfederal data are from BLS.

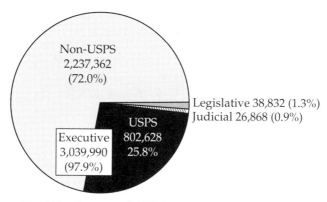

Total Employment: 3,105,690

FIGURE 5-1 Distribution of Federal Civilian Employment by Branch, March 1992.

Source: U.S. Office of Personnel Management, *Federal Civilian Workforce Statistics: Employment and Trends* (Washington, DC: U.S. Government Printing Office, March, 1992).

The percentage of the federal workforce that was female increased from 35 percent in 1976 to 43 percent in 1990. Even more striking during this period were changes in the overall number of both men and women in the federal workforce. While the number of employees in the federal workforce rose by nearly 200,000 between 1976 and 1990 (a 28 percent increase), the number of men in the federal government fell by over 100,000 (an 8 percent decrease).

Most of the changes in the gender composition of the federal workforce were in white-collar professional and administrative occupations. The percentage of women in blue-collar and white-collar technical and clerical jobs changed relatively little from 1976 to 1990. In 1976, less than 20 percent of all professional and administrative employees in the federal government were women. By 1990 however, over 35 percent of federal professional and administrative employees were women.

Throughout the 1976 through 1990 time period, a greater proportion of federal employees were members of racial or ethnic minorities than in the nonfederal workforce. The percentages of minority workers in both workforces increased between 1976 and 1990 at about the same rate. As a result, the federal/nonfederal difference in minority composition was about the same in 1990 as it was in 1976. Despite the increased minority representation in the state and local workforce during this period, the percentage of nonfederal jobs held by minorities in 1990 (20.9 percent) was still not as large as the percentage of federal jobs held by minorities in 1976 (21.5 percent).[13]

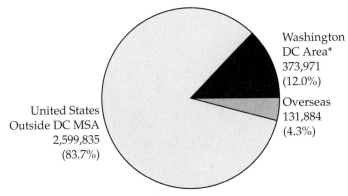

Total Employment: 3,105,690

*Washington, DC Area includes the District of Columbia; Arlington, Fairfax, Loudoun, Prince
William, and Stafford Counties; the Cities of Alexandria, Fairfax, Falls Church, Manassas, and
Manassas Park in Virginia; and Calvert, Charles, Frederick, Montgomery, and Prince Georges
Counties in Maryland.

FIGURE 5-2 Distribution of Federal Civilian Employment by Major Geographic
Area, March 1992.

Source: U.S. Office of Personnel Management, *Federal Civilian Workforce Statistics: Employment and Trends*
(Washington, DC: U.S. Government Printing Office, March, 1992).

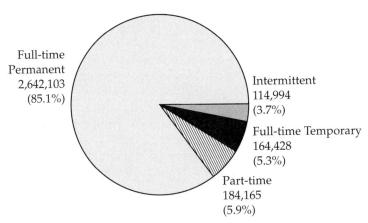

Total Employment: 3,105,690

FIGURE 5-3 Distribution of Federal Civilian Employment by Work Schedule/
Appointment, March 1992.

Source: U.S. Office of Personnel Management, *Federal Civilian Workforce Statistics: Employment and Trends*
(Washington, DC: U.S. Government Printing Office, March, 1992).

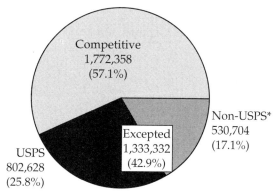

Total Employment: 3,105,690

*Includes: Congress, Judiciary, Schedules A,B,C, foreign nationals overseas, National Guard, Veterans Readjustments, TVA, FBI, Foreign Service, Veterans Affairs physicians and nurses.

FIGURE 5-4   Distribution of Federal Civilian Employment by Service, March 1992.

Source: U.S. Office of Personnel Management, *Federal Civilian Workforce Statistics: Employment and Trends* (Washington, DC: U.S. Government Printing Office, March, 1992).

Each sector's changes in minority composition between 1976 and 1990 varied considerably by racial and ethnic group. The change in the percentage of the workforce that was Hispanic was greater in the nonfederal sector than in the federal sector. Conversely, the increase in African American representation was greater in the federal sector. In both 1976 and 1990, the federal government had a smaller percentage of White and Hispanic employees and a larger percentage of African American and Asian American and employees belonging to other minority groups than in the nonfederal workforce.

In addition to the differences between the federal and nonfederal workforces in terms of their gender, minority, and age characteristics, there were also differences in these characteristics within the federal government by agency and geographic region. There were differences as well among agencies and regions in the degree to which they changed between 1976 and 1990. While the proportion of an agency's workforce that is female or belonging to a minority group provides a good indication of the degree of workforce diversity in the agency, that statistic alone can tell only part of the story. Of at least equal relevance is the degree of change in those demographic characteristics over time. Table 5-4 shows changes between 1976 and 1990 in the percentage of female and minority employees in the federal agencies examined.

TABLE 5-4   Some Federal Agencies' Gender and Minority Composition Changed
More Than Other Agencies' Between 1976 and 1990

	Percentage of workforce					
	Female			Minority		
Agency	1976	1990	Change	1976	1990	Change
Agriculture	26.7	39.4	+12.7	13.9	16.4	+2.5
Air Force	27.1	34.9	+7.8	17.9	22.9	+5.0
Army	30.5	38.6	+8.1	16.7	23.0	+6.5
Commerce	39.2	50.2	+11.0	21.1	28.0	+6.9
Defense	35.1	44.1	+9.0	22.7	29.0	+6.3
Education	[a]	58.1	[a]	[a]	46.1	[a]
Energy	[a]	37.6	[a]	[a]	20.0	[a]
EPA	35.9	48.7	+12.8	11.8	25.9	+14.1
FDIC	30.2	51.3	+21.1	11.8	21.2	+9.4
GSA	33.6	41.2	+7.6[b]	40.0	37.0	−3.0[b]
HHS[a]	60.7	64.9	+4.2	31.4	36.9	+5.5
HUD	44.5	57.7	+13.2	26.9	39.1	+12.2
Interior	28.8	37.5	+8.7	26.7	27.2	+0.5
Justice	31.4	38.1	+6.7	20.9	30.5	+9.6
Labor	46.3	46.4	+0.1	30.6	31.2	+0.6
NASA	19.1	30.0	+10.9	8.4	16.0	+7.6
Navy	23.5	30.9	+7.4	20.5	26.3	+5.8
State	43.7	47.2	+3.5	26.4	30.7	+4.3
Transportation	17.7	25.4	+7.7	13.3	17.3	+4.0
Treasury	45.6	57.8	+12.2	21.0	31.6	+10.6
VA[c]	49.7	55.0	+5.3	28.7	32.5	+3.8
All agencies	34.9	42.8	+7.9	21.5	27.0	+5.5

[a]The Departments of Education and Energy did not exist in 1976. HHS was the Department of Health, Education, and Welfare in 1976, from which the Department of Education was created.
[b]Some of the differences between 1976 and 1990 at GSA may be due to transfers of National Archives and Records Administration employees in 1985 and building operations employees at various times during this period.
[c]The Department of Veterans Affairs was the Veterans Administration in 1976.

Source: *The Changing Workforce: Demographic Issues Facing the Federal Government* (Washington, DC: US General Accounting Office, 1992), 58.

TABLE 5-5 Private and State/Local Workforces Were Somewhat
Different in Gender, Race/National Origin,
and Age Composition in 1990

Gender	Private	State/local	Nonfederal
Male	54.6	43.4	53.0
Female	45.4	56.6	47.0
Race/national origin			
White	79.3	77.4	79.1
Black	9.8	13.9	10.4
Hispanic	7.8	5.7	7.5
Asian/other	3.0	2.9	3.0
Age			
16–19	6.4	2.1	5.8
20–24	12.4	6.4	11.5
25–34	30.4	24.4	29.5
35–44	24.5	31.4	25.4
45–54	15.4	21.4	16.2
55–64	8.7	11.8	9.1
65+	2.4	2.6	2.4

Source: *The Changing Workforce: Demographic Issues Facing the Federal Government* (Washington, DC: US General Accounting Office, 1992), 77.

The nonfederal workforce includes both private sector employees (about 88 million workers in 1990) and state and local government employees (about 14 million workers in 1990). There are some differences in the demographic composition of private sector and state and local government workers. As Table 5-5 shows, in 1990 the state and local government workforce had a much higher percentage of female employees, had a somewhat larger percentage of African American employees, and had a smaller percentage of workers below the age of twenty-five than did the private sector. Because the private sector had about six times as many employees as state and local governments, the nonfederal labor force generally resembled the private sector more than state and local governments.[14]

EQUAL OPPORTUNITY AND AFFIRMATIVE ACTION

Equal employment opportunity refers to "the idea that no person should be denied the opportunity for employment because of discrimination based on race, color, religion, sex, national origin, or physical disability."[15] While *equal opportunity* is essentially a passive concept, *affirmative action* is an active one.

In some ways, equal employment opportunity redefines the merit system to emphasize that the merit philosophy not only recruits, selects, and advances employees on the basis of their relative abilities, but also calls for a work force that is representative of all the people. Equal opportunity is principle among the ideas that fuel the American way of life. Affirmative action implements equal opportunity for minorities and women. Honest people often agree on the lofty goals of equal opportunity, but disagree on the manner in which such a sometimes vague philosophy is carried out.

As a passive strategy, equal opportunity implies nondiscrimination. Equal opportunity and nondiscrimination are passive instruments of public policy because they rely on families, schools, and pertinent forces in U.S. society to abolish stereotypes and prejudices that prohibit creation of a balanced work force. Affirmative action is an active strategy, intended to ensure equal opportunity.

With the possible exception of trade unionism, which we shall examine in a subsequent chapter, no issue in the post World War II era has engaged public personnel administration as the quest for equal opportunity. Public administration is an integral part of modern society and, as such, is not impervious to society's pressures and concerns. As the campaigns for the rights of women and minorities emerge and accumulate legitimacy and recognition, they shake and buffet public personnel administration right along with the rest of American life. There is no question that personnel administration needed the shake-up. The federal government itself has a somewhat questionable record in equal opportunity.

The controversy over affirmative action follows from the noble aspiration of providing equal employment opportunity for all Americans. As we noted earlier, in private administration the law generally tells administrators only what they cannot do, and in public administration, the law tells administrators what they can do. The implementation of equal employment opportunity and affirmative action is therefore, grounded upon a host of federal, state, and even local laws.

The following items have been crucial in the attempt to achieve social equity through proportional representation in the nation's work force: the Civil Rights Act of 1964, Executive Order 11246 of 1965, and the 1972 Equal Employment Opportunity Act.

AFFIRMATIVE ACTION BECOMES INSTITUTIONALIZED

"The curtailment of affirmative action may mean less than is generally expected. . . . Affirmative action is now a firmly established institutional practice, indeed virtually a reflex of many university, corporate and political decision makers. (As Mr. Bush's appointment of Clarence Thomas illustrates, even conservatives need the legitimacy of multiracial representation.) Just as discrimination did not end with formal rulings against it, neither will affirmative action end with formal rulings."

Source: Paul Starr, "Civil Reconstruction: What to Do Without Affirmative Action," *The American Prospect* No. 8 (Winter 1992), 7–14.

The development of the affirmative action concept began in the mid-1960s with the passage of the most far-reaching civil rights law since Reconstruction. The Civil Rights Act of 1964 prohibits job discrimination on the basis of race, sex, religion, national origin, age, and physical disability, and the Equal Employment Opportunity Commission was simultaneously created for the purpose of administering the law. The law gives operational meaning to the 1954 Supreme Court desegregation case of *Brown v. Board of Education,* which holds that the previous doctrine of "separate but equal" facilities for the races will no longer satisfy Constitutional requirements and specifically that blacks everywhere are permitted to attend the same public schools as whites.

President Lyndon Johnson signed Executive Order 11246 in 1965. It repeated nondiscrimination and affirmative action language used earlier, requiring all government contracts to prohibit discrimination by the contractor and to use "affirmative action" to ensure that workers are employed without regard to race, creed, or color. The 1972 legislation also requires state and local governments to develop affirmative action plans.

Other legislation of significance for affirmative action includes the Equal Pay Act of 1963, amendments to the Fair Labor Standards Act of 1938, the Age Discrimination in Employment Act of 1967 as amended in 1978, Title VI of the Vocational Rehabilitation Act of 1973, and the Vietnam Veteran's Readjustment Assistance Act of 1974.[16]

A parallel theme of affirmative action is the concept of *comparable worth.* The phrase signifies "equal pay" for work of comparable value, requiring a job to be paid the same as any other job judged to be equally demanding. Since many jobs typically held by women frequently pay less than many jobs typically held by men, the comparable worth principle would primarily benefit women. Comparable worth refers to jobs dissimilar in content and demand on the worker, which are ranked by objective criteria. Jobs of the same worth or value should merit equal pay.

AMERICANS WITH DISABILITIES ACT (ADA)

The purposes of the act are to provide a clear and comprehensive national mandate for the elimination of discrimination against individuals with disabilities. Access to employment, housing, public accommodations, education, transportation, communication, recreation, institutionalization, health services, voting, and public services is afforded to more than 43 million Americans with one or more physical or mental disabilities. ADA defines "qualified individual with a disability" as a person with a disability who, with or without reasonable accommodation, can perform the essential functions of the job that such individual holds or desires.

ADA prohibits discrimination on the basis of disability in employment, public services, and public accommodations. New buses and trains must be accessible to the disabled. Telecommunications companies must operate relay systems that allow hearing- and speech-impaired Americans to use telephone service. Equal Employment Opportunity Commission (EEOC) issues regulations to carry out requirements of the act.

According to *The Dorsey Dictionary of American Government and Politics*, by Jay M. Shafritz (Chicago: The Dorsey Press, 1988), comparable worth is

> *equitable compensation for doing a job by determining its value to an organization compared to other jobs in the organization. . . . For example, should graduate nurses be paid less than gardeners? Or should beginning librarians with master's degrees be paid less than beginning managers with master's degrees? Historically, nurses and librarians have been paid less than occupations of comparable worth, because they are considered women's jobs. Comparable worth as a legal concept and as a social issue directly challenges traditional and market assumptions about the worth of a job. (page 120)*

Implementation of comparable worth statutes and programs in state and local government has occurred through litigation, collective bargaining, changes in evaluation factors, and legislation. The courts have reacted to factual evidence of discrimination, focusing on unequal pay for equal work, but have stopped short of recognizing the broader concept of comparable worth as a legal principle.

In the government workplace of the 1990s, the feminist agenda squarely confronts conservative traditionalism. Tradition calls for women to focus their energies upon kitchen, children, and school, expecting all women to find satisfaction in feeding the family, comforting their husbands, raising children, praying and obeying, and teaching youngsters about God and country. This traditional view runs against the new and increasingly important presence of women in the marketplace or workforce.

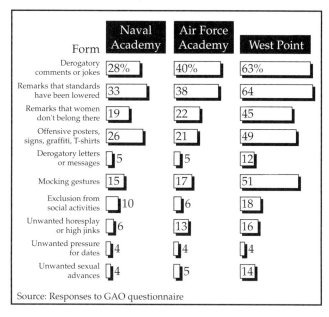

Form	Naval Academy	Air Force Academy	West Point
Derogatory comments or jokes	28%	40%	63%
Remarks that standards have been lowered	33	38	64
Remarks that women don't belong there	19	22	45
Offensive posters, signs, graffiti, T-shirts	26	21	49
Derogatory letters or messages	5	5	12
Mocking gestures	15	17	51
Exclusion from social activities	10	6	18
Unwanted horseplay or high jinks	6	13	16
Unwanted pressure for dates	4	4	4
Unwanted sexual advances	4	5	14

Source: Responses to GAO questionnaire

FIGURE 5-5 Sexual Harassment: Percentage of Female Students Indicating They Experienced Harassment at Least a Couple Times a Month.

Source: *The Washington Post*, June 3, 1992, page A1.

The Clarence Thomas/Anita Hill sexual harassment hearings before the U.S. Senate Judiciary Committee brought sex out of the proverbial closet and placed it on the political agenda and thrust it into the marketplace of ideas. The broader issues raised include a woman's evolution and/or liberation from the more restrictive roles of children, church, and schools. A woman's right to choose an abortion and economic opportunity in the workforce (including freedom from sexual harassment and other forms of sex discrimination) constitute the new moral value. The sexual harassment hearings featuring Thomas and Hill are only symbolic of greater, more significant economic changes in U.S. society.

Social conservatives call for government to put the "father knows best" genie back into the bottle of traditional values. But this attempt to "legislate morality" flies in the face of pragmatism and economic reality. Economically and politically, women—as their economic power in society grows—will cast aside the yoke of male authority, if not domination. The issues of sexual harassment and affirmative action plans in the workplace divide males and females of all races. Women do not want to be patronized, fondled, or harassed. They seek respect for their professionalism, and—sooner if not later—they will demand it. As Figure 5-5 shows, the incidence of sexual harassment at the U.S. Naval Academy, U.S. Air Force Academy, and U.S. Military Academy (West Point) is a matter of record.

REVERSE DISCRIMINATION

The problem of reverse discrimination emerged in the Supreme Court cases of *Regents of the University of California v. Allan Bakke* (1978) and *Weber v. Kaiser Aluminum and Steel Corporation and United Steelworkers Union* (1979).

The Bakke case was a public sector concern; the Weber case was a private sector matter. The distinction is crucial, since it is important to note that legalism in general and laws in particular circumscribe and influence the operation of a public institution more than a private one.

Bakke was a white male suing the Medical School of the University of California at Davis for admission, claiming that the Medical School rejected his application in favor of less qualified minority students. In a voluntary attempt to correct years of minority discrimination, the Medical School established a quota for minority students for each entering class. The Supreme Court's ruling agreed that Bakke had been unfairly denied admission, but the scope of the decision was carefully narrowed.

First, the Medical School is a public institution, supported by taxpayers. Second, the case was one of admission to a public university, not a public sector employment matter. Third, although the court outlawed the quota system, it "played" a different kind of judicial politics as well. If public sector bureaucracies avoided an inflexible quota system, affirmative action programs would remain constitutional. In this way the court allowed for consideration of racial and sexual differences in accepting students. In other words, quotas were made illegal for the public sector; however, race and sex remain acceptable for consideration in entrance requirements. The Bakke decision confused employers, bureaucrats, lawyers, and court watchers alike.

If the Bakke case left the constitutionality of affirmative action in doubt, the Weber Supreme Court decision made some headway in settling the issue, at least in part. Because the Kaiser/Weber was a private concern, no public sector monies were involved. As free agents in a democratic society, the Kaiser Aluminum Company and United Steelworkers Union cooperated in establishing an affirmative action program for minority employees.

Brian Weber, a white lab technician with more seniority than two black applicants, filed suit, claiming reverse discrimination against both the company and the union. By placing minorities in 50 percent of the openings in a training program, and thereby establishing a quota system, management and labor created a voluntary program which afforded special preferences to blacks. The Louisiana plant was located in a region where 39 percent of the local work force was black. Fifteen percent of the employees of the plant were black, but only two percent of the skilled craft workers were black. Therefore, the Weber case raised not only the issue of equal employment opportunity, but also a concern for a representative work force.

The Supreme Court decided in favor of the affirmative action program sponsored by a joint effort of management and labor, concluding that Title

VII of the Civil Rights Act of 1964 was passed for the particular purpose of improving the economic plight of black Americans. In other words, private sector employers could voluntarily establish a hiring and promotion program grounded upon improving the employment skills of blacks. To repeat an earlier distinction, the law generally tells the manager only what he cannot do in the private sector, such as the Kaiser case; however, the law tells the administrator what he can do in the public sector.

We should point out that technically court cases address only the particular set of facts of any court case. To a large degree, the courts in the U.S. are passive units of very fragmented and decentralized federal and state judicial bureaucracies. Courts consider only cases that merit jurisdiction before particular tribunals. Plaintiffs must take their particular set of grievances into court. To do so, plaintiffs need the skills of talented lawyers, money to finance such actions, and the patience and ego strength to see things through, win or lose.

We may conclude that affirmative action issues concern quotas, layoffs, work environment, and compensation. The most controversial issue posed by affirmative action focuses upon the establishment of quotas for making employment decisions. Quotas, of course, specify that a precise percentage of appointments have to be minorities, women, and/or handicapped persons.

DECLINING IMPORTANCE OF AFFIRMATIVE ACTION

David H. Rosenbloom maintains that the importance of affirmative action began declining in the 1980s because: (1) there is no strong consensus favoring affirmative action, which reduces the organizational coherence and political integrity of affirmative action programs; (2) there is a continuing constitutional stalemate as shown by the nonlinear direction of various Supreme Court cases over a 15-year period; and (3) there are new concerns receiving priority such as executive leadership, retrenchment, and productivity.[17]

Given the pros and cons, what is the significance of affirmative action in our society today? Affirmative action causes headaches for many public managers and heartaches for some employees, but we should not overlook the benefits of representativeness in public bureaucracies. Affirmative action raises the issues of potential and real discrimination confronting women, minorities, and handicapped employees. The visibility of the affirmative action issue has heightened awareness of discrimination.

Affirmative action has spawned a great deal of rhetoric; however, the definitive impact, in terms of concrete results, for the purported beneficiaries is questionable. Until the affected groups attain more education and experience, change will be incremental. To its credit however, affirmative action forces public agencies to broaden and intensify their recruiting efforts, to examine the validity of their examinations, and to question the

---

WORK FORCE MORALE AND GOVERNMENT PERFORMANCE

The ability of the Federal Government to function effectively and efficiently is related in no small measure to the quality, competency, and motivation of its work force. Despite generally positive attitudes towards their jobs and the work they do, only about half of the respondents would recommend the Federal Government as an employer, while over one-fourth say they definitely would not.

Several factors that are traditionally viewed as reasons to remain in Federal employment have lost strength as retention factors between 1986 and 1989 surveys conducted for the Merit Systems Protection Board. These include: the intrinsic value of the work itself; salary; current health insurance benefits; and opportunity to have an impact on public affairs.

The components of the Federal Government's performance management program are not creating an atmosphere that strongly encourages quality performance. Relatively large percentages of employees believe that their work units can increase the quantity and quality of the work they perform with the same people.

Source: *Working for America: A Federal Employee Survey* (Washington: US Merit Systems Protection Board, 1990).

---

value of recruitment and promotion criteria. It stimulates innovation and opens up governmental organizations. The administrative branch becomes, as a result, more representative of the population it serves.

The bottom line is that affirmative action has contributed to the process of public administration, if not to its substantive contents. Affirmative action forces governments to hire, promote, and fire employees under the auspices of procedures and administrative due process.

PERFORMANCE RATINGS

If an organization is going to use merit rather than sheer seniority as a basis for promotion or demotion, then just how does one determine job performance? The most common device used is for a superior to give a subordinate a performance rating. The system seems simple, but in practice it generates complications and controversies.

The nub of the performance rating problem lies in the lack of objective data and procedures for making these systems work effectively. Even when a supervisor desperately wants to be fair and impartial, there is often little in the way of neutral criteria that can be applied and that will be immune to personal whim and supervisors can be capricious indeed.

However difficult these ratings systems are to administer, they are almost universally present in the public administration workplace. Table 5-6 is a typical performance rating form.

TABLE 5–6 Personnel Evaluation for Managers Form DPA 57, The Commonwealth of Massachusetts

Name of Person Evaluated	Position Title and Grade	Organizational Unit	Period covered by this evaluation
			Month Day Year
Name of Evaluator	Position Title and Grade	Organizational Unit	From _____ To _____

Instructions: At the beginning of each evaluation period, the manager to be rated should review this form and be informed of the factors on which his or her performance will be evaluated. All ratings must be done by persons who have supervised the manager for at least 90 days. This rating will represent your evaluation of the manager's actual performance on his or her present job.

Suggestions: Consider only one factor at a time. Don't let your rating in one influence your rating of another. Base your judgement on the requirements of the job and the manager's performance in it as compared with others doing similar work. Carefully read the description of each factor before making each entry, and assign the rating which most nearly describes your opinion.

Grading: Performance will be evaluated by the immediate supervisor (*) and, when necessary, the reviewing supervisor (**) by placing a check mark (✓) in the appropriate box in the numerical scale from 1 to 10, based on the following standards:

If the manager's performance demonstrates ability that is—
—outstanding and far exceeds job standards, check the box numbered 10.
—above average, exceeds job standards, check box 7, 8 or 9.
—average, meets job standards, check box 4, 5 or 6.
—below average, does not meet job standards, check box 1, 2 or 3

	Evaluation			
Factor	Below Average	Average	Above Average	Outstanding
Job Knowledge Adequacy of professional skills, experience and knowledge to do the job.	1*|** 2*|** 3*|** Lacks the understanding, skill and experience to perform the job. Requires constant supervision.	4*|** 5*|** 6*|** Has sufficient knowledge, skills and experience to perform tasks with a minimum of guidance.	7*|** 8*|** 9*|** Has a good knowledge of the work to be performed. Above average understanding of procedures.	10*|** Has a thorough understanding of the job and all related procedures, laws, regulations and technical tasks. Extensive professional skill and experience.

Continued

TABLE 5–6 Personnel Evaluation for Managers Form DPA 57, The Commonwealth of Massachusetts, continued

Factor	Below Average	Average	Above Average	Outstanding
Productivity Meeting established standards of quality and quantity of work production.	1 | 2 | 3 | Fails to meet established deadlines. Production does not meet established standards. Requires a high degree of assistance.	4 | 5 | 6 | Work is generally accurate and complete. Meets established standards and deadlines.	7 | 8 | 9 | Completes assignments on time with above average results. Accepts additional tasks when requested.	10 | Consistently completes complex assignments quickly and accurately. Regularly does more than required with exceptional competence.
Communication: Oral Oral facility with language which expedites results while maintaining relationships; maintain channels.	1 | 2 | 3 | Frequently fails to achieve understanding from listeners. Speaks in poorly organized fashion. Has difficulty articulating thoughts.	4 | 5 | 6 | Has adequate ability in making an oral presentation. Occasionally is required to repeat or amend position to achieve desired response.	7 | 8 | 9 | Presents ideas and material in an effective manner. Has above average ability to obtain agreement and support for desired goals.	10 | Outstanding ability to present ideas and articulate thoughts to diverse audiences and organizations. Expedites results through ability to command positive responses.
Communication: Written Presenting and explaining ideas clearly and effectively in writing; developing written work in a logical and comprehensive manner.	1 | 2 | 3 | Lacks the ability to provide written communications in a logical, understandable and timely manner. Requires constant re-write and editing.	4 | 5 | 6 | Written communications are readable and understandable with only occasional need for editing and rewriting. Usually completes written assignments within prescribed time limits.	7 | 8 | 9 | Effectively presents thoughts in writing in a very understandable style with very little need for interpretation or repetition.	10 | Consistently writes complex directives, letters, reports, etc. in a clear, concise, highly understandable style. Writing is convincing and timely, and achieves desired results.
Leadership Inspiring teamwork and productivity; maintenance of discipline; stimulating suggestions; checking the work of subordinates.	1 | 2 | 3 | Is unable to motivate staff to meet organization goals in an efficient and effective manner.	4 | 5 | 6 | Maintains effective work output by utilization of available personnel resources.	7 | 8 | 9 | Effectively utilizes the skill of available staff to obtain a high degree of productivity. Maintains good level of morale; promotes teamwork.	10 | Obtains outstanding productivity and quality of work while maintaining excellent morale. Maintains positive relationships with other agencies.

Category	1 | 2 | 3 |	4 | 5 | 6 |	7 | 8 | 9 |	10 |
Management Skills Efficient use of staff and budget to achieve agency goals; establishing and shifting priorities as necessary; effective delegation of authority; implementing policies and procedures.	Has difficulty utilizing staff and resources efficiently. Overlooks priorities of goals and objectives. Lacks understanding of management skills required.	Accepts established priorities and utilizes resources to meet them. Plans activities and directs subordinates while achieving average results.	Uses staff and budgetary resources efficiently. Implements policies and procedures and has above average ability to adjust priorities to meet goals and objectives.	Achieves agency goals and objectives through superior management skills. Outstanding use of human and budgetary resources to meet priorities. Delegates authority effectively.
Problem Solving and Decision Making Logical and practical thinking; objectivity and deliberation in decision making; application of knowledge and skills to new situations; foreseeing consequences or recommendations.	2*|** |2*|** |3*|** Is unable to adapt to problems of above average difficulty. Does not analyze all facts of problem. Will not make decisions, or makes them hastily or too slowly.	4*|** |5*|** |6*|** Recognizes problems as they occur and contributes to their resolution. Makes suggestions for improvement. Usually coordinates decisions to achieve desired objectives.	7*|** |8*|** |9*|** Applies a highly logical approach to problems presented. Makes suggestions for improvement and carries them through promptly. Suggest conclusions that are accepted. Provides alternate approaches when necessary.	10*|** Anticipates and analyzes difficult situations before they become problems. Logically and quickly applies corrective action with superior results. Generates new and innovative ideas.
Affirmative Action Demonstrating active support of AA goals; knowledge and communication of AA information; monitoring and evaluating activities and progress.	Fails to implement AA goals, activities monitoring and evaluation.	Accepts responsibility for achieving goals. Informs staff. Works to resolve problems and implement policy.	Analyzes situations and provides solutions to achieve goals with above average results.	Outstanding ability to achieve agency goals. Initiate action, expedite results.

Continued

TABLE 5–6 Personnel Evaluation for Managers Form DPA 57, The Commonwealth of Massachusetts, continued

Factor	Below Average	Average	Above Average	Outstanding
	1 | 2 | 3 |	4 | 5 | 6 |	7 | 8 | 9 |	10 |
Initiative & Responsibility Self-starting action; willingness to take the lead and be responsible for decisions, enthusiasm for improvement; working independently with success; open-mindedness toward opposing views.	Is reluctant to accept more than what is perceived to be the required job. Displays little or no initiative. Objects to suggestions for improvement.	Will accept responsibility for work assigned. Displays initiative on selected projects. Seldom seeks out additional work.	Works independently with success. Obtains above average results with self-initiated projects. Is open minded to opposing views.	Develops new and original programs with constant success. Takes responsibility for all actions and results. Exceptional ability to adapt to relevant objections or suggested improvements.
	1 | 2 | 3 |	4 | 5 | 6 |	7 | 8 | 9 |	10 |
Staff Development and Training Development and training of new employees through instruction and by example. Setting and measuring standards of performance; conducting instructive performance appraisal discussions.	Does not set standards for agency tasks nor evaluate employees' performance. Fails to train or develop staff for job improvement and upward mobility.	Periodically measures workers performance against set standards. Routinely instructs staff and assists in improvement of work habits.	Sets standards and measures degree of achievement with individual workers in a cooperative manner. Implements training to improve performance. Sets above average example.	Exceptional ability to develop staff through participative management and regular performance review. Supports upward mobility through the efficient utilization of training programs.

Evaluator's comments (to include recommended areas and methods for improvements):   Total numerical rating ____

_____
Signature

Reviewing Supervisor's comments (Reviewing supervisor must evaluate the employee when the evaluator's rating totals more than 95 or less than 40):   Total numerical rating ____

_____
Signature and Title

Comment of person evaluated: I have reviewed this rating and it has been discussed with me.

_____   _____
Signature   Date

TABLE 5-7   General Schedule Providing a Pay Increase Effective in January 1993

	1	2	3	4	5	6	7	8	9	10
GS-1	$11,903	$12,300	$12,695	$13,090	$13,487	$13,720	$14,109	$14,503	$14,521	$14,891
2	13,382	13,701	14,145	14,521	14,683	15,115	15,547	15,979	16,411	16,843
3	14,603	15,090	15,577	16,064	16,551	17,038	17,525	18,012	18,499	18,986
4	16,393	16,939	17,485	18,031	18,577	19,123	19,669	20,215	20,761	21,307
5	18,340	18,951	19,562	20,173	20,784	21,395	22,006	22,617	23,228	23,839
6	20,443	21,124	21,805	22,486	23,167	23,848	24,529	25,210	25,891	26,572
7	22,717	23,474	24,231	24,988	25,745	26,502	27,259	28,016	28,773	29,530
8	25,159	25,998	26,837	27,676	28,515	29,354	30,193	31,032	31,871	32,710
9	27,789	28,715	29,641	30,567	31,493	32,419	33,345	34,271	35,197	36,123
10	30,603	31,623	32,643	33,663	34,683	35,703	36,723	37,743	38,763	39,783
11	33,623	34,744	35,865	36,986	38,107	39,228	40,349	41,470	42,591	43,712
12	40,298	41,641	42,984	44,327	45,670	47,013	48,356	49,699	51,042	52,385
13	47,920	49,517	51,114	52,711	54,308	55,905	57,502	59,099	60,696	62,293
14	56,627	58,515	60,403	62,291	64,179	66,067	67,955	69,843	71,731	73,619
15	66,609	68,829	71,049	73,269	75,489	77,709	79,929	82,149	84,369	86,589

Executive Schedule

I	$148,400
II	133,600
III	123,100
IV	115,700
V	108,200

Senior Executive Service

ES-1	$92,900
ES-2	97,400
ES-3	101,800
ES-4	107,300
ES-5	111,800
ES-6	115,700

Senior Level

Minimum	$77,080
Maximum	115,700

Administrative Law Judges

AL-3/A	$72,865
AL-3/B	78,470
AL-3/C	84,075
AL-3/D	89,680
AL-3/E	95,285
AL-3/F	100,890
AL-2	106,495
AL-1	112,100

JOB CLASSIFICATIONS

Nearly all public personnel organizations have some system of job classification. The federal government, for example, divides its positions into 15 basic grade levels, ranging from GS 1 to GS 18. Each level is paid more and, ostensibly, requires more in terms of ability and output than the level below it. Within each grade level there are 10 steps, each paying more than the preceding one. The upper steps of any grade actually pay more than the lower steps of the grade just above it. Consequently, an employee who is working at the 10th step of grade 12 will be earning more than an employee who is at the first step of grade 13. Advancement from one step to another takes place chiefly on the basis of seniority. Advancement from one grade to another is based in theory on merit, although in practice seniority often plays a larger role.

The premise underlying classification schemes is the fact that different jobs require varying degrees of ability and impose varying amounts of responsibility. The adoption of a classification plan has long been considered essential for the effective operation of a merit system, for it is designed to place the emphasis on *what* rather than *who* a person knows. It provides a basis for, although it does not guarantee, a neutral and workable personnel operation which, without fear or favor, can reward good performance and penalize bad. It can in principle, do this in open and objective ways.

One crucial question is, "How many classifications should there be?" Should the various jobs be strung out into a large number of separate grades and levels, or should they be compressed into a comparatively few broad categories? If the federal government's personnel system features 18 grades with 10 steps each, is this too many, too few, or just about right?

The problem is obviously a relative one to which there can be no precise answer, since there are no precise criteria defining narrow and broad classifications. To some, the federal government's 18 grade levels may seem too many; to others they may seem too few. We do know, however, that moving in either direction will yield various advantages and disadvantages.

A personnel system employing numerous narrow classifications will be able to tailor its jobs more precisely to each level. If there are two classifications for typists rather than one, better typists can be placed in the upper class and less-capable typists can be put in the lower one. In principle, if typist A does better work than typist B, then A can be given a higher rating than B. It is further assumed that A will be given not only more money and more status, but also more difficult and more responsible assignments. In this sense, using many relatively narrow categories can be fairer to all concerned. Narrow categories also permit more extensive use of promotion as an incentive. More levels mean more possibilities for moving up, and at the same time, such promotional opportunities can be used as a sanction against those who fail to perform adequately.

Many public organizations have relatively few classification levels, particularly in the lower range of jobs. Postal workers, police officers, firefighters, and others can usually move up only to a position of command. Since there are relatively few such positions in most organizations, opportunities for promotion remain limited.

Narrow and therefore numerous job classifications present distinct difficulties, however. The more classifications there are, the more personnel work the organization must do. Each classification must be carefully described and demarcated, and then each job must be carefully plugged into the right classification. This results in a system that is not only costly but also cumbersome and complicated.

Although utilization of numerous and narrow classifications can alleviate discord, since those performing somewhat more demanding tasks can then more easily receive recognition for doing so, it can, for the same reasons, create tension. "Why should he be classified higher than I am when my job requires as much or more responsibility as his?" is a constant complaint. Arguments frequently flare up over whether a position should be put in one class or another. For example, in a regional office of one federal agency, a personnel officer balked at classifying a job at grade level 14, despite pleas and exhortations from the agency's other top officials that he do so. It seems the personnel officer himself held only a grade 13 position, and it was felt that he could not bring himself to categorize the new post at a higher level than his own.

Generally, the more classification levels there are, the more personnel games may be played. One of these is called "job evolution." An employee finds herself stuck at her present level and unable to move up, due to the lack of openings above her; so she strives earnestly to get her existing job reclassified upward. A sympathetic supervisor may assist by adding to her job some new duties, thereby strengthening her case. If the employee is finally successful, then others seek to follow suit, and so the game begins all over again. Jobs have a tendency to keep evolving upward.

Probably the most important impediment that a highly scaled classification scheme imposes on effective administration is inflexibility. The more numerous and narrow the classifications, the harder it is to rotate people from one job to another. In similar fashion, it becomes more difficult to change the nature of the work assigned to any individual, for the new assignments may mandate a change in grade level. An employee may protest vigorously that a new task does not fall into the assigned grade level.

One final aspect of the classification issue is also worthy of note. The broader the classification scheme it uses, the more egalitarian the organization is likely to be. Numerous, narrow classifications can result in a complex pecking order that creates many social and economic distinctions between employees. To take what might be called the limiting case, assume that an organization had only one job classification. It would then be completely egalitarian as far as its personnel system went. The more an organization approaches this situation, the more "democratic" it is likely to become.

What are the trends for the future? Contemporary society is generating considerable pressures on public organizations to hold down administrative costs, to encourage innovation and flexibility, and to increase democratization. For these reasons, it seems likely that the direction of personnel

---

PERSONNEL BUREAUCRACIES

The Civil Service Reform Act of 1978 (CSRA) constitutes a major restructuring of federal civil service in the United States, and the Civil Service Commission (CSC), in particular. The functions once administered by the CSC (1883) are allocated to three separate personnel bureaucracies. The Office of Personnel Management (OPM), as the central personnel agency directly answerable to the President, aids the President in establishing rules for administering civilian employment; advises the President on all employment matters; executes, administers, and enforces civil service laws, rules, and regulations; coordinates research to enhance public personnel administration; and maintains and upgrades existing personnel practices such as examinations, executive development, and performance evaluations.

OPM has no authority over employee appeals. The appellate and quasi-judicial responsibilities previously implemented by CSC are vested in the Merit Systems Protection Board (MSPB). The MSPB decides most appeals and complaints, issues regulations regarding the nature and scope of its review, establishes time limits in which appeals must be settled, and orders corrective and disciplinary actions against employees or departments and agencies if appropriate. As an independent federal agency, MSPB is constituted as a bipartisan organization, consisting of three board members who are appointed by the President and confirmed by the Senate.

The CSRA's final structural change created the Federal Labor Relations Authority (FLRA). The FLRA determines appropriate units of representation, supervises labor organization elections, decides unfair labor practice cases, rules on negotiability issues, rules on exceptions to arbitration awards, mediates disputes, settles impasses, and prosecutes unfair labor practices.

---

administration will be toward broader rather than narrower classification schemes, as we will see later. At this point it is useful to keep in mind that such a trend may increase administrative effectiveness in many ways. Research indicates that the fewer the differences in prestige and status within a group, the more stable the group tends to be and the more likely its members are to accept internal leadership. In addition, communication probably will improve. It is possible that some organizations will need to retain relatively narrow classifications and some might benefit from even more classifications than they now have. But the overall tendency seems to be toward simplification.

SUMMARY

- The quests for *representativeness, neutral competence,* and *executive leadership* are norms of public personnel administration. Value, mediation, and core functions are factors affecting public personnel practices.
- Key merit system principles are: recruiting, selecting and advancing employees on the basis of their abilities, knowledge, and skills; providing equitable and adequate compensation; training employees to assure high-quality performance; guaranteeing fairness for applicants and employees; and protecting against coercion for political purposes.
- Public organizations in the United States use two methods of establishing and operating personnel systems: 1) *political appointment* and *election,* and 2) an objective determination of *merit.* Test validity for predicting on-the-job performance and other selection criteria pose problems for public agencies grounded in merit principles.
- Representative bureaucracy is a basic policy goal pursued by public personnel managers. A separate but related policy choice is whether to pursue that goal *passively* or *actively.* A passive strategy is *equal opportunity.* An active strategy is *affirmative action.*
- Despite huge federal deficits and inefficiency in the federal bureaucracy, in the last 20 years state employees' numbers have increased more than five times faster than federal workers'.
- The average age of federal civilian non-postal employees is 42.5 years; length of service is 13.5 years; 35 percent have Bachelor's or higher degrees; 56 percent are men and 44 percent are women; and 27.7 percent are minority group members.
- To serve the public interest, local, state, and federal governments must attract high-quality job applicants, hire a reasonable share of the high-quality applicants, train and develop employees, motivate employees to perform at their best, and retain good performers and remove poor ones.
- The demographics of the federal workforce are changing. The percentage of the workforce which was female increased from 35 percent in 1976 to 43 percent in 1990. The percentage of the workforce which were minorities increased from 21.5 percent in 1976 to 27 percent in 1990.
- Affirmative Action measures and procedures are becoming firmly established institutional practices and made routine in both the federal and nonfederal workforces.
- The premise underlying *job classification* schemes is the fact that different jobs require varying degrees of ability and impose varying amounts of responsibility.

- Public personnel administration, more than anything else, is a process encompassing *procedures, rules, and regulations.* The recruitment, selection, and promotion phases are grounded in law, reflecting the values of accountability and responsiveness to the public.

The following example shows how complex a personal matter can get. How does the issue of merit come into play in this situation?

CASE STUDY

Personal Dilemma: Terminate or Retain[18]

In a reorganization of the State Department of Education, a planning commission was established to coordinate activities and programs of its more than 50 sections and divisions and to institute and carry out comprehensive programs for the public schools and institutions of higher learning. Commission members were the Superintendent of Public Instruction, the Secretary of the State Board of Education, and the directors of the Federal Program, Finance, and Instruction divisions of the department. Staffing of the commission was provided by the State Board of Education, headed by Dr. Frank Jordan.

In July, Dr. Jordan received funds to hire an additional secretary to perform secretarial and clerical services for the planning commission. The Board at one time had only one secretary for six professional staff persons, and this secretary could not handle that work load and take on additional duties for the commission.

Jordan's administrative assistant, Barbara White, who served as personnel officer and supervisor of the clerical staff, began working with the Department of Personnel to classify the new position and announce the opening. She consulted with the Board's Office Planner, Pamela Goldsmith, and the Facilities Coordinator, John Rodriguez, to determine the classification for the new position. No one was sure what duties would be assigned to the person hired other than that he or she act as Secretary to the Planning Commission. The job would include making arrangements for meetings, preparing agendas, recording and transcribing minutes, and providing data and materials requested by Commission members. It was thought that the person would also serve as secretary to Goldsmith and perhaps do some work for Rodriguez.

After reviewing the anticipated duties with Dr. Jordan, White submitted a job summary to the Department of Personnel requesting a Secretary Grade I classification. The qualifications for this position were graduation from high school, one year of secretarial experience, and the ability to type 45 wpm and take dictation at 80 wpm. The classification was approved and the opening was announced.

The Department of Personnel submitted a list of four eligible applicants to the board and, after interviewing them, Dr. Jordan and Barbara White decided to employ Edith Reichel. Her experience was not entirely what was wanted—she had held only one secretarial position and had worked the past three years as a clerk in the state auditor's office—but she was enthusiastic about getting the job and expressed a willingness to improve her skills and take on new responsibilities. In addition, she won Dr. Jordan's sympathy because she was divorced and had two small children to support.

After Reichel began working, it soon became apparent to Barbara White that employing her had been a mistake. Reichel was a heavy smoker and cigarette ash covered her desk and papers. She was restless and disrupted office work by visiting with other staff members, and she was inattentive when receiving instructions, often making mistakes that resulted in her work having to be redone. Moreover, the position required abilities Reichel did not have. Goldsmith was working on a comprehensive plan for reorganizing the filing system of the department and needed assistance in her studies that she could not entrust to Reichel.

Antagonism also quickly arose between the Board's regular secretary, Hazel Holmberg, and Edith Reichel. Instead of lightening Holmberg's onerous work load, Reichel added to the burden. Because of Reichel's inefficiency, Holmberg had to assist her in collecting material for the Commission meetings and, since Reichel's shorthand was poor, Holmberg had to take the minutes as well. As a consequence, Holmberg complained to White and threatened to seek a transfer unless something was done.

White consulted Pamela Goldsmith about Reichel's performance and found that she, too, considered it unsatisfactory. They held a counseling session with Reichel, who, apologetic, blamed her deficiencies on problems with her two children and promised to improve. For some weeks her work was almost satisfactory, and it looked as though the problem was resolved. But Reichel soon slipped back into her old habits, and Rodriguez discussed getting rid of Reichel while she was still on probation. None of the three supervisors, however, was willing to assume the responsibility for taking action.

The question of whether to start proceedings to release or retain Reichel remained in limbo until near the end of the fifth month of her employment when she failed to report for work one morning. The planning commission was to meet at ten o'clock, and telephone calls made to Reichel at her home to find out where she had placed the data and papers required for the members went unanswered. Fortunately these items were discovered by Holmberg just before the meeting began. Reichel called the office at 11 o'clock to say that she had taken a bus to visit friends in a neighboring town the night before and had missed the bus back. She did not return to work until the next morning.

White reported the difficulties encountered with Reichel to Dr. Jordan, informing Dr. Jordan that only a few more weeks remained on her probationary period. If no action were taken, Reichel would become a permanent employee and it would be hard to remove her, even if her work continued unsatisfactory. Although Jordan was busy trying to meet a deadline for completing the department budget, he promised to talk the situation over with Reichel. When she appeared in his office, he was so preoccupied with budgetary matters that he merely told her there had been some complaints about her work and urged her to try to improve it, which he felt sure she could.

After leaving Dr. Jordan's office, Reichel related to White what had occurred, saying that he had been "very nice" and reassuring about the quality of her work and her future in the department. Later, discussing the matter with Goldsmith, White said that apparently Dr. Jordan, rushed in getting the budget together, would not take the time to deal with such a minor matter as a Grade I secretary's deficiencies. To this end, White arranged for Reichel to attend a week-long secretarial training workshop to brush up on her typing and shorthand. At the end of the probationary period, Reichel became a permanent employee.

Reichel's good intentions did not last long and she lapsed again into her old ways. Other staff members, believing her poor performance placed an extra burden on them, complained of her slipshod work to employees in other offices at the capitol. Through friends, word of this got back to Reichel. She exclaimed that she wished she had never taken the job in the first place and that there had never been any fault found with her work in the state auditor's office. Dr. Jordan and White, she said, had not been honest with her.

Repeated complaints of staff members to Jordan finally persuaded him that to restore staff morale he would have to get rid of her and arrange for someone else to do the secretarial work for the planning commission. Since there was no really strong basis for firing Reichel, he decided to reclassify her position to a Secretary Grade II and reassign her to work in one of the auxiliary programs attached to the department.

QUESTIONS AND INSTRUCTIONS

1. How would you allocate the blame in permitting Reichel to complete her probation and become a permanent staff member?
2. Would an orientation and training program and closer supervision have prevented the situation from developing?
3. What do you think of the manner in which the problem was finally resolved?
4. Do you think that Reichel was correct in her belief that her superiors had not dealt honestly with her?
5. Is it fair to the state for administrators to keep an employee who performs poorly out of sympathy for his or her personal problems or because they find reprimanding or firing a person too painful an experience? How tough must administrators be?

ENDNOTES

1. Quoted in John Franklin Campbell, *The Foreign Affairs Fudge Factory* (New York: Basic Books, 1971), 139–140.

2. *Ibid.*, 47.

3. Quoted in George E. Berkley, *The Administrative Revolution: Notes on the Passing of Organization Man* (Englewood Cliffs, NJ: Prentice-Hall, 1971), 141.

4. Herbert Kaufman, "Emerging Conflicts in the Doctrines of Public Administration," *The American Political Science Review,* Vol. 50 (December 1956), 1057–1073.

5. Donald E. Klingner and John Nalbandian, *Public Personnel Management: Contexts and Strategies* (Englewood Cliffs, NJ: Prentice-Hall, Inc., 1985).

6. Quoted in Paul Van Riper, *History of the United States Civil Service* (New York: Harper & Row, 1958), 36.

7. Steven W. Hays and T. Zane Reeves, *Personnel Management in the Public Sector* (Boston: Allyn and Bacon, Inc., 1984), 16.

8. Cited in Patrick V. Murphy, *The Criminal Justice System in Crisis* (Syracuse, NY: Maxwell School of Citizenship and Affairs, 1972).

9. U.S. Merit Systems Protection Board, *Attracting Quality Graduates to the Federal Government: A View of College Recruiting* (June 1988), page vii.

10. The Hudson Institute, *Civil Service 2000,* A Report Prepared for the U.S. Office of Personnel Management (June 1988), page 10.

11. *The Washington Times,* May 25, 1989, page B5.

12. *The Changing Workforce: Demographic Issues Facing the Federal Government* (Washington, DC: US General Accounting Office, 1992), 3.

13. *Ibid.*, 40–45.

14. *Ibid.*, 76.

15. Ralph C. Chandler and Jack C. Plano, *The Public Administration Dictionary* (New York: John Wiley & Sons, 1982), 246.

16. Klingner and Nalbandian, *Public Personnel Management,* 62–69.

17. David H. Rosenbloom, "The Declining Salience of Affirmative Action in Federal Personnel Management," *Review of Public Personnel Administration,* Vol. 4 (Summer, 1984), 202–205, 248–249.

18. "Personnel Dilemma: Terminate or Retain," in *Practicing Public Management: A Casebook,* by C. Kenneth Meyer and Charles H. Brown (New York: St. Martin's Press, 2nd edition, 1989), 178–181. Reprinted with permission of St. Martin's Press.

6

☆ ☆ ☆

PUBLIC SECTOR UNIONISM

On August 3, 1981, air traffic controllers in the United States went on strike. Federal law prohibits such a strike. Then-president Ronald Reagan fired the strikers. The controllers, belonged to the union known as PATCO—the Professional Air Traffic Controllers Organization. The 17,500 member union accounted for just 1 percent of the federal civilian work force.

During its 20-year existence, PATCO had a stormy labor-management relationship with the federal government. There were work slowdowns and "sick-outs" staged by the union. There were court battles between PATCO and the Federal Aviation Administration.

The issues involved in the disputes included wages, working conditions, FAA policies, and even the number of "orientation" rides the controllers received from the airlines. An orientation ride was, simply, a free plane trip.

A year before the strike, in the presidential election year of 1980, the controllers announced a "withdrawal of enthusiasm"— a work slowdown that managed to delay flights until the FAA secured a restraining order against the union. That year, PATCO's leadership decided to back the candidacy of Reagan. With their candidate later winning the White House, the union readied a new list of demands.

The controllers who worked in the extreme high pressure atmosphere of airport control towers, were earning at that time a base salary of about $30,000, which, with overtime, brought their average earnings to about $34,000. They could retire from their demanding jobs at age 50 with a minimum of 20 years of service. The union's first demand on the Reagan Administration was for a $73,000 salary and a 32-hour workweek. PATCO soon scaled back the salary demand to $60,000.

The Reagan Administration offered PATCO an 11.4 percent pay hike, far below the union demand, but far more than the new Republican administration was prepared to offer any other federal union. PATCO leaders approved the offer, but the rank and file rejected it and the leaders quickly sided with the members. On August 3, 1981, more than two-thirds of the nation's 17,500 air traffic controllers walked off their jobs.

The Reagan Administration threatened to dismiss the strikers if they did not return to work within 48 hours. Only 1,000 went back to work, leaving 11,000 on the picket lines and out of work.

From his California ranch, Reagan said, "There is a law that federal unions cannot strike against their employers, the people of the United States. What they did was terminate their own employment by quitting."

The dispute between PATCO and the federal government is a vivid example of the conflict that can flare up when public sector labor and management don't see eye to eye. This chapter explores the delicate relationship between public employee unions and public administrators.

TABLE 6-1   Private and Public Sector Membership and Density
in the U.S., 1953–1991

Year	Membership (000's)		Density (percent)	
	Private	Public	Private	Public
1953	15,540.2	789.8	35.7(a)	11.6
1962	14,731.2	2,161.9	31.6	24.3
1970	16,978.3(a)	4,012.0	29.1	32.0
1973	16,803.5	5,077.8	26.6	37.0
1976	16,166.8	5,980.3	25.1	40.2(a)
1983	13,142.6	5,410.7	17.8	34.4
1989	10,520.0	6,422.0	12.4	36.7
1991	9,909.0	6,627.0(a)	11.9	36.9

(a) denotes historic peak.

See *Unions in Transition: Entering the Second Century* (1986), edited by Seymour Martin Lipset, page 82.

Sources: Leo Troy and Neil Sheflin, *Union Sourcebook* (West Orange, NJ: IRDIS, 1985); Bureau of the Census, U.S. Department of Commerce *Statistical Abstract of the United States 1991* (Washington, DC: 1991), page 425; Bureau of Labor Statistics, U.S. Department of Labor, *Employment and Earnings* (Washington, DC: January, 1992), page 229.

TRANSFORMATION

Unions in the United States originally arose to combat the terrible work and wage conditions of the early Industrial Revolution. After the Great Depression of the 1930s, organized labor, which then existed only in the private sector, was thriving and calling for macroeconomic policies advocating high employment and high wages. Since then, membership in public sector unions such as teachers' and fire fighters' unions has grown, while unionism in general is declining.

Public sector unionism is a product of the Great Society of the 1960s and has changed the overall labor movement emphasis from high employment and high wages to an emphasis on redistribution of society's economic resources. Today, public sector unions represent a larger percentage of the U.S. labor movement than ever before. Table 6-1 shows that in a dramatic thirty-year period, 1953 to 1983, private union membership ebbed while public unions experienced meteoric membership increases. This enhanced importance of public sector unionism as a component of the overall U.S. labor movement is leading to increased demands for more government intervention in the economic arena.

Leo Troy, in describing the rise and fall of American trade unions from Franklin Roosevelt to Ronald Reagan, argues that organized labor has changed its philosophy of "more" for its clients to a philosophy of "more government intervention" in America's political economy.[1] Troy says there is a philosophical split between America's private sector unions and public sector unions concerning the definition and implementation of "more government intervention" in our economy and society. Private sector unions wish to enhance their clients' incomes; public sector unions argue, in effect, for raising taxes so that client salaries may be increased.

Troy perceives public sector unions and private sector unions to be on a collision course. "On one hand, private sector unions want government to vigorously apply macroeconomic policies to stimulate economic growth and avoid depression; on the other hand, public sector unions want a redistribution of the national income from the private to the public sector in the form of social services and transfer payments."[2]

Despite being larger than private sector unionism, public sector unionism is in *transformation*. The rise of public sector organized labor activities in the 1960s and 1970s was followed by a leveling, or maturation, of such activities through the 1980s and into the 1990s. Public and private unions are both in decline and are not as strong as they once were, but neither shows signs of extinction.

From a global perspective, unionism in general is not simply in a period of maturation—it is in decline throughout the world. Data from England, France, Italy, Japan, and West Germany imply similar trends toward maturation or decline.

The U.S. peak year for the labor movement, measured in terms of "union density," came in 1953. Union density refers to the extent of union membership in the total work force. That year, trade union membership accounted for 25.9 percent of the labor force and 32.5 percent of nonfarm employment. By 1983, the density had shrunk to 16.6 percent and 20.7 percent respectively. Total union membership topped out in 1975, but from the middle 1970s to 1986, overall union membership declined by almost 4 million members.

David Lewin cites key factors for the rise in public unionism during the decline in overall unionism.[3] Among those factors at work from 1960 to 1975 are the passing of state laws permitting collective bargaining by state employees and the rapid growth in public employment.

During the late 1970s and throughout the 1980s however, political and economic factors changed. From a political and economic environment that promoted employee unionism and collective bargaining rights, the recent and current attitude emphasizes imposing penalties for illegal strikes by public employees.

PUBLIC UNIONISM: PRO AND CON

At the beginning of the 1960s, not a single written contract existed between a teachers' union and a U.S. school system. Today, thousands of such contracts are in effect and cover more than two million teachers. The principle teachers' union, the National Education Association, has become the second largest union in the nation. It has also become the most powerful single lobbying group in many statehouses and one of the most powerful lobbies in Washington.[4]

As with the teachers, so with other groups of government workers. As previously cited, the 1960s and 1970s were times of unprecedented growth in public sector unionism. In these times of union decline, The National Education Association is a primary example of a public sector union expanding and growing with enthusiasm and purpose. Many think that's good; many others disagree.

PRO

The numerous accusations that can and have been made against public employee unionism do not shake the faith and determination of the movement's supporters. They continue to stand firm, not only in discounting the negative but also in affirming the positive aspects of public sector unionism. A rationale does exist for viewing the growth of unionism as a beneficial factor in the development of public administration.

Unions will, it is true, usually insist on having input into administrative policy, but such input need not constitute a roadblock to administrative improvement. Unions naturally tend to favor at least some administrative practices generally recognized as positive. For example, they will usually fight against favoritism, for favoritism benefits a few over the many, and the many always means more potential votes at union meetings. Unions may, therefore, resist any policies that permit discriminatory or arbitrary treatment. In order to improve the prestige of their membership, union leaders may also seek to raise recruiting requirements and promote professionalism. Some unions even run career development programs. Union publications usually carry some material concerning new developments in the vocational fields of the membership.

When it comes to innovation and change, unions can also play a constructive role. Public employee unions have the unique ability to effectively bring public-sector problems before the public. Teachers' unions have often done this with positive results for their members.

In summary, unions usually prevent strikes or shorten those that do occur. Union leaders much prefer to resolve disputes by negotiation. Public employee unions bring public sector problems before the public.

CON

Opponents of public employee unionism claim that it is unjustified and unwarranted. The public employee does not labor to provide a profit to his employers. No basic divergence of interest exists, therefore, between management and labor employers since the former do not benefit by depriving the latter. All are public servants, charged with executing the people's wishes as expressed through their elected representatives, votes on referenda, and other means. Trade unionism in general and collective bargaining in particular, say the opponents, erode the whole concept of government work as a public service.

Unions are also accused of perpetuating and even expanding some of the worst features of public personnel systems. These include promotion by seniority and rigid tenure rules, which make it difficult to fire or demote a delinquent or deficient employee. Public employee unions, say the critics, encourage public organizations to meet challenges and solve problems by simply adding more people. Unions are accused of impairing innovation and increasing the political involvement of public employees. Public employee unions probably exert the most influence in those large cities with partisan elections.

More recently, some government officials have pointed out that certain natural restraints on union demands exist in the private sector but not in the public sector. A union that seeks too much from a business firm may only put the firm, and eventually itself, out of business. Governments, however, rarely go out of business. Instead they simply seek to exact the additional costs from their constituents. The absence of an automatic lid on employee demands, say the critics, has led to excessive demands and, when not met, to excessive strikes. Given government's role as a provider of welfare and protector of the public safety, virtually any strike at all can, say unionism's critics, be called excessive.

In summary, trade unionism erodes, however, the concept of government as a public or civil service. Unions perpetuate some of the worst features of personnel systems. Unions diffuse responsibility and make accountibility more difficult to pinpoint. Unionization greatly increases the political involvement of government employees.

THE BARGAINING PROCESS

An administrator who is entering into negotiations with a recently established union will often feel like an early Christian entering a lion-filled arena. A union usually arises as the culmination of a long and mounting series of disputes, the union's first negotiations are often the most militant.

Add to these problems the fact that a new union's representatives are also inexperienced and untested. They know that their members are waiting to see what they can do, and so they feel they must prove themselves.

As a result of these conditions, the initial phases of union-management relations are likely to prove much more trying than later ones. If administrators fail to keep this in mind, they may let themselves in for more turmoil and trouble than necessary. Later, when collective bargaining becomes an established and even routine procedure in organizational life, they may find the atmosphere starting to ease. Rarely will such negotiations become a simple, cut-and-dry operation, and each round of talks presents its own problems, but administrators who have weathered many such bargaining sessions have usually developed a series of strategies to deal with them. While each may have his or her own special techniques, there are a few general rules that many have found helpful.

1. To bargain effectively with unions, an administrator must believe in such bargaining. This is essential for two reasons: (1) a negative feeling toward the process is likely to be communicated to the labor representatives and will, in turn, make them hostile, and (2) no administrator can ever learn how to make full use of collective bargaining—of how to turn it to his or her agency's advantage— unless he or she believes that such a possibility exists.

2. It is important for administrators involved in contract negotiations to encourage the involvement and support of middle management and even first-line management/supervisors. This is not always easy to do, since many low-ranking managers identify with the rank and file. Indeed, the union may bargain indirectly for these people as well as for its own members because a pay increase for rank and file will usually bring a pay increase for middle management as well. In some agencies, the pay of first-level supervisors is fixed at a certain percentage over that of the people they supervise.

   Despite these difficulties, it is worthwhile to seek middle management support, since middle and first-line managers can often contribute substantially to the bargaining process. They usually know best what the rank and file really want and what will satisfy them. They will also be the ones who will have to implement the new contract. This means that the contract is likely to prove more workable if their input is obtained before the contract is worked out. Finally, excluding middle managers or paying little heed to what they have to say may only alienate them all the more from the administrative side and intensify their identification with those they supervise.

3. The public manager should also take care to come to the bargaining table with proposals of his or her own. In other words, management should not simply react to labor's demands but make some demands itself. Furthermore, a manager will be well advised not to negotiate all the union's demands first. Instead, he or she should press forward with settling some of management's claims before all the union's requests have been dealt with, lest management lose all its leverage before its own concerns are thrashed out.

   Administrators should be careful, on the other hand, to see that the union's negotiators do not leave the bargaining table empty-handed. They must be given some victories. Managers who seek to undermine union representatives succeed only in making these representatives and the membership more intractable. The management negotiator should remember that his or her union counterpart may have to contend not only with competition from within but also from without, for other unions may be eager to supplant the existing one.

4. The union representatives will almost always be needed to enforce whatever settlement is achieved. Weakening their position is not going to help management in accomplishing this enforcement task.

5. For some of the same reasons, administrators would do well not to let the negotiations drag on too long, for this, too, may make the membership more militant and hence more difficult for their representatives to control. And once issues have been negotiated, the settlements should be put in writing so that the unions cannot easily repudiate them if they later find the situation more propitious for making even stronger demands.

   One final fact should be kept constantly in mind. In the public sector, as in the private sector, trade unions are not primarily economic organizations, and their fundamental role is not merely to secure economic benefits. They are essentially a means whereby employees seek to ameliorate their dependent position, to assert their right to self-determination and to avoid *manipulation*. The economic issues that so often dominate the dialogue, while by no means unimportant, are still often secondary. The more fundamental issues are those that involve human dignity and human rights.

WHEN COLLECTIVE BARGAINING FAILS

In those cases where a stalemate is reached and the bargaining process breaks down, alternatives are available for avoiding a strike.

A device that is sometimes used when labor-management negotiations flounder is *mediation*. The mediator, or in some cases mediators, actually help carry out negotiations between the disputing parties. They may group both sides around a table and try to find ways to open up previously entrenched positions or to point out possibilities for conciliation. When a dispute has gotten out of hand and tempers have reached a boiling point, the mediator may even put the two sides in separate rooms and run from room to room in a continuing effort to break the deadlock. Some jurisdictions authorize fact-finders to shift to mediation when their recommendations have failed to dissolve the differences separating the parties involved.

Mediation is obviously quite an art. According to one experienced practitioner, a good mediator should:

- have a good sense of timing, knowing when to advise each side on when to make each move;
- avoid relieving the parties themselves of responsibility to solve the dispute;
- be able to distinguish the power contest between the negotiating parties from internal power struggles (such as union leaders fearful of losing face with their own members);
- avoid passing on the merits of the respective positions.[5]

Another alternative is what is called *fact-finding*. Under this process, an individual or, more frequently, a mutually acceptable panel is set up to review the disputed issues and make recommendations. These recommendations are not binding, but if the fact-finding machinery has been properly constituted, and if its analysis of the facts is accurate, both sides will be under a good deal of pressure to accept its suggestions.

Neither mediation nor fact-finding assures a peaceful settlement to a labor dispute. For that type of guarantee we must turn to a third alternative, *interest arbitration*. This device differs from the other two in just one crucial respect: it produces a definite decision and usually one that is binding on both sides. When binding arbitration has been agreed upon, the arbitrator's word is final and there is no further appeal.

If arbitration is not accepted by either party at the outset, it obviously does not guarantee a peaceful resolution, but it is rarely utilized without such prior agreement. One typical way of going about setting up arbitration is for each side to choose a representative and for the two representatives to choose a third member of what then becomes an arbitration panel.

Administrators tend to view third-party proceedings such as fact-finding, mediation, and arbitration with some suspicion. While they recognize that such devices help considerably to avoid strikes, they often feel that they result in decisions that are injurious from a management perspective. Third parties have nothing at stake except their own future arbitration or mediation business. They show a tendency, it is felt, to split the issue down the middle, with perhaps some leaning toward the labor side. Some administrators question not only the leaning toward labor but also whether most disputes should automatically be split down the middle in any case.

BARGAINING HOMILIES

Be sure that you have set *clear objectives* on every bargaining item and that you understand on what ground the objectives were established.

Do not hurry.

When in doubt, *caucus.*

Be *well prepared* with firm data support for clearly identified objectives.

Always strive to keep some flexibility in your position—don't get yourself out on a limb.

Do not concern yourself with only what the other party says and does—*find out why.* Remember that economic motivation is not the only explanation for the other party's conduct and actions.

Respect the importance of *face saving* for the other party.

Constantly be alert to the *real intents* of the other party—with respect not only to goals, but also to priorities.

Be a good *listener.*

Build a reputation for being *fair* but *firm.*

Learn to control your *emotions*—don't panic. Use emotions as a tool, not an obstacle.

Be sure as you make each bargaining move that you know its *relationship* to all other moves.

Measure each move against your *objectives.*

Pay close attention to the *wording* of every clause negotiated; words and phrases are often the source of grievances.

Remember that collective bargaining negotiations are by their very nature part of a *comprehensive* process.

There is no such thing as having all the pie.

Learn to *understand* people and their personalities—it may mean a payoff during negotiations.

Consider the *impact of present negotiations* on negotiations in *future* years.

Reed C. Richardson

Source: *Collective Bargaining by Objectives: A Positive Approach* (Englewood Cliffs, NJ: Prentice-Hall, Inc., 1977), p. 150.

They feel many issues simply do not lend themselves to that type of decision. In any case, management loses control in such proceedings, and decisions are made by those who cannot be fully aware of all their implications, and who, in any case, do not have to live with them.

Unionists have tended to look more favorably on third-party intervention. They have particularly favored arbitration. As a fire fighters' union official once expressed it, without compulsory arbitration in the background, collective bargaining for employees becomes collective begging.[6]

COLLECTIVE BARGAINING FOR FEDERAL EMPLOYEES

The Federal Service Labor-Management Relations Statute, Title VII of the Civil Service Reform Act of 1978, allows nonpostal federal employees to bargain collectively through labor organizations of their choice and thereby participate with agency management in the development of personnel policies and practices and other decisions that affect their working lives.[7] The past three decades have seen the federal labor-management relations program evolve from a simple executive order that provided for consultation between agency management and employee organizations to a formal collective bargaining program established by law.

The program is enforced by an independent administrative agency, the Federal Labor Relations Authority (FLRA), as well as by the federal courts. The latest available data from the Office of Personnel Management (OPM) shows that as of January, 1989, about 1.3 million federal employees, or 60 percent of the total nonpostal federal workforce, were represented by unions. They were represented by 101 labor organizations in 2,266 bargaining units.

The Lloyd-LaFollette Act of 1912 established the right of federal employees to belong to labor organizations as long as the organizations did not impose a duty on employees to engage in or assist in a strike against the government, but it was not until 1962, when President Kennedy issued Executive Order 10988, that a federal labor-management relations program was officially established.

The order was the result of a presidental task force study that found that 33 percent of federal employees, mostly in the postal service and among blue-collar workers, belong to employee organizations. Since they lacked guidance, the various agencies of the government had proceeded on widely varying courses in dealing with these organizations. Some, such as the Tennessee Valley Authority and various units of the Department of Interior, had engaged in close to full-scale collective bargaining with the trade unions that represented their employees, but most had done little or nothing.

Among other provisions, Executive Order 10988 recognized the right of federal employees to join, or refrain from joining, employee organizations and established procedures for granting recognition to federal employee organizations. These organizations were given the right to consult or negotiate with agencies on matters that concerned working conditions and personnel policies, within the limits of applicable federal laws and regulations.

Certain other matters, including the agency's mission, its budget, its organization and assignment of personnel, and the technology of performing its work were deemed "management's rights" and therefore nonnegotiable. The order also allowed individual agencies to establish procedures to deal with grievances, appeals, and negotiation impasses, but it specifically precluded strikes or binding arbitration as means of resolving such disputes. Arbitration hearings by private arbitrators were permitted for employee grievances so long as the arbitrators' decisions were advisory and not binding on agencies.

In 1969, a review of the program by an interagency study committee indicated that the policies of Executive Order 10988 had brought about more democratic management of the workforce and better employee-management cooperation, and that negotiation and consultation had produced improvement in a number of personnel policies and working conditions. The review also found that union representation of employees in exclusive bargaining units had expanded greatly to include 52 percent of the total federal workforce subject to the order.

As a result of the study committee's recommendations, Executive Order 11491 was issued on October 29, 1969. The new order retained the basic principles and objectives underlying Executive Order 10988 and added a number of fundamental changes in the overall labor-management relations structure. A Federal Labor Relations Council (FLRC), composed of the Chairman of the Civil Service Commission, the Director of the Office of Management and Budget, and the Secretary of Labor, was established as a central body to administer the program and make final decisions on policy questions and adjudicate three types of labor management disputes:

(1) negotiability appeals;
(2) exceptions to arbitration awards;
(3) appeals of decisions by the Assistant Secretary of Labor for Labor-Management Relations on unfair labor practice and representation cases.

Although the Federal Service Labor Management Relations Statute was modeled after the National Labor Relations Act applied to the private sector, it also carried over many policies and approaches of the executive order program. As a result, federal labor relations bargaining is different from labor-management relations programs in the private sector in several ways:

• "Bread and butter" issues, such as wages, fringe benefits, and many other issues relating to hiring, firing, promoting, and retaining employees— which are the focus of private sector bargaining—generally cannot be negotiated in federal contracts. Since the first executive order, federal sector bargaining has been generally limited to the way personnel policies, practices, and procedures are implemented.

- Traditional bargaining incentives, i.e., strikes and lockouts, are prohibited.
- "Agency shop" or "fair share" representation fees, are prohibited. Under the federal program, employees are entitled to select a union to represent them, but they cannot be compelled to join or pay a fee for the representation that the union is required to provide.

In 1991, the U.S. General Accounting Office conducted a large-scale survey of those involved in public sector labor relations concerning the effectiveness of the federal labor-management relations program. Among those surveyed were officials responsible for program operations in federal agencies, leaders of federal employee unions, and neutral parties, including current and former officials of the Federal Labor Relations Authority (FLRA) and other third-party agencies, arbitrators, and academics.[8]

Agency officials represented the Departments of Defense, Air Force, Navy, Health and Human Services, Labor, Transporation, Veterans Affairs, the General Services Administration, Government Printing Office, Internal Revenue Service, and Immigration and Naturalization Service. Union officials included presidents of the three largest federal unions—the American Federation of Government Employees, the National Treasury Employees Union, and the National Federation of Federal Employees. Neutrals included six incumbent and former FLRA officials, including the Chairman, General Counsel, a regional director, and three former chairmen.

GAO's work was accomplished in two parts. First, GAO interviewed a total of 30 experts in federal labor relations to get their views on the state of the program. Next, using the information gathered in these interviews, GAO developed a questionnaire to survey union and agency representatives who were involved in day-to-day program operations at federal facilities throughout the country to obtain their perspectives on the federal labor-management relations program. GAO asked union and agency representatives to evaluate various components of the program, such as collective bargaining, dispute resolution procedures, and labor management cooperative efforts. The questionnaire sample consisted of 510 agency representatives and 664 union representatives.

In the end, the GAO report called for a major overhaul of policies and processes governing federal labor management relations, providing a new framework that

- motivates labor and management to form productive relationships to improve the public service;
- makes collective bargaining meaningful;

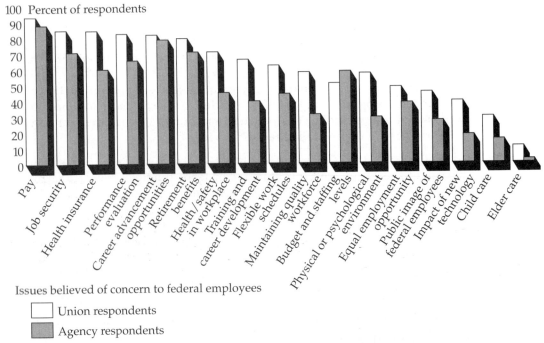

100 Percent of respondents

Issues believed of concern to federal employees

☐ Union respondents

▨ Agency respondents

FIGURE 6-1   Percentage of Agency and Union Respondents Rating Issues to Be of "Great" or "Very Great" Concern to Federal Employees.

Source: *Federal Labor Relations: A Program in Need of Reform* (Washington: U.S. General Accounting Office, 1991), 30.

- improves the dispute resolution processes; and
- is compatible with innovative human resource management practices that emphasize employee involvement, teambuilding, and labor-management cooperation.

CONFLICTS IN STATE CIVIL SERVICE AND COLLECTIVE BARGAINING SYSTEMS

Joel Douglas, professor of public administration at City University of New York, and arbitrator of government employee relations, explores the impacts of the emergence of public-sector labor relation systems on the legal structure and design of state civil service systems. According to Douglas, many jurisdictions have developed "dual personnel systems" with civil service and collective bargaining provisions existing side by side.

Collective bargaining and state civil service merit systems often contradict each other. As of 1990, 28 states had enacted public sector collective bargaining legislation covering state employees. Under collective bargaining, 28 statutes allow state employees new forms of governance where bilateral negotiations regulate the terms and conditions of their employment. Collective bargaining is utilized by 6.3 million public employees, accounting for 37 percent of the public sector work force, in these states. Public sector unions were largely responsible for passage of collective bargaining legislation. Pubic sector collective bargaining includes: (1) mandatory subjects that must be negotiated; (2) prohibited subjects that may not be negotiated; and (3) permissive subjects that may be negotiated.

In the 28 states where collective bargaining is allowed, there are four categories of statutory relationship between collective bargaining legislation and civil service systems. In the first category, legislation guarantees the continuation of, and adherence to, merit systems. Protection of merit system principles and systems varies from broad-scale philosophical encouragement to requirements for civil service commissioners to be politically neutral. Alaska, California, Vermont, New Jersey, Washington, Maine, and New Hampshire have civil service merit systems protected, in some form, by legislation.

In the second type of statutory relationship civil service merit systems may not be within the scope of bargaining, but they are statutorily protected by designating certain topics as under their exclusive domain. Negotiation is limited as appointments, conduct of exams, grading of examinations, grievances, hiring and selection, performance rating, position classification, promotion, and retirement are identified in one or more states as legislatively excluded from the bargaining process. These subjects are placed under the exclusive jurisdiction of civil service merit systems. New Hampshire, Kansas, Iowa, Ohio, Connecticut, New York, and Wisconsin are among the states which enacted legislation reserving specific subjects to civil service merit systems and restricting the scope of bargaining.

Still other states have statutorily selected a third approach: protecting collective bargaining agreements which supersede existing civil service merit systems. The labor contract is presumed superior and preempts existing civil service law. Civil service is deemed inferior to the strength of public sector union politics. Several states, such as Hawaii, Florida, and Illinois, limit contract supremacy to certain subjects.

Finally, 11 states find management-rights states where topics are removed from the scope of bargaining and are declared to be a management right that is not subject to the collective bargaining process. This method attempts to statutorily protect civil service and limit subjects negotiable by collective bargaining. Montana, Nebraska, Minnesota, and Kansas follow this approach.

Labor relations systems supersede but do not replace existing civil service merit systems. State legislatures fail to terminate procedures for civil service merit systems, yet they have not successfully integrated labor relations systems with civil service merit systems, resulting in numerous problems. Dual personnel systems develop in many jurisdictions. Douglas reveals that dual personnel systems are commonplace, but they are not recommended. Collective bargaining and civil service merit systems do not blend very well. Civil service merit systems flourish where there is a statutory commitment to merit, subjects have been removed from bargaining and reserved to merit systems, and management rights are designated and are not subject to bargaining.[9]

The structure of civil service and labor relations legislation is consistent, in as far as civil service statutes predate collective bargaining laws in every state. The silence of legislatures enhances the scope of negotiations and allows issues to be litigated. Confusion exists however, over primary and concurrent jurisdiction, scope of bargaining, and election of forum as bilateralism replaces unilateralism in the public sector workplace decision making process. Table 6-2 depicts the status of labor relations legislation in all 50 states.

PERCENTAGES OF ORGANIZED FULL-TIME PUBLIC SECTOR EMPLOYEES

The percentage of organized full-time employees varies by type of government. 39.7 percent of state employees are organized; 34 percent of county employees are organized; 51 percent of municipal employees belong to labor organizations; 31.4 percent of special district workers are unionized; and 52.5 percent of employees of school districts have joined labor unions. Of all these public employees, 45.3 percent are part of labor organizations.[10] Table 6-3 shows percentage of full-time employees belonging to an employee organization, by type of government.

The percentage of organized full-time employees also varies by function. 64.9 percent of the fire fighters are members of labor organizations; 58.1 percent of teachers; 53.7 percent of police officers; 50.2 percent of sanitation workers; 48.9 percent of welfare workers; 44.4 percent of highway workers; and 38.6 percent of hospital employees belong to labor unions.[11]

TABLE 6-2   Labor Relations Legislation for State Employees

State	Statute	Date
Alabama	No comprehensive statute	N/A
Alaska	Collective Bargaining in Public Employment Act	1972
Arizona	State Employees: Payroll Deductions Act	1983
Arkansas	State Employees: Payroll Deductions Act	1983
California	Collective Bargaining: State Employee Organizations Act	1971
Colorado	State Employees' Grievance Procedure Act	1973
Connecticut	State Employee Relations Act	1965
Delaware	Public Employees' Right to Bargain and Organize Collectively Act	1965
Florida	Public Employee Relations Act	1974
Georgia	Strikes by State Employees Act	1982
Hawaii	Collective Bargaining in Public Employment Act	1970
Idaho	No comprehensive statute	N/A
Illinois	Public Labor Relations Act	1983
Indiana	No comprehensive statute	N/A
Iowa	Public Employment Relations Act	1974
Kansas	Public Employee Labor Relations Act	1971
Kentucky	No Comprehensive Statute	N/A
Louisiana	Public Employees: Dues Checkoff	1966
Maine	State Employees Labor Relations Act	1969
Maryland	No comprehensive statute	N/A
	State Employees' Grievance Procedure	1977
Massachusetts	Collective Bargaining by Public Employees Act	1973
	State Employee Grievance Procedures	1965
Michigan	Public Employment Relations Act	1978
Minnesota	Public Employment Labor Relations Act	1971
Mississippi	No comprehensive statute	N/A
Missouri	Collective Bargaining by Public Employees Act	1967
Montana	Colelctive Bargaining for Public Employees Act	1973
Nebraska	Public Employees Bargaining Act	1967
Nevada	State Employees: Checkoff	1981
New Hampshire	Public Employee Labor Relations Act	1975

TABLE 6-2   Labor Relations Legislation for State Employees, continued

State	Statute	Date
New Jersey	Employer-Employee Relations Act	1968
	Public Employees: Dues Deduction	1981
New Mexico	Labor Management Relations in the Classified Service Act	1978
New York	Public Employees' Fair Employment Act	1967
North Carolina	Public Employee Membership in Labor Unions Act	1981
	State Employees: Checkoff	1981
North Dakota	No comprehensive statute	N/A
	Public Employee Dispute Mediation Act	1969
Ohio	Public Employee Bargaining Act	1983
Oklahoma	No comprehensive statute	N/A
Oregon	Collective Bargaining Public Employment Act	1975
Pennsylvania	Public Employee Relations Act	1970
Rhode Island	Collective Bargaining by State Employees Act	1958
South Carolina	State Employees' Grievance Procedure	1982
South Dakota	Public Employees' Unions Act	1969
Tennesee	No comprehensive statute	N/A
	State Employees' Dues Deductions	1980
Texas	Public Employee Collective Bargaining Ban Act	1947
	Public Employees: Checkoff	1967
Utah	No comprehensive statute	N/A
	State Employees' Grievance Procedure	1979
	Public Employees: Checkoff	1969
Vermont	State Employee Labor Relations Act	1969
Virginia	Strikes by State Employees Act	1970
	State Employees' Grievance Procedure	1982
Washington	Public Employees' Collective Bargaining Act	1967
	Union Security Agreements—State Employees Act	1977
West Virginia	State Employees: Checkoff	1982
Wisconsin	State Employment Labor Relations Act	1966
Wyoming	No comprehensive statute	N/A

Source: Joel M. Douglas, "State Civil Service and Collective Bargaining Systems in Conflict," *Public Administration Review*, Vol. 52, No. 2 (March/April, 1992), 172.

TABLE 6-3   Percentage of Full-Time Employees Belonging
to an Employee Organization,
by Type of Government, October 1987

State	Employees	
	State (%)	Local govt. (%)
Alabama	21.2	33.2
Alaska	68.1	59.9
Arizona	15.6	34.8
Arkansas	15.5	19.1
California	47.3	56.7
Colorado	37.5	33.0
Connecticut	83.1	68.2
Delaware	42.3	65.5
Florida	10.7	46.2
Georgia	21.8	13.5
Hawaii	82.7	95.7
Idaho	29.0	35.5
Illinois	35.1	48.4
Indiana	12.1	37.6
Iowa	21.7	47.5
Kansas	11.3	29.7
Kentucky	2.1	31.8
Louisiana	16.7	25.7
Maine	70.7	57.7
Maryland	42.0	61.6
Massachusetts	77.0	74.8
Michigan	60.1	67.5
Minnesota	81.7	65.4
Mississippi	9.1	7.9
Missouri	15.1	35.9
Montana	54.0	42.1

TABLE 6-3 Percentage of Full-Time Employees Belonging, continued

State	Employees	
	State (%)	Local govt. (%)
Nebraska	14.3	47.7
Nevada	32.5	51.2
New Hampshire	58.7	51.9
New Jersey	71.3	66.9
New Mexico	15.4	27.4
New York	78.5	75.1
North Carolina	22.9	25.7
North Dakota	34.7	52.3
Ohio	47.9	42.4
Oklahoma	20.0	35.7
Oregon	46.5	62.8
Pennsylvania	54.9	63.1
Rhode Island	81.0	65.6
South Carolina	31.1	6.0
South Dakota	18.0	41.1
Tennessee	29.2	27.0
Texas	14.1	23.0
Utah	34.0	54.1
Vermont	47.8	45.0
Virginia	17.6	25.8
Washington	38.3	69.1
West Virginia	19.9	37.0
Wisconsin	49.1	58.8
Wyoming	16.3	30.9
U.S. Total	39.7	47.5

Source: U.S. Bureau of the Census (1991). *Labor-Management Relations*, Vol. 3, *Public Employment* (3), U.S. Government Printing Office, Washington, D.C. See Richard C. Kearney, *Labor Relations in the Public Sector* (New York: Marcel Dekker, Inc., 1992, Second Edition), pp. 30–31.

FEDERAL EMPLOYEE UNIONS

American Federation of Government Employees, AFL-CIO, 80 F Street NW, Washington, DC 20001. Telephone 202-737-8700.

National Air Traffic Controllers Association, MEBA-AFL-CIO, Suite 845, 444 North Capitol Street NW, Washington, DC 20001. Telephone: 202-347-4572.

National Association of Agriculture Employees, P O Box 20825, Atlanta, GA 30320. Telephone: 404-763-7716.

National Association of Government Employees, 285 Dorchester Avenue, Boston, MA 02127. Telephone: 617-268-5002.

National Federation of Federal Employees, 1016 16th Street NW, Washington, DC 20036. Telephone: 202-862-4400.

National Treasury Employees Union, 901 E Street NW, Suite 600, Washington, DC 20004. Telephone: 202-783-4444.

National Weather Service Employees Organization, 400 North Capitol Street, Suite 326, Washington, DC 20001-1151. Telephone: 202-783-3131.

United Power Trades Organization, P. O. Box 26, Dallesport, WA 98617. Telephone: 503-767-4773.

Source: Don Mace and Eric Yoder, Editors, *Federal Employees Almanac 1992* (Falls Church, VA: Federal Employees News Digest, Inc., 1992), page 284.

The membership of national, state, and local employee organizations illustrates the political power of their numbers. The National Education Association (NEA) numbers 2 million (1990), the American Federation of State, County, and Municipal Employees (AFSCME) registers 1,090,000 (1989), the American Federation of Teachers (AFT) includes 780,000 members (1990), the Service Employees International Union (SEIU) numbers 475,000 public sector members, the Fraternal Order of the Police (FOP) brings together 230,000 union members (1990), and the International Association of Fire Fighters (IAFF) includes 142,000 members (1989).[12]

ROLE OF LABOR LAWS IN PUBLIC SECTOR LABOR RELATIONS

The impact of law in public sector unionization is hotly debated. Richard B. Freeman and Casey Ichniowski offer five broad conclusions about the role of labor law in the rise of collective bargaining in the public sector.[13]

1. The legal environment is critical in determining whether or not public sector employees bargain collectively with their workers.

The probability that a municipal department is governed by a collective contract is enhanced by favorable state public sector labor laws. According to Freeman and Robert G. Valletta, "state public sector laws are a prime determinant of the likelihood that municipal workers are covered by collective bargaining and have a moderate impact on wages and employment of public sector workers."[14] The enactment of laws mandating arbitration

TABLE 6-4   Number of States with Laws Governing
             Collective Bargaining Rights

	1955[a]		1984	
	No Law	Law	No Law	Law
State Employees	44	4	8	42
Police	45	3	8	42
Teachers	45	3	3	47

[a]There were only forty-eight states in 1955.

Sources: Robert G. Valletta and Richard B. Freeman, "Appendix B: The NBER Public Sector Collective
Bargaining Law Data Set," in *When Public Sector Workers Unionize,* edited by Richard B. Freeman and
Casey Ichniowski (Chicago: University of Chicago Press, 1988), 404–405. See also: Henry S. Farber, "The
Evolution of Public Sector Bargaining Laws," in *When Public Sector Workers Unionize,* edited by Richard B.
Freeman and Casey Ichniowski (Chicago: University of Chicago Press, 1988), 130.

results in virtually all police departments bargaining contractually for their
workers.[15] Favorable public sector laws likely bring substantial growth in
the extent of bargaining coverage.[16]

   2. *Economic benefits and costs do not readily explain the timing of public sector
labor laws.*

   Public sector labor laws call for legalization of union activities, requiring managers to "meet and confer" with unions, require managers to
bargain with unions, and mandate arbitration or certain final closure
mechanisms to provide a contract.[17] A review of comparative state literature does not explain why certain states enact laws earlier rather than later.[18]

   By the mid-1980s, eight states had no legislative policy for laws governing collective bargaining rights for state employees, eight states prohibited bargaining, six states permitted but did not obligate the employer
to negotiate with the union, four states granted the union the right to
present proposals and/or meet with the employer, and in 24 states, the
employer had the duty to bargain with the union. Nevada, Kentucky, Texas,
Tennessee, Georgia, Alabama, Virginia, and North Carolina prohibited state
employees from collective bargaining.

   By the mid-1980s, eight states had no legislative policy governing collective bargaining rights for police, four states prohibited bargaining, nine
states permitted but did not obligate the employer to negotiate with the
union, two states allowed the union the right to present proposals and/or
meet with the employer, and twenty seven states mandated that the employer has the duty to bargain with the union. Tennessee, Alabama, Virginia, and North Carolina prohibited police from collective bargaining.

   By the mid-1980s, three states had no legislative policy governing collective bargaining rights by teachers, four states prohibited bargaining,
twelve states permitted but did not obligate the employer to negotiate with
the union, one state allowed the union the right to present proposals and/

or meet with the employer, and thirty states mandated that the employer has the duty to bargain with the union. Georgia, Alabama, Virginia, and North Carolina prohibited teachers from collective bargaining.[19]

3. Public sector laws favorable to collective bargaining raise wages in nonunion as well as union departments but have substantial adverse employment consequences only for nonunion departments.

Laws enhance the bargaining power of unions and affect economic outcomes and alter management decisions making in both union and nonunion departments. Public sector union members in states favoring collective bargaining receive 6 percent higher salaries than those workers in municipal departments in states with unfavorable laws. Salaries of nonunion municipal workers are approximately three percent higher in states with comprehensive public sector labor laws than in other states, implying that nonunion municipal employers pay better salaries because of concerns that their employees too may organize.[20]

4. Among states that obligate employers to bargain, wages are no higher with compulsory arbitration than with other dispute resolution mechanisms, whereas wages are noticeably higher with strike-permitted laws.

Potential arbitration creates an environment in which municipalities accept high negotiated settlements as public sector officials fear arbitration processes will result in even higher wages. Everything else being equal, municipalities in states with compulsory arbitration would pay more for comparable labor than municipalities in states requiring state employers to bargain with unions. Compulsory arbitration states would pay more for labor than duty-to-bargain states.

Arbitration impacts wages little in states that encourage bargaining, however. Evidence indicates that arbitration laws reduce strike rates. Although compulsory arbitration states do not differ noticeably from duty-to-bargain states, states that permit strikes pay between 2 and 9 percent higher salaries than states prohibiting strikes. In other words, strike permitted state laws raise pay; arbitration permitted states' laws have effectively no impact on pay.[21]

5. Arbitrators do not favor one side or the other nor respond greatly to the facts of a case when labor and management make "reasonable" proposals; rather, they tend to "split the difference."

Arbitration occurs in a wide range of settings. Most involve a third party arbitrator or panel of arbitrators hearing and deciding how a dispute is to be resolved. Laws generally bind disputants to arbitration awards. "Conventional arbitrators tend to split the difference between the parties' final offers with little additional systematic reference to the facts of the case," states Bloom.[22] Arbitrators weigh facts but do so differently, and since offers and facts are often unrelated, arbitrators "split the difference" when employers and employees propose alternatives which reflect diverse sets of facts. Table 6-5 outlines the legal environment for state, local, police, fire fighters, and teachers in the 50 states.

TABLE 6-5 State Bargaining Legislation, 1992

State	State	Local	Police	Fire fighters	K-12 Teachers
Alabama	—	—	—	Y	—
Alaska	X	X	X	X	X
Arizona	—	—	—	—	—
Arkansas	—	—	—	—	—
California	Y	Y[b]	Y[b]	Y[b]	X
Colorado	—	—	—	—	—
Connecticut	X	X	X	X	X
Delaware	X	X[b]	X	X	X
Florida	X	X[b]	X	X	X
Georgia	—	—	—	Y	—
Hawaii	X	X	X	X	X
Idaho	—	—	—	X	X
Illinois	X	X	X	X	X
Indiana	—	—	—	—	X/Y
Iowa	X	X	X	X	X
Kansas	Y	Y[b]	Y[b]	Y[b]	X
Kentucky	—	—	X	X	—
Louisiana	—	—	—	—	—
Maine	X	X	X	X	X
Maryland	—	X[b]	—	—	X
Massachusetts	X	X	X	X	X
Michigan	Y[a]	X	X	X	X
Minnesota	X/Y	X/Y	X/Y	X/Y	X/Y
Mississippi	—	—	—	—	—
Missouri	Y	Y	—	Y	—
Montana	X	X	X	X	X/Y
Nebraska	X	X	X	X	Y
Nevada	—	X	X	X	X
New Hampshire	X	X	X	X	X
New Jersey	X	X	X	X	X
New Mexico	X	X	X	X	X
New York	X	X[b]	X	X	X

TABLE 6-5   State Bargaining Legislation, 1992, continued

State	State	Local	Police	Fire fighters	K-12 Teachers
North Carolina	—	—	—	—	—
North Dakota	Y[c]	X[c]	Y[c]	Y[c]	X
Ohio	X	X	X	X	X
Oklahoma	—	X	X	X	X
Oregon	X	X[b]	X	X	X
Pennsylvania	X/Y	X/Y	X	X	X/Y
Rhode Island	X	X	X	X	X
South Carolina	—	—	—	—	—
South Dakota	X	X	X	X	X
Tennessee	—	—	—	—	X
Texas	—	—	X[b]	X[b]	—
Utah	—	—	—	—	—
Vermont	X	X	X	X	X
Virginia	—	—	—	—	—
Washington	X	X	X	X	X
West Virginia	Y[d]	Y[d]	Y[d]	Y[d]	Y[d]
Wisconsin	X	X	X	X	X
Wyoming	—	—	—	X	—

X: collective bargaining provisions;

Y: meet and confer provisions;

X/Y: collective bargaining on some issues; meet and confer on other issues.

[a]Negotiations may be established under civil service regulations.

[b]Local option permitted.

[c]Meet and confer established by attorney general opinion.

Source: Compiled from various sources, including issues of *Government Employee Relations Report* and *Monthly Labor Review*, and *Issues and Answers: The Value of Bargaining Laws* (AFL-CIO, Public Employee Department, 1990). See Richard C. Kearney, *Labor Relations in the Public Sector* (New York: Marcel Dekker, Inc., 1992, Second Edition), pp. 70–71.

THE RISE AND FALL OF UNION CLOUT

As the growth of unionism continued into the 1970s, its attendant problems seemed to be overshadowing its benefits. Public employee organizations were flexing their muscles in ways that had started to arouse increasing anxiety and alarm. It was at the state and local level where the clout of public unionism proved most powerful.

The significant and growing number of victories scored by the unions had not occurred simply through political pressures. Union leaders had become quite proficient in using more traditional tactics as well. One of these was the "whipsaw." This stratagem calls for the union to make a breakthrough by scoring a special success in negotiating with a particular community or with a particular agency. Having made the "breakthrough," it then often becomes easy to broaden the front by seeking comparable concessions from other agencies and/or communities.

The case of the professional air traffic controllers mentioned earlier illustrates the potential for such developments. Not only did President Reagan stress his duty to ensure that the laws declaring public sector strikes illegal were enforced, but he also set a tone for labor management relations in general by establishing higher ground for the administration's "philosophical warfare" against labor. PATCO represented only 17,500 employees; the postal unions represented a work force of more than 500,000 persons. In taking a tough stand Reagan sent labor a message, and the postal unions subsequently settled their contract differences with management.[23]

Eventually and inevitably, a negative reaction against growing union power arose. It was catalyzed, if not caused, by the increasing financial strain that governments of all kinds, but especially those of the larger cities, were undergoing. Even before California's Proposition 13 signaled the start of taxpayer rebellion, Cleveland, Baltimore, Detroit, and other major cities had started to pare down their work forces, despite strong and strident resistance from their municipal unions.

SEARCHING FOR SOLUTIONS

During the early years of public unionism, the solution most often advanced to avert clashes and to promote equity was binding arbitration. As we saw earlier, however, this solution seemed to receive more favor from labor than from management. By the late 1970s, the antipathy of public managers to this device had grown and hardened.

Arguments against arbitration centered on the alleged failure of arbitrators to take into account the overall impact of their decisions. Such decisions, said its opponents, often had a "ripple effect," prompting other public employee groups to seek for themselves whatever favorable conditions resulted for the group whose case had been arbitrated. Arbitrators were also accused of being too narrow in their approach and, in general, of being too prolabor.

By this time a new form of arbitration had arisen that offered the hope of eliminating or at least modifying some of the method's more objectionable features. Called "Last Best Offer," or LBO, it provides that each side, once collective bargaining has reached an impasse, submit its last best offer to an arbitrator. The arbitrator then simply picks the offer that seems the best. It was felt that the desire to have their last best offer selected would move both sides to a more responsible position. At the same time, it would prohibit the arbitrator from devising his or her own settlement and imposing it on the disputing parties.

How has it worked? The final results are not yet in, so no definitive judgment can yet be made. In Wisconsin, LBO appears to have generally led to less generous awards. However, the Badger practice is accomplished without prior fact-finding, and lower awards to unions usually occur when fact-finding has been omitted. In Arlington, Massachusetts, where LBO was used to resolve a pay dispute with the community's fire fighters, the results, as far as the town manager was concerned, were almost disastrous. The arbitrator had picked the union's last best offer and this broke the parity then existing between the town's fire and police departments. This, in turn, caused the police as well as other town employees to seek new pay increases.[24]

In the view of critics, LBO tends to favor the unions as much as normal binding arbitration, if not more so. Under LBO, the unions know by the time an impasse is reached what management is prepared to give, so they supposedly have nothing to lose by scaling their demands somewhat higher and taking a chance that the arbitrator will pick their offer instead. LBO also has been accused of delegating power to a third party and thereby thwarting democratic rule by representative government officials. (The same criticism, to the extent that it may be valid, could, of course, apply to normal binding arbitration as well.) Finally, LBO, like other forms of arbitration, detracts from the desire of the parties to resolve their disputes through the collective bargaining process itself.

Another novel solution that has been suggested to improve labor-management negotiations, or at least their outcomes, is open bargaining. In other words, allow the press and the public to sit in on the negotiating sessions. Such a system, so it is said, would make both sides behave and bargain more responsibly.

The secret to handling all or most of the labor troubles that occur in the public sector is simply good management. Nearly all sides consider this the sine qua non of good labor relations, and mediocre management probably causes more labor trouble than militant union leadership. Many management people agree with this statement as well. Union excesses, say some, spring perhaps most often from managerial misdeeds and mistakes. The real key to achieving peace on the public labor front may lie in developing better policies and better administrators.

Future of Public Sector Unions: Stagnation or Growth?

The reasons for union growth in the public sector include (1) changes in the legal environment; (2) changes in public attitudes; and (3) changes in economic conditions. Recent changes in each of these areas will certainly affect the future of public sector unionism, just as they have affected their course for the last thirty years.

The changes in the legal environment brought about the striking expansion in public sector union participation between 1960 and 1976. From 1976 through 1986 there was little or no growth in union expansion in the public sector. The proportion of government workers affiliated with unions or union-like organizations hovers unchanged at around 36 percent.

Changes in public attitudes towards unions paralleled the expansion of public sector union expansion between 1960 and 1976. By allowing public employees to bargain collectively, legislatures recognized that the sovereignty of state government was not threatened by union activities. The 1976–1986 period witnessed a consolidation of public unions. Public attitudes towards public sector unions became less favorable during this period.

Unlike private unions, the political power of public sector unions affects demand for government services, budgets, and outcomes of local elections. Growth in government employees and budgets results directly from citizen demands for increases in government services. Since 1986, the growth in citizen demand for public services has declined. The slowdown in the growth of income and urbanization and the aging of the baby-boom population are two reasons for the decline in demand.

Changes in economic conditions affected growth in public sector employees, programs, and budgets. In the 1960–76 period, the gross national product averaged an annual rate increase of 8.1 percent, state and local government expenditures expanded at 10.7 percent, and state and local employment moved from 11.2 to 15.3 percent of total nonagricultural employment. When the economy slowed over the next decade and a half, the demand for public services naturally did likewise.

The future of public sector unionism rests on these same three factors. Changes in the legal environment, changes in public attitudes, and changes in economic conditions will shape the future of public sector unionism. Legislation and executive rulings will again be crucial. Union supporters advocate a uniform national law permitting all government employees to join unions and requiring all public sector employees to bargain collectively, but public support for unions has not grown in recent years. Women and part-time workers change the composition of the work force. Demographic trends may again influence the demand for public services, leading to more schools, teachers, and related public services. An increase in the number of school teachers will enhance the leverage of government workers. An increase in the number of elderly will proportionally increase the demand for government services. The demand for public services may be met through more privatization of government functions, but not all public services are suitable for private sector implementation.[25]

SUMMARY

- Public sector unionism is a product of the Great Society of the 1960s and changed the overall labor movement emphasis from high employment and high wages to *redistribution* of society's economic resources.
- Despite being larger than private sector unionism, public unionism is in *transformation*. Today about 37 percent of government workers engage in collective bargaining. Future government unionization depends upon organized labor's ability to organize the unorganized, which is not promising.
- Unions usually prevent strikes or shorten those that do occur. Union leaders much prefer to resolve disputes by negotiation. Public employee unions bring public sector problems before the public.
- Trade unionism erodes however, the concept of government work as a public service. Unions perpetuate some of the worst features of personnel systems. Unions diffuse responsibility and make accountability more difficult to pinpoint. Unionization greatly increases the political involvement of public employees.
- In the public and private sectors, the fundamental role of unions is not merely to secure economic benefits. They are a means by which employees seek to avoid manipulation.
- When collective bargaining fails, alternatives for avoiding strikes include *fact-finding, mediation,* and *arbitration.*
- The increasing financial strain experienced by all levels of government in the 1980s brought on a reaction against growing union influence. While the rate of public employee union growth is now leveling off or is perhaps in decline, government workers now constitute more than 37 percent of all union members. As private sector union membership decreases, this proportion will increase.
- AFL-CIO private sector unions lost 165,000 members in 1990, while government unions, representing 37 percent of public employees, gained 150,000 members.

- "Bread and butter" issues generally cannot be negotiated in federal government contracts. Strikes, lockouts, and "agency shop," practices are prohibited in the public sector.
- Civil service statutes predate collective bargaining laws in every state. In order to determine the relationship between the potentially conflicting merit and collective bargaining systems, states have enacted statutes to specify the role of collective bargaining. Public sector collective bargaining includes: (1) mandatory subjects that must be negotiated; (2) prohibited subjects that may not be bargained; and (3) permissive subjects that may be bargained.
- The percentage of organized full-time employees varies by type of government. Of all public sector employees, 37 percent are part of labor organizations.
- The legal environment, economic benefits and costs, favorable collective bargaining laws, compulsory arbitration, strike-permitted laws, and labor-management arbitrators account for many developments in the emergence of collective bargaining in the public sector.
- Explanations for union growth in the public sector include: (1) changes in the legal environment; (2) changes in public attitudes; and (3) changes in economic conditions.
- The major federal employee unions are: American Federation of Government Employees, National Air Traffic Controllers Association, National Association of Agriculture Employees, National Association of Government Employees, National Federation of Federal Employees, National Treasury Employees Union, National Weather Service Employees Association, and United Power Trades Organization.
- Approximately 35 states, the District of Columbia, and the Federal Government permit some form of collective bargaining law for selected public sector workers. Prospects appear dim for public employee union leaders enhancing the power of collective bargaining laws in the remaining state legislatures and in the U.S. Congress.
- State legislatures have enacted employee organizations for fire fighters in 38 states, for teachers in 35 states, for police officers and certain local workers in 33 states, and for state workers in 28 states.
- The absolute prerequisite for good labor relations is *good management*.

The following story offers an interesting glimpse at the nuts and bolts of public sector union negotiations. While you're reading, try to see the situation from the viewpoints of both the union and the city.

CASE STUDY

Union Contract Negotiations in Springfield[26]

The city of Springfield began negotiations in June with the American Federation of State, County, and Municipal Employees local for a three-year contract. The city's negotiations were conducted by City Manager Adam Arbuthnot under guidelines recommended by the Labor Negotiations Committee of the City Council and approved by the full council. The union demanded an across-the-board wage hike of 10 percent and increased fringe benefits.

Progress in the negotiations and the positions of the union local were reported regularly to the committee and council over the next several months, and the council held three special meetings, each lasting more than two hours, to hear from department heads and to discuss wages and benefits. The council reviewed data on wage increases for the past five years and compared these rises to the cost-of-living index. The data revealed that nearly all employees had received pay hikes equal to, and in many instances exceeding, the rise in the cost of living during the period. Springfield's employees, according to statistics, had fared better than workers nationally, and the council considered that its past wage actions had been reasonable.

In determining the wage increase for employees in relation to the cost of living, the council decided that increases in benefits mandated by the federal government during the year should be considered. These included the city's share in the Social Security tax increase and unemployment compensation insurance premiums. The council also decided to take into consideration the employer's share of insurance premiums. It concluded that a wage increase for the next year should not exceed 4.59 percent for all employees.

The council was largely composed of small business managers who hired only a few employees. These managers believed they were familiar with pay and working conditions in the community and felt that city employees were adequately compensated in comparison with employees in the private sector. They were bolstered in this belief since turnover was small in nontechnical and semitechnical positions in city employment.

The city, however, was forced to modify its 4.59 percent limit on wage increases because of the union's firmness in its demands and continued rises in the monthly cost-of-living index. It increased the rate to 5.95 percent in August, to 6.3 percent in September, and, finally, to 6.5 percent in October. Council members believed 6.5 percent was a very reasonable offer in that fringe benefits (retirement, Social Security, workers' compensation, and unemployment compensation) would raise the de facto pay and benefits increases to 7.2 percent.

Council members acknowledged that the average cost-of-living index would exceed 7.5 percent but maintained that their offer was fair because last year the city had given a cost-of-living increase that exceeded the actual cost-of-living rise by 0.5 percent. In further justification, they maintained that the increases in the federally mandated Social Security tax and unemployment compensation tax plus health insurance cost increases raised benefits another 1 percent. The overall increase offered by the city (taking into consideration the proposed wage and benefits increase of 7.2 percent, the previous year's increase of 0.5 percent, and benefits increase of 1 percent) amounted to 8.7 percent.

By late October all issues between the city and union were tentatively resolved, except for the union's insistence on a 7.5 percent rather than the city's 6.5 percent wage increase. An impasse having been reached, the union filed a request for conciliation and fact-finding with the state labor commissioner. Upon his recommendation, a three-year agreement calling for a 7.0 percent increase for the next year and additional increases the next two years at the rate of increase in the cost of living was accepted by both parties and signed on December 19.

Meanwhile, a dispute began to develop over what seemed to be a minor matter—filling a vacancy in the Municipal Light Department—that was to upset the agreement. Two electric line workers (one the union steward and the other the secretary of the local) approached Mayor Thomas Wentwaller and asked to appear before the City Council to express employee concerns about employing an additional line worker. The line workers suggested that money could be made available for hiring better qualified workers by charging for services that the city had been previously providing at no cost to electricity users. The council approved their suggestion and imposed a new service charge that permitted a pay increase for line workers.

The council believed that the increase was made with the full knowledge of the union, since the two line workers were members and officers and the president was also a line worker. In the past the union had also left decisions on merit increases and individual wage adjustments to the city. The council thought this situation was no different from others in which adjustments had been made and no complaints had been filed.

Although there was some grumbling about this action among the rank and file of the union, it took no formal action until April when it filed a complaint with the state labor commissioner. It accused the city of violating collective bargaining procedures and interfering with the union's affairs. The union contended that the city was required to hold to the 7 percent salary increase, that it had improperly given raises above that figure to a selected occupational classification (electric line workers), and that it had made special provisions for rates of pay and wages for specific individuals in the bargaining unit without inclusion of the union representative.

The union recognized the need for the city to award the pay increase to the line workers in order to compete with the private sector, especially the Southern Public Utility Corporation, but felt that competitive salary and wage problems existed in every department and that the same considerations and adjustments should be given to all employees. The union further believed that the city's unfair labor practice was creating a serious morale problem among employees that could have an effect on the amount and the quality of work performed. The union asked that the city be ordered to return to the bargaining table and renegotiate rates of pay and wages for all employees covered by the bargaining unit.

The city itself saw the need for a higher percentage across-the-board increase than the 7.0 percent in the contract because of continued rises in the cost of living but decided to hold the increase because of the complaint of engaging in improper practices filed with the labor commissioner. The city's defense filed with the commissioner made the following points:

1. The city's wage scales were competitive overall, but a salary raise was necessary to fill the vacant line worker position.

2. The city had used benefits paid its employees as part of the percentage raise offered the union.

3. Union members had bypassed their official representatives in requesting the increase for the line workers.

4. Merit raises had never before been the subject of grievances against the city.

5. The unlawful labor practice suit was not filed until five months after the contract was signed.

QUESTIONS AND INSTRUCTIONS

1. If you were the labor commissioner, how would you rule in the case?
2. As a student learning about public personnel administration, how would you react to the following observations?
   a. The line worker should not have been recognized for purposes of salary and wage negotiation by the City Council.
   b. The basis for the wage increase should have been that it was a merit increase rather than an adjustment to the salary schedule.
   c. The city manager was the official negotiator for the city and therefore should have been the party who conducted negotiations with the union.
   d. Street Department employees are not as skilled as line workers and therefore should not expect the same salary schedule.
   e. Regional competition for obtaining line workers is greater than for obtaining help in such departments as Street Repair, Sanitation, Water, and Police; the latter jobs are competitive only locally.

3. Do you think that public employees should have the right to form unions for the purpose of collective bargaining? Why?
4. Do you think public employees have the right to strike?
5. In the area of labor-management relations, what functions should the mayor perform? the city manager? the City Council?

Endnotes

1. Leo Troy, "The Rise and Fall of American Trade Unions: The Labor Movement from FDR to RR," in *Unions in Transition: Entering the Second Century*, edited by Seymour Martin Lipset (San Francisco: ICS Press, Institute for Contemporary Studies, 1986), 75–109. See also: Leo Troy, "Is Unionism in Permanent Decline?," *The Chicago Tribune* (September 1, 1986), Section 1, page 11.
2. *Ibid.*, 106.
3. David Lewin, "Public Employee Unionism in the 1980s: An Analysis of Transformation," in *Unions in Transition: Entering the Second Century*, edited by Seymour Martin Lipset (San Francisco: ICS Press, Institute for Contemporary Studies, 1986), 241–264; see also: Chimezie A. B. Osigweh, "Collective Bargaining and Public Sector Union Power," *Public Personnel Management*, Vol. 14 (Spring, 1985), 75–84; Douglas M. McCabe, "Labor Relations, Collective Bargaining, and Performance Appraisal in the Federal Government Under the Civil Service Reform Act of 1978," *Ibid.*, Vol. 13 (Summer, 1984), 133–146; and R. Douglas Collins, "Agency Shop in Public Employment," *Ibid.*, Vol. 15 (Summer, 1986), 171–179.
4. For an interesting insight into the power of teacher groups, see John C. Wahlke et al., *The Legislative System* (New York: John Wiley, 1962). See also Stephen A. Woodbury, "The Scope of Bargaining and Bargaining Outcomes in the Public Schools," *Industrial and Labor Relations Review*, Vol. 38 (January, 1985), 195–210; Joseph W. Garbarino, "Faculty Collective Bargaining: A Status Report," in *Unions in Transition: Entering the Second Century*, edited by Seymour Martin Lipset (San Francisco: ICS Press, Institute for Contemporary Studies, 1986), 265–284; and Lewis L. Jones, "The Impact of Faculty Unions on Higher Education: A Reconsideration," *Public Personnel Management*, Vol. 15 (Summer, 1986), 181–188.
5. George Bennet, "Tools to Resolve Labor Disputes in the Public Sector," *Personnel*, Vol. 50, No. 2 (March–April 1973).
6. *Boston Herald-American*, March 28, 1973.
7. *Federal Labor Relations: A Program in Need of Reform* (Washington: U.S. General Accounting Office, 1991). GAO Publication GAO/GGD–91–101.
8. *Ibid.*
9. Joel M. Douglas, "State Civil Service and Collective Bargaining Systems in Conflict," *Public Administration Review*, Vol. 52, No. 1 (January/February, 1992), 162–172.
10. U.S. Bureau of the Census. Labor-management Relations, Vol. 3, *Public Employment* (3) (Washington: US Government Printing Office, 1987).

11. *Ibid.*

12. Richard C. Kearney, *Labor Relations in the Public Sector* (New York: Marcel Dekker, Inc., 1992), page 36.

13. Richard B. Freeman and Casey Ichniowski, "Introduction: The Public Sector Look of American Unionism," in *When Public Sector Workers Unionize,* edited by Richard B. Freeman and Casey Ichniowski (Chicago: University of Chicago Press, 1988), 1–15.

14. Richard B. Freeman and Robert G. Valetta, "The Effects of Public Sector Labor Laws on Labor Market Institutions and Outcomes," in *When Public Sector Workers Unionize,* edited by Richard B. Freeman and Casey Ichniowski (Chicago: University of Chicago Press, 1988), 81–103.

15. Casey Ichniowski, "Public Sector Union Growth and Bargaining Laws: A Proportional Hazards Approach with Time-Varying Treatments," in *When Public Sector Workers Unionize,* edited by Richard B. Freeman and Casey Ichniowski (Chicago: University of Chicago Press, 1988), 19–38.

16. Gregory M. Saltzman, "Public Sector Bargaining Laws Really Matter: Evidence from Ohio and Illinois," in *When Public Sector Workers Unionize,* edited by Richard B. Freeman and Casey Ichniowski (Chicago: University of Chicago Press, 1988), 41–78.

17. Freeman and Valletta, *op. cit.*

18. Henry S. Farber, "The Evolution of Public Sector Bargaining Laws," in *When Public Sector Workers Unionize,* edited by Richard B. Freeman and Casey Ichniowski (Chicago: University of Chicago Press, 1988), 129–166.

19. Robert G. Valletta and Richard B. Freeman, "Appendix B: The NBER Public Sector Collective Bargaining Law Data Set," in *When Public Sector Workers Unionize,* edited by Richard B. Freeman and Casey Ichniowski (Chicago: University of Chicago Press, 1988), 404–405.

20. Freeman and Valletta, *op. cit.*

21. Freeman and Valletta, *op. cit.,* 97–99.

22. David E. Bloom, "Arbitrator Behavior in Public Sector Wage Disputes," in *When Public Sector Workers Unionize,* edited by Richard B. Freeman and Casey Ichniowski (Chicago: University of Chicago Press, 1988), 122.

23. William J. Lanouette, "Sending Labor a Message," *National Journal,* Vol. 34 (August 22, 1981), 1516.

24. *Boston Sunday Globe,* January 26, 1975.

25. Linda N. Edwards, "The Future of Public Sector Unions: Stagnation or Growth?" *AEA Papers and Proceedings,* Vol. 79, No. 2 (May 1989), 161–165.

26. "Union Contract Negotiations at Springfield," in *Practicing Public Management: A Casebook,* by C. Kenneth Meyer and Charles H. Brown (New York: St.Martin's Press, 2nd edition, 1989), 196–199. Reprinted with permission of St. Martin's Press. For this chapter, see also: Gerald W. McEntee, "Political Action '86—Why It Matters," *Public Employee,* Vol. 51 (October 1986), 4–5. See also McEntee, "Rebuilding Labor's Strength," *Ibid,* Vol. 51 (November/December, 1986) 4–5; and Steven W. Hays and T. Zane Reeves, *Personnel Management in the Public Sector* (Newton, MA: Allyn and Bacon, Inc., 1984), 317–347.

The opening section of this chapter on the Professional Air Traffic
Controllers Organization PATCO is based largely on news reports
published at the relevant times. Of special interest are accounts published
in *Time,* 24 August 1981, an editorial in the *New York Times,* August 9 1991,
and an Associated Press dispatch of March 17, 1992. See also David Nagy,
"How Safe Are Our Airways?," *U.S. News & World Report,* Vol. XCI (August
24, 1981), 14–17; Jeffery L. Sheler, "A Hard Line Against State, Local Unions
Too," *Ibid.,* 20–21; Marvin Stone, "Strikes Against the People," *Ibid.,* 76;
Jonathan Alter, "Featherbedding in the Tower: How the Controllers Let the
Cat Out of the Bag," *Washington Monthly,* Vol. 13 (October, 1981), 22–27; Bill
Keller, "Most Pro-Reagan Unions Rewarded," *Congressional Quarterly Weekly,*
Vol. 40 (August 28, 1982), 2116; Kevin P. Jones, "Are the Only Good Air
Controllers. . . . The Union Workers Fired?" *National Journal,* Vol. 43
(October 26, 1985), 2436–2437; Stephen Gettinger, "Congress Wrestles With
Air Safety Concerns," *Congressional Quarterly Weekly,* Vol. 43 (November 9,
1985), 2293–97.

7

☆ ☆ ☆

LEADERSHIP

During the late 1930s, J. Robert Oppenheimer seemed to have found happiness teaching theoretical physics at the University of California at Berkley. A shy and nervous man, he was pleased with the fact that he seldom had to venture into the laboratory, let alone the workday world outside the campus. Instead, he could spend much of his time working out equations on his blackboard and indulging in his favorite hobby, reading mystical Hindu poetry in the original Sanskrit. True, he contributed money to political causes that seemed to meet his ideals, and he did enjoy a reasonable social life, but he was largely occupied with theoretical physics and esoteric poetry when World War II broke out.

The war wrought great changes in Oppenheimer's peaceful and sheltered existence. In a few short years, he found himself assembling and directing a task force of over 1,000 scientists and technicians in developing the atomic bomb. This involved, among other things, running an entire community, since the scientists and their families were forced to live in sealed-off seclusion in an isolated area in New Mexico. As everyone now knows, the Los Alamos community stayed together, the scientists accomplished their work, and the bomb was built. Afterward, many of the physicists involved agreed that no one but Oppenheimer could have done it.[1]

AN OVERVIEW OF LEADERSHIP

Oppenheimer made a rapid transformation from a shy, nervous professor into a forceful and effective administrator. His experience is an extreme example of one of the most fascinating phenomena in administration—the mystery of leadership. Leadership and the qualities it demands have puzzled and perplexed many an administrative theorist over the course of time. Peter Drucker, a noted business writer and management consultant, reports:

> *Among the effective executives I have known and worked with, there are extroverts and aloof, retiring men, some even morbidly shy. Some are eccentrics, others are painfully correct conformists. Some are fat and some are thin. Some are worriers and some are relaxed. Some drink quite heavily and others are total abstainers. Some are men of great charm and warmth; some have no more personality than a frozen mackerel.*[2]

Anyone who hopes to spell out the qualities of a leader is engaged in a perilous and problematic mission. One helpful observation, however, can be made at the outset. Leadership is, to a great extent, determined by the needs of the situation. "It is more fruitful to consider leadership as a relationship between the leader and the situation than as a universal pattern of characteristics possessed by certain people," Douglas McGregor notes.[3]

In a similar vein, William J. Reddin, after surveying the research on management style, concludes that "no single style is naturally more effective than others. Effectiveness depends on a style's appropriateness to the situation in which it is used."[4] There is, in short, no ideal leadership style and most probably no ideal leader who can ably handle all situations.

Adolf Hitler provides an interesting illustration of this principle. His gruesome career as leader of Germany is certainly well known. Less well known is his army career during World War I. Although he served over four years in combat and twice won medals for bravery, Hitler ended his military service as a corporal. Since promotion comes quickly in wartime to those who survive, anyone assessing Hitler's record in 1918 would have rated him a poor prospect to become even a shop foreman in civilian life, let alone the most powerful single individual in the world of his time.

Hitler's peculiar leadership abilities needed a particular situation in which to flourish. They required not only the conditions that existed in Germany during the postwar period, but also that Hitler have the leading role in any movement or government with which he should become connected. In a subordinate post, no matter how high it might have been, *der Fuhrer* would most likely have been a washout. Some leaders simply cannot lead unless they occupy the pinnacle position. As Paul Appleby once noted, "There are men who would be poor as ordinary section heads in a bureau but who would be able and effective as Secretary of the Department."[5]

If some leaders can lead only when no one is above them, others can only lead successfully when the reverse is true. There are people who would do well in the second highest position of a very large organization but who would flounder if placed in overall command of even a quite small one. In other words, they are natural seconds-in-command. Arthur Schlesinger puts Dean Rusk, who served as secretary of state during the Kennedy and Johnson administrations, into this category. Writes Schlesinger of Rusk:

> He was a superb technician: this was his power and his problem. He had trained himself all his life to be the ideal chief of staff, the perfect number-two man. The inscrutability which made him a good aide and a gifted negotiator made him also a baffling leader. When assistant secretaries brought him problems, he listened courteously, thanked them, and let them go; they would depart little wiser than they came. Since his subordinates did not know what he thought, they could not do what he wanted. In consequence, he failed to imbue the Department with positive direction and purpose. He had authority but not command.[6]

Situational differences requiring different leadership styles do not just concern matters of hierarchical position. Different types of organizations may also demand different types of leaders. Many a successful business executive has failed miserably after attempting to transfer with all his or her administrative prowess, to the public sector. Few public-sector executives have had the opportunity to test their leadership skills in commanding a business firm, but they would probably produce a comparable failure rate. Furthermore, an organization may need different leaders at different stages of its existence.

The relationship of leadership ability to the particular situation that calls the leader into being makes the task of defining and detailing a list of general leadership qualities elusive and difficult. Certain qualities do, however, seem to characterize most leaders in most situations. Although this list does not constitute a formula—one could possess all the qualities on the list and still be unable to lead—it does provide something of a basis from which the student may gain a perspective on one of the most intriguing and enigmatic aspects of the administrative craft.

LEADERSHIP QUALITIES

Probably no quality is more pertinent and pervasive among successful leaders than the quality of *optimism*. To lead successfully, one must believe that his or her leadership will make a difference. No matter how dark and dismal the journey, the leader must be able to see a light at the end of the tunnel.

Harlan Cleveland, who served successfully in many leadership roles, lays particular stress on this quality of leadership. "Prophecies of doom," he reminds us, "do not in fact move people in action."[7] Indeed, they are more likely to have the reverse effect. In order to be happy, one must believe in the possibility of happiness, the great Russian writer Tolstoy once suggested. The same holds true for leadership. In order to exercise leadership, one must believe in its possibilities.

That *energy* and *enterprise* must accompany such optimism should be fairly obvious. This does not mean that every luminary in the ranks of leadership has been a whirlwind of activity, but one cannot hope to meet leadership's obligations without some deliberate and diligent application of one's talents. Leaders often do not seem to be working hard at their jobs, but such appearances can be deceptive. A leader may be relaxed and easygoing, but laziness and indolence will usually lead to failure.

What about *intelligence*? Certainly, it is rare to find a leader who is both dumb and successful, and some have been extraordinarily brilliant. Take Napoleon and William Pitt, those young titans who confronted each other across the English Channel at the beginning of the 19th century. Each was at home in a variety of disciplines, including mathematics, languages, and the law. In this country, and during the same period, a president (Thomas Jefferson) had come to power who was accomplished in architecture, science, agriculture, law, political theory, and many other fields of study. Nevertheless, when it comes to correlating intellectual ability with leadership, some qualities seem much more crucial than others.

One vital intellectual skill is *verbal ability*. Communication skills generally accompany leadership ability, no matter what the particular situation may be. A ditch digger who becomes the foreman of the work gang will most probably be able to communicate better than all, or at least most, of the other members of the gang.

An interesting study on this point was done many decades ago. Researchers tested people from various occupations as to their vocabularies. It was a multiple-choice test that presented the subjects with numerous words, ranging from the commonplace to the obscure. Each word was followed by four others, one of which was a synonym. The object was to pick the synonym. The group that placed highest on the test consisted of business executives who outscored all the professional groups, including college professors. The test was given at a time when relatively few business people had a college education. Yet, as a group, they demonstrated the greatest facility at word recognition.

An ability to communicate, at least when he wanted to, apparently played a key role in Dean Rusk's rise to administrative prominence. Although sharing Arthur Schlesinger's view that Rusk was more suited for a number-two than a number-one position, journalist David Halberstam points up this valuable Rusk quality in his book, *The Best and the Brightest*. "A brilliant expositor, he had a genius for putting down brief, cogent, and forceful prose on paper—a rare and much needed quality in government."[8] It was this ability, reflected in the cables that he sent back while serving with the army in India during World War II, that led to Rusk being "discovered" by his superior and being slotted for the wider opportunities that came his way when the war ended.

Much more complex is the question of *creativity* and *judgment*. The problem is the fact that these two qualities are not always compatible. Good idea people, as Katz and Kahn point out, tend to be enthusiastic and somewhat impulsive and may fail to subject their ideas to searching criticism. They frequently have a hard time translating ideas into action, and when they do succeed in doing so, they may fail to follow through because they soon sprout another idea that they want to work on.

Katz and Kahn maintain that leadership puts more of a priority on reasoned judgment than creativity, and if a leader can have only one of these qualities, he or she is better off with the former. One can always make up for lack of creativity by surrounding oneself with people who are in fact creative.[9] This, to a great extent, was true of Oppenheimer. Although a brilliant physicist, he was not considered a particularly creative one. His talents lay in being able to analyze the work of others and, in so doing, to spur them on to greater efforts.

The question of judgment leads us to another quality that is still more difficult to define. Perhaps an illustration will serve as the best introduction to its discussion. The story is told of the president of a major steel company who was inspecting one of his plants. He suddenly noticed two men puffing on cigarettes in an area where smoking was forbidden. He went over to the two men, handed each of them an expensive cigar, and said good-naturedly, "Smoke these outside, boys."

This simple incident conveys some of the flavor of successful leadership. Good leaders rarely lose their heads or give in to their emotions. Instead, they deal with situations and the people involved in a disinterested manner best designed to achieve the results they have in mind. This observation is confirmed by research. Burleigh Gardner cites one study of several hundred executives, which showed that they maintained a detached, objective view of their subordinates. Other studies, says Gardner, tend to corroborate this finding.[10] This does not mean that a good leader should be a cool and clammy individual, lacking all the human qualities of warmth and empathy. It rather indicates that he or she should be able to keep personal feelings in check and to appraise objectively the needs of the situation.

Of course, the chronicles of history overflow with accounts of petulant and peevish people who have scored successes as leaders, and certainly some situations seem to require such qualities as detachment and objectivity much less than do others, but many who appear to have disregarded these principles have not really done so. Adolf Hitler is one example. While undoubtedly a neurotic, if not a psychopath, he could, nevertheless, at least at the earlier stages of his career, assess situations with a cool and shrewd eye and act accordingly. Hitler's chief architect and subsequent minister for war production, Albert Speer, tells in his memoirs of the first time he saw Hitler. The Nazi leader had come to address the students at Berlin University prior to Hitler's assumption of power.

> His appearance . . . surprised me. On posters and in caricatures I had seen him in military tunic, with shoulder straps, swastika arm band and hair flapping over his forehead. But here he was wearing a well-fitted blue suit and looking remarkably respectable. Everything about him bore out the note of reasonable modesty. Later I learned that he had a great gift for adjusting—consciously or intuitively—to his surroundings.[11]

His speech itself, notes Speer, also showed that Hitler knew his audience. Instead of an intellectually vapid harangue, the Nazi leader delivered to the students a rather carefully worded lecture on history that was mixed with a good deal of humor.

The Swiss psychologist, Jean Piaget, well known for his pioneering work with children, offers an observation that may aid in summing up this rather illusive leadership quality. Piaget points out that when a child stands in front of another person, the child will tend to identify the other person's left arm as the right and vice versa. This is because the arm of the person the child is facing is on the same side as his or her own. The child is unable to put himself or herself in the other person's shoes.

As people grow older, they usually manage to make this change, at least to the point of distinguishing between the right and left sides of a person they are facing. But everyone still retains some degree of difficulty in seeing situations from the other person's position, particularly when more than physical position is concerned. The good leader will be able to do this better than most. By coolly assessing situations from the various points of view and acting accordingly, he or she exercises the influence that leadership betokens.

QUALITIES IN QUESTION

The preceding list of leadership qualities is admittedly a short one and may seem more notable for what it omits than for what it includes. Left out are at least three characteristics that are usually associated with leadership—*technical proficiency, decisiveness,* and *charisma.* Let us examine the first two qualities, then take an in-depth look at charisma.

Technical Proficiency

Government in the United States has traditionally placed a great emphasis on *technical competency* in selecting leaders for its various administrative agencies. Americans generally insist that school superintendents be educators, public health commissioners be doctors, and public works commissioners be engineers, or at least persons with some engineering background. Appointing technically trained people to administrative positions is often equated with progressive government and is considered a repudiation of administration by political hacks. A city-manager-run city will more likely appoint a professional law enforcement specialist as its police commissioner than will a city dominated by political bosses, although the latter also seems to be bending to this trend.

Many European countries, however, view the matter quite differently. They stress administrative skills and background rather than demonstrated technical expertise. When France consolidated its two major police forces in 1968, the government appointed as its new policy head a man who had previously been the chief of staff in Ministry of Education. He was neither an educator nor a police officer, but simply a professional administrator.

Which is the correct approach? Certainly technical expertise has much to recommend it. People who understand the actual work of their subordinates will possess tangible advantages when it comes to directing them. Katz and Kahn cite studies done on railroads, power plants, and heavy industry that indicate that those supervisors who were the most technically competent were generally the supervisors whose work teams were the most productive.[12] At a minimum, a supervisor who is technically expert can gain the respect of his or her subordinates in a way that a nontechnician would be unable to do.

Administrative theorists even in this country have long looked askance at the "specialist syndrome," however. The leader of an organization or an organizational unit must be able to relate the unit to its external environment. This, so the claim goes, is best done by a professional administrator. He or she is much more likely to possess the expanded frame of reference that the leader needs to manage the organization in a productive manner. Failure to assess the external environment can be, and often has been, disastrous to many organizations.

The technically trained and experienced leader has usually built up a network of prior associations and preferences as well. The leader's very background makes him or her more prone to favor some activities over others and to listen to some people more than others. He or she may lack the overall and objective perspective that the generalist administrator can provide.

These considerations take on heightened importance the more one moves up the organizational ladder. As many writers have pointed out, the higher the administrative level, the more time the administrator spends on "external" in contrast to "internal" matters. As Katz and Kahn note, the larger and more complex an organization becomes, "the greater will be the commonality of their management substructures."[13] This indicates that since organizations are becoming larger and more complex all the time, their administrative positions are becoming more and more alike and are therefore demanding fewer specialist skills.

Other factors also lend support to the oft-heard administrative adage that "the technician should be on tap and not on top." As David E. Lilienthal has said, the technician's work usually has a terminal point. There is the bridge to be built, the vaccine to be discovered, the patient to be cured and discharged. The administrator has to think in different terms. His or her task is never done, because in administration there is never any real completion.[14]

Some of these problems were evident in the administration of the Vietnam War. According to former Undersecretary of the Air Force, Townsend Hoopes, the military leaders could think only in terms of winning the war. They avoided the question of whether some means of achieving victory might produce more problems than they solved or whether it would even be in the United States' interest to win the war in the first place. Theirs was a "can do" policy, which, while productive and useful in some situations, can prove disastrous in others.[15] Instead of questioning the usefulness of air power to begin with, for example, military officials during the Vietnam War devoted their efforts to trying to make it more efficient. The failure to evaluate the means used in achieving limited goals had devastating results.

One thing is certain—the abilities that make a person a proficient specialist in his or her field do not automatically equip him or her for administrative leadership in that field. The first-rate teacher all too often turns into the third-rate principal. In writing about scientists and administration, C. P. Snow observed that "to be any good, in his youth at least, a scientist has to think of one thing, deeply and obsessively, for a long time. An administrator has to think of a great many things widely, in their interconnections, for a short time."[16] Of course there are exceptions, such as Oppenheimer, or, for that matter, Snow himself, but more often than not the qualities that make for excellence in a specialty do not coincide and frequently conflict with the qualities that make for excellence in administering organizations devoted to that specialty.

We may posit then that technical competence in the field is an advantage to an administrator, presuming that everything else is equal. The problem is that everything else is usually not equal. While such competence may be useful, particularly at the first level of supervision, it tends to pose increasing disadvantages as one moves to the higher reaches of organizational life. It is, consequently, omitted here as a necessary quality for administrative success.

Decisiveness

A quality that is often imputed to successful administrators is the ability to make quick decisions. To be sure, decision making is what administration is basically all about. George C. Marshall maintained that the capacity to make decisions was the rarest gift that the gods could give a person. When one scrutinizes the record of many notable government executives however, one frequently finds not a chronicle of speedy decision making, but almost its opposite. Historians have constantly commented on Franklin Roosevelt's penchant for procrastination. Some claim it was his most characteristic trait. Winston Churchill was also not keen on making decisions that did not demand immediate action. Unless it was imperative to make a major decision at once, Churchill would approach it by calling a meeting and asking for various views. Then he would request memoranda on the subject and hold another meeting. It is also interesting to note that while John F. Kennedy sought to present himself as a firm and decisive leader, his favorite book was a biography of a British prime minister named Melbourne. Lord Melbourne was a leader who ardently espoused and acted on the belief that "when in doubt what should be done, do nothing."[17]

PERSONALITY AND CHARISMA DO MAKE A DIFFERENCE

In an age of complexity, change, large enterprises, and nation–states, leaders are more important than ever. Leader effectiveness depends on his or her personality and charisma, and not solely on his or her control over bureaucratic structures. In a model of leader effectiveness, age of U.S. Presidents accounts for approximately 20 percent of the change in presidential needs for power, achievement, and affiliation. Needs of the President and leader self-restraint in using power, the President's age, and crises account for 24 percent of diversity of presidential charisma. A combination of the President's age, crises, needs, and charisma predict from 25 percent to 66 percent of changes in presidential performance.

Source: House, Robert J., Spanger, William D., and Woycke, James. "Personality and Charisma in the U.S. Presidency: A Psychological Theory of Leader Effectivenss," *Administrative Science Quarterly*, Vol. 36, No. 3 (September 1991), 364–97.

Business leaders sometimes show the same trait. Alfred P. Sloan, Jr., the man who is credited with building General Motors into the giant it is today, never made a decision involving personnel the first time it came up. He might make a tentative judgment, but even doing that might take him several hours. Then he would put the matter aside and tackle it again in a few days time. Only when the same name came up two or three times in a row would he proceed. It was this practice, says Peter Drucker, that helped give Sloan his wide reputation for picking winners.[18]

The Sloan example illustrates why successful leaders may often seem loath to exercise the foremost prerogative of their position—decision making. They realize the complexities and implications that may arise from any significant decision they may make. This is particularly true in government where there are so many different interests to contend with. A decision by a governmental administrator may cause reverberations throughout the staff, other governmental agencies, the legislative branches, clintele groups, the press, and the public—all of which must be taken into account. A good decision maker must be like a good billiard player: every time he or she goes to hit the ball, the decision maker must figure out just what will happen when that ball hits another ball, which in turn will hit another. Any decision of consequence is likely to set off a chain of events where the ultimate impact may prove difficult to anticipate.

For reasons such as these, speedy decision making does not always make for good decision making, and good decision makers have usually taken cognizance of this fact. While there is little disputing the fact that any administrator has to be able to make decisions before time runs out, many of the best executives have persistently preferred to stretch the time limit to the near maximum. As society and the apparatus that governs it become increasingly complicated, we may find that quick decision making, although it occasionally will be necessary, will become less and less characteristic of success in administration.

Charisma

The capacity to be colorful and heroic, to stir the emotions of people and capture their hearts and minds, has long been regarded as a powerful leadership tool. Many of those we regard as outstanding leaders have possessed these traits. They include not just political leaders such as Franklin Roosevelt, Winston Churchill, John F. Kennedy, and Ronald Reagan, but also some more purely administrative leaders such as Robert Moses, New York City's famous builder of bridges, highways, and parks, and Harry Hopkins, FDR's dynamic aide.

While a charismatic leader has the ability to inspire and convince followers, reliance on charisma alone is full of pitfalls.

> *Charisma, according to Katz and Kahn, is a means by which people abdicate responsibility for any consistent, tough-minded evaluation of the outcome of specific policies. They put their trust in their leader who will somehow take care of things. Charisma requires some psychological distance between leader and follower. The immediate superior exists in the work-a-day world of constant objective feedback and evaluation. He is very human and very fallible, and his immediate subordinates cannot build an aura of magic about him. But the leader in the top eschelons of an organization is sufficiently distant from the membership to make a simplified and magical image possible.* [19]

When the Iran-Contra scandal rocked the Reagan administration in the later years of his presidency, many blamed the charismatic president's "distant" leadership style for the fiasco. George Bush, the prototype "organization man," was unable to escape more immediate implications in the scandal. Reagan painted himself as "victim" while Bush's role appeared to be more complicated in efforts to cover up the scheme.

A charismatic leader may fail to fully develop the abilities of subordinates, as they become overly dependent upon the leader. When the leader is absent, the organization will tend to flounder, and when he or she departs for good, it may fall to pieces.

Charismatic leadership also may inhibit communication. Subordinates become reluctant to give the leader unpleasant information or advise against policies that may be unwise. Often they lose the ability to discriminate between wise and unwise policies, for they have surrendered much of their capacity for independent judgment. This can be crucial, since a charismatic leader may not only be forceful but also foolish.

MAJOR CONCEPTS IN LEADERSHIP

A *leader* is a person who has the authority to decide, direct, and represent the objectives and functions of an organization.

A *manager* is a person who has the authority to direct specific organizational resources in order to accomplish objectives.

Authority is the license by an organization that grants an individual the rights to use its powers and resources.

Credibility is the recognition by an organization that one is competent to use its powers.

Technical credibility is established when the organization believes that an individual is competent in areas of technical specialization.

Ethical credibility is established when the organization believes that an individual will uphold and support the ethical standards of the organization.

Interpersonal credibility is established when the personnel within the organization believe that an individual understands and cares about what happens to them.

Source: Portnoy, Robert A. *Leadership: What Every Leader Should Know About People* (Englewood Cliffs, NJ: Prentice-Hall, Inc., 1986).

History provides numerous examples of charismatic leaders who vigorously led their nations down the road to ruin. Hitler and Mussolini are two examples, but we do not have to use such extreme examples to find instances of how charismatic leadership can malfunction. Robert Moses may have built more bridges, tunnels, and highways than any man in recent history, but many New Yorkers today are questioning the wisdom of all his activity. His final masterpiece, the New York City World's Fair of 1965, turned out to be a startling economic disaster.

The case of University of California physicist Ernest Lawrence offers another illustration of how charisma can lead to catastrophe. Lawrence, a charismatic leader, became head of an important laboratory at the university and persuaded many younger scientists to work with him in building two highly expensive devices, both of which turned out to be unworkable. Physicists elsewhere had branded both projects silly and impractical from the start, but the charismatic Lawrence had wrangled sufficient funds, and his star-struck subordinates gave him enthusiastic support.

While charisma is positive in many ways, its main danger in public administration is the possibility that a charismatic leader's personality may block out important advice and challenges from subordinates and citizens.

RECOMMENDATIONS FOR ENHANCING THE EFFECTIVENESS OF MANAGERS

To begin with, good administrators exert every effort to obtain the best possible subordinates. They put aside any fears that their subordinates might outclass them or show them up. They know that the better the subordinates' performance the more the organization will achieve. The more the organization achieves, the more successful they, as leaders, will be. Top-notch people will stimulate and spur the leaders on to performing more effectively.

Many administrators, to be sure, do not take this approach. In this way they signal their own shortcomings. Princeton mathematician, Andrew Weil, has promulgated what he calls Weil's Rule. According to Weil's Rule, a first-rate person will surround himself or herself with equals or betters; a second-rate person will surround himself or herself with third-rate people; and a third-rate person will be able to tolerate only fifth-rate subordinates and co-workers. C. Northcote Parkinson has said much the same thing. In his own inimitable style, he notes that, "If the head of an organization is second-rate, he will see to it that his subordinates are all third-rate; and they will, in turn, see to it that their subordinates are fourth-rate. There will soon be an actual competition in stupidity. . . ."[20]

Top-notch subordinates do present problems. Aside from their propensity to outshine their chief and to insist on speaking up for what they believe, both of which are assets to an administrator, they will very likely not stay with him or her very long. They will tend to seek out other opportunities when they feel they have pretty much exhausted the possibilities of their present position. Since they are high-caliber people, they will usually experience little difficulty in finding something better or at least something different. This is a situation that a wise administrator is prepared to live with, and will even boast about the many subordinates who have gone on to make their mark.

In short, the capable administrator will appreciate the lines that steel magnate Andrew Carnegie chose for his tombstone: "Here lies a man who knew how to bring into his service men better than he was himself."

DELEGATION

When Moses assembled his people for the Exodus, he picked the ablest among them and put them in charge of groups of varying numbers. Those selected were given the authority to settle all lesser matters and make all lesser decisions themselves, passing up to the prophet only the most important issues. Delegation has played a crucial role in administration ever since. No administrator can hope to do everything himself or herself. He or she must delegate. This is even more urgent if the administrator is wise enough to pick the best possible people for subordinates, for they will insist on substantial chunks of authority in order to exercise and hone their capabilities.

Administrative history abounds with examples of the success that can come when an administrator knows how to delegate authority to others. It was one of the reasons responsible for the success of George C. Marshall. As secretary of state, Marshall always divested himself of his authority when he had to leave on a mission. As Acheson puts it, "General Marshall was so meticulous that when the door to his aircraft closed, the command passed. He even on occasion asked for instructions when a wholly novel and unexpected point arose."[21]

Another military man who showed an unusual capacity for delegation in handling a civilian position was General Ismay, Churchill's chief civilian aide during World War II. Ismay had two assistants whom he allowed almost as much authority as he retained himself. Contrary to traditional military practice he did not, for example, require all matters to pass through his hands before going to Churchill. As a result, whenever any one of the three men was absent, the other two had no trouble filling in. The fact that his assistants could deal with any situation directly prevented bottlenecks from arising.

The value of delegation has also been substantiated by more systematic research. According to Katz and Kahn, "The extent of delegation has proved to be one of the predictors of productivity of many kinds."[22]

Avoiding the perils and pitfalls of delegation requires only adherence to a few guidelines. First, the leader should not just delegate trivia. He or she should, rather, delegate substantial assignments and the authority to carry them out. Sending a subordinate on a mere errand is delegation of a sort, but it is not the sort that makes for wise and effective administration. The administrator should remember that when it comes to delegating an important assignment, the subordinate, perhaps less knowledgeable and experienced than the delegator, will likely be able to devote more time, effort, and zeal to the task than will the superior.

Beware of delegating to too few people. The administrator who relies on just one or two subordinates to handle major assignments may end up as their captive. Moreover, as Seymour Berlin and his associates point out, "They can become screens and filters rather than eyes and ears, and they can get between you and the rest of your agency. To accomplish your mission, you need numerous ties into your agency."[23] President Eisenhower, who relied heavily on Sherman Adams, and President Nixon, who depended greatly on his aides, John Ehrlichman and H. R. Haldeman, were both brought to grief partly as a result.

Finally, the administrator should bear in mind that some things cannot be delegated. These include ultimate responsibility for:

- creating the climate of the organization;
- representing the organization;
- establishing the basic policy of the organization;
- the overall performance of the organization.

Participation

In a sense, participation in decision making is merely delegation writ large. In another sense, delegation of authority is participation writ large. In any sense, both are interwoven strands of the same tapestry.

Participation differs from delegation in that it can take in many more people and many more aspects than are commonly included in the notion of delegation. Essentially, it means allowing as many people as possible to make as many decisions as possible and to share to the maximum extent possible in making other decisions. It means giving subordinates a "piece of the action."

How big a piece? The answer usually given to this question is "as big a piece as they can handle," and how much they can handle is all too often wrapped up with the superior's estimate of their abilities in this respect. Many modern-day theorists believe that the average subordinate can participate much more than he or she is allowed to do, with positive results for all concerned. The real problem, they claim, is that managers are reluctant to permit or unable to stimulate such increased participation. A bureau or office head may call in subordinates, tell them of a decision he or she has reached, and then ask for their comments. This, the manager may feel, is participatory management. So it is, after a fashion. Others, however, would say that the better approach would be to call in people *before* making any decision. The administrator would then explain the problem and get subordinates' suggestions first. In the former instance, subordinates may be too intimidated to give frank reactions once they know what the manager has in mind. Even if this were not the case, their framework for thinking would be somewhat curtailed by the presence of a tentative decision already lying on the table.

Participation can take many forms. Employees can be allowed to determine many of their work conditions, such as hours. They can be asked to contribute their ideas to overall organization policy. They can even play a role in selecting their own superiors.

The advantages of participatory decision making are many. It generally leads to more informed and better decisions, since more minds and more varieties of experience have gone into making them. It also leads to better executed decisions, for those who are to carry them out have had some say in their formulation. It may stimulate employee development as well. "One of the most important conditions of the subordinate's growth and development," wrote McGregor, "centers around his opportunities to express his ideas and to contribute his suggestions before his superiors take action in matters that involve him."[24]

Participatory decision making does have drawbacks. For one thing, it delays, sometimes extensively, taking action. It does not always lead to a better decision and occasionally may produce a worse one. It can be terribly time-consuming to all involved and can lead to increased bickering. As we noted in discussing delegation, the responsibility remains in the hands of the person in charge, and he or she must bear the brunt of the burden if the decision turns out to have been wrong.

Sometimes participatory decision making is hampered by the reluctance or the inability of the employees themselves to make use of it. Many may react with fear and distrust at being offered such a new role. Others may rush in before they realize the responsibility it entails. Public managers wishing to encourage participation are usually well advised to begin by taking small steps, letting their employees first share in the making of minor decisions and then gradually proceeding to more major ones.

EDUCATION AND ROTATION

If participation can improve the employee's knowledge and skills, then it is only one of many devices for doing so. The perceptive public manager will make use of a variety of techniques for encouraging employee growth. These may include formal education and training, and rotation.

In rotation, employees enlarge their work experience and increase their abilities and knowledge. They also acquire a broader and deeper understanding of the organization and how its various parts interrelate. Even if their main job is comparatively limited, they will be able to perform it better if they see how it fits in the overall scheme. Rotation also helps to keep people from becoming bored or growing stale, as well as preparing the better ones for more responsible roles.

The Forest Service has made extensive use of rotation, and one reason why it does so is to develop the ranger's capabilities. As Herbert Kaufman writes:

> The Service does not wait until vacancies occur; it shifts men to replace each other in what looks like a vast game of musical chairs but has actually the serious purpose of giving them a wide range of experience in preparation for advancement to positions that require a broader understanding of national forest administration than can possibly be gained in long assignments at a single duty station.[25]

Too much rotation, however, can produce adverse effects for both the organization and the employees. If employees feel that they are mere pawns being shuttled arbitrarily about at will, they can become quite dispirited. Even if they perceive the value and need for such rotation, they may, if it occurs too rapidly, fail to immerse themselves deeply in any one assignment, preferring merely to keep things running smoothly until they go on to something else.

It can be argued that the State Department, among all its other ills, suffers from too much rotation. It is unusual for an assistant secretary of state to serve more than two or three years, which does not give time enough to master the intricacies of the position. As for Foreign Service officers, they are regularly rotated from post to post as part of department policy. In his book, *Anatomy of the State Department,* Sloan Simpson says this encourages them to spend too much time thinking about their future opportunities and to spend too little time confronting their existing challenges.[26]

While it does have its limits and can be abused, rotation is still a valuable tool for increasing employee and organization performance. It can and should be applied on an interorganizational basis as well. Employees should be allowed and encouraged to move from one organization to another. Here, suitable organizational policies like transferable pensions and possibilities for early retirement will facilitate interorganizational mobility and keep employees from "drying out" in an organization. They make organizational change easier and create promotional opportunities. Good circulation can be almost as vital to a healthy organization as it is to a healthy human organism.

SPEAKING UP FOR SUBORDINATES

McGregor once told of a mechanical superintendent with a small manufacturing company who swore at, drove, and severely disciplined his men. Yet, somehow he managed to maintain remarkably high morale and productivity in his shop. His behavior did not bother his employees as much as it did a staff group that was organizing a human-relations program in his shop. They could not understand how he managed to break all the "rules" of good management and still do as well as he did.

When they examined the situation further, they found other factors at work. First, the barking superintendent was considered a "square shooter," who, if he behaved rather roughly, also behaved with scrupulous fairness. He took a genuine interest in his subordinates and was always ready to advance them a few dollars until payday or to render some other form of aid without adopting a patronizing attitude.

The most noteworthy means by which he elicited his men's loyalty was his constant readiness to go down the line for them with his own superiors. During a ten-year period he had twice stormed into the "big boss's office,"

THE FUNCTIONS OF INSTITUTIONAL LEADERSHIP

The relationship between leadership and organizational character is more transparent when examined in the context of the leader's key tasks.

1. *The definition of institutional mission and role.* The setting of goals is a creative task that entails self-assessment and discovery of the true commitments of the organization, as determined by effective internal and external demands. The failure to set aims in the light of these commitments is a major source of irresponsibility in leadership.
2. *The institutional embodiment of purpose.* The task of leadership is not only to make policy but to build policy decisions into the organization's social structure. This too is a creative task. It means shaping the "character" of the organization, sensitizing the organization to the complex dynamic of thinking and responding, so that increased reliability in the execution and elaboration of policies will be achieved according to their spirit as well as their letter.
3. *The defense of institutional integrity.* The leadership of any policy fails when it concentrates on sheer survival: institutional survival, properly understood, is a matter of maintaining values and distinctive identity.
4. *The ordering of internal conflict.* Internal interest-groups form naturally in large-scale organizations, since the total enterprise is in one sense a polity composed of a number of sub-organizations. The struggle between competing interests always has a high claim on the attention of leadership. This is so because the direction of the enterprise as a whole may be seriously influenced by changes in the internal balance of power.

Source: Selznick, Phillip, *Leadership in Administration* (New York: Harper & Row, 1957), pages 61–63.

---

as his men fondly recalled, to protest a decision that he felt was unfair to "his boys." When in one of these instances the boss rejected his protest, the superintendent promptly resigned, clamped his hat on his head, and strode out of the yard. The "big boss" actually ran after him, caught him as he was going out the gate, and capitulated on the spot.

According to McGregor, the story illustrates a valuable principle of leadership: *The leader must be willing, and must be able, to represent subordinates to superiors.* The leader must have influence higher up and must use it to protect the rights of his or her own subordinates.[27]

McGregor's observation and the story of the brusk superintendent are supported by more systematic research. Katz and Kahn cite a study done at the Detroit Edison Company that found that supervisors who were following what are considered good human-relations practices were not developing any greater morale or productivity in their units than those engaging in less desirable supervisory practices. Further study indicated that the "good guy" supervisors were not effectively relating either themselves or their subordinates to those higher up.

"The conclusion urged on us," say Katz and Kahn, "is that the most effective leader in a pivotal organizational role is not the perfect bureaucrat (rational, role-actuated, heedless of primary bonds) but rather the successful integrator of primary and secondary relationships in the organizational situation."[28]

PRAISE, CENSURE, AND SANCTIONS

People have ego needs, and any organization would do well to acknowledge them. The same holds true for the organization's leaders. They should make adequate provision to recognize the ego needs of their subordinates. The easiest and cheapest way of doing this is by praise. A few laudatory words cost the giver little while they may mean much to the recipient. Praise is a device that belongs in every administrator's tool kit. Praise is not quite so cheap as many imagine however. Like money, the more of it there is, the less it is worth. An abundance of praise depreciates its value. Consequently, an administrator will do well not to lavish it about. Only when used sparingly (though not stingily) does it achieve its greatest effect. If an employee needs continual praise, then something is usually wrong, either with the employee or with the organization. The latter may have created conditions that require the employee to look for continual reassurance.

George C. Marshall was a leader who was far from prodigious in giving praise. This made his employees appreciate it all the more. Dean Rusk, who served under Marshall in the State Department after World War II, says he only once evoked a favorable comment from his chief. As Rusk was wearily getting ready to leave after having worked a fourteen-hour day, Marshall remarked, "You've earned your pay today, Mr. Rusk." Commented Rusk later, "So I took that lesson from the greatest man I've ever known. If you have very good people, it isn't necessary to compliment them. They know how good they are."[29]

Not all public managers will want to be as parsimonious with praise as was George Marshall. They will certainly find it useful not to overspend in this direction however. They may also find some other guidelines helpful:

- Praise at the appropriate time. A compliment loses its value the longer it is delayed.
- Praise the deed, not the person. It is not who the person is but what he or she does that is important. Praising the person can lead to all sorts of problems, including, oddly enough, an increase in the individual's insecurity. He may become too fearful of falling from favor.

- Praise in descriptive terms, not qualitative terms. Do not say simply, "That was a good report." Say, rather, "That report covered all the matters I needed to know about."

What holds true for praise also, to a great extent, holds true for censure. All employees will need criticism at one time or another, but here too it should be rendered at an appropriate time and on a somewhat impersonal basis. Martin R. Smith offers some helpful pointers in this regard:

- Stress the positive aspect, encouraging the employee to build up skills and proficiency in the area in which he or she has proven weak.
- Concentrate on performance and those aspects of personal behavior that are distinctly job-related.
- When possible, be indirect, but make sure that the employee gets the message. One device is for the manager to talk about his or her own past mistakes.
- Pick the right time. A good occasion for giving criticism is one when the manager is also conferring praise. Calling attention to weaknesses while singling out strengths makes the censure more acceptable.[30]

Smith stresses that criticism, to be effective, must be directed toward a correctable fault that is substantially detracting from a person's performance. It does little good to criticize someone for something that does not bear on the job, and it may do harm to criticize the employee for something he or she cannot change. Peter Drucker goes a step further. He urges executives to focus on what a person can do rather than what he or she cannot do. Everyone has weaknesses, notes Drucker, but the effective executive, instead of becoming overly concerned with weaknesses, concentrates on the subordinate's strengths. These the supervisor seeks to build and utilize while, at the same time, looking for ways to minimize the impact of the employee's liabilities. Drucker claims this is what makes Japanese organizations function with such remarkable efficiency, despite the fact that they almost never fire anyone. They accept a person for what he or she basically is and concentrate their attention on developing whatever assets the person may have.[31]

These are wise admonitions for an administrator to follow. Yet even the best of administrators will come across employees who seem unable or unwilling to make any positive contribution at all to organizational goals. Invoking sanctions, such as suspension or transfer, may help in some cases but not all. The manager will then be faced with the question of dismissal.

Firing an employee is often the hardest job an administrator has to do. It is always unpleasant, not only to the subordinate and the superior, but to others in the organization as well. For the public manager, it poses particular problems, since he or she often has to deal with civil service regulations that make dismissal difficult. Usually, the superior can only take such action when he or she is prepared to go before an appeals board and offer solid grounds for the dismissal, backed up by reasonably hard evidence.

Discharging the hopeless employee can, on the other hand, confer benefits on all concerned. Not only does it make the manager's subsequent task easier but also, in most cases, it lightens the load of other employees. As Parkinson says, "All experience goes to prove that the effective leader must be pitiless toward the disloyal, the careless, and the idle. If he is not, the work falls too heavily on the willing men. The sense of belonging to a picked team is soon lost in an organization where the useless are still included."[32] The head of a large chemical laboratory had similar sentiments in mind when he said he would like to automatically fire his lowest-producing employee every year. When asked, "Why?" he replied, "Simply to keep up the morale of all the others."[33]

There are two additional people who are likely to benefit whenever the dismissal process is appropriately invoked. One is the person who could and wants to do the job that the malfunctioning employee is holding. The other is the dismissed employee. "Any person holding down a job that he is unable to do is tense, angry, and frustrated," says Smith. "This situation is almost certain to affect his health and his family life."[34] Often a malfunctioning employee could do well at some other post. Retaining the employee only keeps him or her from realizing his or her own potential. If the problems are too severe for the employee to hold any job, and if he or she refuses to take any action on these problems while employed, then dismissal may help the employee to finally confront them.

Dismissal does not need to be unnecessarily difficult. In many cases the manager may wish to call in the employee for a talk about performance and in the midst of the conversation raise the suggestion that the employee might be happier working somewhere else. He or she may offer to ease up on the person's duties to let the employee shop around for a more congenial position.

Some leaders have resorted to other stratagems. When Franklin Roosevelt wanted to get rid of an official, he would gradually reduce the man's authority and responsibility while also consulting the official less and less. Gradually, the official would get the hint and tender a resignation for "personal reasons." Roosevelt would accept the resignation "reluctantly," voicing great public praise for the departing official's "untiring efforts."

John F. Kennedy would proceed somewhat more harshly. He would plant newspaper reports that the official was planning to resign. After reading a sufficient number of these reports, the official would grasp what was happening and turn in his resignation.

Lower-level administrators have made use of both tactics. They will take away a person's assignments and fail to invite him or her to meetings, or they will circulate a rumor through the office that the individual in question is planning to leave. The first tactic is used more widely than the second and is certainly less offensive. A variation of this method is sometimes used whereby the person is simply assigned to something he or she does not want to do. This can also hasten the employee's departure.

But no matter what strategies one may wish to use, any manager must be prepared to fire people on occasion. One of the most important traits a leader can possess, it has been said, is the willingness to give pain. This may be harsh but it is also humane. Almost anyone who has worked in or studied public organization in the present-day United States would agree that a more aggressive policy in dismissing people would diminish rather than increase overall employee frustration, to say nothing of the frustration experienced by clients and taxpayers. The good public manager simply must be prepared to fire people. The manager owes it to all concerned.

MANAGING THE MANAGER

Many of the precepts that managers should use in handling subordinates should also be applied to themselves. They should be as concerned with their own development as they are with the development of their employees. Otherwise, they may find that their administrative skills, instead of improving, may actually decline with accumulated experience. As we will find in the following chapter, employees are reluctant to directly address the supervisor's weaknesses or human frailties, so, leader managers need to be open to such criticisms.

One administrator who zealously followed this rule was Napoleon. "The art of government is not to let me go stale," he once said. He showed in the course of his life that he meant what he said. Napoleon read widely and deeply and made a point of picking the brains of the best men of his time. When he sailed on his ill-fated expedition to Egypt, he took along a group of France's greatest scientists and scholars for his own entertainment and enrichment. While exiled to Elba, he developed an enthusiasm for agriculture and soon invigorated the tiny island's agrarian economy. The fact that Napoleon not only conquered most of Europe but also left France with legal and governmental institutions that exist up to the present day is, in part, a tribute to his almost constant self-development.

Administrators who toil in lesser vineyards can still follow Napoleon's lead. The fact that they work within a democratic setting only adds urgency to the task. They must continually reach out for new knowledge and experience from both within and without their organizations. This can mean more than just reading books or attending executive seminars and conferences, although all these things are important. It can mean joining and participating in other organizations. For example, the Forest Service has found that its better executives usually participate, often quite actively, in civic, fraternal, and religious organizations. They do so on their own time, but the outside expenditure of energies apparently enhances rather than detracts from their work as foresters. Although unfortunately very few public organizations encourage such activities, many private organizations have had the same experience.

In recent years some executives have found more dramatic ways of broadcasting their experience pattern. Trans-World Airlines, for example, actually requires its top officials to spend one day a month at a lower-level job, such as writing out tickets or handling baggage. Few executives may wish to go so far, but it may be a good practice for the head of the clinic to see a few patients and for the head of the welfare office to continue to carry a small caseload of clients. At a minimum, he or she should, on occasion, get "out in the field" and talk with those whom he or she does not normally talk to in the course of daily activities. An administrator who never does anything but administer the activities of others may eventually lose perspective on just what those activities entail.

Sooner or later administrators should start thinking of moving on. "Nobody should be chief executive of anything for more than five or six years," say Robert Townsend. "By then he's stale, bored, and utterly dependent on his own cliches—though they may have been revolutionary when he first brought them to the office."[35] Five or six years may be too early, particularly if the administrator takes advantage of some of the other devices we have already discussed to stay fresh and invigorated, but nevertheless, the time will usually come when he or she has ceased to grow in the job. When that times comes, the good manager will pass over the reins to someone else and move along, for that is the way good managers go on to become still better ones.

LEADERSHIP AND ITS LIMITS

A new textile mill manager once decided, on assuming his new responsibilities, that things would go best if he indicated to one and all that things were going to be run his way. On his first day on the job, he strode into the weaving room, walked up to the union business agent, and after making sure the man was the person he was seeking, announced, "I am the new manager here. When I manage a mill, I run it. Do you understand?"

The business agent nodded and then waved his hand. The workers, who had been closely watching the encounter, promptly shut down every loom in the room. The union official then turned to the manager and said, "All right, go ahead and run it."

This story illustrates one very real, yet often-overlooked or at least underestimated aspect of leadership: *it is very much a two-way street.*

"In a bureaucracy that contains people with brains and consciences," wrote Charles Frankel following his tour of duty in Washington, "an unspoken bargain binds the man at the top to his subordinates. If they are to be the instruments of his will, he must, to some extent, be an instrument of theirs."[36] Most writers on administration would agree. "A manager is often described as someone who gets things done through other people," notes the British organizational theorist, Rosemary Stewart. "We tend to forget that this means he is dependent upon them."[37]

In a complex bureaucracy the problem intensifies. Tsar Nicholas II was one of the few truly autocratic rulers of his time. Yet he experienced constant frustration in getting his smallest orders carried out. "I do not rule Russia," the weary monarch once sighed. "Ten thousand clerks do."[38]

American presidents have consistently discovered their office to provide far less power than they had thought. Franklin Roosevelt depicted Lincoln as a "sad man because he couldn't get it all at once, and nobody can." Roosevelt's own battles with his bureaucracy are almost legendary. He once wearily described his efforts to handle government agencies as akin to boxing a featherbed.

Roosevelt's successors, Truman and Eisenhower, suffered from the same problem. John F. Kennedy took office with the idea of changing Washington bureaucracy. But he found that when he wanted a simple sign taken down, it did not come down, even after he had given the order for its removal three times.

President Nixon, at the time that the Watergate scandals were breaking, was widely said to have amassed a frightening amount of power. Yet Watergate in many respects proved that in fact the opposite was true. He tried to get the Internal Revenue Service to crack down on his enemies, but all he could manage to achieve were a few simple audits, something that almost any citizen could engineer with a well-worded letter to the regional IRS representative. Nixon, or at least his administration, was also thwarted in attempts to halt an antitrust prosecution of International Telephone and Telegraph (ITT), to obtain funds from the Central Intelligence Agency for the incarcerated Watergate burglars, to prevent disclosure of the break-in by his "plumbers" of the office of Dr. Daniel Ellsberg's psychiatrist, to limit certain investigations by the Securities and Exchange Commission, et cetera. The fact that the Nixon administration approved plans for breaking and entering and other felonies is certainly frightening. Yet the fact that it felt constrained to do so may indicate a lack rather than a plentitude of power. In any event, Nixon's master plan was stymied by a bureau chief, J. Edgar Hoover, who was supposedly at the President's beck and call.

The limitations of lesser executives are even greater. To many students, the president of their university may seem like an omnipotent figure, at least as far as their immediate needs are concerned. Yet college presidents usually find themselves walking a very narrow tightrope, having to carefully balance the needs and wishes of trustees, faculty and administrative staff, students, and community officials. As for deans, their plight is still worse. The relationship of a dean to his or her faculty and students, so one dean has said, is that of a fire hydrant to a dog.

Even when he or she seems to possess sufficient power to command obedience, the leader may still find the going rough. Stewart relates how "one unpopular manager worked himself almost into the grave, as his subordinates always did what he asked them to do and never did anything else." She adds, "The more a manager needs the cooperation of his staff—and the more skilled and interrelated the work, the more he will need it—the less he can rely on formal authority to obtain it."[39]

It would seem from all this that the leader's lot is scarcely a happy one. Many who view it with awe and wonder from the outside would find it sheer torture to experience from the inside. Yet it does have its challenges and its charms.

David Lilienthal, who held such posts as the chairmanships of the Tennessee Valley Authority and the Atomic Energy Commission, once defined leadership as a humanistic art. It requires, he said, "a humanistic outlook on life rather than mere mastery of technique. It is based on the capacity for understanding of individuals and their motivations, their fears, their hopes, what they love and what they hate, the ugly and the good side of human nature. It is an ability to move these individuals, to help them define their wants, to help them discover, step by step, how to achieve them."[40]

The challenge of leadership is thus the challenge of humanism itself. Its successful exercise lies less and less in giving orders and more and more in developing the innate capacities of human beings. But to this must be joined a sense of mission, bolstered and buttressed by some degree of vision. The story is sometimes told of three stonecutters who were asked what they were doing. The first replied, "I am making a living." The second, busily at work, answered, "I am doing the best job of stonecutting in the whole country." The third looking up with a gleam in his eye, said, "I am building a cathedral."[41]

The conclusion is obvious. Only the third person can become an effective manager.

SUMMARY

- Anyone who hopes to spell out the qualities of a leader is engaged in a perilous and problematic mission. One helpful observation can be made at the outset: *Leadership* is, to a great extent, determined by the needs of the situation.
- Leadership qualities include optimism, energy, enterprise, intelligence, verbal ability, creativity, and judgment. *Technical proficiency, decisiveness,* and *charisma* pose special challenges for leaders in public organizations.
- *Leadership* and *management* are not the same. Leadership incorporates the functions of management, that is, directing the organization's resources to accomplish objectives.
- In an age of complexity, change, large enterprises, and nation states, leaders are more important than ever. Personality and charisma do make a difference.
- *Charisma* is a means by which people sometimes abdicate responsibility for consistent, tough-minded evaluation of the outcome of specific policies. They put their trust in their leader who will somehow take care of things.
- A *leader* is a person who has the authority to decide, direct, and represent the objectives and functions of an organization.
- A *manager* is a person who has the authority to direct specific organizational resources in order to accomplish objectives.
- *Authority* is the license by an organization that grants an individual the rights to use its powers and resources.
- Credibility is the recognition by an organization that one is competent to use its powers.
- *Technical credibility* is established when the organization believes that an individual is competent in areas of technical specialization.
- *Ethical credibility* is established when the organization believes that an individual will uphold and support the ethical standards of the organization.
- *Interpersonal credibility* is established when the personnel within the organization believe that an individual understands and cares about what happens to them.
- The *functions of institutional leadership* are (1) definition of institutional mission and role, (2) institutional embodiment of purpose, (3) the defense of institutional integrity, and (4) the ordering of internal conflict.
- Recommendations for enhancing the effectiveness of managers are delegation, participation, education, rotation, speaking up for subordinates, praise, censure, sanctions, and managerial accountability.
- In times of budgetary decrementalism, the challenges of leaders are ever more demanding. Partisan, policy, and system leaders must convince employees and clientele to work smarter while doing more with less.

Our discussion of leadership can be enhanced by outlining the qualities of a person who is recognized as one of the greatest leaders of the 20th century. While reading the following case study, keep in mind the situational aspects of leadership.

CASE STUDY

The Supreme Allied Commander[42]

When the New York Times polled a group of historians in 1961 as to how they ranked America's presidents, Dwight D. Eisenhower scored a rating of 22. This placed him in the low average category, rated even below Herbert Hoover. Eisenhower's place in history fortunately does not rest on his presidential record alone. Ten years prior to entering the White House, he assumed command of what has been called "the most extensive and cooperative military alliance in history." His conduct of this command provides an excellent example of administrative leadership and assures Eisenhower an undeniable place in the history of democratic leadership.

When World War II first broke out, Eisenhower was only fifty years old and held only the rank of lieutenant colonel, but, he had already given signs of the promise that was soon to be fulfilled. As a cadet at West Point, he had always remained in the upper third of his class and would undoubtedly have finished near the top if he had not been something of a minor hell-raiser. (He rated in the bottom third of his class in conduct.) Later, he attended the Army War College at Fort Leavenworth and graduated from its one-year course as valedictorian of his class.

His military career itself had also supplied indications that he was no ordinary soldier. He early saw the value of tanks, and while George Patton was writing articles promoting the tank in the *Cavalry Journal,* Eisenhower was doing the same in the *Infantry Journal.* Both men, of course, saw their pleas go largely disregarded. (In France at this time, an elongated colonel named Charles de Gaulle was making the rounds of Parisian publishers with a book urging a greater role for tanks. His superiors had already turned down his outlandish suggestions.) Eisenhower showed equal prescience and even more enterprise when it came to airplanes. Seeing in them another major weapon of the future, he took flying lessons at the age of forty-six and earned a pilot's license. He was not a man to let himself go stale.

Eisenhower had also showed that he understood something about the behavioral side of management. "Morale," he once wrote, "is at one and the same time the strongest and the most delicate of growths. It withstands shocks, even disasters, on the battlefield, but can be destroyed utterly by favoritism, neglect, or injustice." He had also committed himself to the goals of maintaining a mature objectivity in his working life. Among the principles he had written down for himself were "Remember that belligerence is the hallmark of insecurity," and, "Forget yourself and personal fortunes."

Finally, Eisenhower had also demonstrated a capacity for verbal communication. This will come as a surprise to those who are old enough to recall the stumbling syntax that so often characterized his press conferences as president, but, as an aide to General MacArthur in the 1930s, Eisenhower drafted most of the eloquent general's speeches. During his mission as commander of the Allied forces in World War II, he drafted delicate orders that were considered models of tact and understanding, wrote more than one hundred letters to his own commander, George C. Marshall, and managed to carry on a fairly lively personal correspondence as well. In one letter to a former West Point classmate, he wrote, "I think sometimes that I am a cross between a onetime soldier, a pseudo statesman, a jack-legged politician and a crooked diplomat. I walk a soapy tightrope in a rainstorm with a blazing furnace on one side and a pack of ravenous tigers on the other. . . . In spite of this, I must admit that the whole thing is interesting and intriguing."

The above description not only indicates an ability to put ideas into words but also provides a fairly accurate description of just what his job entailed. Heading up the Allied forces turned out to be one of the most challenging administrative tasks in history.

Eisenhower was picked for this difficult assignment by George C. Marshall, who had spotted Eisenhower's abilities and had started grooming him for higher responsibilities once he, Marshall, had become chief of staff. When Marshall found that he could not take on the commander's role himself, since Roosevelt wanted him to stay in Washington, he sent Eisenhower in his place. It proved to be a fortunate choice.

The difficulties confronting Eisenhower stemmed not so much from the military as from the political situation. There were all kinds of people, parties, and pressures that had to be skillfully managed. They included the various British armed forces and their various leaders, British public opinion, British political leaders, many different and often conflicting French interests, other Allied forces and their governments (including the exile governments in London), and then of course, his own troops, their commanders, his military and political superiors in Washington, and the American press and public opinion. All these, plus the persistent pressure to bring the European war to as speedy an end as possible with a minimum of Allied bloodshed, required masterly managerial skills.

Eisenhower approached this Herculean task with modesty and geniality. He would share his thoughts with his subalterns as if they were his coequals, and he framed his commands as if they were advice. In the view of one of his biographers, the British Brigadier General Sixsmith, he was a superb delegator of authority, and yet he was able "to keep his finger on all that was going on. His subordinates were able to see that they were expected to act, they were told what was in Eisenhower's mind, and they knew he would not shrink from responsibility."

Regarding this latter point, Eisenhower issued a directive early in the campaign that newspaper stories criticizing him should not under any circumstances be censored. When it came time for the cross-channel invasion of France, he prepared a statement for use in the event that the invasion misfired in which he accepted full blame for its failure. During the actual campaign across Europe that followed, he shrugged off persistent attempts in the British press to give all the credit for Allied successes to the British generals, Montgomery and Alexander.

One good illustration of Eisenhower's mangerial skill was his handling of General George C. Patton. Eisenhower recognized that Patton was in many ways an excellent combat commander, particularly when it came to tank warfare. He further realized that the Germans had a very high estimation of Patton and feared him as they feared no other Allied combat general. Eisenhower was also painfully aware of Patton's many weaknesses, such as his egoism, his officiousness, and his reactionary cast of mind.

When Patton set off an uproar in the United States slapping American soldiers who had been hospitalized with bad nerves or battle fatigue, Eisenhower refused to take the easy course and relieve him of command. Instead, he ordered Patton to make personal apologies to the slapped men, the medical personnel, and all others concerned. Patton, who was desperate to continue in command, complied. Two years later when the savage Nazi counterattack almost upset the Allies in the historic battle of the Bulge, Patton's adept rescue of the besieged U.S. forces vindicated Eisenhower's action.

He tolerated Patton as long as he could, but after the war ended and Patton insisted on employing ex-Nazis in his zone of occupation, Eisenhower moved to replace him. Even at this point he tried to ease the aging general's humiliation by asking Patton whom he would like as a replacement. When Patton named someone who was acceptable to Eisenhower, the American commander appointed him.

His tact and concern were in evidence not only in handling his commanders. He also regularly toured the ranks, talking with the soldiers, and looking after their well-being. He sharply reproved any base commander who utilized his best facilities for administrative quarters instead of giving them up for the rest and relaxation of the men who were doing the fighting.

Behind his modest geniality lay a great singleness of purpose. He realized that the alliance would falter and flounder unless there was a single overall commander, and he made sure that this was accepted and acknowledged. He also took steps to see that throughout the Allied forces all issues would be discussed and decided on considerations other than national pride. His creation of an integrated command—integrated not only in combining the forces of several nations but also in combining both the army and navy of these nations—is considered his greatest accomplishment.

He also knew how to put first things first. In North Africa he deferred his integration scheme, important though it was, in order to capture Tunis before the bad weather set in and when Roosevelt urged him to lead the troops into Rome, glorifying his own and the U.S. role in the city's liberation, he refused in order to get to England more quickly and have more time to work on the coming invasion of France.

Eisenhower had originally wanted to have an invasion of southern France accompany the cross-Channel attack. Owing to a shortage of landing craft and other factors, he continually had to scale down his plan, but he did not scuttle the idea until the very end. In Sixsmith's view, this decision "was typical of the man," for "he liked to keep his options open."

As a military strategist, Eisenhower did make his share of mistakes. He allowed the German military divisions in Sicily to escape, he balked at sending his airborne division to capture Rome, and he opened up a hole in his front that permitted Hitler to launch the perilous and costly Battle of the Bulge. It took the Allied forces, despite their complete domination of the air and their vast superiority on the ground, nearly a year after the time they crossed the channel to bring Germany to defeat.

He was according to Sixsmith by no means a poor strategist either, constantly beset as he was by conflicting pressures. In the north, Montgomery was insisting that the full Allied thrust be put into his hands. He was supported by feverish public opinion in England, not simply because he was their general but also because they feared the German rockets that were being launched from the area that Montgomery was trying to capture. Farther south, there was Patton, chomping at the bit, demanding more gasoline and other scarce supplies as well as men, and since American public opinion needed a hero of its own, Patton could not be completely restricted. Meanwhile, the French were clamoring for the liberation of Paris, a move that would not only detract from the route of advance but could hinder further advances, since supplies and the trucks to carry them would have to be siphoned off to maintain the city afterward.

On balance, Eisenhower handled his strategist role adequately and his administrative and political role superbly. This is Sixsmith's view, and it seems to reflect the consensus of others who were in a position to know. When Germany finally surrendered, General Marshall, who was not, as we have seen, overly given to effusive praise, sent Eisenhower a long and truly effusive letter of congratulations: "You have commanded with outstanding success . . . you have met and successfuly disposed of every conceivable difficulty . . . you have triumphed over inconceivable logistical problems and military obstacles . . . you have made history, great history for the good of mankind. . . ."

Churchill shared much the same view. Shortly before Roosevelt died, the British prime minister wrote the President, expressing "admiration of the great and shining qualities of character and personality which he [Eisenhower] has proved himself to possess. . . ." But most important of all was the judgment of British Field Marshal Montgomery, the petulant prima donna who chafed and complained at the way Eisenhower had restricted him all during the war. Said Montgomery afterward, in words reminiscent of those used by the Los Alamos physicists to describe Oppenheimer, "No one but Ike could have done it."

But if Eisenhower performed so well in the highly sensitive and highly political role of Supreme Allied Commander, why was he such an undistinguished president?

There are many possible answers to this question, and all of them may contain some element of truth. For one thing, he may not have been such a poor president as historians have believed. Eisenhower himself thought that his greatest contribution was to keep the United States out of war, and in view of the actions of his successors, that accomplishment may not have received its due. Eisenhower, like Kennedy and Johnson, also came under pressure to invade Vietnam, but when such a course was urged on him by his secretary of state and his military chief of staff in 1954, he asked that Congress and other nations be sounded out first. When reaction from both quarters was negative, he scuttled the idea.

Another answer may be found in his age. He was ten years older when he entered the White House than when he took over the supreme Allied command, and while sixty-two is not an unusually advanced age for high political office—Churchill was in his late sixties during World War II and Clemenceau was in his late seventies when he headed France during World War I—the years take their toll on some people more than others. The fact that for more than three years during the war he worked day and night, smoking four full packs of cigarettes a day and getting no exercise, certainly did not contribute toward his later vigor.

But most of all, the answer lies in the point raised at the start of this chapter, and that is the situational nature of leadership. Leaders create their situations, to be sure, but situations also create their leaders. Such was the case with Dwight D. Eisenhower.

QUESTIONS AND INSTRUCTIONS

1. Can leadership be learned? Explain.
2. The ability to make good decisions is crucial if a leader is to be successful. What does this case study say about President Eisenhower's penchant for making decisions?
3. Leaders create their situations, but situations also create their leaders. In Eisenhower's case, which premise are we to believe? Why?
4. Why is Eisenhower considered a more effective war administrator than presidential administrator?
5. How did Eisenhower's network of prior associations and preferences contribute to his success as war administrator, yet detract from his record as presidential administrator? Explain.
6. How did the leadership styles of Eisenhower and General Patton differ?
7. What role, if any, did charisma play in Eisenhower's approach to leadership?
8. Why do leaders place more emphasis upon reasoned judgment than creativity? In roles as war and presidential administrators, did Eisenhower exude creativity, or did he exercise good judgment? Or did he demonstrate both?
9. To lead successfully, a person must believe that his or her leadership will make a difference. In roles as war and presidential administrators, did Eisenhower make a difference? Explain.

ENDNOTES

1. The material on Oppenheimer in this chapter is drawn mainly from Nuel Pharr Davis, *Lawrence and Oppenheimer* (New York: Simon & Schuster, 1968).

2. Peter F. Drucker, *The Effective Executive* (New York: Harper & Row, 1967), 22.

3. Douglas McGregor, *Leadership and Motivation* (Cambridge, MA: MIT Press, 1966), 73.

4. William J. Reddin, *Managerial Effectiveness* (New York: McGraw-Hill, 1970), 35.

5. Paul H. Appleby, *Big Democracy* (New York: Alfred A. Knopf, 1949), 41.

6. Arthur M. Schlesinger, Jr., *A Thousand Days* (New York: Fawcett World Library, 1967), 403.

7. Harlan Cleveland, "A Philosophy for the Public Executive," in *Perspectives on Public Management*, edited by Robert T. Golembiewski (Itasca, Il: F. E. Peacock, 1968).

8. David Halberstam, *The Best and the Brightest* (New York: Random House, 1969), 318–319.

9. Daniel Katz and Robert L. Kahn, *The Social Psychology of Organizations* (New York: John Wiley, 1966, 1st edition), 293–294.

10. Burleigh Gardner, "Successful and Unsuccessful Executives," *Advanced Management* (September, 1948).

11. Albert Speer, *Inside the Third Reich* (New York: Macmillan, 1970), 18–19.

12. Katz and Kahn, *Social Psychology of Organizations* (1st edition, 1966), 328.

13. *Ibid.*, 115.

14. David E. Lilienthal, *Management: A Humanist Art* (New York: Columbia University Press, 1967), 17.

15. Townsend Hoopes, *The Limits of Intervention* (New York: David McKay, 1969), 79–80.

16. C. P. Snow, *Science and Government* (New York: New American Library, 1962), 79–80.

17. Anyone who believes that dynamic dictators are immune to such a tendency may find the following quotation from Adolph Hitler of interest. "Unless I have the incorruptible conviction: This is the Solution, I do nothing—not even if the whole party tried to drive me to action. I will not act. I will wait no matter what happens." Quoted in Walter C. Lanager, *The Mind of Adolf Hitler* (New York: Basic Books, 1972), 81.

18. Drucker, *The Effective Executive*, 32.

19. Katz and Kahn, *Social Psychology of Organizations* (1st edition, 1966), 318.

20. C. Northcote Parkinson, *Parkinson's Law and Other Studies of Administration* (New York: Ballantine Books, 1964), 103.

21. Dean Acheson, *Present at the Creation* (New York: W. W. Norton, 1969), 193.

22. Katz and Kahn, *Social Psychology of Organizations* (1st edition, 1966), 332.

23. Seymour S. Berlin et al., "A Guide for Political Appointees: Entering the System," *Good Government* (Winter, 1972).

24. McGregor, *Leadership and Motivation*, 60–61.

25. Herbert Kaufman, *The Forest Ranger* (Baltimore, Md.: John Hopkins Press, 1960), 176.

26. Sloan Simpson, *Anatomy of the State Department* (Boston: Houghton Mifflin, 1967), 36–37, 39–40.

27. Douglas McGregor, *The Theory of Human Enterprise* (New York: McGraw-Hill, 1960).

28. Katz and Kahn, *Social Psychology of Organizations* (1st edition, 1966), 321.

29. Halberstam, *The Best and the Brightest*, 321.

30. Martin R. Smith, *I Hate to See a Manager Cry* (Reading, MA: Addison-Wesley, 1973), 108.

31. Drucker, *The Effective Executive*, see Chapter 3.

32. C. Northcote Parkinson, *Parkinson's Law and Other Studies of Administration* (New York: Ballantine Books, 1964), 103.

33. William English, retired director of chemical research at Polaroid Corporation, in an interview with Dr. George Berkley.

34. Smith, *I Hate to See a Manager Cry*, 186.

35. Robert Townsend, "Up the Organization," *Harper's Magazine*, March, 1970.

36. Charles Frankel, *High on Foggy Bottom* (New York: Harper and Row, 1968), 56.

37. Rosemary Stewart, *The Reality of Organizations* (New York: Anchor Books, 1972), 48.

38. For an interesting and informative view of some of the Tsar's leadership problems, see the earlier chapters of Robert K. Massie, *Nicholas and Alexandra* (New York: Atheneum, 1969).

39. Stewart, *The Reality of Organizations*, 82.

40. David E. Lilienthal, *Management: A Humanist Art* (New York: Columbia University Press, 1967), 16–17.

41. Peter F. Drucker, *The Practice of Management* (New York: Harper & Row, 1954), 122.

42. The principal source of material for this case study is E. K. G. Sixsmith, *Eisenhower as Military Commander* (New York: Stein & Day, 1973). Another source is Ladislas Fargo, *Patton: Ordeal and Triumph* (New York: Dell Publishing, 1970).

8

☆ ☆ ☆

COMMUNICATION

CHAPTER HIGHLIGHTS

BACKGROUND ON ADMINISTRATIVE COMMUNICATION
FORMAL AND INFORMAL COMMUNICATION
THE OTHER ORGANIZATION
UP, DOWN, AND ACROSS

During World War II, British Prime Minister Winston Churchill wrote a memo to the First Lord of the Admiralty that said: "Pray state this day, on one side of a sheet of paper, how the Royal Navy is being adapted to meet the conditions of modern warfare."

On one side of a sheet of paper.

The fact that Churchill was so concerned about the form of the reply indicates the great importance the Prime Minister placed on communication, especially in time of war. By saying he wanted the reply on one side of a sheet of paper, Churchill was indicating he wanted a clear, concise, to-the-point reply.

From the outset of his administration, Churchill placed a heavy emphasis on the written word. "Let it be clearly understood," he told his war cabinet, "that all directions emanating from me are made in writing, or should be immediately afterwards confirmed in writing, and that I do not accept any responsibility for matters relating to national defense on which I am alleged to have given decisions unless they are recorded in writing."

War administration is crisis administration and can therefore lead to considerable confusion. Orders given in a hurry and quickly passed down can easily be misunderstood, with dire results. Other orders that are vital may go unheeded or become lost in the far-flung and fast-moving governmental machinery. Churchill wanted none of that, and since he had no problem handling the written word, he used this facility to keep intermediaries at a minimum and to stay in direct touch with a vast number of people.

Churchill's use of formal communication, such as personal memoranda, allowed him to personally direct much of Britain's governmental activity. His well known verbal communication skills were used to inspire the British during their darkest hours.

Churchill also invariably kept his lines of communication open to those in lower ranks. As Robin Maugham writes, "Throughout the war, Churchill was more interested in talking to junior officers than to the top brass—partly from pure kindness, partly from his knowledge that it was from the men in the field that he could discover what was really going on."[1] Maugham, who served as a lieutenant in the tank corps during the war, recalls how Churchill asked him after the fall of France if he and his fellows were ready to repel a German invasion. When Maugham replied that many of their tanks could not move for want of a spring in their trackpins, Churchill exploded in fury and immediately set the whole British government into action. By nightfall, the springs had been delivered and were in place.

Administrators often overlook the vital importance of communication in all its forms, but communication was for Churchill, and is for many other successful administrators, a high priority.

Background on Administrative Communication

Through the years, administrators and administrative theorists have placed increasing emphasis on communication. In the 1930s, Chester Barnard called attention to the fact that "a common purpose must be commonly known, and to be known must in some way be communicated. With some exceptions, verbal communication between men is the method by which this is accomplished."[2]

Writing in the 1950s, Herbert Simon put even greater stress on the role of communication. "It is obvious," he noted, "that without communication there can be no organization, for there is no possibility then of the group influencing the behavior of the individual. Not only is communication absolutely essential to organization, but the availability of particular techniques of communication will and should be distributed through the organization. . . ." Simon went on to conclude that "only in the case where the man who is to carry out a decision is also the best man fitted to make the decision is there no problem of communication—and in this exceptional case there is, of course, no reason for organization."[3]

More recent writers have assigned communication an equal, if not more important, role. They consider such organizational ingredients as solidarity and support, along with command and control, to be closely related to organizational communication. Some even view organizations as essentially systems of communication and regard all or nearly all organizational problems as communication problems. Such an approach may well go too far, but it can often prove helpful. For example, Charles Redfield tells of one successful consultant who, when he embarks on an organizational study, stations himself in the mailroom and "by plotting the lines of actual communication, . . . can sometimes build a more accurate organizational chart than the one that hangs on the wall in the president's office."[4]

Communication presents as many problems as any other aspect of administration, if not more. There are, first of all, the *technical* problems. When the Germans invaded France in 1940, they utilized teletypes, advanced field telephones, and other devices to maintain a rapid flow of communication among all the parts of their fast-moving, military organization. The French, however, relied heavily on the old dispatch system, whereby orders issued from Paris would be carried by dispatch runners on motorcycles. This not only seriously slowed down communication but often eliminated it altogether, for the runners sometimes never reached their destinations. They would become either the victims of accidents or of strafings and bombings from German aircraft.

The French had other communication problems besides merely technical ones. Prior to the German onslaught, they had received from Vatican sources the proposed route that the Germans were planning to use through Belgium. Paris refused to believe the report, however, since the proposed route did not seem to them militarily sound.[5] This illustrates a further communication problem—sometimes the information is properly sent and received, and is then simply disregarded.

Many countries have experienced this problem in wartime. During the same war, the Germans paid handsomely for some British battle plans that had been carefully photographed by a valet of the British ambassador in Turkey.[6] Once they obtained the documents, however, the Nazis failed to act on them. Similarly, the Soviet Union was repeatedly warned of an impending German attack in 1941. One source was the famous double agent, Richard Sorge, who supplied the Soviets with the exact dates of the scheduled invasion, but Stalin shrugged them off. In the postwar period, the United States received numerous reports from our embassy in China forecasting the impending collapse of the Chiang Kai-shek regime and the Communist assumption of power. When the predicted event occurred, it caught everybody in Washington by surprise.

Experience alone does not necessarily solve such problems. When World War I broke out, the French general staff fell into possession of authentic German documents clearly indicating that the Germans would march through Belgium. This would normally call for the French to shore up their left flank to counter and turn back the thrust. But the French had based their strategy on a strong center and clung to this position, despite their new information. Their 1940 experience was a duplicate of their 1914 errors.

A more common problem is simply a failure to request information from the right parties. In his memoirs Krushchev blamed Russia's abortive invasion of Finland in World War II on such an oversight. The Soviet intelligence services had known about the powerful Finnish defense system all along, but no one in the high Soviet command bothered to ask intelligence services about it. The disaster cost the Russians nearly one million lives.[7]

Not all manifestations of this problem are so sweeping and dramatic, but they occur all the time. A detective investigating a case may fail to consult the police officer who first handled the case and did the initial investigation. This failure, which happens in police forces all the time, scarcely contributes to efficiency in fighting crime. The detective may spend days and weeks tracking down a suspect when the police officer who first dealt with the matter knows all along where the suspect is living.[8] Nor is it only a failure to consult that makes the work of detectives more difficult than it needs to be. Often the patrol officer will not tell the detective what the officer knows, even when the detective asks—the officer may be angry at not being allowed to pursue the matter or may have a grudge toward that particular detective. Thus, information can be impeded as much, if not more, by intention as by error.

Parties involved in a communications network of any kind may not only *withhold* information but may also intentionally *distort* it. The distortions that come about through maliciousness however, are far and away exceeded by those that occur through mischance.

To obtain an idea of how widespread a problem this is, we have only to examine the most simple and most intimate organization in current society—the married couple. In their highly respected book, *The Mirages of Marriage*, William J. Lederer, M.D., and Don D. Jackson estimate that husbands and wives miscommunicate about 20 percent of the time. To offer an example, the authors cite a case where the wife has a habit of rubbing her nose when she is angry. An occasion arises, however, when, in talking to her husband, she rubs her nose simply because it is itching. The husband, who is well aware of what this usually means, assumes that she is angry. Since he cannot imagine any reason why she should be, he starts to get irritated at her for allegedly becoming so. His defensive tone then starts to make her annoyed, which in turn confirms him in his initial reaction. The marriage has to ride over another bump on the road to bliss.[9]

Communications problems arise not only from information that is too slow, incomplete, or distorted, but also from information that is simply overabundant. This is the problem of *communication overload*. Harold Nicolson claimed that this was one of the greatest problems at the Paris Conference that followed World War I.[10] The Conference's 48 committees generated so much information that it was impossible for anyone, including the Paris Conference's major decision makers, to know what was going on. James MacGregor Burns blames too much communication for the failure of the United States to take advantage of concessions from the Japanese in 1941, concessions that might have averted the Pacific war. "The problem was too much information, not too little—and too much that was irrelevant, confusing and badly analyzed."[11]

Occasionally, this communication problem also arises by intent. For example, school superintendents sometimes purposely flood their school board members with reports and other documents, which, although completely accurate, are so voluminous as to make it impossible for the board members to know what is happening. As the board members struggle in vain to keep abreast of the swelling tide of information, the superintendent calmly proceeds to do pretty much whatever he or she wants to do.

Most overload problems, however, arise from sheer force of circumstances, and the circumstances that make for too much communication are increasing all the time. The growing complexity, specialization, and interdependence of today's organizational world are all adding to the rising flood of information—a process being aided and abetted by the exponential growth of *communications technology*. An organization may take great care and achieve great success in developing excellent lines and flows of communication, only to sink under the profusion of information that may develop as a result.

FORMAL AND INFORMAL COMMUNICATION

Communication falls into two basic categories—formal and informal. They are easily defined. *Formal communication* is written communication; *informal* is oral. Of course, not all informal communication is verbal. Attitudes and even ideas can be transmitted by means of inflection, gesture, and body language, but although nonverbal communication definitely has a place in organizational life, its role is usually not very great and, in any case, it is hard to analyze and define. Consequently, our discussion of informal communication will be directed toward verbal communication.

What factors govern the use of one form of communication over the other? Under what conditions does formal communication take precedence over informal and vice versa?

Generally, two factors foster the use of formal communication. One of these is *organizational*. As organizations grow, they tend to make increasing use of formal communication and, correspondingly, diminishing use of its opposite. The other factor is *public character*. Public organizations tend to rely more heavily on formal communication than do private ones. A brief examination of the merits of formal communication will show why this is true.

ADVANTAGES OF FORMAL COMMUNICATION

Formal communication fosters *accountability*. This factor alone makes it indispensable for governmental affairs, particularly in a democracy. Unless the public and those who serve its information needs, such as the press and legislators, can find out what orders were given and who gave them, it cannot make the judgments needed to ensure truly democratic government.

By facilitating accountability, formal communication places natural restraints on arbitrariness, capriciousness, favoritism, and discrimination. By proceeding on formal instructions and keeping records of their transactions, public officials find it much more difficult, although certainly not impossible, to depart from acceptable standards of impartiality and fairness. Of course, the rules and standards themselves may be unfair, but if so, this is at least a matter of public record and can be easily determined. An administrator with integrity will welcome the opportunity to document his or her actions.

Many of the scandals and sensational political events of recent decades that have shed valuable light on governmental operations illustrate this advantage of formal communication. Take, for example, the case of the *Pentagon Papers*. These disclosed a great deal of valuable information on the country's conduct of the Vietnam War. Had Defense Secretary Robert McNamara not directed that such reports be written, much of this information would have escaped public view.

The Watergate affair also provides a good illustration of the relationship that formal communication has with pinpointing responsibility in government. Had there not been a certain amount of documentation regarding these events, the exposure and prosecution of the misdeeds it involved would have been greatly impeded and possibly nullified. Had there been still more extensive use of formal communication, then many more elements of this nefarious affair might have been more deeply and successfully explored. Without formal communication, the work of the journalist, to say nothing of the work of the historian, would frequently become implausible and even impossible.

Watergate and the Pentagon Papers are only two of the more dramatic incidents that spotlight the utility of formal communication, at least when it comes to serving the interest of the public. Other illustrations occur on an everyday basis. A special commission set up by New York State to investigate New York City's property tax situation found there were no written procedures or manuals to guide the City's assessors in their work. The absence of such formal materials resulted in the "frivolous application of discretionary standards," which, in turn, had opened the door to favoritism and other forms of political abuse.[12]

Let us suppose that all New York City's assessors were deeply committed to performing their tasks accurately and fairly, and let us further suppose that the City administration was determined to let them do so. Could New York City's property tax payers then be assured that they were being treated rationally and impartially? Without a uniform and written set of standards and criteria, the chances are that assessments would still be unevenly imposed and administered. What one assessor is likely to emphasize in making an assessment another assessor is likely to make light of. To one assessor, for instance, high ceilings in a building give it added charm and space and hence add to its value. To another assessor, high ceilings may mean additional heating and cleaning costs and hence detract from a building's value.

Formal communication in this way curbs the disparities and discrepancies which can occur even without express design. With all the good will in the world, distortions can and will creep in when formal communication is totally absent. Written communication allows everyone concerned to receive the same message and to check back on it if he or she is at any time uncertain as to what it says.

This brings us to still another asset of formal communication. It saves *time*. In any large organization, it would be difficult, indeed, to issue all instructions orally. Not only would distortions occur as the message was

---

MISCOMMUNICATION ABOUT INCORRECT ASSUMPTIONS

Many government services are underused because the paperwork is complex and was designed without the appropriate audience in mind. Moreover, most people do not adequately read instructions. Government form compilers make incorrect assumptions concerning the respondents' attitudes, ability, and knowledge. Compilers expect that respondents will read the whole form and have a higher reading level than most possess, while assuming an unavailable background knowledge. In order to make government programs more effective, reductions in the forms' complexity are necessary as well as changing the respondents attitudes toward reading instructions.

Source: Jansen, Carel, and Steelhouder, Michael, *Journal of Technical Writing and Communication*, Vol. 22, No. 2 (Spring 1992), 179–195.

---

relayed from person to person or group, but time would be needlessly consumed. Written communication allows an almost infinite number of people to receive the same message at the same time, and if these people forget any portions of it, they do not have to check back to the sender of the message, for they now have it in front of them.

Written communication can also save time when it travels from the bottom to the top. It would be virtually impossible for any large and complex organization to receive orally all the information that it may need to obtain from its far-flung operations. Its phones would be constantly tied up and its offices would be continually filled with people relaying what they think headquarters needs and wants to know. Putting things in writing can save a superior's time in handling information from subordinates. He or she can usually read memoranda from several different people in the time it takes to talk to just one person. This also allows the supervisor to schedule more efficiently and to allocate periods of the day or week for reviewing such messages.

Written communication also allows information to be more fully developed with all of its ramifications discussed. Issues of any importance usually require such treatment. The document that results can then be circulated to others for still further analysis, until all possible points of view have been solicited and all aspects have been explored.

Finally, written communication not only helps to inform the *recipient* but may also do the same for the *sender*. Francis Bacon once said that an index is chiefly useful for the person who makes it and the same can be said for many of the memoranda, reports, et cetera that flow through the corridors of bureaucracy. By putting down data and ideas in writing, the administrator or an aide frequently sees things that were missed before. Expressing ideas in written form usually helps the person doing the writing to ferret out details previously disregarded and to see relationships and implications that were previously missed. Many a bureaucrat will frequently testify that he or she did not fully understand an issue until after writing a memo about it.

There are many good reasons why the written word looms so large in the operations of government. We should bear them in mind when we discuss some of the less attractive aspects of written communication.

DISADVANTAGES OF FORMAL COMMUNICATION

Shortly after he was appointed secretary of Housing and Urban Development, George Romney held a press conference and displayed a stack of paper that stood two and a half feet high and weighed 56 pounds. This, he said, represented all the paper generated by an application for a single, urban-renewal project.[13]

Although the problem, as Romney explained it, was caused more by faulty organization than by a sheer obsession with formal documents, it does illustrate that one of the ways in which organizational pathologies work is by generating a profusion of paper. The very use of the written word tends to encourage its further use, and many a governmental and private organization have found themselves swamped in a *sea of documentation.*

Romney's display is only one of many incidents that have, from time to time, shed light on this startling problem. During World War II, for example, there was a celebrated price order on fruitcake from the Office of Price Administration that consumed six pages of fine print. It was one of the most famous orders that the red-faced OPA ever turned out.

Although the paper problem is as old as bureaucracy itself, it seems to show a great deal of resistance to correction. A congressional report in 1966 estimated that there were 360,000 forms in use by the federal government. By 1972, the number of such forms was thought to have grown to more than 800,000. Harold Koenig, the head of a National Archives team that was trying to reduce the paper explosion, estimated that at least 30 billion copies of these forms were circulating every year. A Senate subcommittee put the total cost of printing, shuffling, and storing the forms at close to $18 billion.[14] While using computers to store information electronically can be helpful, it can also increase paper work since modern word processing makes it so easy to crank out documents.

Few organizations have managed to escape the ravages of the *paper revolution.* Former Federal Bureau of Investigation Director, J. Edgar Hoover, consistently boasted that the FBI was not a bureaucratic agency, and considering the highly personalized manner in which he ran the agency, he was, to some extent, right. Yet the FBI did not manage to avoid the maze and craze of documentation. Its agent's manual encompassed 32,000 rules

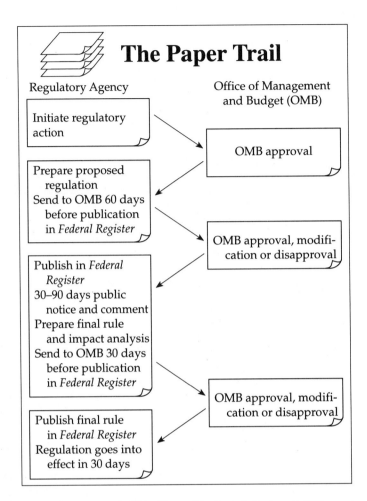

The Paper Trail

Regulatory Agency   Office of Management
                                     and Budget (OMB)

Initiate regulatory
action

OMB approval

Prepare proposed
  regulation
Send to OMB 60 days
  before publication
  in *Federal Register*

OMB approval, modifi-
cation or disapproval

Publish in *Federal
  Register*
30–90 days public
  notice and comment
Prepare final rule
  and impact analysis
Send to OMB 30 days
  before publication
  in *Federal Register*

OMB approval, modifi-
cation or disapproval

Publish final rule
  in *Federal Register*
Regulation goes into
  effect in 30 days

Source: Kitty Dumas, "Congress or the White House: Who Controls the Agencies?" *Congressional Quarterly Weekly Report*, Vol. 48, No. 15 (April 14, 1990), 1133.

and regulations, and its files would have filled an area equal to twelve foot-ball fields. When an agent in Philadelphia was scheduled to speak at a dinner, his office sent out a report on the event to headquarters and thirty-seven other field bureaus and then filed the report under eleven different categories in its own files.[15]

In a desperate effort to stem the ever-swelling flow, Congress enacted the Paperwork Reduction Act of 1980. This legislation gives the Office of Management and Budget near absolute authority to approve all activities, such as requests for information, that would generate more paper. Sponsors of the act claimed that a mere 1 percent reduction in bureaucratic pa-perwork would save the nation a billion dollars. The act also established the Federal Information Locator System to provide an index to information sources within the federal government. Such a system would, it was hoped, encourage federal agencies to share information and keep them from collecting data that other agencies had already compiled.[16]

The main goal of the 1980 paperwork legislation was to reduce the public's paperwork burden by 25 percent. For example, paperwork for federal employment guidelines, defense procurement contracts, and even individual income tax forms was to be reduced. The result of the legislation, however, has been to enhance the power of the White House, especially the Office of Management and Budget (OMB), at the expense of the Congress. In the struggle for control of the regulatory process, the Executive won this battle over the form and content of regulations issued by federal departments and agencies.

Members of Congress argue that they are empowered to oversee departments and agencies. Congressional committees utilize appropriations power to control decisions of executive agencies. OMB insists that the responsibility to determine if regulations are an unnecessary burden on the public belongs to the President. However, more than 50 years ago Congress ceded statutory authority to the executive branch on what and how information was collected by the federal departments and agencies. The struggle between the two branches of government over the content and process of the regulatory paperwork continues.

The formal communication process in this balance-of-powers debate creates a massive paper trail as outlined in the preceding box.

The states, too, have been moving ahead to abridge the rising tide of paperwork. Minnesota, Ohio, Washington, Kentucky—these are only a few of those states that have launched paperwork reform measures. When an inventory in Indiana showed that the state had 68,300 different forms, officials managed to eliminate 20,000 of them within the following two years.

Praiseworthy and productive as such steps may be, one must not lose sight of the fact that the growing crush of paper is in many respects a symptom of other organizational problems, not just a problem in itself. One frequent cause of excess paperwork is an insufficiency of *delegation*. A superior who insists on making all decisions personally and who needs to know everything that is going on, down to the smallest detail, will find his or her desk piled high with memoranda, reports, and requests. In like manner, an agency that has split duties among several subunits when the tasks could be handled by one will also add to its paper problems. This, according to Romney, was the problem at HUD. An urban-renewal application had to travel through the hands of too many assistant secretaries.

Some of the very advantages of written communication lead to its abuse. If it promotes accountability, then it also fosters *self-protection*. People may put something in writing so that they cannot be accused of having done something improperly or so that they can point to the record later on and show where they were right. Harold Macmillan, who served as a British aide to General Eisenhower in World War II, and, as such, was the recipient of a constant stream of written communication, once claimed that "directives are more useful in protecting the writer than in instructing the recipient."[17]

Sometimes people write more than necessary simply to show how industrious they are. Superiors often are quite impressed with such industry. Joseph Califano was a prodigious writer of memoranda when he served on Lyndon Johnson's staff, and although in Califano's case the motivation was probably a genuine desire to reach the president on many issues, his diligence did not go unnoticed. Once when Johnson heard another aide speak somewhat disparagingly of Califano, the president retorted, "Don't criticize Califano. There's never been a man around me who wrote so many memos."[18]

Whatever the causes of paper profusion, its cost can be immense. We have already seen some estimates of the cost involved in printing, storing, and circulating forms, but other costs may also be included. A memo may save the superior's time but may consume inordinate amounts of the subordinate's time; this also bears a price tag. It is not uncommon for a public employee to spend a day or more drafting a memorandum on an issue that could have been settled in a ten-minute conversation with the superior. When this occurs, the time factor involved in formal communication is usually working against the organization instead of for it.

Each piece of paper, we should remember, tends to spawn offspring of its own. One person's contribution evokes a similar or even greater contribution from others. If Ralph sends a memo to Ed, then Ed must often send a memo back. Ed may at the same time send a memo to Mary asking her for comments. Mary may not even have waited for Ed to act. If Mary has heard about Ralph's memo, then she may feel inclined to do some memo writing on personal initiative. In order to make the memo better, Mary may send a memo to Jane seeking some additional information, which, in return, produces a memo from Jane. And so it goes.

Meanwhile, the ever-bulging files start to produce problems other than just the costs of *storage*. J. C. Masterman, in describing Great Britain's remarkably successful effort to convert German agents to double agents during World War II, says the files on some of these double agents grew to over 35 volumes. This, he said, made it "difficult and wearying and time consuming to master the essentials of each case in a reasonable space of time and with some degree of certainty that no essential feature has been overlooked."[19] Completeness of information, carried too far, can lead to less information, or at least informaton that can be used less easily.

Needless to say, all these problems have an impact on the organization's employees. Formal communication by virtue of being formal is less humane. It may have a dispiriting and even deadening effect on human relations.

Indeed, people actually start to "turn off" when too many formal communications pour in on them and the messages themselves end up in wastepaper baskets unread.

Finally, we should note that while formal communication is usually clearer and less liable to be misunderstood than its opposite, this is not always the case. The story is told of how J. Edgar Hoover became irked at the sender of a memo because the sender had not left wide enough margins for the FBI chief to scribble his comments. Since wide margins were a bureau policy, he wrote in it, "Watch the borders." and sent it back. For the next week FBI agents fanned out on the Mexican and Canadian borders in the bewildering belief that their boss wanted them to keep a vigil.

INFORMAL COMMUNICATION

Oral communication offers a solution to many of the problems encountered in written communication. It does not flood the office worker's desk or clog the files. It can evoke immediate feedback, which, in turn, can lead to a resolution of any issues and clarification of any points that may be involved. In so doing, the one who is doing the communicating can be assured that his or her information has been received. Speaking and listening permit the use of shading, emphasis, and gesture. Conversation is also significantly more human and often more humane. People are now dealing together directly.

Technology certainly impacts modes of communication, formal and informal. In an era of faxes, computers, and photostat machines, communication challenges will emerge even more complex, demanding, and technical. Computer electronic mail and telephone answering machines contribute to the narrowing of the gulf between formal and informal communication distinctions.

Technology is crucial in the development of the information highway which would link every home to a fiber-optic network over which voice, data, television and other services would be transmitted. The estimated cost of the nation's proposed data highway, in 1992 dollars, is $200 billion. The cost would be lower if existing coaxial cables or copper wires were used. At $200 billion, the cost of the proposed data highway compares to the cost of the U.S. interstate highway system at $271.5 billion, also in 1992 dollars.

Informal communication is heavily used in Japanese industry and government. The Japanese prefer face-to-face contact and rarely send interoffice memoranda. Superiors spend considerable time "walking the floor" and talking with their employees. Conferences are common at all levels and are often conducted in an informal and relaxed atmosphere. Judging from Japan's growth rates and productivity levels, it does not seem to have hurt their administrative processes.

Efforts are also under way in this country to substitute oral for written communication. President Johnson's task force on cutting red tape, for example, urged federal officials to make more extensive use of the telephone and less use of "time-consuming written communications."[20] It is quite possible that the use of oral communication will grow apace in governmental agencies, although it will most likely never replace formal communication altogether. For reasons that we noted earlier, the written word and the printed document will probably continue to serve as the mainstay of the communications process in any developed democracy.

GRAPEVINES

Any agency that has an informal organization will also have an informal communications system, often referred to as the "grapevine." Since informal organizations are found in almost all organizations, grapevines are ubiquitous.

Grapevines can also be terribly efficient. "With the rapidity of a burning powder train," says Keith Davis, a professor of management who has studied grapevines for over twenty years, "information flows out of the woodwork, past the manager's door and the janitor's mop closet, through steel walls or construction-glass partitions."[21] What is more, Davis claims, well over three-fourths of all this information is accurate.

Even when it is not accurate, says Davis, it may convey a psychological truth, for many rumors that run rampant through an organization are "symbolic expressions of feelings." If the rumor has it that a certain employee is planning to quit, it may reflect the wish on the part of fellow employees that he or she would quit. Or it may simply reflect the employee's own desire to leave.

Davis advises managers to pay careful attention to the grapevine's information, for it may tell them more than they know about what is going on within their organization. He also urges them to disseminate whatever information they have in order to counter whatever errors the grapevine may be spreading. Beyond that, there is little that the administrator can do, because the grapevine, he says, "cannot be abolished, rubbed out, hidden under a basket, chopped down, tied up, or stopped." Managers might just as well accept it, for it "is as hard to kill as the mythical glass snake, which, when struck, broke into fragments and grew a new snake out of each piece."

THE OTHER ORGANIZATION

Elton Mayo concluded from studying the "Hawthorne Experiments" that informal organization is more important in determining worker cooperation than formal organization, that output is set by social norms, not individual abilities, and that the group heavily influences the behavior of individual workers. Mayo's experiment showed how a group of young, female employees at Western Electric Company reacted positively to every change made in their working conditions while they were working in the test room. It is interesting to note, however, that another experiment conducted along the same lines produced quite different results.

Mayo and his colleagues persuaded the management of the company to put in a group of men engaged in making parts of telephone switches on a piece-rate incentive system. Since this new system would allow the men to increase their earnings without undue physical strain, and since these were depression times when most workers seemed desperate to earn more money, both the researchers and the company expected a great jump in productivity. Their expectations came to naught. The output of the men remained the same.

The research group then began to investigate why the workers responded or, rather, failed to respond. Unlike the young, female, relay assemblers, most of whom had expected to get married and leave their jobs before too long, the male workers had developed a work culture of their own. They had become a cohesive and compact group with their own codes, rules, and norms. Among these rules were prohibitions against doing too much or too little work. So solidly entrenched were these understandings among the male employees that they remained impervious to any blandishments from management. The men rationalized that the incentive plan was an attempt to eventually cut out some jobs or to reduce wage rates. The company assured them that such was not the case and pointed to its record, which indicated no instance of its ever having acted in such a manner. The men remained unconvinced and so productivity went on at the same level as before.[22]

Mayo and his associates had come up against the informal organization, grounded in large part on informal communications. This phenomenon has interested and intrigued organizational theorists ever since, and their research shows its ramifications to be far-reaching indeed.

Organizational charts and manuals of procedure, it seems, rarely provide us with an accurate picture of an organization. There is a good deal more lying under the surface, and what is not official or even readily visible is often the most important. Even the most formal organizations, which pride themselves on going strictly "by the book," rarely do so. An informal system of authority, which supersedes, at least to some extent, the formal one, may arise. In the army, for example, the lieutenant clearly outranks the sergeant. But when the sergeant has had twenty years of army service and the lieutenant is fresh from a college Reserve Officers Training Program (ROTC), the sergeant, rather than the lieutenant, may end up running the platoon.

Communication also flows frequently through informal channels. The office grapevine is usually faster and more complete than the office memo. Aboard a ship, for example, the real communications center is often not the captain's office but the kitchen or galley, and navy cooks are usually better sources of news than commanding officers. This is how the term "scuttlebutt" came to have its current meaning.

The informal organization may spawn a network of relationships for which the organization chart and the manual of procedure provide few clues. All employees in the office may hold the same grade, but Jones, the oldest, gets the seat nearest the window, while Smith, the youngest, fetches the coffee for the 10:30 A.M. break. All the employees are assigned the same work, but since Black does better at processing form A while Brown performs better in processing form B, the A forms end up on Black's desk and the B forms on Brown's.

A case study frequently used in public administration courses offers a vivid example of how completely the informal organization can diverge from the formal one. Entitled *The National Labor Relations Board*, or *NLRB Examiner*, it deals with a series of events that occurred in the Los Angeles office of the NLRB during the mid-1930s, when the NLRB was in the early stages of its existence. The head of the office seemed highly partial to employers and to the union organization that was closest to them, the former American Federation of Labor (AFL). The examiners themselves tended to favor the more militant Congress of Industrial Organizations (CIO) and became incensed over what they regarded as their boss's favoritism. So they formed an informal organization of their own, hiding reports and information from the head of the office, leaking material, and otherwise providing aid to the CIO unions while seeking to establish their own connections to headquarters in Washington. Anyone looking at the office's organizational chart and examining its formal rules and procedures would have gained a wholly erroneous idea of just how the NLRB's Los Angeles office was operating in those hectic days.[23]

One of the most extreme examples of how the informal organization can overwhelm the formal organization is the U.S. prison system. Ostensibly, prisons are run by wardens and correction officers according to prescribed rules and regulations. In practice, this has rarely been the case. Sociologists and criminologists who have studied prisons have found out that most prisons have traditionally been run by the prisoners themselves. This does not mean that prisons are democratic institutions; they are indeed far from it. Rather, the supervisory personnel, faced with the enormous difficulties involved in everyday prison operation, eventually surrender basic control to what are often the toughest inmates in the institution.[24]

There is much brutality and ugliness in the typical prison, but those who have studied prisons feel that more often it results from too little, rather than too much, application of official authority. There are some exceptions to this, particularly at smaller institutions, and it should be said that in recent years prison officials generally have been asserting more control over penal facilities, but prisons have traditionally produced a whole subculture of beatings, homosexual gang rapes, and other grim and gruesome rituals, while the prison officials avert their eyes and try to get through the day with a minimum of trouble.

Of course, in most cases, the informal organization does not loom quite so large on the administrative scene, and its role should not be overstressed. It normally colors the formal organization but does not radically alter it. No matter how expert and experienced a sergeant may be, and no matter how naive and nervous the lieutenant may be, it is the lieutenant and not the sergeant who bears the final responsibility for the platoon. There is ultimately a limit as to how much authority the sergeant can acquire and how much the lieutenant may abdicate. Nevertheless, informal elements influence the operation of nearly all organizations, and the administrator must be alert as to what they are and what they do.

There are two aspects of informal organization that merit some special attention. One concerns the role of *informal rules;* the other concerns the role of *small groups.*

WHOSE RULES?

Nearly all organizations seek to prescribe a set of rules and have their members follow them. What they seek they do not always find. If we take the entire country as an organization, we find that from 1919 to 1933 it prohibited the sale of liquor without seriously suppressing drinking. Today, the laws of many states regarding gambling, marijuana, and prostitution are flouted with almost equal impunity.

Employees of organizations, like citizens of nations, tend to obey only those rules they believe in. As sociologist, Alvin Gouldner, has pointed out, workers will accept a rule only if they regard it as legitimate in terms of their values. They will not accept it just because those who issued it had a legal right to do so.

Employees have also become quite adept at evading rules or bending them to suit their needs and desires, and the more rules the organization tends to set down, the more dexterity its members may show. "Any complex maze of rules," write Katz and Kahn, "will be utilized by the guardhouse lawyers in the system to their own advantage."[25] In this fashion the employees may use rules they dislike to defeat, rather than to serve the organization's purposes. Employees do this in some cases by simply enforcing the organization's rules to the letter, thereby creating all kinds of pandemonium. Traffic police have driven their departments to despair by merely giving out a ticket to every motorist who deserved one, flooding the police department with a sharply increased workload and a sharply increased number of complaints from the community's more substantial citizens. In 1970, French customs inspectors, irate over the failure of the government to meet their demands, staged a "strike" by simply inspecting thoroughly every piece of baggage that visitors brought into France. In doing so, they virtually paralyzed operations at France's international airports and generally disrupted travel in Europe.

The informal organization not only achieves frequent and sometimes spectacular success in sabotaging the formal organization's rules, but it also manages to establish and enforce rules of its own. Many of these rules concern work output. Those who exceed the informal quota may be branded as "ratebusters," while those who fail to carry their fair share of the load may earn the title of "chiseler." Seniority is another rule that governs many procedures of many informal organizations. Those with job seniority get the better assignments and the more congenial conditions. The most junior members may not only get the short end of the stick but may also experience various kinds of petty harassments, like being sent to fetch the "left-handed monkey wrench." Sometimes the harassment is not so petty. College fraternities' hazing rituals at one time resulted in frequent injury and occasional death to their initiates.

Probably no informal rule is more widespread than the ban on "squealing." This prohibition is instilled in most Americans during their school years and tends to stay with them through the rest of their lives. The taboo against "tattling" is so widely and deeply ingrained that even those who would stand to benefit from it tend to dislike it. The "informer" or "spotter," no matter how useful he or she may be, rarely wins esteem in the eyes of management, and though the informer may increase his or her earnings, "squealing" seldom enhances chances for promotion.

While the formal organization often encounters difficulty in enforcing its rules, the informal organization usually succeeds quite well in securing support and adherence to its own codes of behavior. Sanctions against offenders can take many forms, not excluding violence. Prisoners who depart from the informal rules can meet injury and even death at the hands of their fellow inmates, and when a New York City policeman named Frank Serpico decided to inform on corruption within the police force, he received several death threats from some of his irate colleagues.[26] The sanction most frequently invoked is the "silent treatment." The erring member is cut off from all social intercourse and all unnecessary conversation. When West Point cadet, James J. Pelosi, refused to resign from the Academy on being accused by his fellow cadets of cheating, he was forced to room alone and to eat alone at a ten-man table in the cadet mess hall. Protesting his innocence, Pelosi stuck out the "silence" until he graduated 18 months later.[27] He was the only cadet in the Academy's history ever to survive such a protracted ordeal. (The next year the cadets abolished the practice.)

Many informal rules, it should be noted, are quite benign. Alvin Gouldner indicates that while the golden rule remains an unattainable goal, it has become a nearly universal governing principle and, as such, governs a good deal of organization behavior. If people do not naturally love their neighbors as themselves, they do tend to help others who have helped them or at least try to refrain from injuring them. Gouldner claims that this norm is as ubiquitous and as important as the incest taboo in modern society.[28] As such, it counteracts the harshness that other rules, both formal and informal, may produce in organizational operations.

THE SMALL GROUP

The basic unit for the formal organization may be the division, the department, the section, or all three, plus others as well. The primary basis for the informal organization is generally the small group. Although many informal norms and rules are organization wide, many others are promulgated and enforced by small work groups. The small group consists of no set number of individuals. Rather, it designates any group whose members are in continual, face-to-face contact with each other. Such groups often follow the structural lines of the formal organization. The small group in the army infantry is typically the squad. In the university it is usually the department. Whether or not it conforms to any formally recognized structure, forces from within customarily dictate a good deal of its behavior.

The importance of the small group springs chiefly from the importance of *primary* relationships over *secondary* relationships in human behavior. Those we work with every day on a person-to-person basis invariably become more important to us than those whom we see infrequently or with whom we conduct relations at a distance. Out of such primary relationships come norms, codes, procedures, and the means for their enforcement. The famed "silent treatment" is most powerfully exercised on those with whom we are in daily contact.

An interesting example of how the small group develops and enforces its own rules is found in Peter Blau's *The Dynamics of Bureaucracy*. Blau reports on an office of a federal agency that had certain law-enforcement powers over business. Many times businessmen caught violating the law by agents would make implicit if not explicit offers of a bribe. The agents uniformly rejected such offers, for it was not only against organizational policy but against their own code to accept them. However, the agents had also learned to make use of these suborning attempts to prod the businessmen, making them settle the case on the agents' own terms. "Being offered a bribe constituted a special tactical advantage for an agent," writes Blau. "An employer who had violated one law was caught in the act of compounding his guilt by violating another one. Agents exploited this situation to strengthen their positions in negotiations."[29]

In refusing to accept bribe offers, the agents were abiding by the organization rules. These rules also called for agents to report such attempted bribes to their superiors however. Here the agents departed from the formal rules, for to them reporting bribe offers constituted "squealing" and "squealing" constituted a cardinal sin. Blau could find only two cases in the recollection of all the current agents when one of their number had reported the offer of a bribe. The agent in one case had left the office. In the second, the agent concerned remained at work but was still undergoing the punishment of ostracism. This agent stoutly maintained his "innocence," claiming he had turned in the businessman only after the latter had pressed his bribe offer vigorously and in the presence of other parties. The agent's protestations were to no avail. None of his colleages would have any dealings with him that were not absolutely necessary for the conduct of office affairs. Such are the workings of small groups and informal organizations.

THE INFORMAL BALANCE SHEET

The informal organization and the small groups that make it up can obviously do a great deal of damage. They may, and often do, subvert the very purposes of the organization, because they show a persistent tendency to do what is most congenial to their members and reject organizational endeavors that may conflict with their own basic goals. The British sociologist, Michael Banton, in his study of a U.S. police organization, was told that "first the front office decides and then the locker room decides."[30] He was left with the distinct impression that it was the locker room's decision that counted.

The informal organization can not only make things difficult for the formal organization, but it can also make things hard for its own members. Not only are the ratebusters or the chiselers usually punished, but sanctions may also be invoked against the member who dresses differently, who espouses radical views, or who in any way speaks or acts in a manner that marks him or her as "different."

Sometimes the informal organization acts in an entirely opposite way, but this can prove even more counterproductive to organizational goals. It may cover up for one or more of its members who fail to do what is expected. The alcoholic who arrives back from lunch in a stupefied state may be allowed to sleep it off in an unobtrusive place while the rest of the group tell the supervisor that he or she is gone on an official errand. Such practices harm not only the organization but also the individual, because it permits him or her to avoid confronting his or her problem and trying to resolve it.

The sense of team loyalty, which the informal organization fosters, can generate a variety of evils. The U.S. Senate Watergate hearings in 1973 provided numerous examples of this. When queried as to why he did not speak up at meetings where "dirty tricks" were planned, Herbert Porter, the youthful scheduling director for President Nixon's re-election committee replied, "I was not one to stand up in a meeting and say this should be stopped. I kind of drifted along." Pressed further as to why he remained silent, Porter added, "In all honesty, probably because of the fear of group pressure that would ensue, of not being a team player."[31]

The informal organization also has a positive role to play, and organizational theorists are coming more and more to accept and avow this fact. Note the following quotations:[32]

> *The incompleteness of the formal plan provides a vacuum which like other vacuums, proves abhorrent to nature. (Simon, Smithburg, and Thompson)*
>
> *No organization chart and no book of policies and procedures can specify every act and prescribe for every contingency encountered in a complex organization. To attempt such specification merely produces an array of instructions so ponderous that they are ignored for the sake of transacting the business of the organization. Moreover, even if such specifications could be provided, they would soon be out of date. . . . (Katz and Kahn)*
>
> *It would not, in any sense, be an exaggeration to assert that any large organization would come to a grinding halt within a month if all its members began behaving strictly in accordance with the structure of responsibility and authority defined by the formal organization chart, the position description, and formal controls. (McGregor)*
>
> *Reduced to its formal power, to the theoretical pact which constitutes it, every organization, every human enterprise is incapable of adapting itself to its environment. (Michael Crozier)*

What these writers are saying is obvious: *The formal organization cannot exist without its informal counterpart.* All organizational design is inevitably incomplete and imperfect, for there is simply too much complexity and variability in the interaction of human beings ever to be compressed into a formal system. As employees come and go, as new technologies develop and new problems arise, the formal plans and procedures, no matter how well designed originally, become increasingly outmoded. Periodic revamping can help but can never hope to keep pace with the rate and sweep of the changes taking place that affect organizational operations. Consequently, the all-important facts of organizational life frequently become the unofficial rules and procedures.

If Ms. Green tends to wield the authority that belongs to Ms. White, then more often than not, Green possesses some competence that White lacks. If the seasoned sergeant exercises more authority than does the neophyte

lieutenant, then undoubtedly many a soldier's life has been saved because
of it. As a matter of fact, young ROTC lieutenants used to be told, "Be good
to your sergeant lest he carry out every order you give." And if small groups
tend to call the shots as they see them, then often they see them much
better than does top management.

This brings us to the question of how the informal organization affects
organizational productivity. We have already noted several ways in which
it can sabotage and subvert organizational goals. However it can also do
the reverse. Elton Mayo and his colleagues found in their Western Electric
studies that informal, work-group norms could affect productivity in a positive way. More recently, Katz and Kahn have stated that the correlation
between the informal group norms and productivity is likely to go in the
way the organization would like to go.[33]

The small group plays an important role in the positive informal organization. Research indicates that the larger the size of the work unit, the
greater the rate of absenteeism and accidents. Small groups meet social and
emotional needs, and whether or not they are the "highest" needs, such
needs remain important for organizational purposes. In another of his
books, *Bureaucracy in Modern Society*, Peter Blau writes that "the effective
enforcement of unofficial standards of conduct in cohesive work groups
has important implications for official operations. "Many studies," he adds,
"have found that the existence of cohesive bonds between co-workers is a
prerequisite for high morale and optimum performance of duty. . . ."[34]

This does not mean that the organization should remain oblivious to the
harm that small groups can do, not only to the organization but also to
their own members. By facilitating and even fostering rotation, organizations can alleviate many of these problems. Promoting organization-wide
activities and stimulating employees to take training outside their subunit,
even outside the organization itself, are other devices that may help prevent small groups from becoming too ingrown and hence too injurious to
all concerned. In general, administrators have shown an increasing disposition to accept the small group and to work with it. To quote Katz and
Kahn:

> *The effective supervisor . . . regards the value of the group to each individual
> as a potential asset rather than as a bureaucratic irrelevancy or a threat to
> authority. As a result, he or she devotes a good deal of effort to creating a
> cohesive work group, a group in which each member finds the fact of mem-
> bership rewarding.*[35]

The ultimate aim is to make the formal and the informal organization
converge. Can this be achieved? According to Chris Argyris, informal organization results from the desires of organization members to satisfy various needs that the formal organization neglects or even thwarts. He reports

---

FOREIGN LANGUAGE STUDY

Some employees of the Food and Drug Administration once decided to compile a dictionary to help people learn "bureaucratese." Here are some sample definitions from the new dictionary:

Infrastructure—(a) the structure within an infra; (b) the structure outside an infra; (c) a building with built-in infras.

Meaningful—(a) opposite of meaningless; (b) the same as full of meaning; (c) when used as "meaningful relationship," it is what used to be called being in love (archaic).

In depth—(a) opposite of shallow; (b) opposite of out of depth; (c) should always be used before words such as study, research, analysis, and review so that readers will think that you didn't do a quick and dirty job . . .

---

on studies he has done of two departments of a business corporation. One department did not attempt to meet such needs, and consequently its members developed informal ways of satisfying them. The other department made ample provision to meet these needs, through job security, personal recognition, variety, and challenge in work assignment. As a result, says Argyris, morale was high, personal relationships were warm, and the need for informal organization was hardly felt.[36]

UP, DOWN, AND ACROSS

Information moves in three basic directions: *upward* from subordinate to superior, *downward* from superior to subordinate, and *horizontally* from one organizational unit to another. No matter which way it flows, however, it runs into problems.

According to Katz and Kahn, communication up the line may occur in many forms, but such information may be reduced to what the person says:

1. about himself, his performance, and his problems;
2. about others and their problems;
3. about organizational practices and policies; and
4. about what needs to be done and how it can be done.[37]

Because the first role requirement of executives and supervisors is to direct, coordinate, and control the activities of persons below them, the basic problematic of upward communication is the nature of the hierarchical administrative structure. Therefore, employees fear that information passed along the hierarchical chain of command may be utilized for control purposes. The employees are unlikely to pass along information that may affect them adversely. This concern makes the upward route the most difficult.

As information winds its way up the organizational ladder, it becomes increasingly stale. Just how severe the problem becomes is a question of the particular situation involved. It may take a fire fighter inside a blazing building only a few minutes to convey information to the immediate superior, but in that few minutes the information may have become tragically outdated. Most matters, fortunately, are not quite so urgent; even so, the information needed to act on them may come too late. The situation may have already changed or at least developed nuances that make the information less satisfactory as a basis for action. This problem affects all communication flow, no matter what its direction. Communicating consumes time, and nearly all delays involve some disadvantage. Of course, delays often turn out to be helpful to an organization in that they permit a reappraisal of the situation or the introduction of new elements into the decision. If it is a question of communicating a specific piece of valid information, then under normal circumstances the quicker it reaches its destination, the more effective it is.

A much greater problem with upward-moving information is the fact that it tends to change as it advances. Although this is a problem for the flow of all communication, it is especially prevalent in upward communication. If Mary relates a message to Ed, and Ed, in turn, relates it to Ralph, then the information that Ralph has received is likely to be a little bit different from the message that Ed received. When Ed is Mary's superior and when Ralph is Ed's superior, however, special factors often magnify the problem.

Consciously or unconsciously, subordinates frequently distort information as they pass it to those above them. They may do this for a variety of reasons. First, and probably foremost, is their simple reluctance to serve as bearers of ill tidings. All too often the bearer of ill tidings becomes identified as the producer of such tidings, and, as such, has incurred the wrath of the recipients. Even when the bearer has no such fears for his or her fate, he or she may still try to soften and shade unwelcome news out of a simple desire to protect the harassed superior from unpleasantness. As former New York City Mayor John Lindsay once wrote, "I think nothing is more dangerous to an executive than isolation from the people and reliance on advisors who, however competent, may tend to tell the executive what they think he wants to hear."[38]

Sometimes subordinates are merely trying to spare their superiors from simple fatigue. George E. Reedy who served for a while as President Lyndon Johnson's press secretary, tells of being called in by one of the President's most trusted assistants and finding him furious over the fact that two separate staff members had submitted memos offering contrary advice on a particular matter. Said the presidential aide indignantly, "That man is exhausted enough and has enough problems on his mind without assistants coming at him from every direction. I think I should send both memos back and tell them to get together before I allow anything to go in."[39]

Subordinates sometimes have more selfish reasons for withholding or manipulating information. They may fear that the action such information would produce would prove disadvantageous to their interests. Or, if others stand a chance of being adversely affected, they may be fearful of being cast in the role of the informer.

This particular problem in upward communication, it should be noted, reflects problems inherent in hierarchy itself. As the French writer, Albert Camus, once noted, "There is nothing in common, in effect, between a master and a slave. One cannot speak or communicate with a subjugated human being. In place of that natural and free dialogue by which we acknowledge our resemblance and consecrate our destiny, servitude causes to reign the most terrible of silences."[40] Of course, bureaucratic relationships are rarely those of a master and slave, but wherever hierarchy is introduced, it will tend to act in this fashion. Chester Barnard once noted that information received from a low-status person will often receive scant attention, while information received from a high-status person may set off a reaction well beyond what was ever intended.[41] Katz and Kahn point out that a superior is supposed to give orders and a subordinate is supposed to receive them. This means that upward communication goes against the organizational grain, for the subordinate is not used to telling things to the superior and the superior is not used to listening to things from the subordinate.[42]

History supplies numerous examples of leaders who succumbed to this weakness and suffered severe setbacks as a result. Among them were such presidents as Woodrow Wilson, Lyndon Johnson, and Richard Nixon. Dictators, however, seem particularly prone to such behavior. When the reign of the last Shah of Iran was rapidly crumbling, it became nearly a crime to mention any bad news in the Shah's presence. Reports of wide-spread unrest in the country were watered down to minor incidents so as not to incur his displeasure.[43]

The Vietnam War provides the administrative analyst with a virtual treasure trove of illustrations as to how the upward flow of communication can become distorted beyond recognition. Vietnamese peasants, being interviewed by U.S. officials in the field, would give the answers that they thought the Americans wanted to hear. The translators would usually touch up the answers still more before rendering them in English. When the information reached Saigon, its negative aspects would be pruned again. This process would continue right into the White House where the aides would cull those items that they thought Walt Rostow, who was Johnson's chief conduit, would most want to receive. Rostow, in turn, would package the information into as agreeable a form as possible and pass it on to the president.[44] Rostow performed a similar tailoring operation on information coming in from other sources as well. As a result, Lyndon Johnson, in some respects, knew less of what was going on in Vietnam than did the average American newspaper reader and television viewer.

Within the military itself, there were numerous instances where the upward flow of communication took an erratic and erroneous course. According to one writer, Morris J. Blackman, the ineffectiveness of the bombing of North Vietnam was consistently distorted, because those who were carrying out the missions did not want to tell the truth to those who ordered them. As Blackman puts it, "It would have taken a certain amount of courage for a colonel to tell a general that the air strike the general had ordered—and for whose success the colonel felt he would be held responsible—was a failure."[45]

Then there were the infamous massacres at My Lai and Song My. On March 27, 1970, the *New York Times* published a story under the headline, "Panel Finds Song My Data Diluted at Each Echelon." The news story recounted how the field investigators of the massacre estimated the number of innocent Vietnamese killed at 175 to 200. (This, in itself, represented a scaling down of other estimates, which had put the reported number of dead at closer to 400.) As the lower figures were forwarded "from echelon to echelon up the military chain of command, the reported number of Vietnamese killed became smaller and smaller," said the *Times*. "By the time these reports reached the headquarters of the American Division, where they stopped, the number of Vietnamese killed had been reduced to an estimate of 20 to 28."

UNPLUGGING THE UPWARD FLOW

Perhaps the most important step that an administrator can take in resolving or at least reducing these impediments to the upward passage of information lies in his or her own conduct. If he or she genuinely believes and acts on the belief that all information should move swiftly and surely upward, then the information is much more likely to do so. If he or she shows subordinates that the bad news should be told along with the good, and in as fresh and pure a form as possible, the subordinates will not only be more inclined to do so but will also be more likely to deal with their own subordinates in the same way.

In an organization of any size and complexity, however, this will not be enough. Fortunately, there are other ways and means of seeing to it that those above are kept adequately informed by those below.

ELECTRONIC ACCESS TO LOCAL GOVERNMENT INFORMATION

In Santa Monica, CA, municipal government installed a city-wide Public Electronic Network (PEN) of microcomputers and terminals to provide its residents with 24-hour access to local government information. PEN bridges the gap between citizens and the bureaucracy of local government by giving users access to city council meetings, community center events, bus line schedules, and other city information. Users can send electronic mail to officials, city departments, or to each other. City officials are dedicated to a 24-hour turnaround in response to questions or concerns. On-going discussions on topics such as crime or schools are read and commented upon.

Source: Michael Artonoff, "Communication: Fighting City Hall at 2400 Baud," *Personal Computing*, Vol. 13, No. 10 (October 1989), 170–74.

One such device is the *trade union*. Informing those on top of what is happening beneath them is one of the major contributions that unions can make to the administrative process. Many an executive who has been shielded by middle management from much of what is going on at the rank-and-file level finds the unions a valuable supplier of needed information. The executive need not worry that the union's representatives will omit any unpleasant news.

Other means for improving the upward information flow are formal devices for hearing *complaints*. These may include grievance committees, appeals boards, and various clientele service units. For example, a mayor who sets up little city halls throughout the city in order to receive and process complaints may find that these complaints will give some excellent clues as to where problems may exist in his or her administration.

Investigatory units can also prove helpful in this regard. Many large police departments have a special unit to investigate police officers. The heads of the "shoefly squad," as it is usually called, can often provide the police commissioner with information that he or she might not hear from other subordinates.

Sometimes executives make their own field inspections, talking directly with rank-and-file personnel. This does not always have to take the form of a formal inspection. When Jerome Kretchmer was Environmental Protection Commissioner of New York City, he made it his practice to leave home once a week at 6:00 A.M. in order to stop off at a car barn and talk to the sanitation workers as they were assembling for work. He would then listen to their complaints and suggestions, usually, of course, receiving more of the former than the latter.[46]

An executive can also disregard the chain of command on occasion and call someone several levels below for some direct conversation. An executive may also stipulate a period each week or month when the office door will be open to anyone within the organization who has a matter to discuss.

Suggestion boxes can also play a helpful role in getting information from the bottom to the top. Not only will the suggestions sometimes be useful in themselves but they may well illuminate problems that the manager may not know about. Surveys and polls of the organization's members and of its clients may also provide valuable information in addition to indications as to how the upward communications process is working.

There are, in short, many means available to ensure a relatively swift and smooth upward flow of communication. Any public manager who truly wants an undistorted picture of what is going on in the organization should experience no great trouble in obtaining it.

COMMUNICATING DOWNWARD

According to Katz and Kahn, communications down the line, from superior to subordinate, are of five varieties:

1. Specific task directives: job instructions.
2. Information designed to produce understanding of the task and its relationship to other organizational tasks: job rationale.
3. Information about organizational procedures and practices.
4. Feedback to the subordinate about his performance.
5. Information of an ideological character to inculcate a sense of mission: indoctrination of goals.[47]

While information may run downward a bit more smoothly than upward, it also encounters numerous obstacles and impediments. When it is oral, downward communication is subject to almost all the alterations that can creep in when it moves the other way. The captain tells the lieutenant to have the soldiers ready at 0800. The lieutenant, for protection, tells the sergeant to have them ready at 0700. And the sergeant, in a further manifestation of the same fear, makes sure the men are ready at 0600. As a result, the captain finds the soldiers sleepy and disgruntled when they are ordered into action.

When communication moves down in written form, it can also develop difficulties. It may be misinterpreted either because it is not complete or because the recipient is simply not willing to accept its message. The biggest problem, however, is probably the inability or the refusal of the recipient to absorb all the information that seems to be cascading downward. As we have already seen, memoranda senders encounter persistent problems in this respect.

Organizations have tried to get around this in many ways. In some organizations, important messages are sent to the recipient's home, occasionally by special messenger, as an insurance that he or she will read it. And at least one school system makes a practice of following up the written messages that it distributes to its teachers in the school by broadcasting the same message through a loudspeaker.

There are other and usually better ways of surmounting this communication difficulty. People will often read material on bulletin boards that they might ignore if placed in their agency mail slots. This is particularly true if the bulletin board also carries other information besides that which emanates from the "front office." Consequently, a notice placed on a bulletin board can score a greater impact than if it were sent individually to each organization member.

Another useful device is the organization publication or house organ. Such publications usually depend for their appeal on the reporting of a wide range of personal items within the organization. The adroit administrator will also seek to sandwich in useful information regarding announcements, company policy, et cetera. Some private organizations have begun using in-house TV. They broadcast interviews with employees, both managerial and nonmanagerial, along with news of what the company is doing. Some also televise the company's annual stockholders' meeting.

Whatever the means used, the wise public manager will develop techniques for making sure that the information he or she has sent has truly gotten through to those for whom it is intended, and the manager will check for feedback as to how employees have responded. Not infrequently, the way in which a decision has been communicated will have a greater effect on agency operations than the substance of the decision itself.

CROSS-COMMUNICATION

A generation or so ago, lateral or horizontal communication received relatively little attention from administrative thinkers. Now it is becoming as important, and in some cases more important, than communication up and down. The growth of specialization and interdependency is making it increasingly vital for information to flow through the organization as well as to move up and down its ranks.

According to Katz and Kahn, communication among peers, in addition to providing task coordination, also furnishes emotional and social support to the individual. The mutual understanding of colleagues is one reason for the power of the peer group. Psychological forces always push people toward communication with peers; people in the same boat share the same problems. On the other hand if there are no problems of task coordination left to a group of peers, the content of their communication can take forms that are irrelevant to or destructive of organization functioning.[48] The communication channels will become dysfunctional if line officials in the organizational hierarchy are charged with initiating all communications. The agency soft-ball team or annual picnic, for examples, should be informal arrangements where someone other than the line officials communicate their directions.

Staff meetings can be particularly helpful in stimulating cross-communication. This assumes of course, that they are genuine interchanges of ideas and data and not just monologues by the person who presides. Within a broader context, interdepartmental committees may also aid the lateral communications process. And house organs, bulletin boards, and many of the other devices already cited can, and usually do, aid in spreading information from one section of the organization to another.

Physical arrangements can also play an important role in either helping or hampering cross-communication. Organizational units put in one building will tend to communicate more than when they are housed separately. Spreading units along the same corridor will usually encourage more communication than placing them on separate floors. And removing partitions that divide offices and work places from one another may greatly assist the cross-communication flow.

Organizational practices designed to resolve other problems may foster cross-communication as well. In-service training, for example, may bring people from various parts of the organization together and result in a good deal of cross-communication taking place. Organization-wide activities, such as bowling teams or hobby clubs, and an organizationally run cafeteria or dining room will also bring employees together and may lead to an interchange of information. Many of the tough problems that arise on Israeli kibbutzes, for example, are solved over the dining room tables in the evening.

Rotation of employees is also useful in improving cross-communication. The rotated employee can give new co-workers a better understanding of how things operate "over there." More importantly, former relationships can be used to maintain some communication flow with his or her former work unit. In any case, the rotated employee is likely to meet ex-colleagues from time to time and fill them in on what is happening at the new assignment.

As the technological society advances, and as organizations become more complex, cross-communication will become increasingly important. It is a subject that administrators will have to devote much more attention to in the future than they have in the past.

Summary

- Administrators and administrative theorists place increasing emphasis on communication.
- Communication problems arise not just from information that is too slow, incomplete, or distorted, but also from information that is simply too abundant. This is a problem of *communication overload.*
- Communication falls into two basic categories—*formal* and *informal.* Formal communication is written. Informal communication is oral. Formal communication fosters accountability, while informal communication does not produce mounds of paperwork.
- Formal communication restrains arbitrariness, capriciousness, favoritism, and discrimination.
- Organizational size and public character are factors affecting the use of formal communication.
- Among the symptoms of organizational pathology is the generation of a profusion of paper—a set of documentation.
- The paper trail includes the regulatory department or agency, the office of Management and Budget (OMB), public notice and comment, and codification of the rule in first the *Federal Register* and finally the *Code of Federal Regulations.*
- The informal communications system is often referred to as the "grapevine."
- Upward communication focuses on the employee, his or her performance, and problems; others and their problems; organizational practices and policies; and what needs to be done and how it can be done.
- Information moves in three basic directions: *upward* from subordinate to superior, *downward* from superior to subordinate, and *horizontally* from one organizational unit to another.
- Downward communication includes job instructions, job rationale, information about organizational procedures and practices, feedback to the subordinate about his or her performance, and indoctrination of goals.
- The growth of specialization and interdependency is making it increasingly vital for information to flow through the organization as well as to move up and down its ranks.
- Informal organization is more important in determining worker cooperation than formal organization. In this "other organization," output is set by *social norms,* not individual abilities, and the *group* greatly influences the behavior of individual workers.
- Employees of organizations, like citizens of nations, tend to obey those rules they believe in. The importance of the small group focuses upon the centrality of primary relationships over secondary relationships in human behavior.

This chapter began with an example of Winston Churchill's communication style. The following case study offers more details on one of history's greatest communicators.[49]

CASE STUDY

Action This Day

Words always came easily to Winston Churchill. As a young man, he engaged in many daring exploits while serving as a lieutenant with the British forces in India and later in South Africa. It was not so much the exploits themselves, however, but his skill in writing about them that gained him the prominence that was to win him a seat in Parliament and launch his political career.

His bitter denunciations of Britain's appeasement policies during the 1930s acquired sharpness and thrust through the pungent language he so often employed. "These are the years when the locust has eaten" was one of the phrases he used to describe that sorry period. When he served as prime minister during the war that ensued, he managed to warm the hearts and rally the spirits of his countrymen with the stirring speeches he delivered in what he called "England's darkest hour."

Churchill's abilities as a communicator also characterized his administration, and they offer an interesting illustration of how a particular administrator sought to handle his many communication problems at a crucial time.

From the outset of his administration, Churchill placed a heavy emphasis on the written word. "Let it be very clearly understood," he informed his war cabinet, "that all directions emanating from me are made in writing, or should be immediately afterwards confirmed in writing, and that I do not accept any responsibility for matters relating to national defense on which I am alleged to have given decisions unless they are recorded in writing."

The message itself indicates one of the main reasons he adopted such a policy. War administration is crisis administration, and as such can lead to considerable confusion. Orders given in a hurry and quickly passed down can easily be misunderstood, with dire results. Other orders that are vital may go unheeded or become lost in the far-flung and fast-moving governmental machinery. Churchill wanted none of that, and since he had no problem in handling the written word, he used this facility to keep intermediaries at a minimum and to stay in direct touch with a vast number of people.

Through the timesaving device of formal communication Churchill was able to personally direct much of Britain's governmental activity. He retained for himself the cabinet post of minister of defense, and there is no indication that wearing two hats in the cabinet impeded Britain's effort in any way. Indeed, most accounts of Britain's history during this time indicate that the country was better off with the prime minister playing such a dual role.

His extended use of personal memoranda, all of which carried the imprint of his personal style and bore his signature or initials, also had an invigorating impact on the whole government. An official several ranks below him might find on his desk a message from the prime minister himself directing him to do such and such. In the words of Cabinet Secretary Lord Normanbrook, such messages often have a "startling effect."

There was yet another reason for Churchill's heavy reliance on written communication—discipline it imposed on him. He was less likely to get carried away by a whim if he made it a point never to give orders that were not confirmed in writing afterward.

Although the profuse stream of memoranda that issued from his office bore his distinct personal style, usually opening with the phrase "Pray tell me . . ." they were by no means literary extravaganzas. He could be remarkably concise, as when he once ordered the mass production of a controversial new weapon. His memo read, "Sticky bombs—make one million—WSC." As he once noted, "It is sheer laziness not compressing information in a reasonable space."

Churchill also insisted that subordinates follow the same policy in dealing with him. He spent little time in interviewing people; instead, they were to address him in writing. All such correspondence was put in a box, and he would work on it at the beginning or the end of the day or at odd moments through the day. When a crisis erupted, he never had to cancel a lot of personal appointments.

He demanded that those who addressed him adhere to the rules of brevity as closely as he did himself, and was particularly hard on the needless use of banalities and truisms. He once replied to an official's memo by pointing out to the hapless fellow that his memo had employed every cliché in the English language except the British men's room admonition, "Please adjust your dress before leaving."

None of this is meant to imply that Churchill disdained the use of the spoken word, rather that he reserved it for those times and occasions when it could be used most effectively. When Eisenhower was in London, Churchill made it a part of his regular schedule to lunch with him every Tuesday. As he said later, nothing but shop was ever discussed on these occasions. He encouraged spirited discussion in meetings, at least at the beginning of his administration, and urged anyone having a dissenting viewpoint to "Fight your corner." When one attendee once remarked, "I have tried to present my case fairly," Churchill growled at him, "That's a very dangerous thing to do."

Churchill made sure that he did not spend all his time talking to higherups. He kept his lines of communication continually open to those below. As Robin Maugham writes, "Throughout the war, Churchill was always more interested in talking to junior officers than to the top brass—partly from pure kindness, partly from his knowledge that it was from the men in the field that he could discover what was really going on." Maugham, who served as a lieutenant in the tank corps during the war, mentions how Churchill asked him after the fall of France if he and his fellows were ready to repel a German invasion. When Maugham replied that many of their tanks could not move for want of a spring in their trackpins, Churchill exploded in fury and immediately set the whole British government into action. By nightfall, the springs had been delivered and were in place.

Despite the personal manner in which he conducted his administration, Churchill did not neglect the use of that traditional British device, the committee. He would frequently set up one group to give him information on a subject and then establish another group to supply him with advice on what to do with the information. On a more informal level, he would often set up dinner parties or after-dinner gatherings with some of the best minds both within and without the government for stimulating, if sometimes rambling, conversation. This institution, which became known as the "Midnight Follies" because of Churchill's predilection for staying up into the wee hours of the morning, was the source of many of the ideas that marked his administration.

His communications style did present drawbacks, however. He would frequently try to handle too much and consequently many matters would go neglected. Things that did not interest him would tend to pile up, and the stack of paper in his box would rise remorselessly until his secretaries could cajole him into spending more time trying to whittle it down. His personality was such that it too easily dominated any meeting at which he presided, and toward the end of the war, when fatigue and possibly age were setting in, he showed himself less and less receptive to ideas from others within the coalition cabinet. The Labour Party ministers protested that his cabinet meetings were becoming monologues.

Although he continued to remain more open to advice on the scientific and technical level, even here he became somewhat more remote as war weariness set in and, perhaps, as he became too infatuated with his own way of doing things. He listened too exclusively to his own science adviser, F. A. Lindeman (later Lord Cherwell), and failed to consult other scientists. He ordered, on the basis of Lindeman's faulty statistics, the rather fruitless and possibly even counterproductive saturation bombing raids on Germany.

Churchill's communications policy reflected his leadership policy and both reflected the man himself. As such, the question becomes one of judging whether his communications style suited the role he had to play at the time and in the circumstances in which he had to play it. On balance, the judgment of history seems to be that it did.

Questions and Instructions

1. How are communication modes reflective of a leader's personal style? What did Prime Minister Churchill's communication style say about his approach to communicating effectively? Explain.
2. Why did Churchill place so much emphasis upon formal communication?
3. How and when did Churchill employ informal communication as Minister of Defense?
4. How did Churchill avoid communication overload?

5. Were Churchill's communications mostly downward, across, or upward? Explain.
6. How did Churchill handle downward communication?
7. Why did Churchill shy away from most modes of informal communication during his war administration?
8. Was Churchill a less humane person because of his penchant for formal, written communications? Explain.

ENDNOTES

1. Material for this section was largely drawn from *Action This Day: Working with Churchill, Memoirs of Lord Normanbrook and Others,* edited by Sir John Wheeler-Bennett (New York: St. Martin's Press, 1969). The quotation of Robin Maugham is from his *Escape from the Shadows* (New York: McGraw-Hill, 1973), 108–109.
2. Chester I. Barnard, *The Functions of the Executive* (Cambridge, MA: Harvard University Press, 1968), 89.
3. Herbert A. Simon, *Administrative Behavior* (New York: Free Press, 1957), 154.
4. Charles Redfield, *Communication in Management* (Chicago: University of Chicago Press, 1953), 7.
5. William L. Shirer, *The Collapse of the Third Republic* (New York: Simon & Schuster, 1969), see Chapters 27, 28, and 29.
6. Ludwig C. Moyzisch, *Operation Cicero* (New York: Coward-McCann, 1950).
7. Edward Crankshaw, editor, *Khruschev Remembers* (Boston: Little, Brown, 1970).
8. Joseph M. Jordan, *Theory Y: An Urgent Need* (unpublished paper, Department of Political Science, Northeastern University, 1972).
9. William J. Lederer and Don D. Jackson, *The Mirages of Marriage* (New York: W. W. Norton, 1968), see Chapter 42.
10. Harold Nicolson, *Peacemaking 1919* (New York: Harcourt, Brace, 1939).
11. James MacGregor Burns, *Roosevelt: Soldier of Freedom* (New York: Harcourt Brace Jovanovich, 1970).
12. *New York Times,* 20 February 1973.
13. Frederick V. Malek, "Executive in Washington," *Harvard Business Review* (September–October, 1972).
14. *Boston Record-American,* 19 November 1972.
15. *Newsweek,* 10 May 1971, 30.
16. *Public Administration Times,* 15 January 1981.
17. Harold Macmillan, *The Blast of War: 1939–1945* (New York: Harper & Row, 1968).
18. David Halberstam, *The Best and the Brightest* (New York: Random House, 1969), 432.
19. J. C. Masterman, *The Double Cross Game* (New York: Avon Books, 1972), 55.
20. *Detroit Free Press,* 28 September 1967.
21. *Time,* 18 June 1973, page 67.
22. F. J. Roethlisberger and William J. Dickson, *Management and Worker* (Cambridge, MA: Harvard University Press, 1946), 552.

23. William H. Riker, *The NLRB Examiner, Inter-University Case Program No. 15* (Indianapolis, IN: Bobbs-Merrill, 1951).

24. Vincent O'Leary and David Duffy, "Managerial Behavior and Correctional Policy," *Public Administration Review* (November–December, 1971).

25. Daniel Katz and Robert L. Kahn, *The Social Psychology of Organizations* (New York: John Wiley, 1966), 350.

26. Peter Maas, *Serpico* (New York: Viking Press, 1973).

27. *New York Times,* 7 June 1973.

28. Alvin W. Gouldner, *Patterns of Industrial Democracy* (Glencoe, IL: Free Press, 1954).

29. Peter Blau, *The Dynamics of Bureaucracy* (Chicago: University of Chicago Press, 1955), 152.

30. Michael Banton, *The Policeman in the Community* (London: Tavistock Publications, 1964), 117.

31. *Time,* 18 June 1973, 19.

32. Herbert A. Simon, Donald W. Smithburg, and Victor A. Thompson, *Public Administration* (New York: Alfred A. Knopf, 1950); and Katz and Kahn, *Social Psychology of Organizations* (1st edition, 1966). Douglas McGregor's statement is from his posthumously published book, *The Professional Manager* (New York: McGraw-Hill, 1967). The quote from Crozier is from *La Societé Bloqueé* (Paris: Editions du Seuil, 1970).

33. Katz and Kahn, *Social Psychology of Organizations* (1st edition, 1966), 379.

34. Peter M. Blau, *Bureauracy in Modern Society* (New York: Random House, 1956), 56.

35. Katz and Kahn, *Social Psychology of Organizations* (1st edition, 1966), 327.

36. Chris Argyris, *Personality and Organization* (New York: Harper & Row, 1957).

37. Katz and Kahn, *The Social Psychology of Organizations* (1st edition, 1966), 245.

38. John Lindsay, *The City* (New York: W. W. Norton, 1969), 89.

39. George E. Reedy, "What the White House Does to Presidents," *Boston Sunday Globe Magazine,* 4 April 1970.

40. Albert Camus, *L'homme Revolté* (Paris: Editions Gallimard, 1951), 340.

41. Chester I. Barnard, *Organization and Management* (Cambridge, MA: Harvard University Press, 1948), see Chapter 9, especially footnote on page 231.

42. Katz and Kahn, *The Social Psychology of Organizations* (1st edition, 1966), 245–246.

43. *Time,* 13 December 1979.

44. Townsend Hoopes, *The Limits of Intervention* (New York: David McKay, 1969), 218.

45. Morris J. Blackman, "The Stupidity of Intelligence," in *Inside the System,* edited by Charles Peters and Timothy J. Adams (New York: Praeger Publishers, 1970).

46. Fred Powledge, "Can Kretchmer Make a Clean Sweep?" *New York Times,* 22 March 1971.

47. Katz and Kahn, *The Social Psycholgy of Organizations* (1st edition, 1966), 239.

48. *Ibid.*

49. Material for this case was largely drawn from Sir John Wheeler-Bennett, ed., *Action This Day: Working with Churchill, Memoirs of Lord Normanbrook and Others,* (New York: St. Martin's Press, 1969).

9

☆ ☆ ☆

TAXING, BUDGETING, AND SPENDING

CHAPTER HIGHLIGHTS

THE FEDERAL BUDGET DEFICIT, TAXES, AND CHOICES
INTRODUCTION TO PUBLIC BUDGETING
CONTEXT OF AMERICAN BUDGETING
TRADITIONAL BUDGETING
BUDGET REFORM TECHNIQUES
DECREMENTALISM AND CUTBACK BUDGETING
CHANGES IN STATE BUDGETING SINCE 1970S

Many students of public administration shudder when the course turns to the subject of taxing, budgeting, and government spending. They regard the budget as a ponderous tome of dreary figures and the process of budgeting as a tedious and humdrum chore that lacks the human interaction that makes things like personnel and leadership so much more palatable. They could not be more wrong.

This chapter attempts to remove the shudders by outlining traditional and reformist approaches that administrators have taken to deal with budgets. With every new administration at every level of government, detailed approaches to budgeting will, of course, vary, but the topics discussed here provide a foundation on which future public administrators can build their budgeting skills. These skills are crucial, since revenues, budgets, and fiscal appropriations are at the hard core of most issues faced by an administrator.

THE FEDERAL BUDGET DEFICIT, TAXES, AND CHOICES

Each year's budget deficit, of course, is simply the difference between revenues and outlays in that year. Federal budget deficits are not new. By any measure, however, they are getting worse. The federal deficit and its gloomy prospects for the future were core issues of Ross Perot's 1992 Presidential campaign. The average deficit as a percent of the gross domestic product (GDP) has *doubled every 10 years* for the past 40 years. Deficits have to be financed, so they add to the debt. For the first 35 years after World War II, the public debt did not grow as fast as the economy. As a result, debt as a percent of GDP declined steadily until 1974.

The ever-larger deficits of the 1980s reversed this trend. More than $1.6 trillion has been added to the debt held by the public since 1980, but the total federal debt, including the amount held by Social Security and other trust funds, increased even more, by $2.3 trillion. As a result, total debt now stands at over $4 trillion and is projected to reach $5 trillion in 1995. During the 1950s, the federal deficit averaged less than 1 percent of GDP. By the 1970s, the average was 2.3 percent. Then in the 1980s it doubled to 4.1 percent. At 6.3 percent of GDP, the Congressional Budget Office's (CBO) projected fiscal year 1992 deficit of $368 billion exceeds these averages.

To understand what has happened to the budget over the years, it is necessary to focus on two major components of the budget. One is the *general fund*, which finances most of the general operations of government, primarily from unearmarked revenue sources such as the individual and corporate income tax. The second major component of the budget is the

TABLE 9-1 Tax Revenues, 1987

(per capita and as a percent of Gross Domestic Product)		
	per Capita in $US	As a % of GDP
United States	5,396	30.0
Japan	5,959	30.2
Australia	3,975	31.3
Canada	5,710	34.5
Italy	4,778	36.2
United Kingdom	4,451	37.5
Germany	6,880	37.6
Austria	6,550	42.3
France	7,099	44.8
Belgium	6,665	46.1
Netherlands	7,012	48.0
Norway	9,546	48.3
Denmark	10,257	52.0
Sweden	10,707	56.7

Sources: Louis Ferleger and Jay R. Mandle, "American's Hostility Toward Taxes," *Challenge*, Vol. 34, No. 4 (July/August 1991), 54; and *Statistical Abstract of the United States, 1991*. Table 1456.

trust funds, in which certain programs are financed from dedicated revenues. Social Security, financed by payroll taxes, dominates this component, along with Medicare and the Civil Service and Military Retirement Funds.

AMERICAN HOSTILITY TOWARD TAXES

The per capita tax level in the United States is not considered high. The people in the United States are not overtaxed. Taxation as a percentage of national income is lower in the United States than in any other major industrialized country (see Table 9-1). The opposition of taxes clearly cannot be traced to a heavy tax burden.

Citizens rebel against paying higher taxes because they believe that governments are inefficient, even wasteful in spending assessed revenues for their various operations.

A BUDGET OUT OF CONTROL

What is the federal deficit?

. . . estimated to reach a record $333.5 billion in 1992, the deficit is the gap between government spending and tax revenue and other government receipts.

Thirty years ago, the deficit stood at $7 billion, and over the next two decades it ebbed and flowed, never exceeding $74 billion. Once, in 1969, the budget showed a small surplus. In 1982, the year after Congress approved President Reagan's major tax cut plan, the deficit rocketed from $79 billion to $128 billion. The deficit has more than tripled throughout the Reagan-Bush era.

What is the federal debt?

. . . the accumulation of all past deficits. At the start of the Reagan administration, the accumulated debt was $709 billion. The accumulated federal debt at the end of this fiscal year will be approximately $4 trillion.

Budget officials have attributed rises in the deficit in recent decades to tax cuts, buildups in defense, the bailout of the savings and loan industry, and rapid growth in spending on federal retirement and medical care programs. As the economy worsened during the Bush administration, demand for entitlement programs such as Aid to Families With Dependent Children and Medicaid increased.

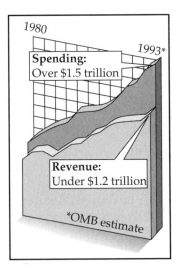

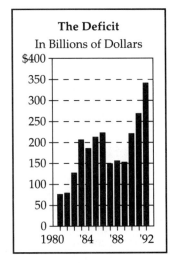

Source: *The Washington Post*, August 4, 1992, page A9.

Source: *The Washington Post*, August 4, 1992, page A9.

Economists believe that heavy government borrowing, coupled with low rates of private saving and growing worldwide demand for capital, divert funds from investment that would enhance U.S. productivity.

Economists and politicians also question the fairness of saddling future generations with massive debt.

How does the government tax and spend?

The federal government operates on a fiscal year that begins Oct. 1.

The president triggers the annual budget and taxing cycle in early February by submitting to Congress a budget request for every agency and program, accompanied with revenue projections and proposals for raising additional revenue.

The House and Senate then must approve nonbinding budget resolutions that set out priorities for spending and taxation.

Authorizing committees, with the power to renew or alter existing programs, conduct hearings and consider reauthorization legislation to extend expiring programs.

Frequently, their deliberations lag far behind the actions of the real powerhouses of spending, the House and Senate Appropriations committees, even though the authorizing committees should act first.

Of the roughly $1.4 trillion in the federal budget, two-thirds is automatically earmarked for mandatory spending programs, like Medicaid and Medicare, and net interest on the debt (see chart below). The remaining third is discretionary funds, which are carved up by the Appropriations committees.

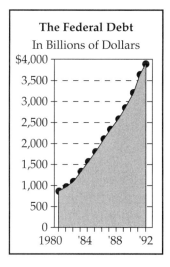

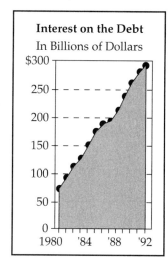

Source: *The Washington Post*, August 4, 1992, page A9.

Source: *The Washington Post*, August 4, 1992, page A9.

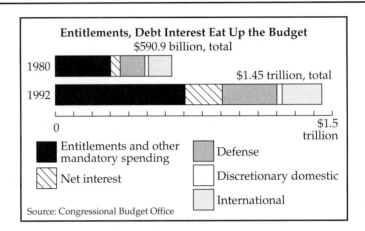

Entitlements, Debt Interest Eat Up the Budget
$590.9 billion, total

1980

$1.45 trillion, total

1992

0 $1.5
                                                  trillion

■ Entitlements and other   ▨ Defense
  mandatory spending

▨ Net interest   □ Discretionary domestic

                                ▨ International

Source: Congressional Budget Office

Source: *The Washington Post*, August 4, 1992, page A9.

Before appropriations bills are drafted, however, the chairmen of the House and Senate Appropriations committees each divide up the available funds among 13 subcommittees. The total available in discretionary funds is dictated by the five-year, 1990 budget agreement, which sets annual spending ceilings for domestic, defense, and foreign operations spending.

Beginning May 15, the House Appropriations subcommittees and full committee begin to mark up the 13 spending bills. Generally, as the House completes work on each one, the Senate Appropriations subcommittees begin their work, with bills sent on to the full committee and then the Senate floor for approval.

Differences between the House and Senate versions are resolved in conference and then a conference report is sent back to the House and Senate for final approval. Unless all 13 spending bills are approved and signed by the president by Oct. 1, Congress must adopt a stopgap spending measure, known as a continuing resolution.

In the event any bills push government spending above caps dictated by the budget agreement, the administration must order across-the-board spending cuts, or "sequestration," to close the gap.

The House Ways and Means Committee and the Senate Finance Committee are responsible for producing all tax legislation. Under the pay-as-you-go provisions of the budget agreement, spending increases must be offset by other spending decreases or tax increases. Moreover, any tax relief measure or increase in entitlement spending must be offset by a tax or revenue increase.

— **Eric Pianin**

Source: *The Washington Post* August 4, 1992, page A9

The huge increases in the debt have been reflected in the rapid growth of interest payments. Gross interest, including interest payments for funds borrowed from Social Security and other trust funds, increased by 222 percent from 1980 to 1989 and is the fastest growing expenditure in the budget. These huge deficits are draining the pool of the nation's savings, which is already historically low. Net savings in the United States have declined from about 9 percent in the 1960s and 1970s to 3.7 percent from 1980 to 1987. The U.S. savings rate is 40 percent of Germany's and only 20 percent of Japan's.

Continuing large federal deficits absorb savings otherwise available to finance investment, either public or private. Deficits have placed a disproportionate strain on federal investment activities. If deficits are not reduced, the government will have no fiscal flexibility to increase its investment in infrastructure, technology, and skills. In a very real sense, bringing the federal deficit down and changing the composition of federal spending represent a test of our ability to build a strong economic future for the generations that succeed us. The key question facing policymakers is not *whether* to undertake major deficit reduction, but *when* and *how*.[1]

The reluctance to save has ominous implications for economic growth. Investment is financed from two sources, *domestic savings* and *capital from abroad*. With the decline in domestic savings and with the budget deficit absorbing a large portion of the savings that remain, the United States has come to depend increasingly on foreign capital. During the past decade, the United States moved from a net creditor position to a net debtor position, transferring enormous wealth to foreign investors in the process. Investment financed overseas is better than none, but it results in foreign ownership of assets.

This means that future generations must pay for these investments in dividends and interest to the foreign owners. If allowed to go unchecked, this practice will seriously erode the nation's future standard of living. The ultimate consequences of the deficit are lower economic growth and a weak competitive position in the world. Without the domestic savings needed to support investment, growth is bound to suffer. The lesson is clear: those who grow are those who save.

There are three basic aspects to deficit reduction:

1. policy changes, that is, cuts in spending programs and increases in revenues from changes in the tax code;
2. interest savings due to the smaller debt; and
3. interest savings due to lower interest rates that should accompany a more restrictive fiscal policy.

A new fiscal policy is essential to the economic well-being of the United States. Not only must the federal government find the will and the way to confront the deficit crisis, it must also encourage savings that will promote economic growth, ease and eventually end United States dependence upon foreign capital, and provide the means to deal with future needs as they arise.[2] Large and persistent budget deficits undermine the future well-being of the country by consuming savings that would otherwise be available to finance investment supporting long-term growth.

Numerous studies, statistical indicators, and everyday observations all strongly suggest that the United States has not been saving and investing enough to achieve the related goals of assuring living standards and preserving a degree of influence in the world adequate for the protection of our basic interests. Long-term improvements in living standards and other aspects of economic strength depend on growth in productivity.

The reduction of the federal deficit is not, however, politically popular. In other words, there are few, if any, votes for politicians who propose cutting the deficit. There is little consensus if the deficit is, or is not, a major issue. Congress hates the budget deficit in general but accepts thousands of specific programs which the deficit finances. A sharp reduction of hundreds of billions of dollars in a fiscal year in government spending and corresponding increase in taxes would drive the economy into immediate recession, if not worse.

The "tax-and-spend" policies of the 1960s and 1970s resulted in the tax, spend, and borrow fiscal policies of the 1980s. The politics of the 1990s are framed around the phrase: "No New Taxes!" The demands for no new taxes, or revenues from citizen taxpayers, resulted in lower budgets at all levels of government. Taxes are what society is all about. We cannot have society without taxes. The core of governance is budgeting. Revenues for budgeting come from taxes. Changes in how budgetary decisions are made imply significant alterations in how government operates.

A review of partisan, policy, and systems politics in the 1980s is necessary in order to place events of these years in larger perspective. Ideas distinguish this nation from other nations around the globe. The United States is the original marketplace for new ideas. Franklin D. Roosevelt, John Kennedy, and Ronald Reagan were presidents driven by ideas. George Bush was the custodian of the presidency, not its innovator.[3] Reagan's economic achievements—cutting taxes, inflation, and interest rates from the Carter years—were, however, accomplished by "voodoo economics" of borrow and spend. The Republican Party's commitments to balanced federal budgets were sacrificed in favor of political pragmatism.

There was little political accountability with respect to the budget in the 1980s. Citizens demanded that Congress fund domestic entitlement programs. Certain federal government programs were reduced, abolished, or assumed by state and local governments. Other government programs were contracted out to the private sector. Presidents Reagan and Bush and Republicans in Congress sought increased defense spending in order to check the military expansion of the late Soviet Union. Conservatives from both political parties saw tax cuts as the way to generate economic growth. Until the early 1990s, the economy continued to grow despite enormous federal deficits and out-of-control domestic and defense spending.

The great American engine of debt and consumption kept the world economy humming during the 1980s.[4] The United States market became the world's designated consumer. From 1982 to 1987, Americans borrowed more than $500 billion from foreigners and spent dollars on imports, resulting in unprecedented trade deficits. As Bush was inaugurated, Americans began to consume less than we produce. The United States, no longer consuming and unable to borrow, is hindered by debt.

Persuasion is what political leadership is all about. After the 1980 election, United States Senate Republicans and President Reagan orchestrated a *political philosophy majority* but not a *political party majority*. The Democratic Party retained control of the United States House of Representatives in number only. Reagan's political philosophy majority, supported by conservative "boll weevil" southern Democrats, was built upon tax cuts. The economy rebounded in record proportions.

The political choices for President Bush in 1989 were either simple or easy. In order that Bush not pay politically for the "Reagan Revolution," citizen consumption needed to be reduced relative to what we produce, the United States needed to cut back on foreign borrowing, and Bush and the Democratic Congress needed to develop a political consensus for reducing annual federal deficits and accumulation of federal debt. Bush did not lead on these crucial issues. Bush hesitated, and worldwide market forces took over.

By comparison to Reagan, Bush did not create a *political philosophy majority* for cutting back on consumer consumption, foreign borrowing, and federal deficit spending and taxing. By not acting decisively early in his term, Bush ultimately paid the political price in the 1992 election.

The American philosophy of taxation is: "Don't tax me. Don't tax thee. Tax the fellow behind the tree." National tax policy illustrates the influence of organized interest groups in policy making. Tax laws permit about one-half of all personal income in the United States to escape taxation through various exemptions, deductions, and special treatments. The unfairness, complexity, and inefficiency of tax laws are directly traced to organized interest groups. Fairness, simplicity, and economic growth—all goals of tax reform—have, as yet, eluded the reformers.[5]

THE WORST TAX AND THE LEAST TAX FOR THE MONEY

The local property tax (25 percent) and the federal income tax (24.5 percent) are in a virtual dead heat as the least fair tax. The sales tax was rated least fair by 15.6 percent, the social security tax by 10.4 percent, and the state income tax by 9.1 percent. Asked from which level of government they get the least for their money, 49 percent of citizens said the federal government gave them the least, followed by 18 percent for local government, and 16 percent for the state.

Source: *Changing Public Attitudes on Governments and Taxes: 1992* (Washington, DC: United States Advisory Commission on Intergovernmental Relations, 1992).

As public spending of all kinds is brought under increasing scrutiny, partisans, policy makers, public administrators, and citizens have three choices:

First, elected officials can abolish local, state, and federal programs. Citizens and politicians must identify what government programs they wish to do without. As of 1992, there are 18,584,000 million government jobs filled by a like number of public administrators. Of that number, 60.4 percent, or 11,228,000 are local government jobs; 23.6 percent, or 4,381,000, are state government jobs; and 16 percent, or 2,975,00, are federal government jobs. As the 1992 elections came, no political consensus emerged on which government programs—and which jobs—to abolish.

Second, elected officials can increase local, state, and federal taxes to pay for programs demanded by citizen clients. Political consensus must be built from the bottom-up to determine what programs are to be retained. Political consensus grounded in the *decrementalism* of cutting back programs is much more difficult to establish than that of the *incrementalism* of adding more programs.

Finally, federal, state, and local legislatures can continue to spend more for government programs, tax less than what is required to pay for those programs, and commit still more of our public treasuries for financing ever increasing deficits.[6]

INTRODUCTION TO PUBLIC BUDGETING

Most, although certainly not all, of the issues and conflicts that spring from the administrative process take the form of contests over monetary allocations. If politics is sometimes defined as the process of deciding who gets what, administrative politics often becomes the process of deciding who gets what amount of money. Consequently, whether one department or individual is favored over another or whether one program or policy is supported over another usually translates into a budgetary decision. In this sense, budgets are political documents.

If budgets are essentially political documents, the politics involved is often thickly veiled. To the untrained eye, a budget often conceals much more than it reveals. Expertise in cloaking some of the political aspects of a budget has advanced more than one administrator's career, while skill in figuring out what was being done has boosted more than one politician's status.

It is not enough, however, to call attention to the political aspects of budgeting in order to define just what budgeting is. Budgets are also instruments of *coordination, control, and planning*. (See Table 9-2.) They govern nearly all aspects of administration and confer a great deal of power on those who prepare them. In New York City, the post of Budget Director is considered the most influential nonelective position in the city government. In Washington, President Nixon transformed the Bureau of the Budget into the Office of Management and Budget, thus giving the budget agency extensive formal power over the entire federal bureaucracy. In Great Britain and Canada, the Treasury Department, which makes up the budgets in these countries, has traditionally exercised many managerial functions as well. Indeed, the Prime Minister of Great Britain was long known as the First Lord of the Treasury.

A fledgling administrator will frequently find that a term of service in an organization's budgetary branch will furnish knowledge and insights obtainable from few of the organization's other units. If an administrator does start out in a line department or other staff unit, he or she will usually discover that budget preparation constitutes one of the unit's most important survival activities, sometimes overriding the unit's main focus of operation in care and concern. As long as resources continue to be relatively scarce, the budgetary process will continue to cast a long shadow over administrative activity.

CONTEXT OF AMERICAN BUDGETING

Budgeting practices in the U.S. today are the result of American ideology, federalism, and decision-making models. The political environment of budgeting is defined by our democratic ideology, which involves varying concepts of representative government. Democratic ideology is, in turn, defined by the idea of capitalism, a system that assumes that a growth-directed economy supports government's ability to appropriate sufficient funds for public services.

TABLE 9-2   History of the U.S. Government Budget. Total Receipts and
Outlays, 1789-1996 (In millions of dollars)

Year	Total		
	Receipts	Outlays	Surplus or deficit (−)
1789–1849	1,160	1,090	70
1850–1900	14,462	15,453	−991
1901	588	525	63
1902	562	485	77
1903	562	517	45
1904	541	584	−43
1905	544	567	−23
1906	595	570	25
1907	666	579	87
1908	602	659	−57
1909	604	694	−89
1910	676	694	−18
1911	702	691	11
1912	693	690	3
1913	714	715	−*
1914	725	726	−*
1915	683	746	−63
1916	761	713	48
1917	1,101	1,954	−853
1918	3,645	12,677	−9,032
1919	5,130	18,493	−13,363
1920	6,649	6,358	291
1921	5,571	5,062	509
1922	4,026	3,289	736

*$500 thousand or less.

TABLE 9-2   History of the U.S. Government Budget, continued

Year	Total		
	Receipts	Outlays	Surplus or deficit (−)
1923	3,853	3,140	713
1924	3,871	2,908	963
1925	3,641	2,924	717
1926	3,795	2,930	865
1927	4,013	2,857	1,155
1928	3,900	2,961	939
1929	3,862	3,127	734
1930	4,058	3,320	738
1931	3,116	3,577	−462
1932	1,924	4,659	−2,735
1933	1,997	4,598	−2,602
1934	2,955	6,541	−3,586
1935	3,609	6,412	−2,803
1936	3,923	8,228	−4,304
1937	5,387	7,580	−2,193
1938	6,751	6,840	−89
1939	6,295	9,141	−2,846
1940	6,548	9,468	−2,920
1941	8,712	13,653	−4,941
1942	14,634	35,137	−20,503
1943	24,001	78,555	−54,554
1944	43,747	91,304	−47,557
1945	45,159	92,712	−47,553
1946	39,296	55,232	−15,936
1947	38,514	34,496	4,018
1948	41,560	29,764	11,796
1949	39,415	38,835	580

TABLE 9–2 History of the U.S. Government Budget, continued

Year	Total Receipts	Total Outlays	Total Surplus or deficit (−)
1950	39,443	42,562	−3,119
1951	51,616	45,514	6,102
1952	66,167	67,686	−1,519
1953	69,608	76,101	−6,493
1954	69,701	70,855	−1,154
1955	65,451	68,444	−2,993
1956	74,587	70,640	3,947
1957	79,990	76,578	3,412
1958	79,636	82,405	−2,769
1959	79,249	92,098	−12,849
1960	92,492	92,191	301
1961	94,388	97,723	−3,335
1962	99,676	106,821	−7,146
1963	106,560	111,316	−4,756
1964	112,613	118,528	−5,915
1965	116,817	118,228	−1,411
1966	130,835	134,532	−3,698
1967	148,822	157,464	−8,643
1968	152,973	178,134	−25,161
1969	186,882	183,640	3,242
1970	192,807	195,649	−2,842
1971	187,139	210,172	−23,033
1972	207,309	230,681	−23,373
1973	230,799	245,707	−14,908
1974	263,224	269,359	−6,135
1975	279,090	332,332	−53,242
1976	298,060	371,779	−73,719
TQ	81,232	95,973	−14,741
1977	355,559	409,203	−53,644

TABLE 9–2   History of the U.S. Government Budget, continued

Year	Total		
	Receipts	Outlays	Surplus or deficit (−)
1978	399,561	458,729	−59,168
1979	463,302	503,464	−40,162
1980	517,112	590,920	−73,808
1981	599,272	678,249	−78,976
1982	617,766	745,755	−127,989
1983	600,562	808,380	−207,818
1984	666,457	851,846	−185,388
1985	734,057	946,391	−212,334
1986	769,091	990,336	−221,245
1987	854,143	1,003,911	−149,769
1988	980,954	1,064,140	−155,187
1989	990,691	1,143,172	−152,481
1990	1,031,308	1,252,691	−221,384
1991	1,054,264	1,323,785	−269,521
1992	1,091,631	1,381,791	−290,160
1993 Estimate	1,147,588	1,474,935	−327,347
1994 Estimate	1,230,300	1,522,700	−269,900
1995 Estimate	1,305,600	1,578,000	−229,600
1996 Estimate	1,378,500	1,644,800	−266,400
1997 Estimate	1,439,700	1,744,700	−305,000
1998 Estimate	1,523,400	1,843,200	−319,800

*$500 thousand or less.

Public sector monies are raised from taxes on *individuals* and *businesses*. It's tough to maintain viable public services if revenues supporting such activities are low or nonexistent. Whether we are providing national defense or unemployment compensation, we need a growth economy to finance such citizen benefits. From a capitalistic economy, we are therefore, able to afford programs that benefit all citizens equally. The appropriate mixture of capitalism and socialism affects the very size and scope of government and, of course, budgeting policies.

Deciding which level of government should provide a certain service is a matter of *federalism,* with its ever-changing division of power. The American system of federalism helps determine the scope, size, and nature of national, state, and local budget priorities. If state law conflicts with federal law, state law gives way. If local legislation conflicts with state or federal provisions, local ordinances are overruled. State boundaries, overlapping jurisdictions, economic decline of certain states and cities, and suburban growth patterns contribute to the dilemmas of budgeting in a federal system.

TRADITIONAL BUDGETING

As might be expected, traditional budgeting is a lengthy process. It usually begins with comparatively small subunits figuring out what they need or feel they need for the coming year. The subunits then submit these figures as requests to higher levels. At each stage, the figures are customarily reviewed and frequently cut back. Eventually, all the requests will converge in the organization's budgetary office or in the office of its chief executive, or both.

From the organization, the figures travel to the government's overall budgetary department, which in the federal bureaucracy is the Office of Management and Budget, or OMB. There they are once again reviewed and often reshaped. The tendency here, as at previous review stages, is to cut rather than expand requested amounts, so agency heads and the budgeting office officials often find themselves to be adversaries. The agency heads stoutly maintain that they need all the money they are requesting and even more, while the budget officials keep insisting the figures are overstated, exceed the organization's ability to pay, and inflate the role the agency plays.

The *traditional budgetary process* revolves around making sense of the federal budget the old-fashioned way—incrementally, or bit by bit. One point of view is the idea that incrementalism represents stability in budgeting practices. Recent changes, such as resorting to top-down rather than bottom-up budgeting, however, question the value of incrementalism as a method for explaining how resources are allocated.

Among the factors traditional budgeting focuses on are inflation indexes, funding for entitlements, single-year allocations, continuing resolutions, baseline reviews for enhancing the status quo of ongoing programs, and incremental or decremental multiyear budget displays. Perhaps the *continuing resolution,* or the authority Congressional grants to agencies to continue obligating funds in the absence of an annual appropriations legislation best illustrates budgetary decision making by incremental procedures.[7]

Cost profiles over time are not developed in traditional budgeting. The single-year cost constitutes merely a down payment for a project requiring numerous allocations. The focus in traditional budgeting is also upon agency inputs (what agencies buy) instead of outputs (what agencies provide), and the value of programs delivered is seldom reported or formally presented. In a nutshell, traditional budgeting is void of comparison between project cost and project benefits.

Nearly 75 percent of the federal budget is already committed by previous legislation to entitlements, or uncontrollables, such as Social Security, railroad retirement, federal employees' retirement and insurance, unemployment compensation, medical care, student assistance, interest on the public debt, and farm price supports. That is why decision makers have a hard time responding to changed priorities or to requirements for macroeconomic stabilization. Administrators, to a great degree, must stick with the traditional ways of doing the public's business.[8]

CAPITAL BUDGETS

Most of America's approximately 80,000 governments divide their budgets into two sections, one for *capital* projects, the other for *expenses*. Often they are considered as two separate budgets.

The rationale for segregating capital expenditures in a separate budget is the fact that such projects require a considerable expenditure that may occur only once in a generation or even once in several generations. Trying to cover the expenditure involved in one year would be troublesome and often impossible. A small community faced with building a new high school could bankrupt many of its citizens if it sought to pay for the project with one year's collection of taxes. Capital budgeting enables the community to break out of the one-year budget cycle and spread the cost over many years. Since such projects are usually financed from the sale of bonds that are to be paid over 20, 30, or even 40 years, placing such expenditures outside the annual expense budget makes a good deal of sense.

Another aspect of capital improvements also warrants spreading out their costs. Capital projects confer benefits for extended periods of time. (Modern-day Rome, for example, is still using some of the sewers built in the time of the Caesars.) Consequently, it is only equitable that those who will subsequently benefit from the expenditures shoulder part of the burden as well. A capital budget permits them to do so.

Because capital projects do not involve immediate expenditures—such projects usually do not get launched until a year or two after they are authorized—there is a tendency to utilize them in political ways. Some state legislatures have been known to pass bloated capital budgets as a way of appeasing their constituencies without imposing any new immediate tax burdens. Legislators can return to their districts boasting about how they have wangled a new highway, postal project, dam, or some other capital expenditure for their constituents while escaping the onus of having voted for new taxes. Of course, eventually new funds will be required to pay off the debts of the approved capital expenditure, but for the present, at least, the lawmakers are home free.

A more flagrant abuse of the capital budget occurs when political leaders cram into it items that properly belong in the expense budget. In doing so, they manage to avoid cutting expenditures or raising taxes. In taking such a step however, they are paying for current expenses with borrowed money—money that must eventually be paid back with interest. Such an expedient only defers and compounds the problem. New York City was using nearly a quarter of its capital budget to pay such operating expenses as policemen's salaries when it went broke in 1975. A few years later, Cleveland, also confronted with collapse, was starting to do the same.

If capital budgeting can lead to political abuses, its absence may produce even worse consequences. The federal government does not use capital budgets, and, in some respects, there seems to be no compelling reason why it should. Unlike states, municipalities, and other governments, federal agencies are rarely faced with one-shot expenditures that would completely disrupt their budget cycles. Federal agencies are so large that capital projects of one kind or another are a continual activity. Furthermore, the federal government, because it controls the money supply, is not compelled to float bonds to finance its projects.

Nevertheless, the hesitancy of the federal bureaucracy to use capital budgeting has drawn fire from many critics in recent years. They claim the lack of a capital budget has promulgated or aggravated an assortment of ills. Why not write a federal capital budget based on the state model? Well, for one reason, there is no state model, so the task of establishing a federal capital budget and ordering the standard version is not that simple. According to a survey by OMB, 42 states utilize a capital budget of one kind or another. These states do not, however, accomplish the same objectives with their capital budgets. None of the state capital budget approaches may be readily transferred to the federal government.

The main goal of a capital budget is to provide a clearer picture of the government's net worth at any given time. Estimating the value of equipment is one method the private sector uses to establish the value of capital. The value of equipment may decline over time; the capital budget will reflect aging of equipment. If a federal capital budget is called for, what elements belong in such an estimate? Do you depreciate a battleship in a capital budget? Does a capital budget cover for large federal deficits? Despite the drawbacks of the current system of federal budgeting, each year's deficit amount is roughly equal to that year's federal borrowing. The primary concern of economists is the government's demand for credit, not the government's net worth.[9]

The absence of a capital budget at the federal level means an absence of systematic review procedures to establish the economic desirability of capital projects. To put it more simply, capital projects are sometimes initiated haphazardly. Many accounting practices do not properly consider total and unit costs. Useful and accurate estimates of the cost savings that a capital expenditure might produce are hard to figure out without the structure of a capital budget.

Despite the fact that the federal government is constantly making capital expenditures, the refusal to segregate them in a separate account may, and often does, make a particular agency head, division chief, or branch manager reluctant to initiate such expenditures. Such outlays will simply loom too large in a current, all-in-one budget and so make the administrator look like a heavy spender. If those who review the budget approve a substantial capital project, they may cut back in other areas as partial compensation. Furthermore, in terms of a professional career, the administrator may not be around to take credit for the economies that such capital expenditures may eventually yield. As a result, an administrator will often feel inclined to let a successor set up the new computer system or purchase the new maintenance equipment.

Capital budgeting makes a good deal of sense for most state and local governments. In theory, a capital format might also prove useful for the federal government as well. It does, however, lend itself to certain manipulations and machinations that have proved costly to some states and municipalities. That is not to say that the expense budget is immune to the playing of political games, as we shall see.

EXPENSE BUDGETS

The basic document in traditional budgeting is the expense budget. This details the operational expenditures for the coming year. Like the capital budget, it is an array of items to be purchased and the prices to be paid. The items include everything from manpower to heat, electricity, and less tangible purchases. Nearly all the basic objects of expenditure are customarily set down clearly in page after page of neat rows.

Some attempt is usually made at categorizing the various objects of expenditure. There may be one account for wages and salaries of permanent personnel, a second for other personnel costs, a third for supplies and material, and a fourth for travel. Within each of these categories, there will most likely be subcategories. There may be, for example, one or more rows in the permanent personnel account listing the number of employees needed for each job classification and the total amount of expenditure these employees represent.

The expense budget is an itemized one. Different kinds of goods and services are classified. In order to expose and control graft and corruption at the turn of the century, reformers called for a uniform classification of accounts in which audits would occur to determine objectively if funds were used properly. All agencies adopted a line-item or expense budget so auditors could utilize the same criteria for evaluating expenditures of any governmental program. In public service programs where wages and related personnel expenditures account for more than half the agency's budget, administrators use the expense budget as a bottom line justification for continuing and enhancing programming.[10]

The traditional, line-item expense budget is often highly detailed. It frequently provides precise data on where every dollar is being spent. The basic problem of traditional, line-item budgets is that they fail to show what the money is being used for in terms of programs. The Public Works Department budget may specify the amount of machinery on hand and what will be needed to keep it in repair, as well as any new machines that may be purchased. The line-item budget may tell us how many employees will be used to operate the machinery and how much they will be paid. The budget may also indicate how many temporary employees may be hired and how much private equipment may be rented to cover specialized tasks or emergencies. It will never tell us just how many miles of streets all this expenditure is designed to tar or pave and whether tarring a street is cheaper than paving it, and, if so, how much cheaper.

Because of this lack of program information, the line-item budget lends itself to stagnation. Possessing little information as to the costs and effectiveness of its various activities, the organization tends to base its budget requests simply on what it has used in the past. Last year's appropriation becomes the basis for this year's requests. Outmoded programs are not phased out and new programs are not eagerly embraced. By failing to provide program information, line-item budgeting tends to perpetuate the status quo.

The status-quo reinforcing effect of traditional line-item budgeting—often referred to as *incremental budgeting* because it concerns itself with increments of change rather than program change—can influence whole governments. The term incremental does imply some change—but this is change that occurs in terms of spending more or less rather than in terms of spending money for different purposes and programs. Until recent efforts by OMB under David Stockman, these changes also tended to go in just one direction. Despite recent top-down budgeting pressures, incremental adjustments almost invariably take the form of more rather than less.

There are many reasons for this, some of them perfectly legitimate as far as administration is concerned. Population tends to grow, hence more public services are needed. Price levels have also shown a pronounced predilection for going up, particularly in the inflation that has characterized most societies since World War II. People seem to expect more and more from government. Increasing prosperity itself takes its toll. The more cars we have, the more highways, parking lots, traffic police, and maintenance are called for.

There are other factors inherent in the incremental budgeting process that tend to push expenditures to ever-higher reaches as well. For one thing, there is little inducement to the administrator to save money. If a parsimonious public manager cuts costs and comes up with a surplus at the end of the fiscal year, superiors and members of the legislative committee that approves the budget may decide that the manager did not need all that money in the first place. Instead of receiving a medal, the public manager will most likely be given a cut in appropriations the following year.

Matthew Dumont, a psychiatrist who once served in the Department of Health, Education, and Welfare, provides a rather pointed analogy to describe how ill-advised an agency head would be to return unspent money that Congress had appropriated for his agency. "It would be like a bum asking for a handout for a cup of coffee. A passerby offers a quarter and the bum returns 15 cents, saying, 'coffee is only a dime—.' "[11]

In the days when the federal fiscal year ended on June 30, Washington bureaucrats used to speak of the "spring spending spree." This term denoted the desperate haste with which federal agencies went about spending or committing whatever funds remained in their accounts as the fiscal year drew to a close. One chief of naval operations even dispatched telegrams to his commanders urging them to proceed full speed ahead in meeting their "outlay targets" for the current fiscal year in order to avoid "reluctant adverse effects" on next year's appropriations.

Changing the federal fiscal year from October 1 to September 30 only transformed the spring spending spree into a late summer one. Efforts to curb this practice by requiring all agencies to report their unexpended balances every three months proved unsuccessful. During one summer, for example, a conservation camp operated by the U.S. Fish and Wildlife Service purchased over 1,000 pairs of protective leg coverings and nearly 3,800 pairs of gloves for its 136 enrollees. As one budget watcher once remarked, "The political process abhors a surplus."

Incremental budgeting not only provides an administrator with few inducements to cut costs; it actually adds to the pressures to increase costs (i.e., to ask for money). Thomas J. Anton points out that an administrator must try to appease three audiences:

1. The administrator's own *employees*, who look to the administrator to preserve and, if possible, enhance their working conditions and their status. Such considerations can be met by increasing the organization's appropriation.

2. The agency's *clientele group*. The people from this group also desire increased funds for the agency, since they are usually the most direct beneficiaries of the agency's expenditures. These first two pressures for budgeting increases would probably exist under any form of budgeting.
3. Finally, there are the *review officials*, including superiors, budget bureau officials and legislators. All of these, but particularly the latter, have an interest in being able to cut the budget. In making cuts, they achieve a sense of fulfillment and importance.[12]

As top-down budgeting pressures mount, agency administrators, employees, clientele, hierarchical superiors, budget bureau officials, and legislators are confronted with making the best case possible for continued, and certainly new, funding.

All these factors translate into the process that characterizes budgeting throughout the U.S. political system. Agency heads inflate their appropriations request; review officials continually pare them down. The agency is then more often than not allowed some additional funding. With pressures to justify spending priorities, however, there is less wholesale inflation of budgetary requests unless accompanied by relevant supportive data. If the funding is granted, advocates inside and outside the agency have not simply made a good case, but the best one.

In the past, when incremental enhancement of the agency's funding base was taken for granted, many administrators became quite adroit in procuring increased allocations. They usually asked for money for one of their more popular activities, regardless of whether or not all or even part of the new funds would actually be targeted for that purpose. With cutback management now the name of the game and accountability measures in place, such a practice is taboo. In the past, administrators may have advocated a popular cause or concept and said they needed the money to do something more or something new in response to it. Or they may have asked to undertake a new activity and sought only limited funds to get started. This was known as the "foot in the door" approach. However, once launched, the new enterprise tended to cost more and more. In times of decrementalism, however, such practices are less likely to be effective.

In the late 1960s, the Department of Defense made frequent use of the "foot in the door" approach. DOD set down a low initial cost to get a program started, and Congress often granted the money without fully realizing what the final bill would be. Another related device employed by DOD focused on creation of shortages. The department would overextend its commitments and then urgently plead for more money. The army would set up a goal of so many divisions and then bemoan the fact that it lacked the funds to maintain them. "The worst thing you can do to a service," one observer once noted, "is to take away its shortages."

Similar stratagems are employed by other organizations as well. Colleges and universities are by no means exempt. As Katz and Kahn point out, an academic department may ask to teach new courses, claiming it can do so with existing personnel. It may be perfectly sincere, but as its work volume expands, it finds itself asking for additional funds. Under the auspices of cutback management however, the best case will continually have to be made for future appropriations. In the public education environment of the early 1990s, units may have to demonstrate several years of effective, successful implementation of a worthy program before senior administrators agree to fund the project.

The pressures and policies of incremental budgeting often converge to force the level of spending to ever-higher appropriations. In his study of budgeting in the state government of Illinois, Anton compares the budget document "to a huge mountain which is constantly being pushed higher and higher by geologic convulsions." He describes the governor as a blindfolded man "seeking to reduce the height of the mountain by dislodging pebbles with a teaspoon. . . ."[13]

Of course, elected officials are not completely powerless in this situation. Except for "earmarked" funds that are appropriated because of constitutional restrictions, prior commitments, and more pressing constituent demands, officials can wield the scalpel as deeply as they wish. In addition to various outside political pressures—such as the agency's clientele group—many other considerations may stay their hand, for budget cutting can be a hazardous game.

The problem is related once again to the lack of program direction and content in the traditional line-item budget. As a result, a budget cut can be translated into various forms. Sometimes such budgetary practices may end up actually increasing costs. A line-item budget will generally include categories for personnel, equipment, and maintenance, among others. An administrator confronted with a general slash in funds will often cut maintenance costs first and personnel costs last. The reasons are fairly obvious. In the short run, reductions in maintenance disrupt an agency's operation the least. Reductions in personnel are apt to disrupt operation the most, particularly when the morale of those remaining on the job is taken into account. Unfortunately, equipment and buildings not properly maintained eventually increase an agency's costs over what would otherwise be the case.

To be sure, administrators will sometimes respond to a budget cut by actually phasing out whole programs or dismissing personnel, but all too often this is done for the express purpose of generating pressure for their restoration. For example, when a new administration in one major U.S. city attempted, as part of a needed austerity program, to cut the budget of its main library, the library's director announced that he would be forced to close the library building two evenings a week and on Saturdays. As it so happens, Saturdays and evening hours were the most popular periods of library use. (During the morning hours, the library actually had more staff than readers on its premises.) The public outcry that ensued from the library director's announcement forced the mayor to temper this proposed cutback in funds. Administrators, however, should be warned not to bluff with drastic action; budget decision makers with more clout and an enhanced global perspective of the organization's tasks may take mid-level officials at their word and agree to drastic action.

As budget constraints beleaguered most U.S. cities in the 1980s, some of them responded by first making unnecessarily deep cuts in their police and fire departments. These, of course, are among the most essential of city services, and such cuts were apparently made with the hope of generating support for increased funding from an alarmed public. Even in the not-for-profit public sector, supply and demand, as a negotiating philosophy, has its advocates.

In addition to promoting static, but swollen administration, incremental budgeting has also been criticized for many other ills. Although its numerous detailed expenditures would seem to make it a likely candidate for public scrutiny, the reverse may be the case. Indeed, the more detailed the data on objects of expenditure are, the more they may obscure. Large, bulky documents filled with page after page containing row after row of expenditure items may reveal very little of what an agency is doing and how well it is doing it. Appropriations for any one activity may be scattered throughout the budget and be almost impossible to piece together.

Incremental budgeting has also been accused with some justification of making liars out of honest people. Requesting more money than one needs or expects simply to satisfy the rules of the game would scarcely seem a way to promote rationality and honesty in administration. As the system has proved more demanding for all concerned, however, empirical supportive data and accountability for priority spending are challenging administrators, employees, and clientele to be more productive, and, perhaps, more honest.

These complications have spurred efforts to find new and better ways of dealing with the budgetary process in modern administration. It is to some of these efforts that we will now turn.

BUDGET REFORM TECHNIQUES

As governments grew in size and complexity, dissatisfaction with traditional budgeting grew apace. Line-item budgets failed to show the impact of expenditures on programs, to show future costs and effects, and to show relationships between capital and operating costs. These problems came to rankle more and more of those who were dedicated to improving administrative performance. Surely, they reasoned, there must be a better way of budgeting than simply drawing up a list of expenditures every year, a list that, based as it is on last year's list, tends to change only in becoming more inflated. A better method of budgeting, one more conducive to change and evaluation, was needed.

By the early 1950s, the Hoover Commission proposed a new type of federal budget. It would be a budget "based upon functions, activities, and projects." Such a budget would be a "performance" budget; it would include, along with the mass of itemized spending, some additional information as to what all this expenditure was to provide in the way of public services. If the Public Works Department was to spend a sum of money for personnel, equipment, and the rest, how many miles of streets would be paved as a result? Early performance budgeters attempted to provide this information by adding a column in the traditional budget and setting down within it the actual work to be performed. Performance budgets became the catalyst for several budgetary reforms that have come and gone as the decades passed.

Reforms we will outline here are performance budgets, program budgets, and zero-base budgets.

PERFORMANCE BUDGETS

Performance budgets focus upon departmental objectives and accomplishments. They do not emphasize the purchase of resources utilized by the department. This technique dates to the mid-1910s in New York City and accounts for the cost of performing measured accomplishment units during the fiscal year. A performance budget includes sections on demand, workload, productivity, and effectiveness.

- The demand section lays out the expected operating environment for the fiscal year, including past and current comparisons.
- The workload section tells how the operating unit plans to meet that expected demand by allocating staff time.
- The productivity section presents the cost per activity.
- The effectiveness section shows criteria that indicate whether the unit is accomplishing its planned objectives.

Performance budgets, in practice, provide a powerful analytic tool for increasing management responsibility and accountability. They cause legislatures to change reviews and appropriations from traditional line-items to departmental activities. They also provide a more suitable environment for "management by objectives" programs.

The quality of a performance budget hinges on the credibility of its measures. Performance budgets do not establish if a task is worth doing, but rather consider whether the task is being accomplished at low cost.[14]

PROGRAM BUDGETS

In a program budget, the focus is on output. The concept rests not on what governments purchase, nor on the tasks in which government is involved, but upon the outputs of government, as nearly as may be defined. This technique delineates the goals of a department and categorizes tasks contributing to each goal. The focus is on product, not input.

A good example of a program budget is Planning Programming Budgeting Systems, or PPBS, initiated by the defense department in 1961. By effort and attention, PPBS has been the major budgetary phenomenon of modern times. It has also been a failure.

According to Samuel M. Greenhouse, PPBS calls for a "sharp-edged tool for defining priorities and evaluating accomplishment."[15] The concept of accountability is the lone philosophical basis for PPBS. Summarizing its overarching focus, Greenhouse describes the PPBS concept and how it is different from previous budgetary reforms: "The PPBS concept is that each Federal agency is accountable to the President (and Congress) for the production of goods and services, and more particularly, for the distribution of these goods and services to the American people."[16]

From the premise of accountability, each agency is charged with carrying out explicit market objectives—the emphasis is on adopting a program for pursuing agency objectives. A program, in this sense, includes summation of all agency efforts to meet objectives. Integral to the PPBS hierarchy of language and idea-relationships is the global concept of program alternatives for reviewing the output of objectives, based upon agency accountability.

Output is defined in the following manner:

- It is a product (either a good or a service).
- It is produced by a federal agency, or is produced under the agency's auspices.
- It is a tangible outgrowth of a particular program (i.e., it is the result of a calculated program effort).
- It is the sort of product which can be appropriately singled out as an indicator of program results. (Logically, therefore, it must be a program end-product, and an important one, at that).
- It is considered by the agency as satisfying an explicit market objective (or related set of objectives).[17]

Not only must output be defined, but progress must be measured, which brings several questions for the administrator working in PPBS. What does PPBS want to measure? What does PPBS consider progress in a given program? Has the expected output materialized as planned? Is the intended output distribution completed?

In summary, PPBS is a way of relating outputs, throughputs, and inputs to a given program objective, based upon accountability in the citizen market. The philosophy conveniently omits reference to particular details of agency operation, because the "concept PPBS" is more significant than the "practice PPBS." Allen Schick reduces the potential of PPBS to three benefits. *First,* it usually spotlights the worst programs, even if it cannot always delineate the best ones. *Second,* it usually provides some improvements in existing programs. *Third,* it encourages administrators, politicians, and even the public at large to start thinking along different and more constructive lines.[18]

The third benefit is considered the most important. It is the process, not the product, that counts the most. As one federal official observed, "The numbers are lousy and always will be in the civilian area. But the need to produce them pushes people in the right direction."[19]

Since the heyday of PPBS, progress in this direction has been made but the pathways selected have been varied. In some cases, they have taken the form of various versions of PPBS. In other cases, different, but nonetheless related, budget systems have been adopted. Other non-budgetary devices, such as productivity measures, program evaluation, and management by objectives, have also emerged. While they are certainly not PPBS, they do exhibit some of the same methodology and approach that characterize PPBS. As Harry S. Havens, formerly of the U.S. General Accounting Office, noted:

> *PPBS really consisted of two distinct parts. One was a formal structure through which passed volumes of paper. The other was an analytical concept—a way of thinking about problems. The formal structure of PPBS is now dead; the analytical concept is very much alive.*[20]

If PPBS was a more rational approach to budgetary decision making, why did it fail? Theorist Aaron Wildavsky has noted that PPBS fostered budgetary decision making focused on output categories of governmental goals, objectives, and end products rather than inputs of personnel, equipment, and maintenance. Once priorities among objectives were established, the PPBS budgetary procedure determined the mixture of expenditures in the annual appropriation that would reap the greatest gain in future benefits. This is how PPBS works on paper. Why did it fail in practice?

PPBS difficulties rested in its objectivity, its centralization, and its political content. Locating and establishing objectivity in program content is as clear as separating means from ends. What categories should constitute the most useful programs and program elements? The conclusion is not obvious. The way programs are structured is another major question for government and a crucial political difficulty for PPBS. Under our fragmented federal system, programs are scattered throughout the entire federal establishment and decentralized to state and local authorities as well. The problem with PPBS as a program budgeting model was its centralizing bias. PPBS also stumbled over conflicts between political rationality and technical, legal, social, or economic rationality. The political solution is always basic and prior to others. Find a political solution, and resolution of other concerns will soon follow.

Wildavsky asks why "ugly old politics beat up nice young PPB?" He argues that PPBS was an irrational method of analysis which led to suppression rather than correction of error. The budget theorist concludes:

> PPB is not an embodiment of rationality; PPB is irrational. If the goal is to alter the allocation of resources in a more productive way, or to generate better analyses than those that are now used, PPB does not (because it cannot) produce results. PPB is not cost effective. It produces costly rationales for inevitable failures. . . . By separating policy analysis from organizational power, PPB is simultaneously rendered unintelligent and impotent.[21]

Program budgets are not necessarily a cure-all for budgetary illnesses. Many public programs contribute to several public objectives and, as mentioned, programmatic classification is not all that simplistic. One set of policy choices will always be at the expense of others. The meaningfulness of cost estimates for public decisions is not scientifically defensible. Resources utilized by the department may be shared and not attributable to a single program. Finally, program budgets give way to the traditional budget format because legislatures, lobbyists, and governmental agencies often prefer the budget format to which they are accustomed.

Zero-Based Budgets (ZBB)

This reform technique owes its origins to private industry. Texas Instruments started the system when it ordered its departments and divisions to formulate their budgets anew each year. When Peter Pyhrr, treasurer of Texas Instruments and creator of ZBB, wrote an article about the concept for the Harvard Business Review, the newly inaugurated governor of Georgia, Jimmy Carter, was impressed with what he read. Carter brought Pyhrr to Atlanta to help implement the system in Georgia's government.

Carter scored a number of successes with ZBB, and upon his assumption of the presidency, eagerly sought to implement ZBB throughout the federal bureaucracy. Pyhrr's book on the technique, *Zero Base Budgeting: A Practical Management Tool for Evaluating Expenses* (1973), soon became a Washington best seller. As one seasoned bureaucrat was heard to remark,

"Never has a management fad more completely taken over this town." One of the attractive aspects of ZBB lies in its ease of execution. ZBB requires its practitioners to adopt two words of basic terminology and three procedures for implementation.

The terms are *decision units* and *decision packages.* A decision unit has been defined as a "meaningful element," that is, any activity, large, isolated, or "meaningful" enough to require its own budget. A decision unit does not have to be big enough to constitute a whole program—often a subprogram or even less will suffice—but whatever its scope, a decision unit does need to possess enough discretion and dimension to warrant its own budget.

The second term, decision package, signifies any particular level of effort by any designated decision unit. For example, if an agency's microfilm unit was considered to have sufficient size and scope to be a decision unit, then a decision package would be drafted for each possible volume of activity which the agency might want to consider for the microfilm unit.

There are three procedural steps of ZBB; *identification, formation,* and *ranking.* The initial step an agency must take to implement ZBB is the *identification* of its decision units. This is not a strictly scientific process, for the agency may exercise a certain degree of discretion in deciding which of its activities constitute separate decision units. Once the decision units have been designated, the agency is ready for step two, the *formation* of the decision packages. Administrative leaders of decision units single out several possible gradations of activity and illustrate what resources each will require and what outputs will be generated. This information becomes a decision package; there should be a separate package for each designated level of effort.

How many levels of effort should be considered? The answer varies depending upon the proficiency of the practitioner and the zealousness of superiors. The first level, as ZBB suggests, could be zero. In theory, up to 10 levels may be utilized; in practice, usually no more than five, and often no more than three, are employed. When only three are used, it usually becomes a case of considering a reduced level, the current level, and one improvement level.

Remember that each level considered requires a separate decision package. Once the agency formulates its decision packages, administrators rank them. The *ranking* of decision packages constitutes the final and most controversial procedural step in the ZBB process.

Like PPBS, ZBB has not lacked for critics. Many prestigious and perceptive observers are quick to point out its alleged deficiencies. In most instances ZBB has failed to produce sweeping or even substantial changes in program operations and costs. ZBB also made the budgeting process more expensive and exhausting. Despite disappointments and doubts, ZBB forced the budgeting process out of the financial office and produced an understandable budgetary procedure for managers. In many instances, ZBB helped identify program initiatives and improvements, and in some cases produced rather spectacular savings.

ZBB provides no magic elixir, no all-pervasive panacea to guarantee administrative effectiveness and cost efficiency. It does, however, furnish the public manager with a potentially useful tool for tackling the troublesome administrative tasks of today's and tomorrow's world. ZBB promotes flexibility in government, identifies low-yield programs, and forces administrators to analyze the total program on an annual basis. In attempting to prevent a budget process that focuses exclusively on program increases, ZBB responds to changed service demands without government reorganization or loss of the line-item format.[22]

FEDERAL BUDGET CUTTING IN THE 1980s: MUCH TALK, LITTLE ACTION

On coming to power in 1981 the Reagan Administration did not offer reforms to solve the problem of government spending and huge federal deficits. Reagan argued that big government in Washington crippled economic prosperity that is produced in free markets. Reagan's OMB leader, David Stockman, instead adopted strategies of top-down budgeting and budgeting for legislative advantage.[23]

Top-down budgeting, as implemented by Stockman, focused upon several changes in the traditional budgeting process. By the spring of 1981, Stockman was convinced that deficit spending must be addressed because a large structural deficit in the Reagan program was emerging. In top-down budgeting, Stockman dealt with the total budget, not particular programs. Budgeting for legislative advantage became his second strategy for attempting to master the budget process and the ever-increasing deficits. The former Michigan congressman ran OMB more like a congressional office than an executive institution. The aims of budgeting for legislative advantage were to hammer home the perception that the Reagan mandate for tax and spending cuts had not eroded and to use the ponderous budget procedures of Congress against itself.

The task Clinton has now is much more difficult than was Reagan's. In order to have a balanced federal budget, the politicians would have to cut programs and raise taxes. Persuading the politicians to cut taxes in 1981 was "easier" than convincing the politicians to raise taxes in 1993. The political conservatives would "lose" with a balanced federal budget. Although the budget might get a closer "balance," the role of government (classic liberalism) would be enhanced because citizens would demand that a certain level of services be maintained.

Reagan was aided on Capitol Hill in the early part of the decade by a fellow believer in such political strategies, Phil Gramm, who holds a Ph.D. in economics from the University of Georgia and who later became a college professor of economics at Texas A&M University. Gramm was elected to the U.S. House of Representatives as a Democrat in 1978. Once in Congress, however, Gramm parted from the leadership of Democratic Speaker, Tip O'Neill. He co-authored the Gramm-Latta budget, adopted May 7, 1981, and the Gramm-Latta II Omnibus Reconciliation Act, which changed existing law to reduce the level of expenditures for 250 federal programs. He also mandated the Reagan tax cut and implemented the Economic Recovery Program, signed into law on August 13, 1981. For his transgressions, Gramm was denied his seat on the House Budget Committee. He resigned from Congress, ran as a Republican for his House seat, won, then ran as a Republican for the U.S. Senate in 1984 and won an even larger political prize.

In 1985, Phil Gramm, along with Republican Senator Warren Rudman of New Hampshire and Democrat Fritz Hollings of South Carolina, pushed for the successful passage of the Balanced Budget Act of that year. Known as Gramm-Rudman-Hollings, the legislation calls for savage cuts in domestic programs and defense if annual deficit targets are not reached, leading to a balanced budget by 1991. Gramm argues that the Act has had "a profound impact on government spending and on the relationship of government to the people."[24] Rudman calls the legislation a *mentality* rather than a *mechanism*, surmizing that there is a moral imperative to get the deficit down. Hollings, even more philosophical, states that Congressional enactment and implementation of the Balanced Budget Act means that "the truth has increased, not the deficit."[25]

The Balanced Budget Act had little, if any, success in holding down annual federal deficits and the national debt. The deficit problem is actually two problems. One is *numerical*, relating to the reduction of this year's deficit. The second is *political*, relating to fundamental questions of priorities. Advocates will have to make convincing arguments for Congress to decrease spending in all areas. The U.S. Senate's sum-zero rule requires that any spending increases or tax cuts that would bust the Act's deficit target would be offset with deficit cuts. As California Congressman and Director, Office of Management and Budget (OMB) for the Clinton administration, Leon Panetta surmized: "You can build whatever kind of system you want, but the bottom line is still politics and guts."[26]

PPBS, ZBB, and balanced budget proposals are conceptual approaches and guidelines for resolving the taxing and spending dilemmas confronting the American people. In making decisions concerning the role of government in society and establishing priorities for the country's future, however, the American people and their representatives have yet to muster the political will for implementing appropriate fiscal policies.

DECREMENTALISM AND CUTBACK BUDGETING

George Bush, who was part of the Reagan administration as Vice President, inherited Reagan's budgetary legacy of huge deficits. More federal spending was added to the national debt during Reagan's tenure than was added during all previous administrations combined. Perhaps Reagan's chief contribution to budgetary politics, on the other hand, was calling attention to excessive middle-class entitlements and in moving from incremental budgeting to decremental estimates. From domestic to defense spending, the representatives of the American people have yet to find the line-items for equal sacrifice in implementing federal budgetary policies.

In times of retrenchment in government programs, incremental budgeting changes its assumptions when confronted with cutback management alternatives. The incremental budgeting process is *decentralized*; the decremental mode, calling for funding cutbacks, necessitates *centralization*. Fragmented, substantive decision making dominates incremental budgeting; decremental budgeting calls for a comprehensive effort. Incremental budgeting calls for increases, although oftentimes modest, in funding allocations; decremental budgeting, meanwhile, spells decreases in legislative appropriations.

Incremental budgeting demands little intellectual inquiry because the increment, not the base, is considered. Incremental decision making entails routine, requires negotiations and accommodation grounded upon mutual respect, is delegated to specialists, and is almost invisible. It seems merely distributive, historical, annual, repetitive, predictable, and automatic. It is rewarding and can create stable coalitions.

Decremental budgeting, on the other hand, is chaotic and conflict-laden. It may result in coercion, involve confrontation, and generate mistrust. It is clearly redistributive, breaks precedents, is multiyear, erratic, unpredictable, painful, can foster unstable coalitions, and requires active leadership for overcoming such obstacles.

Incremental budgeting distributes only the increment, but takes nothing away from anyone; decremental budgeting, meanwhile, redistributes resources from people who absorb cuts in appropriations. Incremental budgeting rewards increments to everyone, as credit for such enhancement is to be shared; decremental budgeting engenders blame for the pain of losing accustomed funding.

The incremental model minimizes the intellectual task of creating a new budget every year, facilitates the political task of adopting a budget and appears ethical. Such a model, accepting the base as a given, eliminates the necessity for rethinking everything. The political task of building a coalition to support this year's new budget allows a majority of political interests with economic stakes to form and take hold. No one appears hurt; everyone gains a little in incremental budgeting. Even if the balance struck a decade ago has little or no ethical or political relevance today, the overall equity is never examined. Numerous interests may be unhappy with the process and results, but everyone knows what would be received under incrementalism. No one knows with certainty what new assumptions decrementalism would bring.

Decremental budgeting met with a good deal of political support in the 1980s. The Omnibus Budget Reconciliation Act of 1981 sliced the 1982 federal budget by $35.1 billion. It was passed by voice vote in the House of Representatives; an 80 to 14 Senate vote approved the measure. The Social Security Act Amendments of 1983 also entailed significant benefit reductions; the House passed the Amendments by 243 to 102; the Senate approved the decrements by 58 to 14. What unique set of politics was required to support decrementalism?

The overarching consideration was the definition of the political issue itself. *Cutback management* strategy saw the dominant issue as something more important than the consequences of individual cuts. The President glossed over the individual cuts; he spoke only of the big picture. In the case of the 1983 Social Security cuts, the overriding issue focused upon was preventing the economic collapse of the Social Security system. The redefinition of the issue provided a reason for voting for the cutback legislation.

A second consideration fueling such a decremental coalition concerned *parliamentary procedures*. David Stockman, former Director of the Office of Management and Budget, developed a reconciliation strategy whereby members of Congress voted only on the entire package and not on individual programmatic cuts. Your congressman voted to save the national economy, or Social Security, not to cut back your widowed mother's pension. *Equity* constituted a third consideration. Everyone—the self-employed, beneficiaries, workers, new government employees, and the better-off among the retired—assumed some of the economic hardship. The philosophy of equal sacrifice boosted the prospects for decrementalism.

Definition of the political issue, voting procedures, and equity, however, are often not enough. Leadership may emerge from the speaker of the House, the majority leader of the Senate or the chairmen of the budget committees; however, the President occupies the best position to define the issues and exert political pressure. The President, or governor, or mayor, defines the overarching issue, focuses public attention on the problem, and constructs blocs of support behind decrementalism efforts. The executive occupies the position with leverage for employing restrictive parliamentary procedures demanding controversial votes, which redistribute limited resources rather than distributing increments from revenue growth.[27]

Decrementalism suggests a centralized political system dominated by what is called top-down budgeting. Incrementalism explains budgeting as a bottom-up process. What's the difference? The budgeting process includes the countervailing forces of centralization and decentralization, autonomy and interdependence, micropolitics and macropolitics. The President and his key advisors dominate the top-down process. A limited number of people are involved in such an approach; the developments are less visible to the public. Top-down strategy confronts the mixture of defense and domestic components of the budget, the budget's size, the impact of the budget upon fiscal policies, and the executive's policy initiatives to force cutbacks. As suggested in our discussion of decrementalism, routine is not a common feature of the top-down process (see Table 9-3).

There have been top-down characteristics of the budgetary process since the passage of the Budget and Impoundment Control Act of 1921. Top-down elements are more difficult to document as the process is less routine, involves fewer people, and receives less publicity, and as such have garnered less attention than the bottom-up developments. Researchers find it difficult to observe, conceptualize, and explain the top-down process. According to budget theorists Barry Bozeman and Jeffrey D. Straussman, such features are often ignored or relegated to historical "disturbances."[28]

Incrementalism reflects the bottom-up budgeting process. Budget theorist Aaron Wildavsky reports that incrementalism focuses on the significance of adjusting the margins from last year's budgetary base with little, if any, examination of the baseline so assumed. Why the emphasis upon the bottom-up process? *First*, incrementalism is explainable; budget variations may be explained by utilizing simple projections. *Second*, incrementalism gives an adequate account of the bottom-up process. *Third*, incrementalism is emphasized by authors of public administration and budgeting textbooks. *Finally*, incrementalism dominates policymakers' perceptions of how budgeting actually occurs and portrays the actual experience of policymakers themselves.

Top-down and bottom-up processes are operative in every budget cycle. As the demands of the budget cycle change with developments in fiscal policy, presidential leadership, economic growth, foreign conflict, congressional assertiveness, and other factors, the utilization of the respective processes changes. Although the top-down process of federal budgeting grew more important in the Ford and Carter Administrations, the Reagan Administration implemented perhaps the most important shift in budget policy—determining that the "controllable" portion of the budget includes entitlements offering social services to the middle class.

The baseline federal outlay projections for entitlements consist of social insurance programs such as Social Security, Medicare, unemployment insurance, and railroad retirement; means-tested programs such as Medicaid, food stamps, assistance payments, supplemental security income, veterans'

TABLE 9–3 Outlays by Agency: 1962, 1972, 1982, 1992 (in millions of dollars)
Percentage Distribution of Outlays by Agency: 1962, 1972, 1982, 1992

Department or other unit	1962	1962	1972	1972	1982	1982	1992	1992
Legislative Branch	196	0.2	499	0.2	1,367	0.2	2,641	0.2
The Judiciary	57	0.1	173	0.1	710	0.1	2,435	0.2
Executive Office of the President	11	*	46	*	95	*	214	*
Funds Appropriated to the President	3,178	3.0	2,982	1.3	7,940	1.1	13,491	0.9
Agriculture	6,437	6.0	11,053	4.8	45,700	6.1	66,844	4.5
Commerce	215	0.2	850	0.4	2,054	0.3	3,031	0.2
Defense-Military	50,111	46.9	77,645	33.7	180,714	24.2	281,883	19.2
Defense-Civil	1,863	1.7	5,415	2.3	17,927	2.4	28,415	1.9
Education	825	0.8	5,612	2.4	14,808	2.0	28,883	2.0
Energy	2,755	2.6	2,299	1.0	11,639	1.6	17,196	1.2
Health and Human Services— except social security	3,529	3.3	26,264	11.4	98,020	13.1	275,595	18.8
Health and Human Services— social security	14,365	13.4	39,620	17.2	155,120	20.8	284,903	19.4
Housing and Urban Development	826	0.8	3,600	1.6	15,232	2.0	24,961	1.7
Interior	600	0.6	1,610	0.7	3,948	0.5	7,122	0.5
Justice	299	0.3	1,182	0.5	2,617	0.4	10,001	0.7
Labor	4,134	3.9	10,136	4.4	30,745	4.1	48,191	3.3

Continued

TABLE 9-3 Outlays by Agency: 1962, 1972, 1982, 1992 (in millions of dollars), continued

Department or other unit	1962	1962	1972	1972	1982	1982	1992	1992
State	259	0.2	495	0.2	2,186	0.3	5,245	0.4
Transportation	4,138	3.9	7,932	3.4	20,007	2.7	36,204	2.5
Treasury	8,560	8.0	21,863	9.5	110,318	14.8	296,146	20.2
Veterans Affairs	5,608	5.2	10,713	4.6	23,941	3.2	33,907	2.3
Environmental Protection Agency	70	0.1	763	0.3	5,081	0.7	6,461	0.4
General Services Administration	382	0.4	655	0.3	165	*	359	*
National Aeronautics and Space Administration	1,257	1.2	3,423	1.5	6,155	0.8	14,317	1.0
Office of Personnel Management	1,017	1.0	3,776	1.6	19,983	2.7	35,765	2.4
Small Business Administration	230	0.2	452	0.2	773	0.1	1,891	0.1
Other Independent Agencies	2,606	2.4	6,295	2.7	10,625	1.4	60,225	4.1
Undistributed offsetting receipts	−6,707	−6.3	−14,672	−6.4	−42,165	−5.7	−117,111	−8.0
(On-budget)	(−5,878)	(−5.5)	(−11,909)	(−5.2)	(−38,448)	(−5.2)	(−87,372)	(−5.9)
(Off-budget)	(−830)	(−.8)	(−2,763)	(−1.2)	(−3,717)	(−.5)	(−29,739)	(−2.0)
Total outlays	106,821	100.0	230,681	100.0	745,706	100.0	1,469,166	100.0

Source: Historical Tables: Budget of the United States Government, Fiscal Year 1992 (Washington, DC: Executive Office of the President, Office of Management and Budget, 1992), pp. 49–52. See Table 4.1—Outlays by Agency: 1962–1996; and Table 4.2—Percentage Distribution of Outlays by Agency: 1962–1996.

pensions, guaranteed student loans, and child nutrition; civilian and military employee retirement and disability; and programs offering veterans' benefits, farm price supports, general revenue sharing, and other social services. The projected expenditure for such programs for fiscal 1989 was $570 billion.[29]

The desire to curb the development of middle-class entitlement spending, promote economic changes, alter public perception of economic issues and economic thinking encouraged Reagan Administration policy-makers to adopt top-down strategies. Bozeman and Straussman state that conventional budgeting wisdom did not keep pace with events. Concluding that budget theory should be reformulated, these theorists argue that the political and economic environments changed and led to a perceived demand for cuts in the rate and level of spending. Such cutback management, they argue, may be achieved only through coordinated fiscal management with top-down strategies. Under such conditions, incrementalism becomes a less satisfactory explanation of federal budgeting.[30]

The Reagan Administration left a budgetary legacy for George Bush and future presidents that is best described by John Shannon: "The creation of a fiscal environment that forces state and local officials to become more self-reliant stands out as the primary impact the Reagan Administration has had on our federal system."[31]

CHANGES IN STATE BUDGETING SINCE 1970S

The recession of the early 1990s hit the states especially hard. The governors and state legislatures felt the fallout as 50 percent of the states could not fund their fiscal 1992 budgets despite the more than $16 billion increase in state taxes in fiscal 1991. Personal income and business income tax collections naturally fall during an economic slowdown. In turn, state revenues decrease, but the economic distress causes citizens to pressure state governments for relief. Service costs in education, health care, welfare, and corrections are made worse by budget shortfalls. Compared with fiscal 1981, state governments in fiscal 1990 appropriated less for education, highways, and more for corrections, debt service, and human services.[32]

Two events of the 1970s contribute to the state budget shortfalls of the 1990s. First, the tax revolt movement swept the country. The trend was symbolized by Proposition 13, the California property tax revolt in 1978. Second, the decline of federal assistance in real, per capita terms to state governments resulted in "fend-for-yourself," or "go-it-alone" federalism. The Reagan and Bush administrations promoted the pull-out of federal grants to state and local governments.

The structural budget deficits confronting state governments in the 1990s originated in the 1980s. From fiscal year 1981 through fiscal year 1990, trends in state government spending, revenues, and employment indicate that some state governments acted responsibly to replace lost federal aid, others were forced by federal or state court orders to spend more on schools and prisons, some states assumed higher state employees' health and pension costs, and still other states were victimized by ambitious politicians who promised more public services to their constituents. The states have more government than citizens are inclined to pay for. Cutbacks in state spending necessitated by these shortfalls especially affects programs for the poor. Despite efforts to reduce state government spending, 28 state legislatures— trapped between services and deficits—passed tax increases in fiscal 1992.

Our examination of the fiscal policies of the 1980s illuminates the changes in state budgetary processes during the 1970–1990 period. As a result of fiscal policies of the past few decades, functions relatively uncommon in 1970 but common in 1990 are:

- dollar-level ceilings and policy ceilings issued by the executive to agencies for preparing budget requests;
- guidance in preparing budget requests based upon current levels of service;
- instructions for agencies ranking requests by priority;
- overall policy guidance—written and otherwise;
- program effectiveness and productivity information required for requesting new and revised programs;
- computer usage in agency budget preparation, analysis of agency requests by the budget office, and preparation of the governor's budget;
- inclusion of effectiveness and productivity measures in budget documents;
- conduct of effectiveness and productivity analysis by the central budget office and the legislature;
- use of analysis in decision making by the executive and legislative branches;
- accounting systems that collect information by appropriation, department, organizational unit, program, and levels within a program;
- Master's degree education of professional budget office personnel;
- academic disciplines other than business and accounting constituting a majority of budget office personnel.[33]

Summary

- If politics is sometimes defined as the process of deciding who gets what, administrative politics often becomes the process of deciding *who gets what amount of money*. If budgets are essentially political documents, the politics involved are often veiled.

- It is not enough to call attention to the political aspects of budgeting in order to define budgeting. Budgets are also instruments of *coordination, control,* and *planning.* They govern nearly all aspects of administration and confer a great deal of power on those who prepare them.
- Public sector budgets are raised from taxes on individuals and businesses. It's tough to maintain viable public services if revenues supporting such activities are low or nonexistent. Whether we are providing national defense or unemployment compensation, we need a *growth economy* to finance such citizen benefits.
- Most of America's approximately 80,000 governments divide their budgets into two sections, one for *capital* projects, the other for *expenses.* Often they are considered two separate budgets. The main goal of a capital budget is to provide a clearer picture of the government's new worth at any given time. The traditional budgetary process revolves around making sense of the federal budget the old-fashioned way—incrementally, or bit by bit. The basic document in traditional budgeting is the expense budget. This details the operational expenditures for the coming year.
- The status-quo reinforcing effect of traditional line-item budgeting—often referred to as *incremental budgeting* because it concerns itself with increments of change rather than program change—can influence whole governments. A line-item budget will generally include categories for personnel, equipment, and maintenance, among others.
- As governments grew in size and complexity, dissatisfaction with traditional budgeting grew apace. Line item budgets failed to show the impact of expenditures on programs, future costs and effects, and relationships between capital and operating costs. Performance budgets, program budgets, zero-based budgets, and the Gramm-Rudman-Hollings Balanced Budget Act of 1985 constitute budgetary reforms.
- *Incremental budgeting* demands little intellectual inquiry because the increment, not the base, is considered. Incremental decision making entails routine, requires negotiations and accommodation grounded upon mutual respect, is delegated to specialists, and is almost invisible. Incrementalism explains budgeting as a bottom-up process.
- *Decremental budgeting* is chaotic and conflict-laden. Decrementalism suggests a centralized political system dominated by what is called top-down budgeting.
- The Reagan Administration significantly affected budgeting allocations and processes in the states and the nation. Reagan created a fiscal environment in which state and local officials had to become more self-reliant, shifting financing responsibility from the national treasury to the states and localities. Large federal deficits, increased defense spending, and high levels of federal spending for Social Security and Medicare caused all public sector administrators to do more with less.

- Each year's budget deficit is the difference between revenues and outlays in that year. Continuing large federal deficits absorb savings otherwise available to finance investment. A new fiscal policy is essential to the economic well-being of the United States.
- The federal debt is the *accumulation* of all past deficits. As President Reagan entered office in 1981, the federal debt was $709 billion. Twelve years later the debt is more than $4 trillion.
- The tax and spend policies of the 1960s and 1970s resulted in the tax, spend, and borrow fiscal policies of the 1980s. There was little fiscal and political accountability in the 1980s. Political consensus grounded in the decrementalism of cutting back government programs is much more difficult than the incrementalism of adding programs.
- The per capita tax level in the United States is *not* high with respect to America's economic competitors. The people of the U.S. are not over-taxed. Taxation as a percentage of national income is lower in the U.S. than in any other major industrialized country.
- Two events of the 1970s contribute to the state budget shortfalls of the 1990s: the *tax revolt* and the *decline of federal assistance*. The structural budget deficits confronting state governments in the 1990s originated in the 1980s.

Public administrators realize that some hard decisions must be made when setting down the details of a budget—decisions that not everyone will agree with. This case study illustrates some of the tough budget decisions a typical town faces each year.

CASE STUDY

Cutting Back at City Hall[34]

The Smithville City Council meeting of June 23 had aroused more public interest than its usual weekly sessions because it was the time set for presenting the completed operating budget for the fiscal year starting July 1. The budget specified the estimated revenues and expenditures for personnel services and the maintenance and operation of the city. On the table before each council member was a copy of the proposed budget over which department heads, the controller's staff, the city manager, and the council had been struggling for months—a neatly bound book with a light blue cover containing 163 pages of tables and charts. A public hearing would be held on the proposed budget before it was presented to the council for final approval at its last regular meeting in June.

In presenting the budget, City Manager James Harmsworth said the fact that it was a balanced one was due to the hard work put into it by city employees and council members. Failing revenues and higher operating costs made it seem early in the year as if there would be a shortfall, ranging from a "best-case scenario" of $1,739,495 to a "worst-case scenario" of $5,139,000.

State law prohibited deficit spending by municipalities, and so figuring out a budget that would meet this requirement was not an easy task. Earlier Harmsworth had presented to the council the capital budget, down about $2 million, or 39 percent, from last year. He believed the completed operations budget was equally successful.

The grim situation that Smithville, population 65,000, faced early in the year was due in part to a general business slump in the state that had affected the city's revenue. The city's income from services was down, sales tax receipts had dropped, and there was a loss in federal revenue sharing.

Early in the year Harmsworth had told the council: "This is one of the most critical times in my ten years as city manager. But the problem is a manageable one if the council will respond to it. During the year we must try to alleviate the situation. A year from now, if something isn't done, it will no longer be a manageable problem."

Recognizing that Draconian measures were needed, city negotiators had resisted demands for pay increases by the three employees' unions, the Fraternal Order of Police (FOP), the International Association of Fire Fighters (IAF), and the American Federation of State, County, and Municipal Employees (AFSCME). FOP members had asked for pay raises of 7 percent, then lowered their demand to 4 percent, and finally accepted, by a 55 percent vote of the membership, no increase at all in the face of the bleak prospects presented to them. Similarly, the fire fighters had dropped their first request of an 8.5 percent increase to a 6.5 percent one and then were forced to settle for none at all; AFSCME members had abandoned their more reasonable request of a cost-of-living increase of 3 percent.

Union leaders had objected strongly to what they considered "taking the brunt" of retrenchment, arguing that instead of lowering salaries and cutting down on personnel, the city's revenue could have been raised if officials had taken proper prevention measures to offset declines in the sales tax and utilities income.

John J. Patrick, FOP president, had told a council budget study session: "It's up to City Council to determine whether they want a cut in the quality and efficiency of police services. It has known for months that sales taxes have not been up to budgeted estimates, and it could have acted to avert the present crisis by changing the city charter." He pointed out that a charter provision required that 70 percent of the one cent sales tax be used to fund capital improvements. "Other cities can cut capital improvements and give their employees a little raise," Patrick had said. "Smithville has made the wrong choice between capital improvements and its employees."

Judith Weintraub, president of the employees' federation, had been critical of officials for meeting rising utility costs by taking money from the general fund. "I realize that the city charter requires residents to vote approval of increases in the water, sewage, and trash-removal rates," Weintraub had said, "but officials have allowed the present inadequate rates to go on for years."

To these criticisms officials had replied that it was difficult to persuade the public to approve increased rates for services and higher taxes in a period of business decline. A vote on such matters at a time like this would undoubtedly reject the needed increases, and it could be several years before the time was right for seeking a second vote.

Harmsworth briefed the council on the proposed budget and presented enlarged tables and charts on a screen. He first displayed a budget summary showing estimated revenues for all funds—general, capital, cable television, room tax (on hotels and motels), street and alley, revenue sharing, Smithville Municipal Authority, Smithville Utilities Authority, and the sinking fund. The budget summary revealed a total income of $35,018,179 and total expenditures of $34,710,324, well under the anticipated income.

Harmsworth presented a table comparing the projected expenditures for the new fiscal year with those for the past year that illustrated dramatically the budgetary task facing the city. The city had planned to spend $49,507,154 for the past year. Fortunately, it had been possible to reduce this amount by almost $12 million using carryover funds from previous years, placing a moratorium on buying supplies, dropping training programs, eliminating travel expenses and automobile use reimbursement, postponing the filling of vacant positions, and employing other money saving devices.

When pressed by council members to discuss the fiscal year 1988 operations and maintenance budget of the General Fund not itemized in Exhibit 1, Harmsworth indicated that $1,343,310 was spent for electricity, natural gas, and telephone service; $1,248,520 for landfill fees; $763,470 for gasoline, oil, tires, and vehicle and equipment repair parts; $238,800 for insurance; $376,460 for membership in the Lake Region Master Water Conservancy District; and $205,090 for water treatment chemicals. Harmsworth, as a seasoned and politically astute city manager, was quick to add that the "O & M portion of the budget would be decreased by 11.7 percent for FY '89 and that no part of the budget would remain unaffected by the sharp knife of Smithville's retrenchment plan."

Harmsworth said the worst aspect of cutting down on costs was the impact it would have on personnel—lowering the already inadequate pay of the men and women who protect the people from criminals and maintain order, who save people and buildings during fires, who collect trash and garbage, who provide a clean and adequate water supply, and who keep up the streets, parks, and public buildings. They were the human element in government budgeting, he said, and a significant proportion of the general fund went for their services. Such personnel services in the new fiscal year, Harmsworth explained, were estimated to be $17,772,324 out of a total expenditure budget of $23,725,446.

The council budget committee and officials, Harmsworth continued, had worked out a plan that would save the jobs of employees—a plan calling for a reduction in force of only forty persons. Last year there had been 683 persons on the city's payrolls, the most ever employed, and the projection for the new fiscal year was 643 persons. The reduction in force, however, would not substantially affect the essential services of the fire, police, emergency medical, and sanitation departments, whose combined work force numbered 361 persons. Instead, the forty proposed layoffs would occur in the areas of professional and management level employees, clerical staff, and so forth.

To minimize the salary cutback of employees, $400,000 would be transferred from the capital improvement budget and $175,000 would be saved by reducing street lighting to every other street. Additional salary funds would also be obtained from reduced health care and insurance premiums and by deletion of a separation and retirement budget. Thus, personnel would be penalized only by a 5 percent salary reduction and a freeze on merit pay and furloughs once a month for all employees. These changes would result in net savings for the following categories: salary reduction, $820,000; merit raise freeze, $343,000; and furloughs, $750,000.

QUESTIONS AND INSTRUCTIONS

1. In developing the Smithville budget, officials endeavored to make reductions easy on employees. From this standpoint, how do you evaluate their success in the following: hiring freeze, cost-of-living pay freeze, merit pay freeze, furloughs, reduction by attrition, cutting back on force, elimination of training programs, and freeze on travel?

2. Other methods of cutting back include putting ceilings on positions, load-shedding, demotions, personnel transfers, and reclassifying positions. Do you believe Smithville officials should have done more in these areas?

3. Officials could have quickly solved most of the budget-cutting problems by a 10 percent reduction in the work force. Do you think they were wiser to choose instead the complex program they did?

4. Is the criticism of union leaders valid who faulted officials for failing to attempt to alter the city charter permitting increases in utility rates or reducing the 70 percent of the sales tax going to capital improvements, when city officials knew long beforehand that revenue would be substantially lowered?

5. Do you agree with the president of the Fraternal Order of Police that in the Smithville budget capital improvements were allowed at the cost of "a little" raise for employees?

6. Do you think it fair not to make reductions in force for essential services such as fire and police protection and to place the burden of retrenchment almost wholly on employees providing other services?

7. Do you think it is possible that efficiency and productivity might be in fact increased after a retrenchment program has been effected?

8. Researchers have reported what they consider negative results in retrenchment in government: (a) an increase in polarization—management vs. labor, whites vs. blacks, political appointees vs. career officials, and veterans vs. nonveterans; (b) increases in waste, fraud, and failure to maintain standards; (c) an increase in the age of the work force; (d) a higher level of organizational chaos—disruption of programs and processes; (e) a decline in morale; and (f) an increase in decision-making uncertainty. How serious are these findings?

ENDNOTES

1. United States General Accounting Office, *Budget Policy: Prompt Action Necessary to Avert Long-Term Damage to the Economy* (Washington: 1992), Publication Number: GAO/OCG-92-2.

2. United States General Accounting Office, *The Budget Deficit: Outlook, Implications, and Choices* (Washington: 1990), Publication Number: GAO/OCG-90-5. See Donald F. Kettl, *Deficit Politics: Public Budgeting in Its Institutional and Historical Context* (New York: Macmillan).

3. William Schneider, "Bush Will Pay for Reagan Revolution," *National Journal* Vol. 21, No. 1 (January 7, 1989), 50.

4. Lawrence J. Haas, "New Fiscal Realities," *National Journal*, Vol. 20, No. 2 (January 9, 1988), 62–69; "Who'll Pay the Price?" *Ibid.*, Vol. 20, No. 8 (February 20, 1988), 444–449; and Jonathan Rauch, "The Growth Machine," *Ibid.*, Vol. 20, No. 10 (March 5, 1988), 580–590.

5. Thomas R. Dye, *Understanding Public Policy* (Englewood Cliffs, NJ: Prentice Hall, Inc., 1992). See Chapter 10: Tax Policy, Battling the Special Interests, 268–292.

6. John Rouse, "Tax/Debt Choices Harder When Leadership Fails," *The Muncie Star*, September 6, 1992, page 12A.

7. Bernard T. Pitsvada and Frank D. Draper, "Making Sense of the Federal Budget the Old Fashioned Way—Incrementally," *Public Administration Review*, Vol. 44, No. 5 (September/October, 1984), 401–407.

8. John L. Mikesell, *Fiscal Administration: Analysis and Applications for the Public Sector* (Chicago: The Dorsey Press, 1986), 135–140.

9. Jonathan Rauch, "A Capital Idea for the Budget," *National Journal*, Vol. 18, No. 49 (December 6, 1986), 2948–2949.

10. Fremont J. Lyden and Marc Lindenberg, *Public Budgeting in Theory and Practice* (New York: Longman, Inc., 1983), 66–69.

11. Matthew Dumont, "Down the Bureaucracy!," *Trans-action*, Vol. 7, No. 12 (October, 1970), 11.

12. Thomas J. Anton, "Roles and Symbols in the Determination of State Expenditures," *Midwest Journal of Political Science*, Vol. 11, No. 1 (February, 1967), 29.

13. ———, *The Politics of State Expenditure in Illinois* (Urbana, IL: University of Illinois Press, 1966), 146.

14. John L. Mikesell, *Fiscal Administration: Analysis and Applications for the Public Sector* (Chicago: The Dorsey Press, 1986), 135–155.

15. Samuel M. Greenhouse, "The Planning-Programming-Budgeting System: Rationale, Language, and Idea-Relationships," *Public Administration Review*, Vol. 26, No. 6 (December, 1966), 271–277.

16. *Ibid.*, 272.

17. *Ibid.*, 274.

18. In remarks made by George Berkley to a seminar on PPBS for Boston city officials, May, 1970.

19. "Putting a Dollar Sign on Everything," *Business Week*, 16 July 1966. Reprinted in James W. Davis, Jr., editor, *Politics, Programs and Budgets* (Englewood Cliffs, NJ: Prentice-Hall, Inc., 1969).

20. Harry S. Havens, "MBO and Program Evaluation, or Whatever Happened to PPBS," *Public Administration Review,* Vol. 36, No. 1 (January/February, 1976), 43.

21. Aaron Wildavsky, *The Politics of the Budgetary Process* (Boston: Little, Brown, and Co., 1984), 196.

22. See Peter A. Pyhrr, "The Zero-Base Approach to Government Budgeting," *Public Administration Review,* Vol. 37, No. 1 (January–February, 1977), 1–8; see also Allen Schick, "The Road from ZBB," *Public Administration Review,* Vol. 38, No. 2 (March–April, 1978), 177–180.

23. Hugh Heclo, "Executive Budget Making," in *Federal Budget Policy in the 1980s,* edited by Gregory B. Mills and John L. Palmer (Washington, DC: The Urban Institute Press, 1984), 255–291.

24. Rauch, "Is It Really Working?," *National Journal,* Vol. 19, No. 5 (January 31, 1987), 245–248.

25. *Ibid.,* 245.

26. *Ibid.,* 248.

27. Robert D. Behn, "Cutback Budgeting," *Journal of Policy Analysis and Management,* Vol. 4, No. 2 (1985), 155–177.

28. Barry Bozeman and Jeffrey D. Straussman, "Shrinking Budgets and the Shrinkage of Budget Theory," *Public Administration Review,* Vol. 42, No. 6 (November/December, 1982), 509–515. See also LeLoup, 16–21; see also Robert D. Behn, "Cutback Budgeting," *Journal of Policy Analysis and Management,* Vol. 4, No. 2 (1985), 155–177.

29. Murray L. Weidenbaum, "Budget Dilemma and Its Solution," in *Control of Federal Spending,* edited by C. Lowell Harris (New York: The Academy of Political Science, 1985), 47–58.

30. Bozeman and Staussman, "Shrinking Budgets and the Shrinkage of Budget Theory," *Public Administration Review,* 511.

31. John Shannon, "The Return to Fend-for-Yourself Federalism: The Reagan Mark," *Intergovernmental Perspective,* Vol. 13, No. 3/4 (Summer–Fall, 1987), 34–37.

32. Henry J. Raimondo, "State Budgeting in the Nineties," in *The State of the States* (Washington, DC: Congressional Quarterly, Inc., 1993), 31–49.

33. Robert D. Lee, "Developments in State Budgeting: Trends of Two Decades," *Public Administration Review,* Vol. 51, No. 3 (May/June 1991), 254–262.

34. "Cutting Back at City Hall," in *Practicing Public Management: A Casebook,* by C. Kenneth Meyer and Charles H. Brown (New York: St. Martin's Press, 2nd edition, 1989), 166–170. Reprinted with permission of St. Martin's Press.

10

☆ ☆ ☆

THE PRODUCTIVITY CHALLENGE: WORKING SMARTER WHILE DOING MORE WITH LESS

CHAPTER HIGHLIGHTS

PUBLIC SECTOR PRODUCTIVITY AS EXCELLENCE

Productivity in the public sector refers to excellence in individual and collective performance—especially in times when public employees are expected to do more with less. The employees could be public school teachers, occupational safety inspectors, highway patrol officers, fire fighters, air traffic controllers, maintenance crews removing snow from the streets, or sanitation workers removing waste and technological excess from communities.

In all of these areas of worker expertise, there are widely divergent views as to what excellence really is. *Excellence,* in its various forms, is based on the cultural context of a particular function. Therefore, measuring productivity is a problematic assignment. The public sector usually deals in services, which, because they are intangible and often widely variable, almost always present problems in productivity measurement.

How does one compare the productivity of heart surgeon A versus heart surgeon B? Surgeon A may perform more operations per week and patients may show a greater recovery rate, but how does one know that surgeon A's patients are suffering from roughly the same heart problems as surgeon B's cases? And what if surgeon A's patients are richer and can afford more follow-up care or are more educated and thus are perhaps more likely to adhere to recommended diets and other advice than are the patients of surgeon B?

Even if one analyzes what might seem to be a fairly routine operation in health care, the administration of chest X rays for instance, one can encounter measurement difficulties. X-ray unit A may consistently outperform X-ray unit B in number of chests examined each week. But perhaps unit B operates in poorer areas where people can't afford X rays. Or perhaps B's unit handles more children than A's, and children, it turns out, are harder to x-ray.

Many government experts concede that some public sector functions are simply not measurable with the tools currently at hand. Posing particular difficulties for analysis are numerous staff operations, such as personnel work and social casework. As for the latter, one has only to think of the complexities involved in trying to measure the productivity of a caseworker in a public welfare office. Should the caseworker be rated on how many cases he or she clears from the welfare rolls or on how many people he or she adds to the welfare rolls? Using either standard can produce all kinds of distortions.

EFFICIENCY AND EFFECTIVENESS

Related to these problems is the central task of distinguishing between efficiency and effectiveness. Efficiency means doing things well, while effectiveness means doing the *right* things well. Efficiency, essentially, is the input or contribution of labor, capital, and other resources into an effort matched against the output of product produced or measured, regardless of the mechanism selected to gauge output. Effectiveness, meanwhile, calls for a preestablished standard of comparison, a focus upon a certain quality of production, an ability to mobilize, organize, and direct resources for specified purposes, taken within a certain cultural context. As one commentator noted, a man might be efficient in driving nails into a table. Effectiveness enters the picture when we question whether he should be driving nails into a table at all.

Questions regarding quality make the public productivity measurer's task still more of a hazard and a hassle. A fiddler isn't necessarily producing more by fiddling faster. Nor can a pianist be hailed as especially productive for playing Chopin's Minute Waltz in 50 seconds. On a more mundane and realistic level, a narcotics squad that makes a lot of arrest quotas for their narcotic divisions had to change them when they realized that such productivity measures were not producing "quality" arrests, i.e., arrests of major dealers.[1]

The problem of productivity measurement may produce behavior that is actually antithetical to good results. Correction officials may release inmates before they are rehabilitated, sending them out of the state to hold down their recidivism rates. Hospitals, if subject to carelessly drawn productivity measures, could end up turning away the hopelessly ill because they would not show up well on the balance sheets. Deceptive practices may also find favor. Some drug shelters established to house and cure addicts have reported "cure" rates of 50 percent or higher. In some cases, however, they were counting only those who had stayed in the program until completion. Since about 75 percent of those who were entering such programs dropped out before completion, the "cure" rate represented only 50 percent of the one-fourth who finished the program.

Productivity measures can produce counterproductive behavior in employees, even when the organization itself is attempting to use such measures for perfectly legitimate ends. Peter Blau has described a public employment agency where interviewers were evaluated on the number of applicants they interviewed each month. This led the interviewers to dismiss clients who would require too much of their time. The agency then

---

PERFORMANCE OF PUBLIC WORKS

Asked to grade the performance of key public works services on a 4.0 scale (A=4—F=0), Americans rated roads and bridges at 2.14; water supply, 2.70; and solid waste disposal, 2.32. How would Americans prefer to raise needed additional revenues to improve public works? Dedicated taxes are the choice of 35 percent, followed by 29 percent for user fees, 12 percent for general taxes, and 13 percent for no increase in spending or revenues (volunteered).

Source: *Changing Public Attitudes on Governments and Taxes: 1992* (Washington, DC: United States Advisory Commission on Intergovernmental Relations, 1992).

---

changed its system to judge interviewers on the number of jobs they actually filled. This caused the interviewers to try to outdo each other in getting hold of the slips that reported job openings, even to the point of hiding the slips from each other.[2]

Sometimes, an agency may know which measurement device to use but not how to scale it. One summer the Division of Social Security placed college students in offices of the Internal Revenue Service to check Schedule C forms of tax returns. (It is a very simple exercise that can be executed at a speedy pace.) Social Security officials set a work norm of 4,500 a day per student. However, it was found that in an office where no norm had been set, the students were checking 9,000 to 12,000 per day!

Accounting problems contribute to the administrator's dismay in setting productivity measures. Shall man-hours or cost-per-output be used? Cost-per-output is sometimes almost impossible to measure, while man-hour tabulations may not reflect the cost of new equipment. Another item that is often hard to figure is overhead costs. Then there is the problem of a changing, and usually rising, price level. Shall the costs be figured in current dollars, which do not adjust for price-level changes, or shall they be calculated in terms of constant dollars, which do? Both approaches create difficulties. And what about the problem of side costs, which the private sector can often ignore but which the public sector cannot? A new street cleaning program may show measurable improvements in productivity but may also require more police costs. Or it may require residents to bring their trash cans to the curb. In this latter case, whose productivity has been increased, the sanitation crew's or the residents'?

Legal problems can also impede and impair the use of productivity measures. Civil service rules and regulations are examples of these. New York City's former Deputy Mayor, Edward K. Hamilton, has claimed that "parts of state civil service laws sometimes appear to have been written precisely to frustrate a productivity effort."[3] Even laws not specially related to public employment can bog down a productivity drive. One New York State law requires all medical admissions into hospitals to be recorded in handwriting. With admission to some hospital emergency wards having risen 400 percent and more during the past decade, one can see why the New York hospitals are having admission problems.

Labor unions may and often do resist productivity measurements. Many work contracts are written in such a way as to nullify the use of nearly all such criteria. Fortunately, unions, if properly handled, can help as well as hinder the implementation of productivity measures.

Finally, there are the political problems involved. Like PPBS, to which they are obviously related, productivity measures can collide with the interests of many elements in the politico-administrative process. These include administrative office holders who find such measures threatening to their own pet ways of doing things, legislators who react negatively to measures that may show their favorite programs misfiring, and public interest groups whose preferred projects fail to measure up under the new criteria.

Productivity measures can even prove upsetting to whole sectors of the public who otherwise might be clamoring for increased public sector productivity. For example, conservatives are often in the forefront in demanding more efficient government, but productivity measures may show that incarceration of criminal offenders is much less productive in terms of crime control than parole and probation, or that much of the nation's extensive military hardware produce little in the way of added security. Since incarceration and defense are programs that conservatives tend to favor, they may react with outrage.

Liberals, too, are not immune from the dangers that productivity measures can pose to programs that they ideologically support. Liberals have responded angrily when the use of productivity measures showed that many initial programs designed to help the poor, such as Head Start or Job Corps camps, yielded little or nothing in the way of measurable benefits.

All these factors make the introduction and implementation of productivity measures an exacting and often excruciating undertaking. There are, however, numerous indications that suggest the problems are far from insurmountable and that the task is far from hopeless. Maintaining high levels of productivity is very important for the future effectiveness of public administrators. Progress has been neither smooth nor swift, but it has occurred, and in some instances remarkable successes are being achieved.

GOVERNMENT PERFORMANCE PERCEPTIONS

Before a public administrator tackles productivity issues, he or she should have a good idea about public perceptions of government performance. Those perceptions are not always as negative as is commonly believed. The following section is a brief overview of perceptions and should be kept in mind when exploring productivity issues in this chapter.

There are understandable reasons for the sometimes unfavorable perceptions we have of the way government performs. In a series of interviews with business and government leaders, Mark Abramson found four explanations for the public's dissatisfaction with government performance.[4] The reasons are:

- Democracy is messy.
- Government takes a bum rap.
- Government must shape up.
- The country must shape up.

DEMOCRACY IS MESSY

Democracy is untidy and sometimes disorderly because it is not cost effective. Democratic governments are designed to promote equity and fairness. Because pluralism is central to the way our society is organized, the inherent nature of our government admits of inefficiency and ineffectiveness. Americans, on the other hand, expect only satisfactory performance from the variety of government jurisdictions and their respective functionaries, not optimum performance. We accept that the democratic values of equity, due process, equal opportunity, and openness take prominence over bureaucratic values of efficiency and effectiveness. Human nature dictates, however, that what is wrong with society gets more attention than what's right about how the system is working. The need for improvements gets more press coverage than the task performed without fanfare. Perceptions of performance are crucial.

Despite cost effectiveness dilemmas, there is a need for communicating to citizens the impacts of equity, due process, equal opportunity, and other democratic values concerning government's performance. Administrators and employees must develop more valid methods for judging the performance of public programs to prevent outsiders from doing so. The costs of democracy must be communicated to the taxpayers who will elect politicians; the politicians, in turn, appropriate monies.

In a society where advertisements, music, and sports receive priority over civic education via the nation's radio and television media, citizens must realize the importance of public policies and their corresponding impacts upon their lives. If there is to be political consensus concerning government functions, elected leaders must convince citizens as to the necessity for maintaining solid infrastructures of schools, libraries, highways, hospitals, sanitary facilities, prisons, and public safety functions. Governments cannot be all things to all people. Although sometimes messy, the functions of government must be understood and appreciated by its citizenry.

GOVERNMENT TAKES A BUM RAP

This assertion—that government takes a bum rap—assumes that government's performance is much better than its critics suggest. The media, politicians, academics, and government oversight agencies accentuate what's wrong with public sector bureaucracies. According to Charles Goodsell, public bureaucracy as stereotype, discriminator, and bungler is not an empirical reality.

Surveys and nationwide public opinion polls reveal approximately 75 percent of citizen experiences with municipal, state, and federal departments and agencies are positive. These organizations compete satisfactorily with private companies for service deliveries. According to Goodsell, American bureaucratic performance is superior.[5]

This implies that elected representatives, who supervise public managers, need to be more proactive in advocacy for government performance. According to Abramson, public managers also need to be proactive in explaining the role of the press in covering government activities. There is, likewise, a need for training public managers in public relations, marketing, and communications.[6]

GOVERNMENT MUST SHAPE UP

This perspective maintains that, individually and collectively, as employees and as a system, government needs to improve performance and images. The disincentives for innovation need to be overcome. The role of management needs continued emphasis. Managers must assume responsibility for improving the performance of their programs, for providing continuity and leadership, and for effectively recruiting, retaining, and developing personnel. If the public is to assume that public managers are members of a "profession" responsible for the performance of their colleagues and programs, better incentives are needed to promote such a vision. Support systems of government should encourage and reward public administrators rather than penalize them for taking risks. There is no public philosophy by which to judge the effectiveness of government programs. No popular consensus exists for cutting spending programs not deemed worthy of government support and raising taxes to provide a sufficient "safety net" of societal benefits for all citizens.

Some states, however, are redefining public service, and in a manner of speaking, are "shaping up." Several states are employing information technology to disperse social services to citizens. For example, Maryland implemented an electronic benefits transfer system that distributes benefits. Food stamps and welfare checks are processed through automated teller machines and grocery-store terminals. This innovation is estimated to save the state $1.2 million each year.

In other experimentations with technology, states are using multimedia kiosks in libraries and shopping malls to provide 24-hour government information and services. These touch-screen kiosks permit citizens to register their vehicles, order birth certificates, learn about job opportunities, and get access to information referrals. Such efforts reflect government's attempts "to shape up," reducing bureaucratic waste and offering citizen-customers better services more effectively.[7]

THE COUNTRY MUST SHAPE UP

The special problems of productivity are not unique to the public sector. The performance of the nation as a whole, not just the public sector, is important for a national common purpose. The federal deficits may be traced back to a society grounded in short-term consumerism with little, if any, long-term commitment to values which promote savings and investments for the future.

New creative mechanisms must be established to cause the business community and government to develop more innovative solutions to national problems. Everyone is responsible for maintaining a healthy relationship between productive public sector employees and clientele interfacing government. The country must become more disciplined in its political economy. When asked why is the U.S. falling behind in worldwide economic competition, 41 percent of a national survey conducted for the Council on Competitiveness stated that the U.S. hasn't done enough to adjust to the new challenges of economic competition, 31 percent said the U.S. work ethic and commitment to quality have declined, 19 percent believed countries like Japan ignore the principles of free trade in order to get ahead, and nine percent volunteered other answers or were not sure.[8]

PRIVATIZATION OF THE PUBLIC SECTOR

Privatization, in other words, means that a service previously produced by a government agency is now produced by a nongovernmental organization. The government may sell to private buyers or a private concern may sell to government. Contracting out, as it is often called, is thought to be more efficient because:

- It harnesses competitive forces and brings the pressure of the marketplace to bear on inefficient workers.
- It permits better management, free of most of the distractions characteristic of overtly political organizations.
- It places the costs and benefits of managerial decisions more directly on the decision maker, whose own rewards are directly at stake.[9]

As government at all levels has come under attack, the conclusion that the private sector performs and produces more effectively has received considerable credibility. If privatization is the answer in general, however, no one seems to agree on the particulars, like what products will be produced privately, or what provisions for private entrepreneurship will follow.

Conflicting definitions of privatization center around *provisions*, or providing, and *production*, or producing.[10] Executives, legislators, and judges make and interpret policies that provide a service or services. Government carries out functions as buyer and seller. A good example of services that are privatized to varying degrees is security. A four-part scheme of possible overlap of sectors, government and nongovernment, providing and producing security services follows. Note that of the four possibilities, there are two admixtures of responsibility and two possibilities where one sector or the other takes full responsibility for provision and production of security.

- **Case 1** Government does both—The legislature writes the law and provides the money; the Department of Corrections runs the prison. Neither function is private.
- **Case 2** Production is private—The City of Bloomington decides to provide security when the high school hockey teams play at the city arena and it contracts with Pinkertons for the guards.
- **Case 3** Provision is private—Government sells to a market of private buyers. The North Stars hockey team wants security at Metropolitan Sports Center, and it contracts with the Bloomington city police.
- **Case 4** Both activities are private—A department store decides that it wants uniformed security and employs (or contracts privately for) its own guards. Government performs neither activity.[11]

The policy decision in Case 1, the pure-case public sector, shows government as a public bureau producing the service. Case 2 obviously entails the controversial system of governments contracting out. Case 3 illustrates government as selling services to a private buyer. Case 4 portrays a pure case of a private agency selling to a private buyer.

Of the two words, provision is the more complicated to explain. The word "providing" can be confusing. For example, society (or government) provides medical care to the elderly; however, medical doctors are the providers. To provide in this context means to make policy, to decide, to buy, to regulate, to franchise, to finance, to subsidize. A publicly provided service is described in this manner:

> (a) where the decision whether to have it (and the decisions about who shall have it and how much of it) is a political decision, (b) when government arranges for the recipients not to have to pay directly for the service themselves, and (c) when the government selects the producer that will serve them.

A privately provided service is one

(a) where the individuals and nongovernmental organizations make their own decisions whether or not to have it, (b) where, if they choose to have it, they pay for it in full out of their own resources, whatever these may be, and (c) where they select the producer themselves.[12]

There are mixed cases of public and private provisions as well. Government may provide a service and allow citizens to decide whether to use it or not. The financing of such provisions may be divided between public and private sectors as users finance a portion and the government pays part of the costs. Some citizens (the wealthy) may pay the full cost of provisions while government picks up the complete tab for others (the poor). Government may finance the complete cost but permit the user to choose the vendor. The provision of schools is financed, publicly, via taxes.

Nontax devices, such as regulations and franchising, are used as well. Government regulations require restaurant owners to clean the premises themselves at their own expense; in franchising provisions of water, gas, or electricity, government allows a monopoly to develop, which, in turn, permits an average price, overcharging some customers while subsidizing still others. In privatizing the provision of services, government withdraws or reduces its role as buyer, regulator, standard setter, or decision maker.

Now let us examine the concepts produce, or production, as they apply to activities of government. Government officials decide to produce services that they determine should be provided. In other words, government operates, delivers, runs, performs, sells, and administers services. As emphasized, service production is less complicated than service provision. Production may be divided into line services and support, or staff, services; production may be divided into labor intensive functions, equipment and facilities; production may focus upon the substance of the work itself or the management, or administration, of work. For example, a municipality may divide refuse collection among several garbage collection companies or the management of worker pension funds among several financial institutions.

In privatizing public sector production, the question of competition is an important one. If the shift is merely from a public sector provider to a single private sector one, a monopoly supplier still exists. In recent years, the deregulation of railroads, aviation, trucking, banking, health care, and telecommunications has taken place in the private sphere to encourage competition. Despite such efforts, questions concerning competitiveness still remain.

The neat distinctions between government's primary policy decision providing a service and the secondary decision producing a service are not, in reality, easily discerned. The Federal Aviation Administration admin-

---

PUBLIC VERSUS PRIVATE POSTAL PRODUCTIVITY

Perhaps the most maligned public agency is the U.S. Postal Service (USPS). The cost of a first class stamp has risen in the past and will certainly rise steadily in the future. Statutes prohibit private firms from competition with the U.S. Postal Service for first class service. It is possible that private entrepreneurs could find cheaper, more effective ways to deliver a huge volume of first class mail, but the U.S. Postal Service is more than just a national post office. USPS is a conduit, a catalyst for undergirding capitalism by facilitating consumer advertising through the mails, for bolstering the free press, disseminating information through newspapers and magazines, and for promoting commerce in general.

By comparison, the United Parcel Service (UPS) delivers twice the number of parcels as the U.S. Postal Service, with lower rates, faster deliveries, and an 80 percent lower damage rate, and still makes a profit. But will UPS deliver your favorite fashion catalog, news magazine, or church bulletin for mere pennies? The point is that the U.S. Postal Service subsidizes at a reasonable cost many and varied cultural, economic, and even political activities in the United States.

---

isters air safety for public and private good. The Department of Defense contracts with private providers for base support and maintenance. Pinkerton and Wells Fargo, private security firms, have a long history of public service. Public day-care centers allow young mothers economic opportunities in the private sphere.

Empirical evidence generally shows private enterprises to be more efficient than public enterprises. Public sector productivity is lower than private sector productivity, labor costs are higher in the public sector than in the private sphere, and public utilities are less cost effective than private utilities.[13] On the other hand, no one promised that democratic government would be cost effective, at least when measuring efficiency; fairness is a more accurate standard for ascertaining the effectiveness of government services.

PRODUCTIVITY IMPROVEMENT BARRIERS

It cannot be denied that many of the criticisms leveled against the public sector's law productivity are fair and accurate, but the reasons for the productivity gap between public and private sectors should not be oversimplified. The following are barriers to productivity implicit in the structure of the public sector, and as such are difficult to identify and even more difficult to overcome.

- The budget process is a significant structural barrier to government productivity improvement. The demonstration of improved productivity may result in an arbitrary, across-the-board reduction in budget and staff, thereby penalizing agencies and discouraging such efforts. Managers play the budget game where incrementalism teaches administrators to spend the entire appropriation by the conclusion of the fiscal year. The line-item approach and single-year funding are also budget restraints on productivity innovations.[14]
- Personnel regulations may restrict, delay, or prevent the hiring of qualified personnel, and, likewise, the discharge of non-productive personnel. Rigid job classifications and reduction-in-force procedures constitute barriers as well. Pay increases, incentive awards, promotions, and development opportunities result more from longevity rather than from productivity incentives. Systems facilitating automatic pay increases dilute basic performance-reward relationships. Organizational configurations and administrative regulations of agencies result in multiple layers of line and staff offices and promote numerous administrative regulations governing internal operations. Internal administrative procedures may impede efficiency and effectiveness of productive work.
- Structural barriers may cause problems with centralized decision making. Regional and field offices may duplicate and fragment lines of authority. Numerous organizational layers, populated by inordinately large percentages of administrative support personnel and widely varying supervisor-to-employee ratios, often hinder efforts to promote streamlined efficiency. Lack of accountability is another obstacle to productivity improvement. Unclear agency goals, inadequate productivity measures, poor reporting systems, and top management inaction symbolize lack of accountability for individual and collective productivity.
- Low morale, inadequate pay structure, inexperienced management, senior administrator turnover, and lack of priorities for policy setting constitute serious environmental barriers to productivity improvement. Political appointees and career professionals are often at odds in program purposes and directions, resulting in professionals becoming scapegoats for program problems and failures. Political rhetoric often discredits public employment and devastates employee morale. Examples of good government rarely make headlines in the media.
- Political appointments assume substantial managerial responsibility in the federal bureaucracy but often possess limited administrative experience in carrying out such responsibilities. The managerial experience of top federal managers, who are often politically selected, is yet another environmental barrier since their former professional activities are likely in education, law and politics rather than administration. Administrative

---

SEVEN ELEMENTS OF AN EFFECTIVE PRODUCTIVITY MANAGEMENT REPORT:

1. A manager serving as a focal point for productivity in the organization.
2. Top level support and commitment.
3. Written productivity objectives and goals and an organization-wide productivity plan.
4. Productivity measures that are meaningful to the organization.
5. Use of the productivity plan and measurement system to hold managers accountable.
6. Awareness of productivity's importance throughout the organization and involvement of employees in the productivity effort.
7. An ongoing activity to regularly identify productivity problems and opportunities for improvement throughout the organization.

Source: "Increased Use of Productivity Management Can Help Control Government Costs," *GAO Report*, November 10, 1983, page 36.

---

capability is seldom a reason for choosing top policy makers. With limited administrative experience, it is not surprising that many political appointees are not familiar with the laws, regulations, and programs of their respective agencies. Turnover of political managers is high as the average tenure of an assistant secretary is only nineteen months. Interim mistakes are detrimental to the agency's productivity, and by the time most political appointees find out what's going on, they leave government service.

- The failure of federal managers to consider productivity improvement a priority constitutes a final environmental barrier. Productivity improvement efforts generally exceed the scope and tenure of appointed officials. Political appointees consider effective policymaking and direction more important than achieving managerial efficiency, and voters, reporters, and academicians do not perceive program administration as an issue on which to measure the administrator's overall effectiveness.

FEDERAL PRODUCTIVITY IMPROVEMENT PROGRESS

Productivity improvements need institutionalization; that is, the structural and environmental barriers, if they are to be eliminated, require the commitment and political leadership of executives at all government levels. To this end, the General Accounting Office (GAO) suggested that the Office of Management and Budget (OMB) assume a more active role in eradicating barriers to enhanced federal productivity.[15]

OMB has, indeed, called attention to the issue, outlining goals for productivity improvements that include a 20 percent increase in productivity by 1992 for targeted government functions, short-term improvements required for immediate deficit reduction, and a long-term focus, utilizing an institutionalized productivity program that alters the behavior of managers and efficiency of government functions. In order to realize productivity gains, however, legislation is needed to overcome constraints to improving productivity. Working with Congress, OMB intends to identify and eliminate barriers and disincentives to productivity improvements.[16]

WAYS OF MEASURING GOVERNMENT OPERATIONS

Despite all the difficulties and dilemmas that they engender, productivity measures are assuming increasing importance in public administration. Progress has been neither smooth nor swift, but it has occurred. In some instances remarkable successes have been achieved.

One of the first federal agencies to use efficiency measurements was the Division of Social Security. In the mid-1950s, it began its work-sampling program, where an employee in every office periodically measures the amount of work being done by various employees. These samples are not taken in an attempt to judge the employees' efficiency but to determine how long it takes to handle the various operations that the office is performing. This information from all Social Security offices is then compiled into averages, and each office is subsequently rated as to how it performs in respect to the overall averages for its region and for the nation as a whole.

The averages provide a useful yardstick for measuring how any one office is operating. Of course, numerous factors may make any particular office rate above or below its regional or national average. An office may be so small, for example, that maintenance functions, as opposed to line operations, consume too large a proportion of its man-hours. Nevertheless, once all such factors have been taken into account, the averages provide a tool that indicates which regions, which offices, or even which individuals are performing well and which are not.

In the early 1960s, the Bureau of the Budget (now known as the Office of Management and Budget) decided to see if other federal functions could use productivity measures. It attempted to develop such measures for five federal agencies, and two years later announced that it had succeeded in doing so. In 1971, the bureau teamed up with the General Accounting Office and the Civil Service Commission (now called the Office of Personnel Management) to launch a more all-encompassing attack on the productivity problem. This joint effort soon produced productivity measures covering 56 percent of the federal civilian work force. Pleased with this success,

OMB issued formal instructions to each federal agency with two hundred or more employees to report annually on what progress it was making to promote productivity.

As public discontent with public sector performance mounted during the 1970s, many states and municipalities began following the federal government's lead. One of the more noteworthy efforts occurred in New Jersey, which in 1978 appointed a productivity coordinator for each department of the state government. Using a modified carrot-and-stick approach, New Jersey ordered all its departments to file quarterly reports on what they were doing to improve productivity, while at the same time, the state offered the opportunity to tap a newly established Productivity Investment Fund to finance such initiatives.

The program soon began bearing fruit. By early 1980 the fund had financed 16 proposals among the 100 submitted. Many involved such simple steps as installing food freezers at a mental hospital, thereby enabling the institution to serve prepackaged frozen foods and save $70,000 by reducing personnel costs. More ambitious endeavors included new equipment in the Division of Motor Vehicles, which produced annual savings of a quarter million dollars; a revised recycling program for obsolete paper records, which turned an expense into a financial benefit; and conversion of the state's Vital Statistics and Registration program to microfilm, which cut retrieval time by 50 percent.[17]

It is generally felt that productivity measures lend themselves most easily to certain types of operations. In other words, particular functions rather than whole programs may provide the productivity analyst with the most fruitful terrain in which to toil. It is also possible, at least in many cases, to determine the productivity of a particular facility. Harry P. Hatry and Diana R. Dunn offer some ways of measuring the effectiveness of a recreation facility for example:[18]

- First, one can measure the number of people within so many miles or so many minutes of the facility in order to determine its *accessibility*. If it is a specialized facility, such as a playground, then the measure could be limited to the number of children in the appropriate age group. Census maps, police listings, and other data can be used to discover whether the facility is conveniently located. The proximity to public transportation can also be taken into account.
- From there we can go on to measure *usage*, taking into account how many persons actually use the facility, how often they use it, and for how long. This can be estimated by visiting the facility at representative times and taking random samples of the participants, asking them how often they come, what services they use, how long they stay, and so on. Some estimate of crowdedness can also be made by examining sign-up sheets or by observation of waiting times. The evaluator can also ask users if they feel crowded.

- *Safety* is another factor that should enter into the evaluation. What is the rate of injury? What about crime? These data can be supplemented by asking users if they felt the facility was dangerous. The accidents and the crime that may occur in the facility must be balanced, however, with the accidents and crime that it may have averted elsewhere. Unsupervised swimming and playing on public streets also lead to accidents. Lack of recreational outlets can be linked to increased crime. Has the facility had any impact on crime and accidents in the neighborhoods it serves?
- *Attractiveness* is another, although perhaps lesser, criterion that can be utilized in weighing the productivity of a recreational facility. Does it contribute to the neighborhood's physical design? Does it upgrade the neighborhood? Here, in addition to the opinion of residents, one can check the effect, if any, on property valuations and possibly on the amount of business done by nearby commercial establishments.
- Then there is the final and determining factor of overall *satisfaction*. People in the area served by the facility can be asked such questions as, "Would you say that the recreational opportunities in this community are excellent, good, fair, or poor?" Doing this on a yearly basis will provide some idea of trends.

Much of the evaluation will be achieved through polling. This, however, need not be extensive or expensive, for only a reasonably representative sample is required. The results can be matched against other data. If, for example, the community served by the facility had a population of 100,000 and attendance at the facility came to 50,000, and if a random sample of 100 users showed that they used the facility 2.5 times a year, it can be estimated that about 20,000 people, or one-fifth of the community, are being served.

Hatry and Dunn claim that evaluations of recreational programs can be done at a cost of no more than one or two percent of the recreation budget. It is an expenditure that might be well worth making.

It is also possible to develop productivity measures for entire programs. The Institute of Traffic Management at Northwestern University, for example, has worked out what it calls a law enforcement index for evaluating the effectiveness of a police department in enforcing traffic laws. It is based on a simple equation in long division, the number of citations divided by the number of fatal and personal injury accidents:

$$\text{Enforcement Index} = \frac{\text{citations with penalties}}{\text{number of fatal \& personal injury accidents}}$$

The institute says that the Enforcement Index, or EI, should equal 20. In other words, a police department should give out penalty citations equal to twenty times the number of fatalities and personal-injury accidents caused by motorists.

It should be noted that the approach differs considerably from the more simplistic quota system used by many police departments. Under the latter system, traffic officers are instructed to hand out a fixed number of citations every day or week. The Enforcement Index established a relationship between enforcement and accidents, and, since evidence indicates that accident rates do respond positively to traffic enforcement, the number of citations is allowed to fall as the number of such accidents declines. If a department could reduce the number of such accidents occurring in its jurisdiction to one a year, it would need to give out only twenty citations in order to meet the standard set by the index.

Establishing productivity measures for crime control, however, remains much more illusive. It is possible, for example, that improved police work can bring about an *increase* in the reported crime rate. Why is this? Simply because most crimes do not get reported. If a police department starts improving its operations, including the strengthening of its relationships with the community, this could cause more crimes to be reported. For this, as well as other reasons, crime rates by themselves do not provide a basic, reliable measure of police effectiveness.

Crime rates do tell us something, however, and when used in conjunction with other measures, they may offer valuable clues in assessing the quality of law enforcement. What are some of these other measures? They include such things as attitude surveys (i.e., do people feel they are better protected?); pedestrian flows, particularly at night; merchants staying open after dark; the number of arrests; the number of cases won in court (the latter element is often omitted in reports of cases cleared by the police); the number of complaints against the police; and the number of police officers and civilians killed or injured in police-civilian encounters. The task of evaluating police effectiveness in fighting crime is by no means easy, but it is by no means impossible.

One city that has attempted not only to measure police productivity but also to tie it into police pay is Orange, California. In 1973, this middle class city of 89,000 put into effect a plan to raise police salaries one percent for each three percent drop in the rate of robbery, rape, auto theft, and burglary. Some 16 months later, the rate in those categories of crime had gone down by 19 percent, and the city police officers were looking forward to a pay raise of $119 a month.

Not all observers were impressed with the results. Concern was expressed that the figures might have been juggled in one way or another to make a better showing. The Urban Institute, in an evaluation of the experiment, said in defense of the program, "The incentive agreement . . . appears to have been successful in achieving its immediate goal of reducing the total number of reported rapes, robberies, burglaries and auto thefts."[19]

PRINCIPLES OF ENTREPRENEURAL GOVERNMENT

1. Entrepreneural public organizations act as *catalysts*. The old-model government used bureaucracies, but entrepreneural governments increasingly find other ways to get the job done.
2. Entrepreneural governments are *competitive*. The old-model governments were monopolies and viewed competition in the public sector as waste and duplication.
3. Entrepreneural governments are *mission* driven. Bureaucratic public organizations are driven by rules and by budgets.
4. Entrepreneural governments shift accountability to outcomes, producing *results-oriented government*.
5. Entrepreneural governments are *customer* driven.
6. *Anticipatory government*, the idea of prevention rather than cure, addresses the rapidly changing world in which we live.
7. *Community-owned government* reflects the idea of pushing control of services and public programs into the hands of communities. Enterprising government captures the idea of earning money rather than spending it.
8. Entrepreneural government must be *decentralized* in order to preserve its *flexibility*.
9. Entrepreneural government is *market-oriented* and does not always create programs to attack problems.

Source: Ted Gaebler and David Osborne, "Reinventing Government: An Agenda for the 1990s," *Public Management*, Vol. 74, No. 3 (March 1992), 4–8. See also: *Reinventing Government: How the Entrepreneural Spirit Is Transforming the Public Sector* (New York: Addison-Wesley Publishing Co., 1992).

PAYOFFS OF PRODUCTIVITY: ENHANCING MORALE AND WORK SATISFACTION

Assuming that productivity measures can be developed and implemented, the benefits to public administration and the public in general would seem to be immense. First and foremost, of course, is an increase in output both in terms of efficiency and effectiveness. Katz and Kahn claim that "knowledge of results in itself motivates people toward improving their performance. Level of aspiration studies," they say, "indicate that individuals tend to raise their sights when they see the outcome of their efforts. If there is continuous feedback on the basis of some objective criterion of behavior, people will be motivated to improve their scores."[20]

It must not be assumed that this reaction leads to exhausted, and eventually exasperated, employees. On the contrary, such goal raising is likely to increase employee satisfaction. Marshall Edward and Gladys Ogden

Dimock cite research indicating that employee work satisfaction goes up when standards are raised.[21] Productivity measures, therefore, despite the fears and frustrations that they may initially arouse, should lead to increased employee morale and increased work satisfaction.

Evidence of this has already been seen in New York City. Former Deputy Mayor Hamilton describes how under a productivity improvement program, the city Parks and Recreation Department abolished their policy of assigning one or more employees on a permanent basis to take care of a particular park. Instead, the workers were grouped into three crews of three and sent from park to park as a team. According to Hamilton, not only did the output of the crews double that achieved by persons working alone with permanent assignments, but "the morale of the work force increased noticeably because, as they said, they could see the results of their work and they took the new system as evidence that someone was taking an interest in their jobs."[22]

Productivity measures tend to work for, rather than against, the public employee in other ways as well. In the absence of productivity measures and ratings, the bad often tends to show up more than the good. Attention is more easily aroused when things go wrong than when things go right. Productivity measures make it easier to bring to light superior as well as substandard performance.

In doing this, productivity measurements offer a better method for determining promotions of one kind or another. Use of such measures may obviate the need for traditional efficiency ratings and all the problems that they present. They also may permit a reduced emphasis on seniority. A good set of productivity measures can provide administrators with an impartial method of determining and rewarding merit.

Measuring productivity may also provide a basis for deemphasizing rules, regulations, and even supervision itself. Working with a good set of productivity measures, the employee can often become his or her own boss, at least to a substantial extent. Objective criteria, rather than a supervisor, guide an employee's labors and determine his or her achievements.

All of these factors can foster innovation, for once specific goals have been set, they should tend to become more important than the procedures for achieving them. The increased flexibility that results, along with the spur to use it, can widen and enrich the employee's scope of work. To cite one example, Wisconsin Correction Department officials, responding to a productivity effort, abolished the rule limiting female probation officers to counseling only women offenders. By doing away with this rule, the department was able to equalize work loads and reduce the overall number of probationary employees needed. At the same time, it broadened the work experience of one group of probation officers.[23]

Productivity measures may also augment the positive features of the small group while modifying its less advantageous aspects. The genial alcoholic whose failings were previously covered up by his associates may now find himself forced to confront his problem as his comrades balk at his failure to contribute his share to their measurable output. A member of the group, on the other hand, who may have been ostracized for reading poetry rather than joining in the lunchtime card game, may win a greater measure of acceptance by making a worthwhile contribution to the group's performance.

A change in management's attitude may also result. The U.S. National Commission on Productivity in a 1972 study of British experiences in productivity bargaining found that it "induced management to abandon its defensive posture toward work rules and practices and to take the initiative in improving both the health of the enterprise and the welfare of the workers."[24]

In summary, productivity measures, despite the problems they present and the limitations under which they must work, may have much to offer present-day public administration. At a session of the New York City conference on productivity, former Ford Foundation President, McGeorge Bundy, called such initiatives "the beginning of the kind of human endeavor in which nearly everybody wins."[25]

PROGRAM EVALUATION AND POLICY DEVELOPMENT

When PPBS began to diminish in the federal bureaucracy, many found a replacement in another analytical device—*program evaluation*. Some state and municipal governments have warmly welcomed this technique and have even set up offices to evaluate their program performance.

According to Ralph C. Chandler and Jack C. Plano (*The Public Administration Dictionary*. New York: John Wiley & Sons, 1982), program evaluation is "an assessment of the effectiveness of a program through the application of a research design aimed at obtaining valid and verifiable information on the structure, processes, outputs, and impacts of the program. Program evaluation is an effort to help decision makers determine whether to maintain, modify, or discontinue a specified program. Program evaluation is concerned with whether program activities have been successful in resolving the public problem identified, and the extent to which other factors may have contributed to the problem's resolution (page 91).

There are three phases in program evaluation: (1) selection and identification of goals and objectives of the program; (2) execution of the evaluation according to scientific guidelines; (3) feedback of results and recommendations.

The overall goals of program evaluation, or PE as it is sometimes called, can be simply stated. PE increases our understanding of government activities, leads to governmental improvements, and produces financial savings. The tools it uses also seem familiar—for the most part, they greatly resemble the types of analytical devices developed for PPBS, ZBB, and MBO, Management by Objectives.

Legislative backing and buttressing have played a major role in the flourishing of program evaluation at all government levels. Conservatives looked to the technique to bring out all sorts of failures in the numerous social service programs of the 1960s. Liberals hoped to use it to show the efficacy of such endeavors. Underlying all these partisan or ideological concerns was growing citizen dissatisfaction over rising taxes and what seemed to many a decreasing quality of public services.

Today program evaluation seems quite firmly entrenched in U.S. government. The Congressional Budget Office, Congressional Research Service, General Accounting Office, and Office of Management and Budget evaluate federal programs. Over two-thirds of the states also engage in some form of systematic evaluation, along with a rising number of cities. However, disputes continue to rage over the role and impact of such assessments.

The first task of the program evaluator is to know and state just what he or she is to evaluate. This may sound like a monstrous platitude, yet it frequently presents perplexing problems. The program evaluators may have one thing in mind, the agency for which they work may have another, those operating the program being evaluated may have another, and so on. Some clear-cut consensus should prevail on the specific purpose of the evaluation before those making it start to work.

The desirability of clarifying the specific goals of the evaluation should not cause the evaluators to overlook incidental pieces of information that result from their efforts. Sometimes these incidental results yield more important information than the main thrust of the study itself. To take one example, the Indianapolis Police Department decided to let their police officers take patrol cars home and use them as their regular, off-duty means of transportation. It was hoped that this would create more police visibility and therefore lower the crime rate. An evaluation conducted by the Urban Institute one year after the launching of the program failed to show any significant drop in the rate of crime. It did, however, reveal a rather remarkable reduction in the number of fatal auto accidents. The number of such fatalities declined from 59 to 40, a decrease of almost one-third. Since auto accidents take far more lives than homicides, this "side effect" of the program may have been more important than the program's stipulated goal.

Who should do evaluations? Agencies often like to perform their own, but this obviously presents problems. Some degree of insulation is probably necessary for the program evaluators if they are to do their job properly. On the other hand, insulating them too fully from those who are running the program may make it too difficult for them to discover what is really going on behind the numbers. As it is, they are likely to encounter resistance, for "the lower level program administrator and his/her staff literally see their bread and butter at risk when the program evaluator arrives on the scene."[26]

Low-level administrators are not the only ones who tend to turn skittish when the evaluators come into view. Higher-level administrators and politicians frequently find evaluations disquieting. Large portions of the public itself with a deep financial, ideological, or simply emotional involvement in a particular program may disown or disregard an evaluation that fails to confirm their commitment. Finally, evaluators themselves often come to their jobs encumbered with predilections and prejudices that can contaminate their conclusions.

The difficulties that program evaluations entail have brought concern to many, including some of its initial boosters. While thoroughly complete and careful evaluations are probably rare, reasonably sound appraisals of ongoing and proposed programs have been made and put to effective use. In the early 1970s, conservative Republicans relied on such evaluations to end some of the least productive poverty programs. In the early 1980s, a negative evaluation of the MX missile system helped liberal Democrats in Congress garner enough votes to block the program, at least temporarily. Meanwhile, back at the grass roots, many public managers are using program evaluations, albeit often in an abridged form, to help bring their activities more into step with the demands and desires of a changing and increasingly cost-conscious society.

MANAGEMENT BY OBJECTIVES

Perhaps the most popular device yet developed for promoting productivity, and one that incorporates many of the tools and techniques of productivity measurement and program evaluation, is management by objectives (MBO). It expands the basic elements of productivity measurement and program evaluation into a system for operating the entire organization.

MBO owes its origin to Peter Drucker, and it did much to establish him as the presiding "guru" of modern management theory. Drucker has long insisted that all one can measure is performance and that all one should measure is performance. He evolved MBO as a method of putting this principle into practice.[27]

MBO's central idea certainly poses few perplexities. It simply stipulates that organizations and their leaders should be judged strictly by their results. Personnel practices, communication flows, administrative structure, and all the other ingredients of organizational life become important only to the extent that they contribute to or detract from organizational achievement. Results alone count.

Some may argue that this single-minded focus on results smacks of fanaticism and folly. It also calls to mind the philosophically dubious principle that the end always justifies the means. The priority of ends over means has, however, been recognized since Aristotle.[28] If, in some areas of human activity, the intensive implementation of this principle may lead to morally reprehensible deeds, Drucker and his growing band of believers claim that the results of emphasizing results will be far, far different when applied to management.

MBO starts out with some organizational soul-searching to define its mission. The organization must attempt to answer the question, "For what purpose does our organization exist?" ("What are we here for?") The *missions* of most organizations are essentially ongoing and open-ended; they do not have a fixed, terminated point. But this isn't true for all. Some organizations exist to accomplish a particular purpose, and once they accomplish it, they dissolve. The differences will, of course, be reflected in their stated missions. However, most organizations will adopt broad and inclusive mission statements listing no specific and measurably achievable ends.

Earlier in the book we saw that nearly every organization is a part of another, larger organization. This obviously will influence its mission statement. Normally, an organization's mission will be narrower and less inclusive than its parent organization while broader and more inclusive than those of its own subunits. A state department of conservation, for example, may take as its mission the maintenance of a healthy and attractive environment; its division of air quality may make its mission the maintenance of air that is safe and healthful to breathe; and the air monitoring laboratory within this division may limit its mission simply to the testing of air to see if it meets air quality-control standards.

After determining its mission, the organization must give itself a *goal*. The goal has been defined as "a statement of intended output in the broadest terms. It is normally not related to a specific time period."[29] This makes the goal sound identical to the mission, but an important difference does exist. It is found in the words "intended output." The mission statement generally deals only with the outcome of an agency's activity. The goal statement gives us the output. One way of distinguishing between the two is by noting that the laws setting up an agency usually provide the basis for its mission; its goals will usually be formulated by itself. In drawing up and divulging its goals, top management communicates its decisions regarding the organization's aims and relative priorities and provides general guidance to its employer, clients, political overseers, and so on, as they relate to the organization's proposed strategy.

Once it has defined its mission and designed one or more long-range goals, including the general means intended to achieve that mission, the organization now proceeds to hammer out its *objectives*. Objectives—the results to be accomplished within a certain period of time—should exhibit four essential features: *concreteness, attainability, desirability,* and *measurability.*

Objectives can be major or minor; if major, they will relate much more directly and impact more sharply on the organization's basic goals. They may also be long-term, requiring more than a year for their fulfillment, or short-term, being achievable within the budget year.

Finally, the organization and its subunits will normally establish *milestones.* As the name implies, these are checkpoints placed along the way toward the objectives. If the long-range objective of a school is to reduce its truancy by 30 percent, and if its short-range objective is to accomplish a 15 percent drop in truancy during the current school year, it might well want to check periodically to see how it is doing. Each of these monitoring events will constitute a milestone in its MBO operation.

POLICY DEVELOPMENT

The taxing, budgeting, and government spending priorities place program evaluation at the center, not at the periphery, of policy making in the public sector. In order to improve the effectiveness of program evaluation, such priorities need to assume their rightful place at the center of the policy making and budget making processes. Program evaluation needs consideration alongside financial and political sources of information. According to Larry Polivka and Laurey T. Stryker, the principal purposes of the program review unit are to bring rigorous analytical perspective to influence agency budget requests, to assess agency effectiveness for meeting program objectives as set forth by the legislature and executive, and to develop program performance measures for agency implementation.[30]

The effectiveness of the evaluation unit depends upon the location of the evaluation, the selection process, the implementation of recommendations, and the evaluation strategies. Implementation of recommendations occurs as incorporation of evaluation results are part of the governor's high priority statement, agency policy guidelines, budget development process, performance agreement monitoring, process (or efficiency) and outcome (or effectiveness) of program budget measures, and annual legislation.

PPBS, ZBB, MBO, and similar policy planning and budgeting innovations clarify and rationalize the development of public policy; however, evaluation focuses upon fundamental value choices that contribute to initiate or terminate a policy or increase or reduce program appropriations. Polivka and Stryker, formerly analysts for the Office of Governor, State of Florida, outline certain conditions for maintaining a consistently influential role for program evaluation in the policy and budget development processes of state government.

• Evaluations are done by a unit organizationally close to key decision makers, rather than one buried in the bureaucracy;
• Key decision makers are actively involved in the selection of evaluation topics and the formulation of research designs;
• The policy budget development processes have a formal structure with relatively rational decision making procedures that are heavily dependent on information, including evaluation data;
• Evaluations are clearly designed to address a significant policy issue(s) and are neither more nor less methodologically sophisticated than is required to make a reasonably valid, relevant, and timely contribution to the resolution of the policy issue;
• The evaluator is prepared to play an assertive role in the policy and budgeting processes by clearly articulating and actively defending policy positions most compatible with the findings of his/her study;
• Evaluators are not demoralized by the fact that decision makers will frequently make policy choices that are responsive to factors other than evaluation findings. Political and fiscal conditions change and evaluation findings and recommendations which are initially rejected may later be used in the generation of new or amended policies.[31]

Since the productivity challenge in the public sector is hampered by structural and environmental barriers, the need for evaluation of productivity is always present. In the private sphere, technology becomes an intervening factor between monetary rewards and corporate failures. However, productivity indices in the public sector are grounded in politics with merit principles sometimes receiving less prominence. As citizens, elected officials, and administrators consider the effectiveness of the bottom-line delivery of public services, there will be enhanced interest in proactive, rather than reactive, program evaluations and employee performance evaluations.

SUMMARY

- Measuring productivity has long been an accepted, almost routine, practice in business. This, however, has not been the case in government. Productivity in the public sector refers to *excellence* in individual and collective performance. There are widely divergent views as to what excellence really is.
- Four reasons explain the public's dissatisfaction with government performance. They are: Democracy is messy; government takes a bum rap; government must shape up; and the country must shape up.
- Definitions of the *privatization* of public responsibilities center around provisions, or providing, and production, or producing, of goods and services. Privatization, often called contracting out, means that a service previously produced by a government agency is now produced by a nongovernmental organization.
- *Barriers* to productivity measurement are numerous. The budget process is a significant structural barrier to federal productivity improvement. Personnel systems may restrict, delay, or prevent the hiring of qualified personnel and the discharge of nonproductive personnel. Structural barriers may cause problems with centralized decision-making. Regional and field offices may duplicate and fragment lines of authority. Lack of accountability is an obstacle to productivity improvement, as are also low morale, inadequate pay structure, managerial inexperience, senior administrator turnover, and misplaced priorities for policy making and direction.
- *Efficiency* means doing things well, while *effectiveness* means doing the right things well. Efficiency is essentially the input or contribution of labor, capital, and other resources into an effort matched against the output of product produced or measured, regardless of the mechanism selected to gauge output. Effectiveness, meanwhile, calls for a preestablished standard of comparison, a focus upon a certain quality of production, an ability to mobilize, organize, and direct resources for specified purposes, all taken within a certain cultural context.
- Accessibility, usage, safety, attractiveness, and overall satisfaction constitute preset ways of measuring effectiveness of public services. The *enforcement index*, a mechanism for gauging the effectiveness of enforcing traffic laws, is an example of one of these preset evaluation tools.
- Assuming that productivity measures can be developed and implemented, the benefits to public administration and the public in general are immense. *Measuring productivity* may also provide a basis for de-emphasizing rules, regulations, and even supervision itself. Working with a good set of productivity measures, the employee can often become his or her own boss, at least to a substantial extent. Objective criteria, rather than a supervisor, guide an employee's labors and determine his or her achievements.

- Entrepreneural public organizations act as catalysts to innovation, are competitive, mission driven, produce results-oriented government, are customer driven, anticipatory, community-owned, decentralized, flexible, and market-oriented.
- *Program evaluation,* which may increase our understanding of government activities and lead to improved productivity and financial savings, is firmly entrenched in government. PPBS, ZBB, and MBO are illustrations of attempts to evaluate public programs. The principal purposes of program evaluation are to bring rigorous analytical perspective to influence agency budget requests, to assess agency effectiveness for meeting program objectives established by elected leaders, and to develop program performance measures for agency implementation.

When discussing the area of productivity, it's easy to get wrapped up in theories and forget the human element. This case study is a simple reminder that people and their feelings are key factors in productivity.

CASE STUDY

A Problem of Motivation[32]

As part of a work-force program to make mothers who were recipients of Aid to Families with Dependent Children (AFDC) self-supporting, the State Tourism and Recreation Department employed six women and assigned them to various divisions. Under the plan, the federal and state governments jointly paid the women's salaries while they underwent a six-month training program. At the end of this period, each division had the option of hiring or releasing the women—a decision based on performance and the recommendations of supervisors.

Julie Davis was one of the three trainees chosen for regular employment, assigned to the Tourist Information Office. The mother of two girls, ages six and eight, Davis had received aid from AFDC since her husband was killed in an auto accident five years before. On her marrying she had given up her job as a receptionist and typist in a wholesale grocery firm. Davis had naturally reentered the workforce with some trepidation, given her 10-year hiatus from the workforce. Initially she displayed enthusiasm and performed her duties efficiently. After about six weeks, however, Jeff Baker, her supervisor, noticed she was developing poor working habits such as long coffee breaks, tardiness, and absenteeism.

Baker felt Davis' low performance had resulted from her association with two employees in the Conventions unit of the department. Baker arranged a meeting with her and advised her of the unacceptability of her work behavior. He had received complaints from other employees that she was not carrying her share of the load. "Julie," he said, "generally your work has been very good but lately your job performance has not lived up to expectations. Although our standards are higher than other sections of this department, the chances for promotion and career advancement are a lot better for the hard-working employee. You can do a lot better than you have been doing!" After the session with Baker, Davis' work and behavior immediately improved. She volunteered to assist others whenever her own work was completed and quickly acquired the necessary skills for several other positions in the section. She often worked as a substitute in the absence of other employees.

At the end of the training period, Baker recommended that the agency hire Davis at the level of Grade 5. The quality of her work remained consistently high and she continued to assist others willingly. Six months later, when she had completed a year with the agency, she was promoted to Grade 6 and assigned additional responsibilities. Indeed, a bright future seemed on the horizon.

About two months later, one of the employees Davis had been assisting resigned because of a death in the family. The announcement for the newly opened position emphasized it was limited to employees of the department. Since Davis was familiar with many aspects of the position, she discussed applying for it with Baker, who advised her that even though she was the only staff member familiar with the job, her chance of being on the list of applicants supplied by the Bureau of Personnel was small because she had only fourteen months' experience instead of the required two years. He said she would make the list only if there were no applicants with the required experience. This was possible, though unlikely. Davis decided to apply and hope for the best. There were several applicants with the required experience and she did not make the list.

Davis' attitude changed immediately. She became irritable and her relationship with other staff members deteriorated. She developed intense feelings of insecurity. Each time a new employee was hired she felt as though she might be replaced. As a result of this constant fear she developed an ulcer. In another meeting with her, Baker reassured her of her abilities, explained the steps involved in employee termination, and outlined the grievance procedures available to employees should termination occur. Initially, Davis seemed to gain confidence and her work improved, although not to the level of her previous performance. She had become confused and felt angry toward Baker for what she considered to be unwarranted encouragement.

Since Baker felt he could no longer adequately motivate Davis, he recommended that she be transferred to another supervisor, Malcolm Tate. After a few weeks, her work performance and attitude improved considerably, and Tate soon considered her among the best employees he had ever supervised.

The problem in the department appeared to be resolved, but Tate was to encounter the same problem as Baker. In the next four months, two employees under Tate's supervision were to retire. Both positions were at the Grade 7 level. Davis was now qualified for both, but there were others in the agency better qualified. Even if she made the list, there was a good possibility she would not be selected for the position.

QUESTIONS AND INSTRUCTIONS

1. Was transferring Davis the best course of action Baker could have taken? What other choices did he have?
2. Do rules stating that a person must have two years' experience bear any relationship to the realities of an employee's efficiency and the needs of an organization? Should the rules be reviewed?
3. Do you feel that the manner in which Davis was hired through the work-force program affected her job performance?
4. Do you feel that Davis' home situation may have been the cause of her attitudes toward her job?
5. Should Tate have encouraged Davis to apply for a new position when the possibility of not being selected existed?
6. What could Tate have done to prevent the recurrence of the previous situation if Davis was not selected for one of the Grade 7 positions?
7. Davis seemed to be experiencing stress. What do you think could have been the main cause of the stress? Was the stress-risk behavior related to the actions of others or was it related to her own expectations? What could Baker have done to reduce the level of personal stress that Davis was experiencing? What could Davis have done about her own situation?
8. Did Davis appear to be internally or externally motivated? What are the implications associated with both of these motivations?
9. What follow-up program should the state adopt for graduates of work-force programs now holding jobs?

ENDNOTES

1. *New York Times,* 20 April 1971.
2. Peter Blau, *Bureaucracy in Modern Society* (New York: Random House, 1956), 58–59.
3. Edward K. Hamilton, "Productivity: The New York Approach," *Public Administration Review,* Vol. 32, No. 6 (November–December, 1972), 784–795.
4. Mark A. Abramson, "The Public Manager and Excellence," *The Bureaucrat,* Vol. 14, No. 3 (Fall, 1985), 9–13.
5. Charles T. Goodsell, *The Case for Bureaucracy* (Chatham, NJ: Chatham House Publishers, 1983), 55–60.
6. Abramson, "The Public Manager and Excellence," 11.
7. Mitch Betts, "States Redefining Public Service," *Computerworld,* Vol. 27, No. 16 (April 19, 1993), 1–2.
8. "Campaign '92: Looking Back, Looking Ahead," *Challenges,* Vol. 5, No. 10 (Washington: Council on Competitiveness, December 1992), pages 1, 4.
9. E. S. Savas, *Privatizing the Public Sector* (Chatham, NJ: Chatham House, 1982), 89.
10. Ted Kolderie, "The Two Different Concepts of Privatization," *Public Administration Review,* Vol. 46, No. 4 (July/August, 1986), 285–291.

11. *Ibid.*, 285.

12. *Ibid.*, 286.

13. Steve H. Hanke, "Privatization: Theory, Evidence, and Implementation," in *Control of Spending*, edited by C. Lowell Harris, *Proceedings of the Academy of Political Science*, Vol. 35, No. 4 (New York: 1985), 101–113.

14. Brian L. Usilaner, "Federal Productivity Problems and Progress," *The Bureaucrat*, Vol. 14, No. 2 (Summer, 1985), 54–58.

15. U.S. General Accounting Office, *Increased Use of Productivity Management Can Help Control Government Costs*, GAO/AFMD-84-11, November 10, 1983.

16. Executive Office of the President, Office of Management and Budget, *Management of the United States Government: Fiscal Year 1986* (Washington: Government Printing Office, 1986), 67.

17. Richard F. Keevey, "State Productivity Improvements: Building on Existing Strengths," *Public Administration Review*, Vol. 40, No. 5 (September–October, 1980), 451–458.

18. Harry P. Hatry and Diana R. Dunn, *Measuring the Effectiveness of Local Government Services: Recreation* (Washington: Urban Institute, 1971).

19. *New York Times*, 10 November 1974.

20. Daniel Katz and Robert L. Kahn, *The Social Psychology of Organizations* (New York: John Wiley, 1966), 421.

21. Marshall E. Dimock and Gladys O. Dimock, *Public Administration*, 4th ed. (New York: Holt, Rinehart and Winston, 1969), 377.

22. Hamilton, "Productivity: The New York Approach," *Public Administration Review*, 784–795.

23. Patrick J. Lucey, "Wisconsin's Productivity Policy," *Public Administration Review*, Vol. 32, No. 6 (November–December, 1972), 795–799.

24. U.S. Civil Service Commission, General Accounting Office, and Office of Management and Budget, *Measuring and Enhancing Productivity in the Federal Sector*, mimeograph edition (Washington, D.C.: June, 1972).

25. *New York Times*, 20 March 1973.

26. Thomas V. Greer and Joanne G. Greer, "Problems in Evaluating Costs and Benefits of Social Programs," *Public Administration Review*, Vol. 42, No. 2 (March–April, 1982), 151–156.

27. Peter Drucker, *The Practice of Management* (New York: Harper & Row, 1954). This was his first book to describe MBO. See especially Chapter 11.

28. The opening paragraphs of Aristotle's Nicomachean Ethics not only underscore this point but actually provide some of the underlying premises for MBO.

29. George S. Odiorne, *Management by Objectives: A System of Managerial Leadership* (New York: Pitman, 1965), 18.

30. Larry Polivka and Laurey T. Stryker, "Program Evaluation and the Policy Process in State Government: An Effective Linkage," *Public Administration Review*, Vol. 43, No. 3 (May/June, 1983), 255–259.

31. *Ibid.*, 259.

32. "A Problem of Motivation," in *Practicing Public Management: A Casebook*, by C. Kenneth Meyer and Charles H. Brown (New York: St. Martin's Press, 2nd edition, 1989), 103–105. Reprinted with permission of St. Martin's Press.

11

☆ ☆ ☆

ADMINISTRATIVE LAW AND CONTROL

CHAPTER HIGHLIGHTS

THE IMPACT OF ADMINISTRATIVE GROWTH ON
DEMOCRATIC IDEALS AND ADMINISTRATIVE LAW
TRADITIONAL AND CONTEMPORARY CORNERSTONES
OF AMERICAN ADMINISTRATIVE LAW
WHAT IS ADMINISTRATIVE LAW?
ADMINISTRATIVE DISCRETION AND ITS LIMITS
THE EXPANDING ROLE OF ADMINISTRATIVE LAW JUDGES
ADMINISTRATIVE CONTROLS: INTERNAL AND EXTERNAL
LAW AND CONTROL: HOW MUCH IS ENOUGH?

During the first 100 years of U.S. history, several factors conspired to keep the administrative sector of our many governments comparatively small and weak. Fragmentation and personalism, for example, deterred the growth of large and formalized bureaucracies like those starting to emerge in Europe. The antigovernmental attitudes of the American people probably acted as an even greater deterrent. In the end, our legalistic approach to governmental problems may have served as the greatest deterrent of all.

The ways in which U.S. legalism imposed limits on, and even substituted for, administrative power were noticed by Lord James Bryce, the perceptive British observer who began visiting our shores late in the nineteenth century. In his 1888 book, *The American Commonwealth*, Bryce wrote:

> *It is a great merit of American government that it relies very little on officials [administrators] and arms them with little power of arbitrary interference. . . . [The government] has taken the direction of acting through the law rather than through the officials. That is to say, when it prescribes to the citizen a particular course of action it has relied upon the ordinary legal sanctions, instead of investing the administrative officers with inquisitional duties or powers that might prove oppressive.*[1]

As the quotation suggests, Bryce wholly approved of this approach. Had he been more legalistically trained or oriented himself, he might have pointed to a particular legalistic feature of our system that served as the main roadblock to a greater assumption of power and responsibility by U.S. administrators. This feature is our constitutionally enshrined principle of separation of powers.

The Constitution stipulates that the legislative branch enact the laws and the executive branch execute and enforce them. Through the first century of our existence, the courts—the judicial branch—took a particularly rigorous attitude toward this demarcation of authority. They ruled that Congress could not give away its power, even if it voted in such a manner. Consequently, all efforts to bestow substantial discretion on any administrator or administrative agency drew the Supreme Court's prompt disapproval. Congress, said the Court, could not delegate its fundamental powers. Rules and regulations that would have the force of law would have to be passed by the body charged with passing laws.

As Bryce was writing his 1888 book, however, the Court was getting ready to alter the whole course of U.S. administrative history. Congress, confronted with the pressing need to regulate the country's sprawling railroad industry, realized that it could not possibly devote the continuous time and effort that such a task demanded, and passed the Interstate Commerce Act of 1887. This act set up a new agency, the Interstate Commerce Commission, to carry out this regulatory function. In a landmark decision that signaled a major change in policy, the Supreme Court ruled the Interstate Commerce Act, along with the agency it established, to be constitutional.

It should be pointed out that the newly created ICC was scarcely given carte blanche discretion. Congress set down specific standards regarding its jurisdiction and prescribed rather detailed criteria for use of its discretionary power in policing the railroads. Congress even spelled out the various forms of misbehavior that the ICC was to police, such as rebating, rate discrimination, and pooling. The new regulatory commission was, in the words of Theodore Lowi, "relatively well shackled by clear standards of public policy, as stated in the statute and as understood in common law."[2]

From this time on, Congress, along with most state legislatures, began delegating more and more legislative power to administrative agencies, and the Supreme Court became increasingly cooperative in permitting them to do so. When Congress amplified the ICC's powers, for instance, by passing the Transportation Act of 1920, the Court let the Act stand, even though the increased powers were accompanied by far fewer specific criteria to guide and control their application.

Although the court had backtracked considerably over its once hard line stand on delegation, it was still not ready to capitulate completely. The Court, for example, played havoc with the Federal Trade Commission during the first 20 years of its life, invalidating order after order of the agency on the ground that the congressionally imposed standard of "unfair method of competition," which the agency was charged with enforcing, was too vague. Such vagueness, said the Court, gave the agency too much discretionary power.[3]

The New Deal brought the issue to a head when President Roosevelt, trying to wield broad executive power to pull the country out of the depression, found himself on a collision course with the nation's highest tribunal, leading to a series of hostile Court decisions which culminated in the famous Schechter case of 1934.[4] In this case, a majority of the justices struck down the National Recovery Act and with it the elaborate planning machinery and the wide blanket of administrative power that the act had promulgated.

The Reagan Administration approached things quite differently. According to Harold Seidman and Robert Gilmour, Roosevelt's "New Deal" marked the birth of the positive state, and the Reagan "revolution" was geared to end it.[5] "The evolution from the positive to the regulatory state commenced in the 1960s, but President Reagan was the first to redefine the federal government's role as limited, wherever possible, to providing services without producing them."[6] Reagan worked to privatize government services in an effort to minimize to the negative aspects of big government.

DEFINING ADMINISTRATIVE LAW

Administrative law is an amorphous body of law. . . . Administrative law is created or affected by the activities of government agenices. The term 'administrative law' is akin to many other conceptual terms and is hard to define.
—Joseph J. Simeone

Administrative law controls a system: a system which, in the simplest terms, has only one goal: to deliver government services to its citizens.
—Charles Koch, Jr.

1. That branch of law concerned with the procedures by which administrative agencies make rules and adjudicate cases; the conditions under which these actions can be reviewed by courts. 2. The legislation that creates administrative agencies. 3. The rules and regulations promulgated by administrative agencies. 4. The law government judicial review of adminstrative actions.
—Jay M. Shafritz

Sources: Joseph J. Simeone, "The Function, Flexibility, and Future of United States Judges of the Executive Branch," *Administrative Law Review*, Vol. 44, No. 1 (Winter 1992), 159–161; Charles Koch Jr. *Administrative Law and Practice* (New York: West Publishing Co., 1985); Jay M. Shafritz, *The Dorsey Dictionary of American Government and Politics* (Chicago: The Dorsey Press, 1988).

During the past 50 years, the administrative sector has surged forward, spurred on by what might be called the permissive attitude that the Court has taken toward the delegation issue. Administrative agencies have acquired increasing functions along with more powers to carry them out. They may prescribe rules and issue orders that have the force of law and may impose penalties on those who disobey. Some agencies have even acquired the subpoena power and/or the contempt power. What were once the closely guarded prerogatives of elected officials increasingly have been placed into the hands of nonelected functionaries. The United States has entered the era of the administrative state.

THE IMPACT OF ADMINISTRATIVE GROWTH ON DEMOCRATIC IDEALS AND ADMINISTRATIVE LAW

The administrative presidency, with corresponding implications for state governors, county executives, and municipal mayors, finds philosophical origins in George Washington's first Cabinet. Thomas Jefferson—as the original "outsider" advocating state's rights and decentralization of power—called for the pluralist model of presidential leadership. Alexander Hamilton—our first accountant of the nation's purse—called for a strong chief administrator with direct, accountable lines of program authority.

Jefferson represented values of equality of uniform participation, or democratic ideals, while Hamilton called for efficient administration, articulated in hierarchy and bureaucracy. How has the emergence of the modern administrative state redefined basic democratic principles of our 1787 U.S. Constitution? Tenets of administrative law are grounded in constitutionalism, shared governmental powers, popular government, individualism, and political equality.[7]

Constitutionalism. A constitutional governmental system regards the people, not the government, as sovereign. Rule of law emphasizes supremacy of the law and the notion of limited government. A constitutional government is politically legitimate if it rests securely upon popular consent.

Many Americans believe that the growth of administrative expertise challenges the primacy of democratic constitutionalism. According to this argument, administrative discretion permits public administrators to "govern" the United States, and governmental regulations are threats to democratic constitutionalism. The undemocratic character of administrative experts compromises constitutional democracy. The new cadre of governmental experts forms an administrative elite which evolves into a democratically irresponsible oligarchy.

Shared Powers. The division of powers among the chief executive, administrative, legislative, and judicial branches and among different levels of government permits each political entity a limited check over the powers of other authorities in the governmental system. Decision-making powers in this system are not monopolized by a single governmental branch. Presidents, legislators, and judges tend to delegate more and more of their prescribed powers to government bureaucrats as the weight of increasing governmental regulation increases.

The expansion of administrative policy-making powers is enhanced as other branches of government become increasingly bogged-down with peripheral concerns. Public administrators, for example, absorb more power as constitutionally elected politicians agonize over the role of government in the resolution of moral dilemmas. Many citizens perceive the public administration system a closed, political system which circumvents the open decision-making structure authored by the constitutional framers. Political bureaucracy emerges with a less than well-defined philosophy of the public interest.

Popular Government. Democratic government implies that the ultimate determination of public policy resides with the people. Stressing majority will, individual rights, and liberty, popular government is the opposite of absolutism. The shift of power from political institutions to administrative agencies raises questions about the democratic functioning of popular government.[8]

If public policy making is "farmed out" to government bureaucrats, how "popular" can government be? The administrative state, grounded in structures, functions, and rationality, may not be well suited to the flexibility required to meet the public's demands. A system based on knowledge, skills, and expertise conflicts with a system based on partisan politics and spoils. All government officials—elected and appointed—are servants of the people and should be held accountable for their performance in the public's interest. It can be difficult to ensure that a non-elected official can be that accountable.

Individualism. Freedom, personal well-being, and capabilities of individuals may conflict with the regulation of society by public bureaucracies. According to some, bureaucracy stymies the will of citizens, expressing the powers of the system and not the individual. The tug of war between societal rights and individual rights challenges the political consensus of democratic governments. Regulatory agencies prescribe rules which may destroy the freedom of individuals, with new structures of apolitical power over individuals emerging in their place.

In balancing societal and individual rights, government regulators are called upon to implement guidelines of federal, state, and local laws in a "fair" manner. Issues of administrative law ultimately involve questions of due process of law. The question is: due process or fair treatment for whom? Liberty is sacrificed and our way of life is altered when an administrative agency or a court makes a decision which benefits a larger group at the expense of the individual. The rights of the individual—bolstered by the Fourth Amendment to the U.S. Constitution, which monitors unreasonable searches and seizures, and the Fifth Amendment, which guards against self-incrimination—can be undermined by the exercise of excessive regulatory control.

Political Equality. Grounded in democratic philosophies of equality under the law and equal opportunity for all persons, government is to treat and represent all persons equally. Laws forbid arbitrary treatment of citizens by government officials, but in practice U.S. administrative agencies do not afford complete quality to all persons or groups. The reality of U.S. political bureaucracy is that preferential treatment is given to special interests.

Sexual and racial discrimination are well known and publicized aspects of our society. Since the Great Society of the 1960s, citizen groups have been organized to represent the interests of women and minorities. Affirmative action programs call for special compensatory measures from government to rectify past discrimatory practices by society. In theory, at least, the rule of law principle demands that government bureaucrats treat all

---

WHY ADMINISTRATIVE LAW MATTERS

1. The growth of government by public administrators is the most important political innovation in modern times.
2. In the present day, the effects of administrative government influence us literally every moment of our lives.
3. Bureaucratic government has provided no utopian cure for the shortcomings of free enterprise.
4. Administrative law seeks to reduce the tendencies toward arbitrariness and unfairness in bureaucratic government.
5. Administrative law, a relatively new and open-ended field of law, has not yet succeeded in playing its assigned role very effectively.

Source: Lief H. Carter, *Administrative Law and Politics: Cases and Comments* (Boston: Little, Brown and Company, 1983). 4.

---

individuals equally. Public bureaucracy, as prescribed by Max Weber's "ideal-type," rests upon knowledge, skills, and expertise, and not upon equality or political influence.

Constitutionalism, shared powers, popular government, individualism, and political equality are the political philosophies upon which administrative laws find implementation in modern-day American society. The individual needs the assurance of protection in law from the potential misuse of regulatory power. The conflicts between individual citizens and their governments and the resolution of these conflicts by the law allow understanding of how these philosphies are played out in American life.

TRADITIONAL AND CONTEMPORARY CORNERSTONES OF AMERICAN ADMINISTRATIVE LAW

The traditional cornerstones of administrative law are the independent regulatory agency, a uniform administrative procedure law (Administrative Procedure Act, 1946, as amended), substantial evidence judicial review, and notice and comment ruling.[9]

The *independent regulatory agency*, as a descriptive concept, is a misnomer. All agencies are directly dependent in unique ways upon executive and legislative branches of government and indirectly upon the judicial branch. The independent agencies, as they are called, emerged from the American constitutional provision of separation of powers.

There are three kinds of regulation. The best known is the *old-style economic regulation*. The *new social regulation* is a product of the 1970s. A third kind of regulation is *subsidiary regulation*.[10] Economic regulation emerged from the social and economic challenges of the 1930s. From the devastating consequences of the Depression, the New Deal created the Federal Deposit Insurance Corporation(FDIC), Tennessee Valley Authority(TVA), Federal Communications Commission(FCC), Securities and Exchange Commission(SEC), National Labor Relations Board(NLRB), and Civil Aeronautics Board(CAB). These regulatory bodies were established from 1933 through 1938.

After World War II, other agencies were created to monitor and confront emerging national problems. The Atomic Energy Commission(AEC), Selective Service System(SSS), National Aeronautics and Space Administration(NASA), Federal Maritime Commission(FMC), Equal Employment Opportunity Commission(EEOC), Environmental Protection Agency(EPA), Occupational Safety and Health Administration(OSHA), and Consumer Product Safety Commission(CPSC) were created to administer and regulate, respectively, programs concerning atomic energy, military conscription, space exploration, shipping, employment discrimination, environmental protection, occupational safety, and consumer product safety. In addition, there is a need to regulate the activities of agencies implementing social security, medical care, welfare, food stamps, veterans' benefits, and internal revenue programs.

The development and enactment of a uniform *administrative procedure law* is the second traditional cornerstone of administrative law. The Administrative Procedure Act, enacted in 1946, brings a degree of standardization to administrative practices and procedures and public access to those procedures. Before the enactment of APA, all manner of administrative practice and procedure questions were decided on a constitutional basis. The APA brought order from chaos. Unless they can find justifiable exception, agencies must follow the fundamental outlines of APA's broad and general statute. Such legislation was an advance of immeasurable proportions in administrative law and the protection of citizen rights.

Judicial review is the third traditional cornerstone of administrative law. Substantial evidence review is a dominant feature of administrative practice and procedure. The courts may rule on the merits of agency action if things go askew. Derived from statutory and non-statutory sources, judicial review permits judges to scrutinize allegedly illegal administrative actions. Judicial review, as a basic right, rests on the Congressional grant of general jurisdiction under Article III of the U.S. Constitution.

The *rulemaking* procedure constitutes the fourth, and final traditional cornerstone of administrative law. Rulemaking guides subsequent application of policy, and, it is argued, clear rules promote fairness. Rulemaking is also a forceful, efficient, yet democratic way for agencies to implement their mandates. Prior to the advent of rulemaking, agencies resorted to policy interpretation on a case by case, ad hoc fashion. Rulemaking is a more rational means of policymaking than adjudication, since adjudication is reactive and potentially disjointed. Rulemaking is more comprehensive, facilitating planning and coordination.

The independent regulatory agency, uniform administrative procedure law, judicial review, and rulemaking are traditional cornerstones of U.S. administrative law. Contemporary exigencies have called for new cornerstones of administrative law. These are *public participation* in the administrative process, *administrative process* in informal and discretionary governmental activity, and the *evolving definition of the mission* of administrative agencies and *development of effective oversight* of their activities.[11]

The courts have held that *public participation* is pertinent to sound and equitable decision making in administrative processes. Until the mid-1960s, the prevailing perspective was that the agency itself was representative of the public interest. The courts insisted upon citizen rights to participate in the administrative process; Congress and the agencies themselves soon recognized the validity of public participation as well.

The *administrative process* in formal and discretionary governmental activity is a second contemporary cornerstone. The development of procedural law to cover persons in public institutions, aliens, and the governance of educational institutions emphasizes the broadening development for protecting the rights of citizens in previously neglected areas. Aspects of administration once thought purely discretionary are subject to regulation as well.

A third, and final, contemporary cornerstone of administrative law is the continuing *definition of the mission of administrative agencies* and *development of effective oversight* of their activities. Each new administration advocates regulatory reform, but each administration fails to redefine the mission with sweeping regulatory reform. Congress may strengthen its oversight functions by demanding better analyses of the potential effects of proposed legislation, stronger program evaluation requirements in legislation, greater oversight of program design and development of regulations, and more use of program evaluation information. The final cornerstone, then, is the continuing development and fullfilment of mission and likewise improvement in oversight.

WHAT IS ADMINISTRATIVE LAW?

There is no commonly agreed upon subject matter of administrative law. There are, however, certain "parameters" wherein the application of administrative law is appropriate. Bernard Schwartz argues that administrative law does not relate to public administration in the same manner that commercial law relates to commerce and land law relates to land, rather the definition of administrative law centers around powers and remedies to answer the following inquiries: (1) What powers may be vested in administrative agencies? (2) What are the limits of those powers? (3) What are the ways in which agencies are kept within these limits?[12]

All law may be generally categorized as either procedural or substantive. For example, the Environmental Protection Agency establishes New Source Performance Standards that prohibit emissions from industrial, stoker-fired boilers in excess of 0.10 pounds of fly ash per million BTU of heat input. The Administrative Procedure Act specifies that such a rule be published in *The Federal Register* so that interested persons may comment before the ruling becomes final. The requirement for publishing the rule in *The Federal Register* is procedural; the rule for limiting emissions from stoker-fired boilers is substantive.[13]

The distinction between internal and external dichotomy means administrative law is restricted to agency actions that concern the rights of private parties. Such a limitation excludes legal relationships among governmental officers, government departments, or different levels of government. This narrow definition focuses not upon administrative powers as such, since a violation of administrative law occurs when a governmental representative employs administrative power against the person or property of private citizens. However, internal administrative law questions cannot be fully understood without considering the relevance of intergovernmental relations.[14]

The dichotomy between so-called quasi-legislative and quasi-judicial action constitutes a third narrow definition of administrative law. Although the distinction between quasi-legislative and quasi-judicial activities by agencies is easily blurred, an administrator is acting as a policy maker, similar to a legislator with a limited range of authority when making rules. Due process rights are not involved in a quasi-legislative procedure; citizens have no guaranteed rights of any consequence to have a policy adopted by a legislature or to exercise an active role in the legislative process. Questions involving individuals' rights are associated with quasi-judicial or courtlike proceedings. Quasi-legislative actions basically resemble a policy-making decision; quasi-judicial actions have characteristics of a court proceeding.

Examples of ambiguous, quasi-judicial and quasi-legislative administrative actions include utility rate setting and broadcast station licensing. In rate setting, an administrative decision-maker judges the merits of the utility company's immediate request, but, in making pertinent judgments, acts upon policy decisions for the future. Such judgments resemble a court-like activity; the ambiguity arises where the decision-making process has legislative implications as well.

AD LAW JUDGE UPHOLDS COLLEGE FOOTBALL CARTEL

An administrative law judge, citing lack of jurisdiction, dismissed an FTC antitrust complaint against the College Football Association and Capital Cities/ ABC Inc. The FTC complaint charged that the ABC television network's deal with the football cartel for exclusive broadcast rights illegally restrained competition. The CFA sells broadcast rights for 66 major colleges. The FTC charged that the CFA contract for 1991 violates antitrust law.

The FTC argued that the association is a business and that its member colleges make a profit from the sale of TV rights. The administrative law judge ruled that a nonprofit organization is not a corporation and is outside the purview of the FTC. "CFA, through its television contracts and other programs, fosters intercollegiate football, and that in itself is a proper non-profit purpose," stated administrative law judge James Timony. "The CFA's television rights to college football games, with the proceeds going to the schools to help support their athletic programs, have a nonprofit educational purpose."

Source: "FTC Complaint Dismissed Against Football Group," *The New York Times*, August 7, 1991, page B6.

The licensing of broadcasting, meanwhile, portrays a legislative, decision-making means of regulating a valuable business enterprise for particular companies or individuals, very likely grounded upon past events. However, from a judicial perspective, a disputed claim often is settled. Despite such ambiguity, agency quasi-judicial adjudications determine important questions of legal status or obligation; meanwhile, legislative rules, authorized by a statute, have the force and effect of law, cannot exceed or contradict the statute, and are implemented according to correct procedure.

Administrative law originates primarily from interpretations of legal statements that describe procedures agencies follow. Such judicial interpretations emanate primarily but not exclusively from due process clauses as detailed in constitutions, from applicable administrative procedure statutes, and sometimes from clauses within statutes establishing an agency and also prescribing a procedure to follow.

Administrative law is not regulatory law. The differences between regulatory and administrative law are the subject of the next chapter. Numerous government agencies and departments, cooperating with legislatures, create regulatory laws that affect even the most trivial of activities. Several of the more recognizable regulatory agencies include the Federal Communications Commission (FCC) that regulates broadcasting and interstate telephone rates, the Occupational Safety and Health Administration (OSHA) that regulates the safety of the workplace, and the Food and

Drug Administration (FDA) that tests drugs for marketing and monitors the contents of the food we eat. The laws, consent decrees, rules, and regulations made and enforced by these agencies are not administrative law. Instead, "regulatory law governs the citizenry; administrative law governs the government. We might say that administrative law governs the bureaucracy as other constitutional provisions govern the judicial, legislative, and presidential powers in government."[15] Administrative law applies legal principles originating from statutes, common law, constitutions, and regulatory laws to the government agencies affected.

ADMINISTRATIVE DISCRETION AND ITS LIMITS

Informal activity refers to administrative actions occurring outside formal proceedings. Informal advice from governmental officials could include commentary on the tax-deductible nature of a certain expenditure; the necessity of securing a building permit to construct an addition to a home or a zoning order to operate a particular business in a certain part of the city; or the likelihood that a person is entitled to a governmental benefit and how to go about getting it. The *ombudsman*, which will be described later in this chapter, is also an informal remedy.

The exercise of discretion occurs in context of the informal administrative process. The difficulty lies in ascertaining ways to restrict discretion without unduly limiting the flexibility of the administrator. Administrators need some discretion for implementing their functions in a reasonable and efficient manner; excessive discretion may result, however, in the violation of the rights of private citizens. In order to find the proper balance, author Kenneth Culp Davis suggests that greater utilization of administrative rule-making curbs unreasonable discretion. The tremendous rise in use of rule-making has helped make this dilemma less of a problem in recent years.

Although administrators today find themselves blessed with powers their predecessors little dreamed of possessing, they also find themselves subjected to numerous restraints as well. The legislative and judicial branches of government have not been content to stand aside and let administrators run the country, subject only to broad policy prescriptions and rather vague standards regarding the public interest. These two branches have acted to limit administrative discretion by, among other things, imposing increasingly strict standards on how administrators may use their new prerogatives.

Congress first took action in 1946 through passage of the Administrative Procedure Act (APA). This detailed piece of legislation set down specific rules on the ways in which administrative agencies are to proceed. The

---

POSTAL SERVICE VIOLATES GRIEVANCE PROCEDURES

An administrative law judge found that the Philadelphia, Pennsylvania, division of the United States Postal Service (USPS) violated its contract with the American Postal Workers Union by failing to resolve grievances and schedule cases for arbitration within time limits specified in the contract.

ALJ Richard H. Beddow Jr. ruled that grievances not heard or answered in the duration of the contract would be decided in favor of the union. The USPS Philadelphia district had 3,000 grievances pending arbitration during the contract time frame. The evidence presented during the hearing led the judge to conclude that USPS "has consistently and progressively failed to meet its contractual time obligations" in responding to union grievances.

Source: *The Wall Street Journal*, October 3, 1990, page B6.

---

courts have since taken up the task, and, based on broadened interpretations of the "due process" clauses in the Fifth and Fourteenth Amendments to the Constitution and the Administrative Procedure Act itself, they have subjected administrative actions to progressively stricter review.

It is important to note that judicial review since the Schechter case has focused not so much on matters of substance as on matters of procedure. In other words, the courts have concerned themselves less and less with what the administrative sector is doing and more and more with how it is doing it. The judges have, in effect, admitted that they do not have the expertise to determine whether a drug is safe, a welfare payment is adequate, or a highway route is well designed. As long as the administrative agency can show that its decisions in such matters are not arbitrary but are based on some legitimate rationale, the judges will not be inclined to interfere. They have become increasingly disposed to speak out, however, when they find that the agency is proceeding in a manner contrary to administrative due process.

"Administrative due process," writes Lewis Mainzer, "is that procedure which will normally be accepted by the courts as reasonable under the circumstances, whether or not the judge thinks the substantive decision was correct."[16] Kenneth Culp Davis puts it this way: "The dominant tendency in both state courts and federal courts is toward the middle position known as the substantial–evidence rule . . . the court decides questions of law but limits itself to the test of reasonableness in reviewing findings of fact."[17]

Due process, however, is not fully encapsulated by the criterion of "reasonableness" alone. It also implies what the Supreme Court has referred to as the criterion of "fundamental fairness." In attempting to set up standards for administrative due process, the courts, basing their findings both on the federal government's Administrative Procedure Act and similar state acts and on their new interpretations of the Constitution, have worked out a fairly strict set of rules that administrators must follow to meet due process requirements. The following set of rules has developed as case law on administrative due process accumulates.

1. **Adequate Notice** Before administrators or agencies can take any action that would directly affect one or more persons or institutions, they must generally give such affected parties adequate notice. How much notice is adequate? This depends on the circumstances and often becomes a matter of litigation before the courts. Rarely is a period of less than 30 days deemed to be adequate, and frequently a much longer interval is required.

   The adequacy of the notice, the timeliness of the information, and the proper distribution of the notice are of particular importance. Concerning adequacy, the APA states that: "Persons entitled to notice of an agency shall be timely informed of—(1) the time, place, and nature of the hearing; (2) the legal authority and jurisdiction under which the hearing is to be held; and (3) the matters of fact and law asserted."[18]

   However, in some situations, administrative agencies are empowered to act with scarcely any notice at all. If a building inspector finds a structure so unsafe as to be in danger of collapse at any moment, for example, or a health inspector finds a restaurant serving contaminated food, they can usually order the situation remedied immediately. Unless it can be shown that the public safety demands precipitate action, however, the rule of adequate notice must govern.

2. **Disclosure of Reasons** In addition to giving adequate notice, administrative agencies are usually required to state their reasons for taking their intended action. In most instances, the affected party may demand that the agency put these reasons in writing. This tends to deter agencies from acting in an arbitrary and capricious manner and at least gives the affected party written evidence to use in seeking subsequent redress in the courts.

3. **The Right to a Hearing** Beginning in the late 1960s, the courts began to broaden dramatically the right of aggrieved parties to have a hearing. Motorists deprived of their licenses, welfare clients deprived of their benefits, public-housing tenants faced with eviction, and prisoners sentenced to solitary confinement all sued for the right to be heard with favorable results in the courts.[19] Even the private sector found itself affected by the dictum in certain cases as students faced with expulsion were also granted the right to be heard.

The expansion that has taken place in requiring hearings also affects rule-making. Today, agencies that seek to promulgate new rules must usually schedule hearings and allow those who think differently to state their case. Even those who may not be directly affected by the new rule can have their voices heard.

At one time courts were not prone to require a hearing when benefits were at stake. Starting in 1970, however, the Supreme Court began insisting that benefits such as welfare payments, passports, unemployment insurance, driving licenses, and public housing accommodations could not be denied or removed without an evidentiary hearing, even though these were customarily termed privileges and not rights. Essentially, the Court held that when the government has issued a benefit to an individual, it cannot rescind it on mere administrative and fiscal considerations without a prior hearing.[20]

Hearings, of course, are not court trials, but they are increasingly coming to resemble them. An aggrieved party now can often demand not only the right to appear on his or her own behalf, but also to be represented by counsel. In many instances, the aggrieved party or their legal counsel can cross-examine witnesses who may be testifying on behalf of the agency. The affected party can further ask that the hearing be made public. Here, however, the courts may allow the agency some discretion in denying such a request. In two cases involving students protesting their expulsion, the courts allowed their respective universities to hold closed hearings. In one case, the grounds were the argument that a public hearing might endanger the public safety; in the other, the reputations of innocent students might be injured.[21]

4. **The Right to Further Appeal** If, after a hearing, the protesting party is still not satisfied, he or she may appeal to a higher echelon within the agency and, as a last step, to the courts. Available figures suggest that increasing numbers of citizens are taking this final step.

The aggrieved party may seek judicial redress on the grounds that he or she was not given adequate notice, that the agency's procedures are not clear, that the agency is not abiding by administrative due process or even its own procedures, that it has behaved in an arbitrary or discriminatory manner, or that the agency lacks jurisdiction in doing what it did or plans to do. As Mainzer points out, "Despite the Administrative Procedure Act and mountains of court opinion, the standards of administrative due process are extraordinarily indefinite."[22] Thus, numerous possibilities exist for carrying administrative issues into the courtroom.

There are, at the same time, numerous limitations on utilizing the courts to reverse or mitigate administrative actions. First, the courts will not entertain the case until the petitioner has exhausted all recourse within the administrative agency itself. The courts will likewise not intervene in cases where there is no remedy. Finally, as was previously noted, the courts presently balk at deciding questions of fact or weighing the validity of one expert opinion against another. They prefer to confine themselves to questions of law and procedure.

To see how these limitations work, let us assume that a citizen wishes to contest a decision on a new highway route that will require the taking of her house. She protests the decision to the highway commission, is turned down, and so takes her case to court. She may argue in court that an alternative route would have been a better one and may offer evidence and expert witnesses to support her view. If the highway commission can, on the other hand, show any evidence and bring forth any expert testimony of its own to indicate that it had a valid reason for choosing the route that it did, the court will generally turn a deaf ear to the citizen's plea. If, however, the irate homeowner can show that the highway commission's selection flies in the face of logic and expert opinion, or if she can further show that the commission may have a motive in picking a route that would take her home, then she will stand a chance of getting the commission's action struck down.

OPENING UP THE GOVERNMENT

Citizen access and participation in the administrative process gained much support during the late 1960s and 1970s. The general presumption is in favor of public access whenever possible. There are circumstances where information and participation are denied under the law, but in general, the department or agency searches for an appropriate balance between citizen interests and governmental needs for secrecy. The federal Freedom of Information Act (1966), the Privacy Act (1974), the "government in sunshine" laws, and provisions for increased citizen participation in governmental policy-making and decision-making processes have all made important contributions to opening up the government.

The Freedom of Information Act, or FOIA, is part of the Administrative Procedure Act (1946). Prior to its adoption, governmental information and records could be revealed only to "persons properly and directly concerned." Such records could be subject to secrecy if a policy was "in the public interest" or if said data pertained "solely to the internal management of an agency." The FOIA reversed such practices, guaranteeing openness to "any person." If information is withheld, the burden of proof for the necessity of secrecy is placed upon the agency. The agency has 10 days to respond; if the decision goes against the petitioner, he or she may appeal to a higher level in the agency. Certain items such as "trade secrets and commercial or financial information obtained from a person," deemed "privileged and confidential," and "personal and medical files or similar files the disclosure of which would constitute a clearly unwarranted invasion of personal privacy" are not subject to disclosure.

The FOIA is used frequently. The costs of administering the FOIA are going up. The rise in requests is more significant than the rise in costs over the 1990–91 period. In 1991, all federal departments and agencies received 589,391 FOIA requests, up from 491,299 in 1990. The costs of processing FOIA requests increased from $83,085,690 in 1990 to $91,405,744 in 1991. A total of 72,484 denials were issued in 1991. There were 8,780 appeals to those denials. Agencies collected $6,018,936 in fees in 1991, representing 6.7 percent of the overall reported cost of the FOIA.

Agencies with significant numbers of requests from businesses brought in the largest fees. Fee leaders included DOD, HHS, EPA, Treasury, Transportation, Agriculture, and Labor. Almost 75 percent of the FOIA requests originate from business and law firms. An estimated 91 percent of all requests were honored. A research assistant at a college in California and a newspaper reporter in Oregon asked the Department of Energy for details on the Nuclear Emergency Search Team(NEST). A consulting firm in Maryland asked the Department of the Navy for copies of procurement contracts. An inmate at a prison in the midwest asked the Department of the Army for instructions on how to make a bomb and where to detonate the mechanism in Denver. A hospital in Massachusetts asked for a Quality Assurance Profile from the FDA.[23]

Table 11–1 records the number of FOIA requests, costs, and costs per request from clients for ten selected federal departments and agencies in 1991.

The Privacy Act is a part of the Administrative Procedure Act and addresses what information is collected on citizens and how that information is used, requiring agencies to publicly report the existence of all systems of records maintained on individuals, requiring that the information contained in these record systems be accurate, complete, relevant, and up-to-date, providing procedures whereby individuals can inspect and correct inaccuracies in almost all federal files about themselves, specifying that information about an individual gathered for one purpose not be used for another without the individual's consent, and requiring agencies to keep an accurate accounting of the disclosure of records and, with certain exceptions, making these disclosures available to the subject of the record. The potential conflict with the FOIA is avoided with the disclaimer dictating disclosure as required under Section 552, or the FOIA, section of the

TABLE 11–1   Agency, Number of Requests, Costs, and Costs per Request
              for Selected Federal Departments and Agencies for
              Administering the Freedom of Information Act(FOIA),
              March 31, 1991.

Agency	# of Requests	Costs/Millions	Costs @ Request
Agriculture	63,775	$3.5	$ 55
CIA	4,563	2.3	495
Defense	129,437	23.1	179
Energy	8,267	4.1	491
EPA	38,614	4.5	117
HHS (inc. Health Care Finance Adm. & FDA)	121,297	11.3	93
Interior	4,782	1.7	362
Justice	71,265	13.2	185
State	5,311	5.8	1,092
Treasury	56,017	9.0	161

Source: Harry Hammitt, Editor, *Access Reports* Vol. 19, No. 7 (March 31, 1993), 1–2, 4.

Administrative Procedure Act. The common law right of access to information is an important source for legal development in the states. Nearly all states include statutory counterparts of the FOIA and Privacy Act.

Like FOIA and the Privacy Act, the Federal Sunshine Act, passed by Congress in 1976, is also part of the Administrative Procedure Act. Enhancing access to government operations is the purpose of sunshine laws. The degree of openness varies from statute to statute—most statutes permit exceptions to guarantees of openness, most notably, in labor negotiations and personnel matters. In some states, and on the federal level, a governmental body may enter executive session, and then, by majority vote, close the meeting to the public. In other states, even informal meetings are subject to sunshine statutes.

Citizen participation also opens up government to the public. Citizen-initiated activities, or the citizen action movement, and government-initiated activities, or the citizen involvement movement, illustrate attempts to involve citizens. The second approach is relevant to the practice of administrative law. Because of congressional mandates, hundreds of provisions require or permit some form of citizen participation in administrative policy-making or decision-making. Such legislatively induced participation ranges from creation of citizen advisory committees to requirements that public hearings be conducted prior to adoption of a policy.

THE EXPANDING ROLE OF ADMINISTRATIVE LAW JUDGES

The field of administrative law, even after a century of intense litigation and adjudication, remains alive with issues, and the nature of both administration and the law makes it unlikely that many of these issues will shrivel up and fade away. Legal complications and complexities appear destined to provide a wealth of litigation for lawyers and a wealth of perplexities for administrators for many years to come.

One issue yet to be fully resolved is *hearsay evidence.* Hearsay is a report of a statement made by someone who is not present for cross-examination. It is, therefore, considered second hand evidence and, as such, is excluded from U.S. courtrooms. Should it be barred from administrative proceedings as well?

The Administrative Procedure Act of 1946 ruled out any evidence that would be "irrelevant, immaterial or unduly repetitious," but did not go so far as to outlaw hearsay evidence as such. In 1971, the Supreme Court held that uncorroborated hearsay evidence can constitute "substantial evidence," sufficient to support an administrative ruling.[24] This did not mean that all such evidence was to be indiscriminately accepted. It would have to be relevant, reliable, and supportive of the point for which it was being used. Material "without a basis in evidence having rationality and probative force" would not meet the Court's standard.

Such a ruling does not close the door on the issue but only opens it wider. Heated disputes can erupt at any time on whether a particular piece of hearsay evidence meets the criteria for relevance and probative value. Many, meanwhile, still question whether any hearsay evidence should be allowed to influence administrative action. Since the consequences of administrative decision-making can frequently exceed those of a court trial, it is only right and proper, so the argument goes, that those who would have to bear these consequences should benefit from the safeguards enjoyed by those who are subject to a court trial. Others contend, however, that there is nothing inherently evil about hearsay evidence. Such evidence, as a matter of fact, is admissible in even criminal trials in most countries in the world, including most democratic countries. To bar it from the hearing room, they contend, would only hinder administrative tribunals from making informed and judicious decisions.

A still more lively controversy regarding the administrative process arises over whether an agency should be allowed to play the *double role of a judge and prosecutor.* When an agency discharges or demotes an employee or deprives an individual or a group of some benefit or right, the agency first brings the charges and then, during the hearing, sits in judgment on these charges. In effect, it seems to be sitting in judgment on itself. To many lawyers, this is inherently unfair and contrary to both the spirit and intent of due process. They claim the affected party should possess the right to have the charges decided by a completely external body.

While most administrative agencies adjudicate their own charges and complaints, they usually utilize special employees to do so. These officials are customarily called hearing examiners in most local and some state bureaucracies, but in a few states as well as at the federal level they bear the more prestigious title of *administrative law judges*. Sometimes referred to as "Washington's hybrids" or "the hidden judiciary," they adjudicate cases for federal agencies.[25]

The administrative law judge exercises his or her prerogatives when a corporation or a private citizen disputes the decision of a federal department or agency. For example, if your grandfather is denied a disability pension from the Social Security Administration or if a state university is charged with unfair labor practices by the faculty union, the administrative law judge decides the case.

Until 1978, the 1,100 administrative law judges were called hearing officers. They, according to the United States Supreme Court, are "functionally comparable" to Federal Court Judges. An administrative law judge must have at least seven years' trial experience and pass an examination of general legal knowledge. The Office of Personnel Management certifies the administrative law judge and maintains a central registry from which agencies select judges. The position is a lifetime job in which pay ranges from $72,865 to $112,100 per year.

Administrative law judges interpret Federal regulations enforced by a particular department or agency to which they are assigned. "There's a perception that people are not getting a fair shake from us because we're Department of Labor A.L.J.s," said Nahum Litt, the Labor Department's chief administrative law judge. Some administrative law judges are former staff attorneys for particular agencies and are, on occasion, perceived as officials for those federal bureaucracies instead of independent judges.

More than 800 administrative law judges are employed by the Social Security Administration, 80 in the Department of Labor, and 84 in the National Labor Relations Board. The remaining number are divided among 26 other departments and agencies around the country. Administrative law judges in the Social Security Administration alone hear 300,000 appeals a year.[26]

Although federal ALJs are employees of the agency whose cases they adjudicate, their qualifications and civil service status have given them virtual immunity from normal agency pressures. They have frequently counteracted and contradicted the expressed wishes of their agencies. When the Social Security Administration attempted to use the Reagan Administration's stricter guidelines to pare nearly a quarter million people from the rolls of its recipients, it found itself on a collision course with its ALJs. The ALJs, using the looser and more liberal standards of the Supreme Court, reinstated approximately three-fifths of those who appealed their loss of

TABLE 11–2 Total Number of ALJs on Board by Grade and Agency as of June 25, 1991

Breakdown by grade:	AL-3	1,106	($ 72,865–$100,890)
	AL-2	16	(106,495)
	AL-1	4	(112,100)
		1,126	

Breakdown by agency:	AL-3	AL-2	AL-1
Agriculture Department	4	1	1
Commerce Department	1		
Commodity Futures Trading Com.	4		
Education Department	3		
Environmental Protection Agency	6	1	
Federal Communications Agency	8	1	
Federal Energy Regulatory Com.	21	1	1
Federal Labor Relations Authority	8	1	
Federal Maritime Commission	3		
Federal Mine Safety & Health Review Com.	8	1	
Federal Trade Commission	2		
Health and Human Services Department			
Food and Drug Administration	1		
Department Appeals Board	2		
Social Security Administration	813	1	
Housing and Urban Development Department	3	1	
Interior Department	12		
Justice Department			

TABLE 11–2   Total Number of ALJs on Board, continued

Breakdown by grade:	AL-3	1,106	($ 72,865–$100,890)
	AL-2	16	(106,495)
	AL-1	4	(112,100)
		1,126	
Breakdown by agency:	AL-3	AL-2	AL-1
Drug Enforcement Administration	2		
Immigration Review	4		
Labor Department	76	3	1
Merit Systems Protection Board	1		
National Labor Relations Board	82	1	1
National Transportation Safety Board	6		
Nuclear Regulatory Commission	2		
Occupational Safety & Health Review Com.	14	1	
Securities and Exchange Commission	3	1	
Small Business Administration	1		
Transportation Department			
Office of the Secretary	3	1	
U.S. Coast Guard	9		
U.S. International Trade Commission	2	1	
U.S. Postal Service	2	—	—
	1,106	**16**	**4**

Sources: Joseph J. Simeone, "The Function, Flexibility, and Future of United States Judges of the Executive Department," *Administrative Law Review*, Vol. 44, No. 1 (Winter 1992), 165; Don Mace and Eric Yoder, editors, *Federal Employees Almanac* (Falls Church, VA: Federal Employees News Digest, Inc., 1992), 1.

DID ABORTION PILL IMPORT BAN VIOLATE ADMINISTRATIVE RULES?

In federal court on July 7, 1992, lawyers for the Center for Reproductive Law and Policy argued that the government had violated its own administrative rules by not seeking public comment before determining to prohibit the import of the abortion pill, RU486. RU486 is an antiprogestin that prevents the hormone progesterone from maintaining a pregnancy. Researchers say the drug is a safe and effective method for abortion up to seven to nine weeks after a missed menstrual period.

A single 600 milligram dose (12 pills) of the drug was seized from a pregnant woman entering the country at Kennedy International Airport in New York. "The imposition of this import ban is arbitrary, capricious, unscientific and a clearly political action," said Simon Heller, a lawyer at the center. "The Bush Administration circumvented the democratic process to curry favor with a vocal minority."

The official position of the FDA with RU486 is that if the drug is used without a doctor's supervision, it can pose health hazards. Although the drug has fewer risks than surgical abortion, RU486 can cause excessive bleeding. The FDA allows citizens to import drugs approved in other countries but not in the United States if they are not imported to the United States in commercial quantities.

Source: Philip J. Hilts, "U.S. Sued Over Ban on Importing Abortion Pill," *The New York Times*, July 8, 1992, page A16.

---

benefits. Their actions infuriated the heads of Social Security, who overruled many of the reinstatements. This, in turn, riled the ALJs, who felt they had acted as they should, i.e., as independent judicial officers and not as "mere bureaucrats."

Despite the independence and integrity that ALJs have generally shown, some observers continue to express doubts as to whether an agency employee should preside over a case in which the agency itself is a party of interest. To obviate this objection as well as to make better use of ALJ personnel, eight states have placed their administrative law judges in an agency of their own, assigning them to other agencies to handle cases on a random basis. At least one of these states, New Jersey, says it has also saved money in so doing. Some would like to see the federal government take a similar step.

Another suggestion would have ALJs hand down decisions, not just recommendations. While agency higher-ups could still overrule the findings, presumably they would feel more compunction about doing so if such findings were couched in the form of decisions instead of recommendations.

Suggestions have been made to divorce ALJs completely from any particular agency, setting up, in effect, a new administrative unit in the federal bureaucracy that would assign them to different agencies as cases arose. This would give them still more independence, but would reduce their expertise in the matters under dispute, for they would no longer be specialized in the work of one agency.

Critical examination of the formal agency adjudicative process and the role of the ALJ reveals two trends. First, there is growing dissatisfaction with formal, trial procedures for resolving licensing, merger, and related economic regulation policy issues. Second, the number of benefits and enforcement cases have increased dramatically. Social Security Administration (SSA) ALJs decide 300,000 cases annually; Department of Labor ALJs resolve thousands more benefits cases concerning black-lung benefits claims and longshoremen's compensation. Enforcement is another growth area. ALJs discipline license holders, revoke licenses, issue cease-and-desist orders, or issue civil money penalties.

ALJs license and route certification of transportation by air, rail, motor vehicle, or ship; regulate radio and television broadcasting; establish rates for gas, electrical, communication, and transportation services; monitor compliance with federal standards relating to interstate trade, labor-management relations, advertising, communications, consumer products, food and drugs, corporate mergers, and antitrust; regulate health and safety in mining, transportation, and industry; regulate trading in securities, commodities, and futures; and adjudicate claims relating to Social Security benefits, worker's compensation, international trade, and mining. The brief history of ALJs reflects tension between the need for fact-finder independence and the need for policy and management control.

ADMINISTRATIVE CONTROLS: INTERNAL AND EXTERNAL

In the fifty-first of their famous *Federalist Papers*, James Madison and Alexander Hamilton pointed out,

> *If men were angels, no government would be necessary. If angels were to govern men, neither external nor internal controls on government would be necessary. In framing a government which is to be administered by men over men, the great difficulty lies in this: you must first enable the government to control the governed; and in the next place oblige it to control itself. A dependence on the people is, no doubt, the primary control of the government; but experience has taught mankind the necessity of auxiliary precaution.*[27]

The judicial safeguards so far examined in this chapter constitute an important part of the "auxiliary precautions" that Hamilton and Madison referred to, but they by no means embrace them all. As administration has grown in size and scope, and as it has become increasingly comprehensive and complex, a welter of "auxiliary precautions" have evolved in a continuing effort to keep it within controllable bounds.

As the writers of *The Federalist Papers* perceptively noted, there are two aspects to the subject of administrative control. One is the control that agencies must exercise over their own constituent elements, be they subunits or individuals; the other is the control that must be imposed on the agency itself. These two forms of control overlap and even duplicate in many areas. In other respects, however, they diverge and even conflict. An agency may show itself quite zealous in exercising internal control but equally zealous in contesting external control. The question of administrative control has two quite distinct aspects that, although they often make use of the same techniques and devices, warrant separate consideration.

INTERNAL CONTROLS

Staff units and their personnel frequently perform a controlling function, even when they have no authority or mandate to do so. This is what frequently makes them disliked by people on the line. The school social worker has no right to tell the teacher what to do, but dealing with one or more of the teacher's pupils means contact with the teacher and usually leads, at a minimum, to some joint consultation. While the social worker has no authority to give the teacher orders, the social worker will most likely appeal to the teacher's department head or principal if the suggestions are rejected. In talking with pupils, the social worker is, to some extent, checking up and may disclose what he or she finds to the teacher's colleagues, if not the superior. Although teachers do not commonly regard social workers as enemies and instead often welcome their assistance, an element of control is nearly always present in their relationships. This can breed contempt.

What holds true for the teacher's relationship with the social worker also characterizes the teacher's relationship with the guidance counselor, the school secretary, the custodian, and other nonline personnel. As these people carry out their duties, they are likely to come into contact with the teacher and are likely to become aware of what he or she may or may not be doing. If the teacher is not doing anything untoward, then there is no pressure at all from these contacts, but if the teacher were to "step out of line," word would get around, causing reverberations that he or she would subsequently experience as disquieting. All of these staff personnel may also make demands upon the teacher, and though he or she has the option, in most instances, of refusing them, each refusal is likely to have negative consequences, even if it is only an attenuation of relations that makes the organizational environment a little less pleasant.

In this manner, then, staff services tend to provide internal control, even when they are not expressly designed to do so. Many staff services are, however, expressly designed with a control function at least partly in mind.

One of these is the *personnel department*. If it enjoys a fair degree of authority, as many such departments do, it can wield a considerable influence in determining how line departments and line officials deal with their personnel problems. Even when a personnel unit has no power other than to recommend, it still does not lack influence—there is always a price to be paid for saying no. In this way, personnel departments are inevitably units that perform a controlling function.

When it comes to staff services involving financial matters, the control function becomes still more apparent. The *budget office* of any agency or any government obviously exercises a high degree of control, for it plays a crucial role in deciding who gets what amount of money for what purpose. Since this function has already been the subject of an entire previous chapter, it requires no further elaboration here.

Another staff department that plays a very direct role in exercising financial control is the *purchasing office*. Generally, line departments as well as staff bureaus may apply to the purchasing agent when they want to buy anything other than small, petty-cash-type items. The purchasing agent, in turn, must usually adhere to certain prescribed rules in filling requests. One of the most important of these rules requires putting out for bid contracts to purchase an item or service and accepting the lowest qualified bidder. This stipulation is often waived in whole or in part when the contract is quite small or when it calls for an exceptional type of equipment or service that can only be supplied by one firm. Even in this latter instance, the purchasing agent will normally exercise some care to see to it that the exceptions are justified.

Perhaps the most important financial control unit is the *auditing branch*. Certainly it is the one branch expressly charged with control and with little else. For obvious reasons, auditing is best performed by a unit that is as separate as possible from the activities that it is auditing. As such, it more often falls into the category of external control. Yet, some organizations, particularly large ones, have their own auditing units, and an organization the size of the Defense Department actually has specialized auditing offices.

There have been some important changes in the auditing function in recent years. First, there has been a shift of emphasis from preaudit to postaudit activities. Auditing offices have begun exercising less and less control over expenditures before they are made, and instead have begun centering efforts on checking up afterward. To some this seems like locking the barn door after the horse is stolen. Others point out that this is really just as effective, since awareness that the books will be examined will generally provide the proper deterrent to financial abuses. It also makes for less work by the auditors and is less aggravating to those they are auditing, since employees now do not have to clear every expenditure ahead of time.

Most organizations of any size also utilize a form of control called the *field inspection.* Sometimes these inspections are done by internal investigation units, but more often they are performed by simple field inspectors and sometimes by regular line officials. In any case, it has become customary to try to eliminate some of the aura of "snooping" from these field checkups. Instead, the emphasis is being placed upon the positive aspects of such inspections. The inspectors are ostensibly seeking only to assist the branch or field office they are inspecting. While their protestations of good intent are often greeted with cynicism by those being inspected, still a change in emphasis is taking place.

The goal of trying to make field inspections into a positive rather than a negative phenomenon is best achieved when field inspections are made on an announced and scheduled basis. Unannounced inspections do permit the inspectors to catch the unit unawares and thus unable to put on a deceptive camouflage for the inspection visit, but the costs of unannounced inspections may outweigh benefits. First, the local officials may be away or busy on the day the inspectors have chosen to pounce on them and so they may not be able to supply records, answer questions, and so on. Then the unit itself may be undergoing an unusually critical or unusually slack period. Just because the inspectors have arrived unannounced does not mean that they have caught the unit on a typical day and can fairly judge its overall performance.

The fact that the possibilities of deception are supposedly increased when inspections are announced beforehand should present no great problem. Experienced and alert inspectors, equipped with the proper tools and techniques and oriented toward inspecting for substantive rather than superficial problems, should have no great difficulty in seeing through any deceptive strategy they may encounter.

EXTERNAL CONTROLS

Along with the courts, whose role in providing external control we have already examined, numerous other agents and agencies exist to curb administrative power. Since many of these forces constitute sources of support for administrators, a more detailed analysis of their relationship with administration must await the next chapter. At this juncture, we will limit ourselves to a brief review of their function as agents of restraint and regulation.

The instrumentality that is most expressly charged with controlling administration is the *legislative branch of government*. Legislatures exercise this function in many different ways. The first is by the customary control over expenditures. Even the least powerful of city councils can usually cut a mayor's or city manager's budget, while many city councils, to say nothing of state legislatures and the Congress, can add, cut, and shift around appropriations pretty much as they see fit (subject in most cases to a chief executive's veto). Joseph Harris, in his authoritative work, *Congressional Control of Administration*, emphasizes that Congress's power over expenditures is "perhaps the most important single control over the departments."[28]

This power is largely, although not exclusively, exercised during budget hearings—and it is a power that can strike terror into the hearts of administrators. Richard E. Fenno, Jr., in his book, *The Power of the Purse*, quotes a Washington bureaucrat as saying, "There is not a bureau head here whose blood pressure doesn't go up before the appropriations hearing. It's an ordeal. You don't know what questions they might ask or what case they might bring up."[29] Budget hearings, which are annual affairs in most legislative bodies, provide legislative committees excellent opportunities, not only to make or to pass on key decisions regarding future agency operations, but also to review the agency's activities. Such hearings, thus, can become probing and quite painful proceedings whose outcomes can prove decisive for an agency's continued well-being or even survival.

Another way in which legislative bodies can exercise control over administration is through *confirmation of appointments*. The United States Senate must advise and consent on most presidential appointments to agencies situated outside what is called the Executive Office of the President. Since only a small portion of the federal bureaucracy is situated within the Executive Offices—the Office of Management and Budget, the National Security Council, the Office of Science and Technology, and some others—this confirmation of appointment power gives the nation's upper house a fair degree of at least residual control over the administrative branch. In practice, the Senate usually goes along with the president's nominee. Presidents will also make at least some appointments at the behest of certain key senators. At times the Senate has succeeded in exacting policy commitments from presidential appointees before confirming them and, on occasion, turns down appointees. Many state legislatures and not a few city councils also possess the power to pass on certain gubernatorial or mayoral appointments, and they often exhibit a greater interest in influencing such appointments than does the U.S. Senate.

The most well-known power legislative bodies exercise over administrative ones is the *power to investigate and expose*. Congress, state legislatures, and city councils can generally summon administrative officials to appear before them to answer questions. Legislatures and their staffs may also examine administrative records and documents. Most investigations are conducted by the legislative committee concerned, although at the municipal level it is not unusual for the entire town or city council to become engaged in the probe. Congress, all state legislatures, and some city councils also possess the subpoena power that enables them to command the appearances of witnesses and the production of documents outside the government proper.

One limitation on this power at the federal level involves *executive privilege*. Presidents have often claimed that their personal staffs are not subject to congressional demands to testify and that many of the in-house documents they generate are similarly off-limits to congressional scrutinizers. This power has never been adequately demarcated or defined. In the Watergate investigation, President Nixon allowed his aides to testify at the Senate committee's public hearings, but refused to surrender the tapes of his White House conferences and telephone calls until forced to do so. In 1983 the issue once again came before the court, as the Reagan Administration refused to allow the administrator of the Environmental Protection Agency to give Congress certain records that the legislators were seeking. The president eventually relented and agreed to Congress's request before the court reached a decision.

How effective is the legislative investigation as a tool for controlling administration? Dean Acheson answered the question in this way. "The most publicized weapon of Congress—and one which as often as not proves frustrating to those who employ it—is the investigation."[30] He then went on to quote with approval Woodrow Wilson's opinion on this subject:

> *Congress stands almost helplessly outside the departments. Even the special, irksome, ungracious investigations which it from time to time institutes . . . do not afford it more than a glimpse of the inside of the small province of federal administration. . . .*[31]

Legislative investigations do lack continuity, often becoming one-shot affairs that, although they may result in some sensational public hearings, do not provide for following through on recommendations. They have often been launched and executed with publicity factors in mind, and this, needless to say, limits their depth, and in some cases their desirability. Finally, they tend to focus on negative aspects alone, and this curbs their ability to provide a rounded picture of what is taking place and limits their capacity for offering solutions.

But despite these drawbacks, there are reasons for viewing such investigations in a more favorable light. There is first of all the "lighthouse theory." No one ever knows how many ships a lighthouse may save, and similarly no one knows just how many abuses the investigatory weapon may prevent. Since administrators seldom welcome such probes, the fear of prompting one may well deter much error and wrongdoing in government agencies. The threat of an investigation probably accomplishes more in terms of controlling administration than the actual use of the device.

Another possible benefit is improvement of the possibilities for continuity and follow-up. Legislative committees have begun showing more long-term responsibility in overseeing the work of the department entrusted to their care. The Legislative Reorganization Act of 1946 formally mandated to the standing committees of Congress "continuous watchfulness of the execution by the administrative agencies concerned of any new law the subject matter of which falls within the jurisdiction of such committee."[32] Committee staffing, at the state as well as at the new congressional level, has improved markedly in recent years, providing the basis for more diligent overseeing of administrative agencies.

Civil liberties lawyer Charles Rembar has noted a sharp change in the focus of congressional investigative committees during the past several decades. They are, he says, becoming more responsible and more useful. "The Senate tries to pry information out of an unwilling Executive and present it to the public. Instead of stifling free expression, the committees, by and large, promote it. And the target of investigations at the present time is fact rather than opinion."[33]

Another means by which Congress and some state and local legislative bodies exercise surveillance over their respective bureaucracies is *auditing*. Many state legislatures and city councils appoint an auditor to examine the books of the executive department. Congress maintains for this purpose a department of its own, the General Accounting Office. Staffed by 5,600 men and women with headquarters in Washington but with field offices in the various regions and even at federal installations overseas, the GAO acts as the watchdog of the legislative branch. At its head is the Comptroller General, who, although appointed by the president, holds the post for 15 years, is not eligible for reappointment, and can be fired only by Congress and not by the president. Consequently, there is little dispute over where his or her loyalty lies and whose interests are served.

The GAO has seldom been accused of lack of vigor when it comes to monitoring the activities of the executive branch. Indeed, it has often been accused of being too meddlesome. The auditing office has, however, somewhat shifted its emphasis in recent years. In line with the current trends in auditing, it has taken to concentrating on postauditing rather than requiring agencies to clear expenditures in advance. It has also begun to use sampling techniques rather than make complete examinations of expenditure accounts. At the same time, under a congressional mandate to expand its scope beyond the strictly financial sphere, it has begun using the services of economists, engineers, management consultants, and other specialists. With such added resources, it is now able to undertake what are called "management audits." As former Comptroller General Elmer Staats put it, the GAO has begun shifting its focus away from examinations of "individual mismanagement and waste to some of the broader implications of Government operations."[34]

Congress has begun relying more and more heavily on the GAO. If members of Congress find evidence of something amiss in the federal bureaucracy, they are likely to ask the Comptroller General and his or her staff to investigate and give them a report. In 1972, Congress established a new Office of Federal Elections within the auditing office. The GAO, however, still lacks the subpoena power and this curtails some of its activities. It cannot, for example, examine income tax records unless the Internal Revenue Service chooses to let it do so.

One final means through which legislatures oversee administration is through "casework." Members of Congress, state legislators, and city council members frequently receive complaints against administrative agencies. Checking them out provides these representatives opportunities to discover what these agencies are doing and how they are doing it. The performance of casework frequently leads to other forms of legislative oversight. If a legislator, in looking into a matter brought to his or her attention by a disgruntled constituent, finds an indication of some greater wrong, then the legislator may call for an investigation or ask the auditors to look into the agency or subject the agency's officials to some tough questioning at the next round of budget hearings.

In some countries and in certain jurisdictions in the United States, the processing of complaints is done by an official expressly charged with this task. Such an official is called the *ombudsman*. The term is a Swedish word meaning "representative," and in the Scandinavian countries, where the office originated, the ombudsman functions as the people's representative against the bureaucracy. He or she is always a highly esteemed individual, often a distinguished former judge, who has been appointed for a long term. Although in most cases he or she acts in response to a complaint, the ombudsman can initiate action when there is reason to believe that an administrative agency is not performing its job properly.

The office of ombudsman has a long and successful record in Scandinavia, and during the 1960s other countries began adopting it. Great Britain and many of the commonwealth nations, such as New Zealand, Australia, and Canada, have set up ombudsmen, as have at least ten of the United States and several U.S. cities. The U.S. governmental units that have adopted the ombudsmen concept usually give the office a different title and rarely confer on its holder the sweeping and formal powers that Scandinavian counterparts enjoy. Nevertheless, the concept has made headway and does seem to be bearing fruit. By the end of the 1980s, there were approximately 71 ombudsman offices operating in 20 countries with 18 in the United States, its territories, and Canada.[35]

Citizens are not the only ones who lodge complaints against public agencies. Sometimes the agency's own employees find grounds for rebellion and resistance, and this, too, results in a form of administrative control. The development of public employee unionism can be viewed as a manifestation of this kind of control, as can the emergence of "underground newspapers," which are published and circulated through some agencies by dissident employees. Such publications flourished at HEW's Washington headquarters during the 1960s.

THE EMERGENCE OF THE WHISTLE BLOWER

A more striking, although not necessarily more important, form of employee control has been the rise of the whistle blower. The term "whistle blower" was originated by Ralph Nader to categorize those public employees who, in effect, blow the whistle on acts by their own agencies when they deem such acts to be improper.[36] Some of the more famous whistle blowers during the early 1970s were Gordon Rule, the Navy's Director of Procurement, who challenged extravagant cost overruns and claims for extra compensation by Navy suppliers; A. Ernest Fitzgerald, the Pentagon cost analyst who called attention to similar cost overruns in conjunction with the Air Force's C-5A transport jet; and Frank Serpico, the New York City patrolman whose reports on corruption in his department touched off a wide-ranging investigation that culminated in numerous indictments and shake-ups in the city's constabulary.

Many factors account for the growing prominence of whistle blowers as agents of administrative control. One of them is the development of *administrative law* and the safeguards it extends to public employees. When the Nixon Administration attempted to discharge Fitzgerald, for example, by eliminating his job, he fought back through the courts and won.[37] A midwestern high school teacher who was fired after he sent a letter to a local newspaper criticizing his school board won similar reinstatement. In general, the courts have become increasingly protective of whistle-blowing employees.

A second factor that has encouraged whistle blowing has been the development of the *news media*. In this connection, it is important to note that the press has long played an active and aggressive role in controlling administrative actions. "I fear three newspapers more than I fear 3,000 bayonettes," Napoleon once remarked, while an English contemporary, philosopher Jeremy Bentham, observed that "Without publicity, all checks are inefficient; in comparison to publicity, all checks are of small account."[38]

The development of broadcast journalism, particularly television news, and the growth of public awareness and interest in government generally have made the news media today a form of control that rivals, if it does

---

ETHICS: PUBLIC ADMINISTRATION'S CHALLENGE OF THE 1990s

Honesty, fairness, and productivity are characteristics of American patriotism and must be practiced consistently by every government employee. Even from the point of view of effectiveness it is smart for public administrators to be moral in carrying out government functions. The credibility of government is at stake. Laws, rules, and regulations of government should be grounded in ethics, integrity, and organization commitments.

Government employee performance and policy leadership should reflect emphasis on the following themes:

- Make ethics a part of employee orientation and training programs.
- Include ethics in the performance evaluations and regular feedback provided to employees.
- Publicize ethical dilemmas and the organization's perception of them.
- Review management practices in different parts of the organization to help identify existing or potential ethics problems.
- Develop a code of ethics.
- The actions of top government officials must be consistent with their expectations for employee conduct. Leadership by example is an effective tool to establish an ethical perspective among members of the federal, state, or local government organization.

Source: Stephan J. Bonczek, "Ethics: Challenge of the 1990s: A Local Government Perspective," *Public Management*, Vol. 72, No. 8 (July 1990), 17–19.

---

not exceed, that exerted by legislative bodies. This is particularly true in the United States, which does not have a government-owned television and radio network and which has a long muckraking tradition. The media is not only important for what it does on its own but for the help it provides other forms of control. It has encouraged and strengthened whistle blowing by providing considerable publicity to the whistle blowers. It also has stimulated legislative control by providing headlines and coverage for legislative exposés. Furthermore, many newspapers and radio and TV stations even act as ombudsmen, soliciting citizen complaints against the bureaucracy and then checking them out.

A third instrumentality of control over an administrative agency is its *clientele*. For reasons that will be more fully discussed in the next chapter, administrators, particularly in the U.S., need considerable cooperation from their clientele, and the clientele often seize upon this to exercise some countervailing influence over administrators. Sometimes this takes dramatic and violent forms, such as the client takeovers of welfare offices, the student rebellions of the 1960s, and the prison riots of the early 1970s. More often, however, clients exercise control by simply refusing to comply with policies they do not like.

Finally, a form of control that often receives little attention but that plays an important role in constraining many administrative agencies is the control exercised by *competing agencies*. Agencies are frequently locked in combat over jurisdiction, funding, and so on. In their continual jousting for power and position, agencies tend to control each other. James Madison actually saw this as one of the most effective forms of control. In a well-known passage in *The Federalist* he noted,

> *Ambition must be made to counteract ambition . . . the constant aim is to divide and arrange the several offices in such a manner that each may be a check on the other—that the private interest of every individual may be a sentinel over the public rights.*[39]

Law and Control: How Much Is Enough?

Democratic government rests on such principles as accountability and responsibility. We have seen that the realization of such principles requires a comprehensive system of administrative control. The public has a right to demand and administrators have a need to accept a widespread network of restraints and restrictions on administrative activity. Democratic government is *controlled* government.

Of course, administrators often find such controls irksome and irritating. They are, by nature, active men and women who wish to "get on with the job." It would be strange if they did not frequently chafe at curbs placed upon their actions. In the long run, however, they, too, benefit from a suitable system of control. Such a system will point out their errors before they go too far and will also reassure the public that they are not behaving capriciously or coercively. Many administrators in countries that have ombudsmen, for example, have found that the ombudsmen are beneficial. By giving timely warnings when needed, constructively pointing out errors, and investigating complaints, the ombudsmen may assist the administrators in carrying out their missions.

The idea of bureaucracy as a dominant and power-hungry force in modern life is not the only negative image that administrators have to struggle against. They must also contend with the equally pervasive picture of bureaucracy as the paradigm for sloth and sluggishness. If bureaucratic agencies are frequently accused of becoming too meddlesome and interfering, they are also constantly being flayed for laziness and laxity.

While administrative controls can help allay the first type of criticism, they can aggravate the second. Controls, although they impede administrative abuse, may also inhibit administrative innovation and enterprise. Administrative agencies are continually being rebuked for the "red tape" that seems to engulf so many of their activities. Yet this "red tape" is, in many instances, the direct result of a desire to monitor and control their decisions, and to maintain standards of accountability and responsibility. "Too often in American public administration we assure legality and propriety in hiring, purchasing, building and the like, but prevent not only corruption but action prompt and vigorous enough to be effective," writes Lewis Mainzer. And he goes on to add, "Harmless government is not good enough."[40]

Another writer on administration, Peter Woll, expresses the same concern. "Guaranteeing that agencies will follow certain procedures in no way assures that they will take any action at all," he writes. The issue is an important one, he claims, because, owing to the limitations of the courts and the chief executive in directing and implementing policy, "the bureaucracy inevitably becomes the primary instrument of positive government to maintain the public interest." As a result, "the central problem today is not how to curb its [the bureaucracy's] power, but how to guarantee that it will take the necessary action to deal with critical public needs."[41]

Understood in this light, control, or at least extensive control, can be counterproductive. Carried too far, it can render government ineffectual and even inert, leaving the way clear for less savory and less responsible forces to operate. As we saw in our examination of administrative law, the judicialization of the administrative process has proved to be a bonanza to various business interests that use the safeguards imposed on administrative agents to perpetuate or prolong questionable activities.

Too much control also breeds a climate of conflict and distrust that can result in a great deal of dysfunctional behavior. If it refuses to resign itself to relative immobility, an agency strait-jacketed with a strict system of controls may dissipate so much of its energy trying to overcome obstacles to action that it may have little energy left to serve the public. Furthermore, it may respond to the distrust that extensive control suggests by meriting such distrust. The American statesman, Henry L. Stimson, who served in many high government positions before and during World War II, once observed that one way to make a man trustworthy is to trust him.[42] The reverse may also be true. Certainly, the distrust that pervasive control fosters does little to encourage candor and cooperation.

Control, whether exercised through legalistic or other means, has its limits if the ends of democratic society are to be served. Fortunately some of the changes now buffeting administration may help alleviate some of the problems it poses. Programmed budgeting, productivity measures, management by objectives, and other techniques may increase responsibility and accountability while replacing or reducing the role of negative control, that is, control for its own sake. Some systems of control will continue to be needed and the problems they present will doubtless persist, but the growing professionalism that is also starting to characterize public administration may make extensive and elaborate control systems somewhat less necessary.

SUMMARY

- The principles of administrative law are grounded in constitutionalism, shared powers, popular government, individualism, and political equality.
- Independent regulatory agencies, uniform administrative procedure law, judicial review, and rule making are traditional cornerstones of administrative law. Public participation in the administrative process, the administrative process in formal and informal governmental activity, and the evolving definition of the mission of administrative agencies and development of oversight of their activities are contemporary cornerstones of U.S. administrative law.
- Honesty, fairness, and productivity are characteristics of American patriotism and must be practiced by every government employee. Even from the standpoint of effectiveness, it is smart for public administrators to be moral in carrying out government functions. The credibility of government is at stake. Laws, rules, and government regulations should be grounded in ethics, integrity, and organizational commitments.
- The United States has entered the era of the *administrative state*. During the past 50 years, the administrative sector has surged forward, spurred on by what might be called the permissive attitude that the courts have taken on the delegation of power issue. Administrative agencies have acquired increasing functions, along with more powers to carry them out.
- Franklin Roosevelt's "New Deal" gave birth to the idea of the *positive*, or welfare, state, whereby government provided a "safety net" of programs to enhance the "quality of life." Ronald Reagan's "revolution," that of redefining the federal government's role as limited, or privatizing government services whenever possible, responded to the regulatory, or *negative*, aspects of big government.
- Administrative law and regulatory law act in tandem, but they are not the same. Agencies and departments, cooperating with legislatures, create regulatory law. Regulatory law governs the private activities of citizens; administrative law governs the regulators, applying principles originating from statutes, common law, constitutions, and regulatory laws. The provisions of adequate notice, disclosure of reasons, the right to a hearing, and right to further appeal entail a set of rules that administrators must follow to meet due process requirements.
- After a century of intense litigation and adjudication, the field of administrative law is still alive with issues. Hearsay evidence and the double role of judge and prosecutor are key controversies of administrative law, affecting public administrators and clientele. The majority of *administrative law judges* function as hearing examiners in the Social Security Administration.

- The major aspects of the administrative process include delegation of power, judicial review, the investigatory power, the rule-making process, the right to be heard and adjudicatory policy-making, informal activity and the exercise of discretion, remedies against improper administrative acts, and opening up the government. The Freedom of Information Act (1967) and Privacy Act (1974) are amendments to the Administrative Procedure Act (1946), all of which concern due process guarantees.
- The question of administrative control has two quite distinct aspects—*internal* and *external* controls.
- Democratic government rests on principles such as accountability and responsibility; the realization of such principles requires a comprehensive system of administrative control. The public has a right to demand, and administrators have a need to accept, a widespread network of restraints and restrictions on administrative activity. Democratic government is *controlled* government.

The following case shows the ramifications a single administrative law can have. While reading, look for issues discussed in the chapter, especially administrative due process discretion and concerns.

CASE STUDY

Administrative Discretion at the State Health Services Administration[43]

Heidi Heitzler was excited about what she had just heard at the conference she was attending on aging. As the director of the not-for-profit St. Hillary's Nursing Home and Convalescent Center, she knew exactly how difficult it was to keep the books balanced during a time when the cost of medical and health care was skyrocketing. She also knew that the clients at St. Hillary's were interested in a therapeutic milieu which provided good, nutritionally balanced meals, clean and safe rooms, and caring health care providers—nursing aides, licensed practical and registered nurses, and doctors. The future for geriatric care facilities was destined to be a good one, insofar as the proportion of the aging population which would require care was projected to continue growing. The demographics presented at the conference showed that the percent of the age group 65 and older was growing at twice the national population rate and expected to comprise 20 percent of the total population by 2030.

Although Heitzler's participation in the conference produced what she called a "booked and shooked" frame of mind, she realized that she would have to return to St. Hillary's and face the routine problems associated with day-to-day administration: a nurse with a drug abuse problem; a client who had brought a negligence suit against her chief physician; a client who was injured when she slipped and fell on a freshly-waxed floor; a leaky roof that required immediate repair; a high turnover rate among the center's nursing assistants; and all the planning that was required for the celebration of Thanksgiving. The prospects of successfully resolving all these dilemmas seemed remote; but she was a dedicated administrator who had faced what appeared to be insurmountable obstacles before. She knew the value of perseverance and was certainly no stranger to adversity.

Earlier in the year, the state assembly had responded to the pressures which had been placed on it by enacting additional laws on the regulation of nursing homes for the aged. In fact, the law had given the State Human Services Agency (SHSA) wide authority and discretion to oversee the operations of nursing homes in the state. The reported cases of abuse against nursing home residents had received front page priority in the press, and the article showed the disparities associated with the quality of nursing care across the state, coupled with vast disparities between nursing home facilities. These factors had helped develop a mood among the state legislators that something should be done to alleviate the problem and do something that would benefit the aged.

Delegation by Legislature

The further empowerment of the SHSA by the legislature in its regulatory function came as no surprise for Mr. Henry Ortega. As the director of SHSA, he had long been concerned about the quality of health care provided in the state's nursing homes. On another occasion, he had joined the forces with the American Association of Retired Persons (AARP) and the State Mental Health Association (SMHA) in successfully getting the legislature to pass a patients' rights advocacy law. Now, at the request of the Association of Registered Recreational Therapists (ARRT), he formulated a set of rules which required each nursing home to employ at least one recreational therapist. The president of ARRT was Joliene Eggenberger, a cousin of Ortega and the wife of Senator Oscar "Big Spender" Eggenberger, a veteran chair of the state senate's powerful Appropriations Committee.

Although Ortega did not hold any hearings on his newly promulgated agency rule, he met privately with the Health Care Advisory Board—a group which was generally supportive of his proposals. The Board, after hearing the arguments which Ortega presented in support of the need for an agency regulation requiring recreational therapists, issued a formal recommendation which was broadly supportive of Ortega. Delighted by their response, Ortega complimented the Board for its caring concern for the elderly and issued a statement on the Board's action. He further stated that ". . . no formal hearing was required on the rule since such a hearing would be unnecessary and unduly time consuming, especially since there was a need to take immediate action to ensure the protection of the public interest and the welfare and safety of all nursing home residents."

Heidi Heitzler, upon learning of the new rule regarding recreational therapists, did not question the value which access to this type of therapy meant for her patients. Nevertheless, she felt that this regulation represented another "mindless act" by the bureaucrats in the state capitol. She knew she would not be able to comply easily with the regulation since Great Falls was a small, rural community.

To Comply, or Not to Comply

After examining her options, Heitzler complained to SHSA about the new rule and cited the fact that St. Hillary's could "not afford to hire a therapist" and noted that the only one she was able to locate lived nearly 50 miles away and would be available only two days a week. The Chief of Compliance, B. J. Smith, an experienced administrator who went, as he was fond of saying, to the "College of Hard Knocks," replied to Heitzler's complaint by sending an SHSA inspection team to St. Hillary's.

The inspectors reported that St. Hillary's ". . . met or exceeded all standards," except for the lack of a recreational therapist on its staff. Based on this information, Smith ordered that decertification proceedings be initiated against St. Hillary's.

St. Hillary's, at the initial hearing before James Westin, the SHSA's Hearing Examiner and General Counsel, argued that being a small nursing home in a poor rural area made it very difficult to identify and hire a recreational therapist. St. Hillary's also suggested that the seriousness of the problem was mitigated because their staff were all home town people who cared for the well-being of their elderly residents. In fact, a time-keeping log was produced which indicated that nurses frequently stayed after work to play games, supervise hobby activities, and help with other forms of patient recreation.

Westin was sympathetic to St. Hillary's dilemma, but felt that the law was clear. He found the nursing home to be out-of-compliance and issued a "recommended decertification" to the reviewing officer, Mr. Ortega. While in the process of reviewing the case, a citizen group from Great Falls visited Ortega and lobbied on behalf of St. Hillary's. Ortega ruled that St. Hillary's was in "substantial compliance" and he cancelled the decertification order.

Heitzler was happy with the decision, but Joliene and Oscar Eggenberger and SARRT were not. Senator Eggenberger informed Ortega at an Appropriation Committee meeting in which they were reviewing SHSA's bi-annual budgetary request, that "If I were you, I wouldn't grant any more exceptions to the recreational therapist rule." Ortega responded that he was the expert on nursing homes and that he felt Eggenberger had been intrusive in the affairs of SHSA.

Several weeks later, Hillside Nursing Home, a long-term care facility located in Carter City, requested a waiver exempting it from complying with the recreational therapist rule. The director of Hillside presented a scenario and set of facts that he thought would justify the granting of a ". . . hardship exemption to the rule." That is, Hillside was located in a very poor part of town and residents were disproportionately drawn from a sector that found it difficult to meet the present costs of extended nursing care for the elderly. Requiring the employment of a recreational therapist would also cause the home serious financial difficulties, and, after all, the regulations of the SHSA permitted waivers to be issued by the Chief of Policy, the Chief of Compliance or the Director. Upon reviewing the case, Shirley Jones, without seeking additional counsel, issued a waiver to Hillside.

Mr. Smith, however, had not been informed of the waiver granted to Hillside. Upon learning that Hillside did not have a recreational therapist, he called in his inspectors and inquired about the overall operation of the home. He was told that Hillside had not always measured up to either the letter or spirit of the state codes and that the facility was poorly managed. Prompted by this information, Smith ordered a surprise inspection. The subsequent inspection report showed that Hillside was in minimal compliance on most standards, deficient in some, and clearly in need of a recreational program. Smith issued an emergency decertification notice on Hillside. The notice also included a cease-and-desist order which instructed the home that it would be closed within 30 days unless it came into complete compliance on all reported deficiencies.

As expected, Hillside went to court and sought a restraining order against the SHSA. At the hearing, the lawyer for Hillside argued the following:

1. The legislature had improperly delegated too much authority and discretion to the SHSA.

2. The rule on recreation therapists was not properly related to the issue of good health care; the rule was arbitrary and unnecessary; it was established without a proper hearing; and it came about as a result of a conflict of interest.

3. The emergency decertification was arbitrary, excessive, and not authorized by law.

4. Hillside was being denied equal treatment under the law, whereas St. Hillary's was given an exemption under similar circumstances.

5. The surprise inspection violated the Fourth Amendment.

6. The waiver issued by Jones bound the agency and Smith could not legally overturn the waiver; collectively their actions violated due process of law.

7. The internal structure of the SHSA violated the separation of powers concept. The home could not, therefore, receive a fair hearing from Westin, who authorized the decertification.

8. Hillside could not receive fair treatment from Ortega, since he had a conflict of interest and was politically controlled by Senator Oscar Eggenberger.

In the final analysis, Hillside's attorney asked the court to restrain the SHSA from enforcing its orders and asked it to grant the home a permanent waiver on the rule requiring the employment of a recreational therapist.

The response of the SHSA addressed the legal arguments that were raised by Hillside's attorney in the following ways:

1. The legislature's broad grant of power to SHSA was valid.

2. The recreational therapist rule was related to the proper care of the aged. The rule was formulated with the advice of a statutorily established group of experts that also included input from the State Nursing Home Association. Under these circumstances, no formal rule-making procedures were required.

3. The emergency decertification process was a necessary part of the agency's statutory power to protect public health and safety.

4. Hillside was not entitled to the same treatment as St. Hillary's because Hillside's operation was deficient. Also, Hillside had a past record on poor compliance.

5. Surprise inspections were properly used in license cases and where public health was involved.

6. Mrs. Jones had not followed proper procedure in regard to the waiver granted to Hillside, therefore, the agency was not bound by her decision. Moreover, the waiver did not preclude action to be taken against the home on other grounds, as revealed in the on-site inspection.

7. Mr. Ortega was not Senator Eggenberger's prisoner. Ortega's own response at the committee hearing indicated his sense of independence. Furthermore, no conflict of interest existed, since he was not a member of any of the associations which were interested in the outcome of the implementation or adjudication of the rule.

In closing statements, the attorney for the state argued that while it was true that the court possessed the power to restrain the agency, the court should have deferred to the expertise and primary jurisdiction of the agency. "Finally," the state's attorney opined, "the court did not have the power to waive the therapist rule—that power clearly resided within the discretionary authority of the SHSA."

Exhibit 1

Relevant State Statutes, Regulations and Laws Pertaining to Nursing Homes.

Statutes

Section 101—The Human Services Agency is empowered to promulgate all appropriate rules and regulations for the operations of nursing homes for the aged including procedures for granting and terminating the licenses of such homes as the Director may prescribe.

Section 110—The Director of the Human Services Agency shall be authorized to waive any portion of these laws or regulations of the agency if he/she deems that a home, while technically deficient in some standards, has made a good faith effort to reach substantial compliance.

Section 115—The Human Services Agency is empowered to take any appropriate actions necessary to protect the health, safety, and welfare of all persons residing or working in nursing homes and to take the necessary measures to protect the public interest.

Section 120—There is hereby established a Health Care Advisory Board. This Board shall have the authority to investigate and make recommendations to state agencies on all matters related to health care in hospitals, clinics, nursing homes, and all other health care facilities which are licensed to operate in the state. The Board shall be composed of one representative from each of the State Medical Association, State Dental Association, State Osteopathic Association, State Hospital Association, State Nursing Home Association, State Mental Health Association, State Association of Registered Recreational Therapists, and two members of the general public to be chosen by the governor.

Civil Procedure Code

Section 201—The Federal Administrative Procedures Act shall apply to all state administrative agencies except as may be provided otherwise by acts of the legislature and, further provided that agencies may deviate from the APA in those instances wherein the agency has adopted or is statutorily subject to procedures which are substantially equivalent to those procedures contained in the APA.

Health Services Agency Regulations

Regulation C—The Director hereby authorizes the General Counsel, the Chief of Policy, and the Chief of Compliance to issue waivers and exemptions to the laws and regulations of the agency, according to policy guidelines as established by the Director.

Regulation M—The Chiefs of the Policy and Compliance Divisions shall be attorneys and shall serve as assistant legal counsels to the General Counsel. On all matters which involve the legal interpretation of the laws and regulations of this agency, the chiefs of the above named divisions will consult with the General Counsel before taking final action on such a matter. On all other matters within the scope of their duties, the chiefs of the above named divisions shall report to the Director.

Regulation Q—Before any emergency or summary actions may be instituted, the Chief of the Compliance Division must obtain the authorization of the General Counsel.

QUESTIONS AND INSTRUCTIONS

1. Do administrators like Ortega need to be concerned about the appearance of being influenced by "interest-group" politics? In what ways?
2. If you were the chief inspector, would you have taken action to begin the decertification for St. Hillary's based on its noncompliance with the recreational therapist standard? Justify your response.
3. If St. Hillary's was owned and operated by a municipality, would you see any difference in the way that the SHSA dealt with the rule requiring nursing homes to hire a recreational therapist?
4. How does the study of public and administrative law pertain to the basic activities associated with day-to-day administration?
5. Do you believe that Ortega's action to mandate recreational therapy in all nursing homes constitutes a conflict of interest, given his involvement and support of the SARRT Association? Why?
6. Assume the role of a trial judge and write an opinion in which you deal with the arguments presented by Hillside and the SHSA in court. As you know, you may rule on one point in favor of the agency and on another for Hillside. In the final analysis, who should win the case and why?

ENDNOTES

1. James Bryce, *The American Commonwealth* (1880), quoted in Theodore J. Lowi, *The End of Liberalism* (New York: W. W. Norton, 1969), 128–129.
2. Lowi, *End of Liberalism*, 131.
3. *Ibid.*, 132.
4. *A. L. A. Schechter Poultry Corporation v. United States*, 295 U.S. 495 (1935).
5. Harold Seidman and Robert Gilmour, *Politics, Position, and Power: From the Positive to the Regulatory State* (New York: Oxford University Press, 1986), 119.
6. *Ibid.*
7. Jerre S. Williams, "Cornerstone of American Administrative Law," *Administrative Law Review*, Vol. 28 (1976), v–xii.
8. Florence Heffron and Neil McFeeley, *The Administrative Regulatory Process* (New York: Longman, 1883), 347–371.
9. Williams, v–xii.
10. Kenneth F. Warren, *Administrative Law In The American System* (St. Paul, MN: West Publishing Co., 1982), 111–122.
11. Dwight Waldo, *The Enterprise of Public Administration: A Summary View* (Novato, CA: Chandler & Sharp Publishers, Inc., 1980). See especially "Chapter 6: Bureaucracy and Democracy: Reconciling the Irreconcilable," 81–98.
12. Bernard Schwartz, *Administrative Law* (Boston: Little, Brown, 1976), 2.
13. Stanley A. Reigel and P. John Owen, *Administrative Law: The Law of Government Agencies* (Ann Arbor, MI: Ann Arbor Science, The Butterworth Group, 1982), 4–5.
14. Phillip J. Cooper, *Public Law and Public Administration* (Palo Alto, CA: Mayfield Publishing Company, 1983), 6–7.
15. Lief H. Carter, *Administrative Law and Politics: Cases and Comments* (Boston: Little, Brown and Company, 1983), 60.
16. Lewis C. Mainzer, *Political Bureaucracy* (Glenview, IL: Scott, Foresman, 1973), 62.
17. *Ibid.*
18. 5 U.S.C., 554(b).
19. For an interesting, although scarcely disinterested account of a leading decision regarding prisoners' rights, see editorial, Tom Wicker, "Due Process for Prisoners," *New York Times*, 18 June 1970.
20. "Administrative Law Developments—1971," *Duke Law Journal*, 1972, No. 1, Section 3.
21. *Ibid.* For a more readable, but less profound account of the explanation of this right, see "Toward Greater Fairness for All," *Time*, 26 February 1973, 95.
22. Mainzer, *Political Bureaucracy*, 37.
23. The authors are appreciative to Harry Hammitt, Editor, *Access Reports* Vol. 19, No. 7 (March 31, 1993), 1–2, 4, for providing 1991 data on requests, costs, and fees collected by federal departments and agencies for administration of the Freedom of Information Act. For analysis of the history and management of the FOIA, consult Lotte E. Feinberg, "Managing the

Freedom of Information Act and Federal Information Policy," *Public Administration Review* Vol. 46, No. 6 (November/December, 1986), 615–621. See also Donald D. Barry and Howard R. Whitcomb, *The Legal Foundation of Public Administration* (St. Paul, MN: West Publishing Company, 1981), 331–332.

24. *Richardson v. Perales,* 402 U.S. 389 (1971).

25. "The 'Hidden Judiciary' and What It Does," *U.S. News and World Report,* 1 November 1982.

26. Martin Tolchin, "Are Judge and Agency Too Close for Justice?" *The New York Times,* February 5, 1989, page E3; Joseph J. Simeone, "The Function, Flexibility, and Future of United States Judges of the Executive Department," *Administrative Law Review,* Vol. 44, No. 1 (Winter 1992), 159–188.

27. Alexander Hamilton, John Jay, and James Madison, *The Federalist* (New York: Modern Library, n.d.), 337.

28. Joseph P. Harris, *Congressional Control of Administration* (Garden City, NY: Anchor Books, 1965), 8.

29. Richard F. Fenno, Jr., *The Power of the Purse* (Boston: Little, Brown, 1966), 283.

30. Dean Acheson, *Present at the Creation* (New York: W. W. Norton, 1969), 146.

31. W. Woodrow Wilson, *Congressional Government* (Boston: Houghton Mifflin, 1885), 271. Quoted in Acheson, *Present at the Creation,* 146.

32. Quoted in Mainzer, *Political Bureaucracy,* 76.

33. Charles Rembar, "The First Amendment on Trial: The Government, the Press and the Public," *The Atlantic,* Vol. 231, No. 4 (April, 1973), 47.

34. Quoted by Philip Shabecoff, "Watching the Money," *New York Times,* 25 February 1972, Business and Finance Section.

35. International Bar Association Ombudsman Committee and International Ombudsman Institute, 8 Ombudsman and Other Complaint Handling Systems Survey (July 1, 1978–June 30, 1979).

36. Ralph Nader, Peter Petkas, and Kate Blackwell, editors, *Whistle Blowing* (New York: Bantam Books, 1972).

37. *Ibid.,* 39–55.

38. Quoted in George E. Berkley, *The Democratic Policeman* (Boston: Beacon Press, 1969), 159–160.

39. Hamilton, Jay, and Madison, 337.

40. Mainzer, *Political Bureaucracy,* 89.

41. Peter Woll, "Administrative Law in the Seventies," *Public Administration Review,* Vol. 32, No. 5 (September–October, 1972), 557–564.

42. McGeorge Bundy, *The Strength of Government* (Cambridge, MA: Harvard University Press, 1968), 56.

43. By C. Kenneth Meyer, Professor and Chair, Department of Public Administration, Drake University, Des Moines, IA, and Paul A. Tharp, Jr., *Programs in Public Administration,* University of Oklahoma, Norman, OK 73019, written especially for *The Craft of Public Administration,* 5th edition. The authors retain all copyright privileges.

12

☆ ☆ ☆

CLIENTELE PRESSURES AND REGULATORY BEHAVIORS

CHAPTER HIGHLIGHTS

CLIENTELE RELATIONS
EVOLUTION OF ADMINISTRATIVE REGULATION
ECONOMIC, SOCIAL, AND SUBSIDIARY REGULATIONS
ADMINISTRATIVE RULES AND RULE-MAKING
ADMINISTRATIVE RESPONSIBILITY: PROFESSIONALISM,
PARTICIPATION, AND PUBLICITY

Perhaps nothing differentiates U.S. administrators so much from their European counterparts as the Americans' unending quest to secure support for their agencies and programs. The reasons for this relate very directly to the distinguishing features of the country's political culture. The fragmentation and personalism of our political system in particular tend to make the typical administrative agency something of an isolated entity that must continually develop and maintain its own sources of support.

In his highly regarded and oft-cited essay, "The Federal System," the late Morton Grodzins maintains:

> *The administrator must play politics for the same reason that the politician is able to play in administration: the parties are without program and without discipline. In response to the unprotected position in which the party situation places him, the administrator is forced to seek support where he can find it.*[1]

Francis Rourke sounds a similar note.

> *The political neutralization of bureaucracy is impossible in a country in which the political parties are incapable of performing the functions expected of them in the governmental structure of which they are a part. When the parties do not provide for program developments and the mobilization of political support, executive agencies must perform these tasks for themselves.*[2]

The clientele pressures placed upon public administrators from a variety of perspectives are numerous and continuous.

While these two writers stress the role played by the fragmented nature of our political parties in producing the U.S. administrator's difficult and slippery situation, there are other factors as well. The variability and vigor of the levels of government, the separation of powers in the various governments found at so many of these levels, the hostility, or at least ambivalence, with which the American people tend to regard activist government—all these play a part. The upshot is that the U.S. administrator must indeed cultivate and exercise the skills of the politician and must develop and maintain support if he or she is to achieve success.

Where is one to look for such support? As noted in chapter 11, those elements that control administration also support it. The courts, for example, in clamping procedural restrictions on administrative behavior also give it sanction, for once administrators have abided by the prescriptions of procedural due process, they can then look to the courts for legal vindication of their actions. Similarly, the ombudsman, when he or she investigates a complaint and finds it invalid, tends to bolster the position of the agency in question. Indeed, many administrators in those countries that have ombudsmen have found such investigatory officials to be helpful in deflecting public irritation and encouraging public approval of their actions.

For the most part, however, administrators must assume a more activist role in developing support. They must take affirmative steps to strengthen and promote their relationship with individuals and organizations in their control networks. Although developing support from other administrative agencies is often useful and even necessary, most public managers tend to concentrate efforts in support development in three basic areas—the clientele, the general public, and the political leaders, particularly legislators. While all three sectors obviously overlap and interrelate in developing and improving relationships, each will require somewhat different strategies and skills.

CLIENTELE RELATIONS

United States administrators often work hard at developing what Francis Rourke calls "fervent and substantial constituencies." In many cases, such constituencies are as important to the bureaucrat as they are to the elected politician. They not only help the agency to successfully formulate and implement its programs but, more important perhaps, may also help generate the support necessary to gain approval and funding for these programs. A fervent and substantial constituency can produce an outcry that will make any elected political leader think twice before cutting back an agency's scope or reducing its funding.

What makes a clientele effective? One rather obvious factor is *size*. Other things being equal, an agency with a larger clientele will benefit from more of this kind of support than an agency with a smaller one. A second factor is *dispersion*. An agency with a large clientele that is concentrated in only a few states will seldom gain as much influence and power as another agency with an equal number of clients who are more widely dispersed geographically.

A third and quite vital element in assessing clientele support is the clientele's *degree of organization*. The gun lobby, which generally supports the Department of Defense, is quite well organized. Welfare clients, on the other hand, lack the strong organization that could make them an effective source of support for the Department of Health and Human Services as well as for state and local welfare departments. The fact that programs benefiting the poor suffer from this lack of organized clientele support has often prompted administrators to organize and build up clientele groups on their own initiative. Sometimes this has worked successfully and sometimes not. In the poverty programs of the 1960s which arose as a result of such initiative, for example, a number of organizations purporting to speak for the poor struck many politicians and members of the public as being too demanding and too controlled by a self-seeking minority of the poor. As a result, such clientele support in many instances proved detrimental to building the programs' overall support base.

A fourth factor that must be taken into account is the *degree of ardor* that the clientele may manifest in rendering support. Usually, the degree of devotion that a clientele group manifests in supporting an agency roughly correlates with its degree of dependence on the agency.

How do administrators take advantage of the potential support that a clientele has to offer? It must first secure the clientele's cooperation. To this end, it may appoint members of the clientele group to positions, sometimes the highest ones, in the agency. When Franklin D. Roosevelt named financier Joseph P. Kennedy to head the newly created Securities and Exchange Commission, he was motivated in part by the desire to win the securities industry over to cooperate with the new regulatory commission. For the same reason, presidents today usually appoint a business person to head the Department of Commerce, a labor leader or someone with close ties to the labor movement to serve as Secretary of Labor, and in recent years a Native American to preside over the Bureau of Indian Affairs. Similar tendencies are also becoming more widespread at state and local levels; for instance, the greater concern of minority groups with housing problems has led to frequent appointments of blacks to head municipal housing commissions.

Such efforts at clientele involvement are not confined to the upper levels of administration. At lower echelons, the use of what are sometimes called "paraprofessionals" has become increasingly popular in many areas of U.S. public administration. School departments are using parents as "teacher's aides," police departments are setting up auxiliaries, correction departments have even begun using rehabilitated offenders to rehabilitate other offenders. Chester Barnard maintained that the customers of an organization should be considered as part of the organization. Modern administration has shown an increasing tendency to carry out this dictum and, in so doing, has often increased clientele support.

A related method of securing clientele support is through the awarding of contracts. This, of course, has played a key role in the powerful support the Defense Department has managed to build up through the years. Other departments have used the same strategy with a good deal of success. HHS and, to a lesser extent, HUD have also parceled out work to individuals and institutions outside of the government. This does not mean that the sole or even primary purpose of such contracts is to build clientele support. Often such arrangements are not only useful, but necessary for an agency. The alternative for the Defense Department in contracting with war suppliers would be to set up its own armaments industry, a move that would require a major and controversial reversal of a deeply rooted American attitude regarding the relationship of government to the economy. Such contracts and grants do however foster clientele support.

Important as such activities have become, few agencies can hope to "buy" all the support they need in this manner. They must also learn to gain the backing of their clientele through other means. While space does not permit a full-scale analysis of all the means and methods that administrators have utilized to achieve this end, we can briefly examine three of them before going on to appraise some of the dangers that the task of developing clientele support presents to the administrator and to the society he or she serves.

STRATEGIES OF SUPPORT: ADVISORY COMMITTEES AND TASK FORCES

If administrators are to elicit the favor and not the fury of their clients, then they must set up effective ways of listening to what their clients have to say. One tool for doing this is the advisory committee or the task force.

Ideally, the advisory committee can assist an agency in a variety of ways. It can act as a weather vane, pointing out to the agency what ideological and emotional currents are blowing among its various clientele groups. It can also serve as a sifter for new ideas that the agency may wish to implement. It can further help by serving as a lightning rod, deflecting many of the criticisms and complaints flung at the agency. Finally, it can provide a resource to help the agency carry out its programs.

In order for it to be able to perform all these roles, the advisory committee must be as fully representative as possible of all the segments of the agency's clientele. If it is an advisory committee for a police precinct station in a mixed neighborhood, then it should include residents and business people, blacks and whites, poor and nonpoor, young and old. Often it will be necessary to include divergent interests among its membership. An advisory committee for a housing agency should, for example, include both tenants and landlords. Such a breadth of membership invariably make committee meetings more tumultuous, but they are also more productive. Rourke has observed in this regard that, at best, "The public dialogue as well as the bureaucratic dialogue may be greatly improved by having outsiders participate in the internal deliberations of executive agencies. The bureaucratic dialogue may immediately become more spirited, and the public dialogue may eventually become more informed."[3]

Advisory committees can do more than simply provide useful input for policy formulation. They can, like labor unions, serve as a two-way transmission system for communication, bringing to the agency clients' concerns and bringing to the clients the agency's problems. Advisory committees can explain the agency's problems and help win acceptance for its proposed solutions. In some cases, they can even help implement the solutions.

TASK FORCE ON HEALTH CARE REFORM SHUNS SECRECY

Fifteen working groups, chaired by first lady Hillary Rodham Clinton, on health care reform include between 300 and 400 people from all phases of the health industry. According to the 1972 Federal Advisory Committee Act, the task force's policy making may be conducted in private, but the names of the working group members must be made public.

The labyrinth of medicine, economics, and politics confuses and frustrates providers and patients alike. The U.S. spent about $832 billion on health care in 1992, or one-seventh of the total U.S. economy. Some 35 million people living in the U.S. have no health care coverage; 100,000 people lose their health insurance every month.

With the stakes so high, the best interests of health care policy reform are served when the issues are debated in public forums. Appointed officials seek consensus for reforming an industry which is projected to rise to $1.6 trillion by 2000. Health care policy advocates, as task force members, have no citizen constituency, but they enjoy access to Mrs. Clinton and task force organizers.

Public acceptance of health care reforms requires that the processes of change be accomplished in the open. A political price may be paid for holding advisory committee or task force meetings in secret.

Source: Alissa J. Rubin, "Reinvention of Health Care Is Key to Clinton Overhaul," *Congressional Quarterly Weekly Report*, Vol. 51, No. 11 (March 13, 1993), 595–600.

Using advisory committees in this expanded role requires giving them expanded powers. While many agencies and their administrators have been reluctant, others have taken such a step with some success. One area where clientele advisory committees are assuming more and more authority and responsibility is in public housing. The State Housing Board of Massachusetts promulgated a regulation in 1973 giving representative tenant groups in all the state's housing projects the right to approve all employee hiring. In some cities, tenants have actually won the right to operate the entire project. Meanwhile, the Bureau of Indian Affairs, faced with rising ferment on the nation's reservations, has been moving to shift more responsibilities into the hands of Native Americans themselves.[4]

Such attempts at clientele involvement are by no means uniformly successful. Frequently, they only produce added stresses. The poverty programs offer an example, in some instances at least, of the wrong kind of clientele involvement, since the "grass roots" leadership that developed did not always represent the interests of the clientele. Although the trend toward clientele participation in policy making presents problems and will require caution and care, it seems likely to be a trend that will continue and grow.

COMPLAINT HANDLING

Although involving clients or their representatives in agency operations should do much to allay the fears and appease the demands of the agency's clientele, it can hardly hope to ensure complete and continuous contentment. Any agency, no matter how well run, will always encounter some dissatisfaction on the part of clients. This dissatisfaction will, furthermore, often have a basis in fact, for even the best of agencies creates occasional injustices. Any agency of significant size would do well to establish a formal and expeditious way of receiving and processing complaints.

A good complaint handling system can benefit an agency in many ways. It can provide discontented clients with a means of registering their grievances and, if justified, of having them redressed. Even when the grievances have not been found sufficiently valid for corrective action, the clients will often experience some satisfaction in knowing that at least their complaints were heard and examined.

Another and sometimes more important contribution of good complaint handling is providing the agency with valuable information. If complaints appear to cluster around one particular segment of the agency's operations or seem to be directed against certain individuals, the agency may want to take a closer look at the operations or the individuals in question. Complaints can aid in the process of internal control and can also assist the agency in evaluating present operations, while helping it to plan future ones.

To make maximum use of complaint handling for purposes of building clientele support, exercising internal control, evaluating current operations and planning future operations, administrators may find the following guidelines useful:

1. Adopt an attitude of welcoming complaints and see to it that your agency's clients understand this. Set up a regular procedure and, if possible, a regular branch for receiving and processing complaints, and publicize its operation. Have forms printed up to help complainants record their grievances. Above all, try to avoid giving the complainant the impression that he or she is being given the "run-around."

2. Make sure that your complaint handling procedure provides for following through on the complaint. Too often complaints are accepted, but then disappear. Every complainant should be informed of the disposition of the complaint, along with the reasons why no action is to be taken, if that is the case.

3. To make sure that the complaint handling function is taken seriously by all members of the agency, invest those in charge with some prestige and power. They will need the cooperation of the rest of the agency in checking out the complaint and may experience difficulty in obtaining it unless they can speak with some authority. Furthermore, complainants themselves are more apt to feel that they are being given adequate treatment when their grievances are heard by someone who holds a position of some authority. U.S. Customs Officers, for example, usually refer complainants to their supervisors. At one time, the Customs Service ran short of supervisor badges and so aggrieved parties had to be directed to officials who, while supervisors, were wearing ordinary badges. This compounded the complainants' annoyance and made many of them outspokenly irate. When the new supervisor badges finally arrived, things quieted down considerably.

4. Make sure that you explain the value of and need for a complaint handling procedure to all agency employees, and stress the fact that it should not threaten them in any way. Good employees will actually benefit by receiving a low number of valid complaints. Should such employees receive a high number of complaints, then the problem most likely will come from outside their jurisdiction and investigative action will usually uncover and correct it with benefits to them as well as to the complainants.

5. Make sure you have a system for cataloging complaints. Often an agency may want to multi-index them. For example, a police department may wish to file its complaints according to the area of the city from which they come, according to the type of police work they involve (such as criminal investigation or handling of family disputes), and according to the individuals involved. Only by maintaining a good filing system can an agency make full use of the information that complaint processing can provide.

In recent years, many administrative agencies have begun to institute ombudsmen to handle clientele complaints. These are not ombudsmen in the strict sense, since they are employees of the same agency against whom the complaint is being lodged, but they often enjoy a measure of independence and discretion in seeing that the grievances brought to their attention are heard and, if valid, acted upon.

The U.S. Immigration Service has set up an ombudsman in its New York City office to process both complaints and appeals for help. "One of my primary functions," says Cono Trubiano, who first held the position, "is to cut through red tape and to zoom in on officials who could attend to a case swiftly."[5] The U.S. Department of Commerce has also set up an "Ombudsman for Business," who, working directly under the department's secretary, gives aid and advice to business persons in their dealings with the department. Several large business corporations have attempted to do the same, often giving their complaint handling official the status of vice presidency.[6]

Probably no organization in the country, public or private, creates as much clientele disfavor as the Internal Revenue Service. The very nature of its work brings it into an adversarial relationship with vast numbers of the country's population every year. It gives serious attention to complaints and maintains suggestion boxes in its field offices where such complaints can be submitted. In handling complaints, it also maintains a useful sense of humor. When an irate taxpayer sent in a turnip with his tax return, saying the government agents were welcome to all the blood they could get out of it, an IRS official cut a slice of the turnip and mailed it back to the taxpayer with a letter saying, "Enclosed please find refund. Affectionately, U.S. Treasury."[7] Mechanisms for facilitating complaint handling are ever more important in the 1990s as employees and government programs are under siege from clients and taxpayers.

PUBLIC HEARINGS

The public hearing has, in many instances, become part of administrative due process. Administrative agencies are generally required to hold them before they can change their rules, discharge a tenured employee, and so on. Even when they are not required by law to hold such hearings, agencies have increasingly done so, for they offer opportunities to win support or defuse antagonism. New York City's Board of Education, for example, holds a hearing one evening every month, allowing any citizen to speak for four minutes on any topic of his or her choosing, provided that it is related to the city schools.

As a method of improving clientele relations, the hearing is more useful in "clearing the air" than in mobilizing support. It brings hostilities, complaints, and rumors out into the open and thereby enables administrators to deal with them on a more informed basis. Frequently it provides new information that can be used to modify and occasionally reverse an agency's course of action. At a minimum it offers an outlet for resentment which, if kept bottled up, could eventually explode and cause serious damage to the agency and its goals.

Hearings should be adequately advertised and publicized in advance and should be held at convenient times and places. Some sort of record should be kept that should be available for inspection afterward. The agency holding the hearing should also take care to see that both sides are represented and that no one faction dominates the proceedings. To this end, the agency may alternate limited time periods to proponents and opponents. Those parties that stand to be the most deeply affected by the issue involved may be given first priority in having their views heard. An urban-renewal agency holding a hearing on a proposed project may allow residents and business people in the project area to speak first, for example.

Though sometimes useful, hearings do have their liabilities and limitations. They delay action, consume time (particularly in preparation), and add to expense. More important, perhaps, is the fact that despite all the safeguards an agency may take to see that both sides are adequately heard, the negative side often tends to predominate. Those who are opposed to an action are usually the most vociferous. An agency contemplating a proposed move will often find itself confronted with a preponderance of outspoken antagonists when it holds hearings, even though majority sentiment may be in its favor. News reports based on the hearing may subsequently give the impression that the opposition is much more widespread than it really is. Although hearings can clear the air, they can sometimes do the reverse, embittering already rocky relationships and strengthening entrenched positions.

The pitfalls that public hearings sometimes present have prompted many administrators to become somewhat wary about using them to secure citizen input into administrative activity. While required in many instances to meet standards of administrative due process, and while in some instances useful in improving clientele relations, they nevertheless sometimes prove more harmful than helpful. As a result, many administrators and their organizations look to other devices to muster support.

Public hearings of all types—executive press conferences, legislative committee sessions, and consumer conscience government agencies—are broadcast day and night—literally—by C-SPAN (Cable System Public Affairs Network) on television cable systems throughout the nation. Local cable television franchises may broadcast sessions of municipal legislatures as budget decisions and policy development needs demand access to a wider audience in the community.

CLIENTELE SUPPORT: HOW MUCH IS TOO MUCH?

One of the first major federal agencies to undertake a major program of clientele involvement was the Tennessee Valley Authority (TVA), and it is not difficult to understand why. Censured and condemned from the beginning as a "socialist" and thereby "un-American" enterprise, this New Deal venture faced an urgent need to win local support. To this end, the TVA appointed representatives of influential local institutions to its policy-making body and deferred generally to local customs and sentiments. By assiduously cultivating clientele support, the public power facility was able to prosper and grow.

The authority paid a heavy price for such grass-roots support, however. It ended up discriminating against blacks, retrenching on conservation measures in order to protect local real estate interests, and hindering programs of other New Deal agencies, such as the Soil Conservation Service, which it sought to exclude from operating in the valley area. What started out as a highly progressive undertaking became, in large part, a conservative institution—and this as a result of its responsiveness to its presumed clientele.[8]

The TVA case is by no means unique. As Rourke points out, the relationship between a public agency and its clientele is nearly always a two-way street. An agency may achieve great success in marshaling clientele support, only to find that it has surrendered its independence and, in so doing, has impaired its commitment to the public as a whole. The clientele may manipulate the agency to serve their own limited interests with consequential detriment to general public policy.

Examples of clientele capture abound in the federal bureaucracy. The regulatory commissions, for example, have often been accused of actually being regulated by those they are supposed to regulate. The Department of Veterans Affairs for example has become heavily dependent on and influenced by veterans' organizations, which hold a near veto on much of its policy-making. Even Cabinet departments are not immune. Agriculture, Commerce, and Labor are often regarded as particularly susceptible to clientele dictation, and many presidents have wanted to merge the latter two departments, partly to release them from this bondage.

Agencies that serve only one highly demarcated group are particularly vulnerable to this problem. And when the agency lacks broad support and when its operations tend to attract insufficient public interest, the problem deepens.

Two current trends in public administration may serve only to increase the amount of clientele capture in U.S. public administration. One of these is the trend toward the *clientele basis of organization*. Structuring and orienting public agencies on the basis of clientele, while it often offers many advantages in terms of effectiveness and humaneness, will also open up more possibilities for clientele influence to get out of hand.

A second trend that could create increasing difficulties is the drive toward *decentralization*. "Where considerable authority is devolved upon field officials," David Truman once wrote, "there is always the danger . . . that policy will be unduly influenced by those private individuals and groups who are closer and have more intimate contact with the field than are the superior officers." Such a situation, says Truman, "if carried to any great lengths, is likely to beget such differences of policy between field officers that national policy will be a fiction."[9]

Fortunately, some corrective forces are also at work to counter these trends and possibly redress the whole situation. One is the move toward integration of activities. The interdependence between agencies and programs that characterizes today's bureaucratic milieu may make clientele capture of any particular agency increasingly difficult. Programs intermesh, and sometimes clientele do as well. The sight of a highly differentiated clientele clustered around a highly independent agency may become increasingly rare.

Many developments in public administration, such as programmed budgeting and management by objectives, should likewise make it difficult for a clientele group to induce or coerce an agency to depart from publicly sanctioned policies. The increased visibility accorded public agencies and their activities, while it will also hopefully increase their responsiveness to those they serve, increases their responsibility to policies espoused by the entire community. For example, federal regulatory commissions became much less dominated by clientele groups during the past decade, thanks in part to the increased attention they received from the news media and the public. Such countervailing developments as these may well succeed in offsetting the dangers that increased decentralization and increased clientele orientation may present.

EVOLUTION OF ADMINISTRATIVE REGULATIONS

In 1789, Congress granted the president the prerogative to select an administrator to "estimate the duties payable on imports." Since then, Congress continues to delegate rule-making power to administrative agencies. The full scope of regulatory power, in addition to the power to formulate rules, includes the authority for interpreting laws and regulations, enforcing rules and regulations, trying cases concerning violations of those rules, holding hearings investigating and adjudicating such circumstances, and imposing sanctions on violators. In a single agency, administrative regulatory power combines legislative, executive, and judicial powers.[10]

Administrative power expands as the power and responsibilities of government in our society expand. An industrialized, urbanized, interdependent society requires a more active role for government. The protection of individual rights, mediation of disputes, provision of benefits, and stabilization of the economy reflect accepted activities of modern U.S. government. As the 1980s began, at least fifty-eight federal agencies exercised rule-making authority and issued approximately 7,000 rules and policy statements each year.[11]

FDA GIVES BIOTECHNOLOGY FOOD INDUSTRY GREEN LIGHT

The Food and Drug Administration (FDA), subsidiary of the United States Department of Health and Human Services, responsible to the President and accountable to Congress, established a regulatory policy that foods developed through biotechnology should not require extraordinary testing and regulation before entry into the marketplace. Genetically engineered foods are to be regulated just like ordinary foods unless they contain unusual ingredients. FDA officials conclude that scientific evidence does not warrant special precautions in most gene-altered foods.

Requested by the budding biotechnology food industry, FDA's regulatory policy is based on science. More than a dozen companies have developed almost 70 different crops, including cucumbers, potatoes, and cantaloupes, which contain new proteins, enzymes, or other substances to enhance their quality. In circumstances where safety is a concern, FDA officials pointed out that changes in food resulting from genetic modification may be regulated under food additives rules, which call for premarket testing and approval.

Former Vice President Dan Quayle argued that genetically altered organisms and products are not dangerous because of the techniques used to produce them. FDA critics, such as Dr. Rebecca Goldburg of the Environmental Defense Fund, oppose any regulatory policy that does not require extensive, premarket testing of foods produced through genetic manipulation. "Genetic engineers are taking genes from bacteria, viruses and insects and adding them to fruits, grains and vegetables," Dr. Goldburg stated. "They are producing foods that have never before been eaten by human beings. Without clear and consistent labeling of genetically engineered foods, consumers will have no idea what they are buying."

The demands of the new biotechnology food industry to compete with international rivals and the well-being of consumers require many checks and balances between government regulators and private citizens in the American marketplace.

Source: Warren E. Leary, "Gene-Altered Food Held by the F.D.A. to Pose Little Risk," *The New York Times*, May 26, 1992, pages A1, C9.

Administrative regulatory powers are vested in state and local government agencies as well. State regulatory powers and responsibilities include licensing of physicians, barbers, lawyers, architects, cosmeticians, liquor dealers, and funeral directors. States regulate commerce within their boundaries and supervise the governance of all public educational institutions. Local government agencies enforce building codes, fire, health, and safety regulations and standards. Agencies of state or local governments may also be charged with implementation of national programs via functional federalism.

As stated in the previous chapter, the United States is a regulatory state. The vast majority of direct contacts for most citizens is likely to be with federal, state, or local administrative agencies. We are a society where virtually every activity of organizations and individuals is included in the scope of administrative regulation and control. The responsibilities and powers of administrative agencies include the following partial listing:

1. The rates that consumers pay for telephone service and electricity are determined by administrative agencies, as are the interest rates that savings and loan institutions may pay depositors.
2. Administrative agencies protect individuals from racial, sexual, and age discrimination in the major aspects of their lives: employment, education, and housing.
3. Administrative agencies determine who does and does not get radio and television licenses.
4. Administrative agencies ensure that the food we eat is pure, wholesome, and free from harmful additives and that the drugs that we purchase are both safe and effective.
5. The right to join a labor union and to be protected from unfair labor practices is safeguarded by administrative regulatory power.
6. Administrative agencies are responsible for ensuring the safety of our workplaces, our methods of transportation, and the countless products that we purchase as consumers—from toys to clothing to automobiles.
7. Administrative agencies are responsible for protecting us against monopolies, false advertising, air and water pollution, incompetent health care professionals, subminimum wages and working conditions, unfair and misleading credit transactions, and fraud in securities purchases.
8. Administrative agencies determine who is eligible for welfare, food stamps, veterans benefits, Medicaid, Medicare, and Social Security.
9. Administrative agencies determine how much of our income we get to keep and whether a person may be admitted to or remain in this country.[12]

Independent regulatory commissions, cabinet departments, independent agencies, government corporations, the Executive Office of the President (EOP), and a variety of assorted federal agencies of more and lesser consequence issue administrative regulations daily in *the Federal Register* and annually in the *Code of Federal Regulations*. Overhead units carry out functions for the entire federal government. The General Accounting Office (GAO), Government Printing Office (GPO), Congressional Budget

---

THE FEDERAL REGISTER AND THE CODE
OF FEDERAL REGULATIONS

The Federal Register, published daily, Monday through Friday, provides a uniform system for making available to the public regulations and legal notices issued by Federal departments and agencies. These include Presidential proclamations and Executive Orders and Federal agency documents having general applicability and legal effect, documents required to be published by act of Congress and other Federal agency documents of public interest.

The Code of Federal Regulations is a codification of the general and permanent rules published in *The Federal Register* by the Executive departments and agencies of the Federal Government. The *Code* is divided into 50 titles which represent broad areas subject to Federal regulation. Each title is subdivided into chapters which usually bear the name of the issuing agency. Each chapter is further subdivided into parts covering specific regulatory areas.

The Federal Register and *The Code of Federal Regulations* must be used together to determine the latest version of any given rule. Each volume of the *Code* contains amendments published in *The Federal Register* since the last revision of that volume of the *Code*. Source citations for the regulations are referred to by volume number and page number of *The Federal Register* and date of publication.

Office (CBO), Office of Management and Budget (OMB), General Services Administration (GSA), and Office of Personnel Management (OPM) issue regulations and administer support functions for most of the federal bureaucracy.

Since the creation of the Interstate Commerce Commission more than 100 years ago, independent regulatory commissions have been prominent in the government regulation of business. Such commissions are multi-headed, bipartisan in composition, organizationally separated from other departments and agencies, and not directly in the president's chain of command; they provide nonpartisan flexibility, continuity, and expertise in the regulatory process, assign commissioners with terms longer than the president, protect commissioners from presidential dismissal, and allow lengthy tenure for maximizing commissioner expertise and independence. These characteristics and aspirations may not be realized in each commission on every day of every year; however, these commissions possess widespread responsibilities for regulating specific industries and for protecting consumers and workers.

Examples of prominent, independent regulatory commissions are the Federal Communications Commission (FCC), Interstate Commerce Commission (ICC), Nuclear Regulatory Commission (NRC), Postal Rate Commission, Securities and Exchange Commission (SEC), Federal Maritime

Commission (FMC), Federal Reserve System (FED), Consumer Product Safety Commission (CPSC), and Equal Employment Opportunity Commission (EEOC).

Cabinet departments enjoy similar scope, type, and impact of regulatory power as independent regulatory commissions. Major distinctions between the two types of agencies include administrative form and operations within executive departments or agencies. Cabinet agencies are led by a single administrator; cabinet secretaries are directly responsible to the president for programming. For example, the Food and Drug Administration (FDA), within the Department of Health and Human Services (HHS), is responsible for ensuring purity and safety of food, drugs, and cosmetics; the Internal Revenue Service (IRS), within the Department of Treasury, implements tax laws; the Immigration and Naturalization Service (INS), within the Department of Justice, regulates the entry, residence, and exit by aliens; and the Occupational Safety and Health Administration (OSHA), within the Department of Labor, attempts to ensure that places of work are free from hazards affecting the health and safety of workers.

Independent agencies, such as the Federal Emergency Management Agency (FEMA), Selective Service System, the National Foundation on the Arts and Humanities, and Small Business Administration (SBA), share characteristics in common with independent regulatory commissions and cabinet departments. Independent agencies are accountable to the president for direction and control; they have a single, administrative leader, and they are not positioned within a cabinet department. The government corporations, such as AMTRAK, a passenger railroad; Federal Deposit Insurance Corporation (FDIC), an insurance company; Tennessee Valley Authority (TVA), an electric power generating facility; or the U.S. Postal Service, a post office; issue regulations as well. Such public corporations are multiheaded (with a board of directors); however, the president may dismiss corporation board members.

Distrust and dislike of the chief executive encouraged establishment of independent regulatory commissions. A powerful clientele group, such as the environmental lobby, called for the promotion and protection of a particular concern or interest within a single-headed independent agency. An agency within a department may seek refuge there from hostile or corrupt influences.

The total administrative regulatory process includes ten procedures, or steps. Most regulatory activities do not include touching all ten bases, either because the rule is obeyed without discussion or controversy or the agency does not actively enforce the regulation. The procedures or steps of the administrative regulatory process are identified in Table 12–1.

TABLE 12–1   Steps of Administrative Regulatory Process

Step 1: Authorizing Legislation;
Step 2: Agency Interpretation-Enforcement (rule-making);
Step 3: Complaint;
Step 4: Investigation;
Step 5: Informal Proceedings;
Step 6: Prosecution;
Step 7: Formal Hearing (adjudication);
Step 8: Agency Review;
Step 9: Judicial Review;
Step 10: Agency Enforcement.

Source: Florence Heffron and Neil McFeeley, *The Administrative Regulatory Process* (New York: Longmans, 1983), page 17.

ECONOMIC, SOCIAL, AND SUBSIDIARY REGULATIONS

Despite partisan efforts by Presidents Reagan and Bush to bring regulatory policy relief to the American economic and social system, regulatory expenditures in real terms increased 21 percent between the 1981 budget and 1990 budget. Reagan did not stop the growth of federal regulatory spending, but he was able to slow the growth of federal regulatory spending.

Between 1970 and 1975, there was dramatic expansion of the regulatory establishment. Between 1975 and 1980, regulatory expenditures increased 27 percent. From 1980 to 1985 costs decreased by 3 percent. Reagan's attempts to shut down the regulatory establishment came to a halt in 1984. Growth in the regulatory establishment resumed between 1985 and 1990, rising by 18 percent, making up lost time for the previous period.

Priorities for the broad, regulatory categories changed significantly in the 1970–1990 period. Spending for job safety and other working conditions increased by 217 percent between 1970 and 1980 and decreased by 13 percent between 1980 and 1990. Between 1970 and 1980 spending for industry-specific regulation increased by 66 percent but decreased by 23 percent from 1980 until 1990, reflecting Reagan's attempts to halt regulatory activities. Consumer safety and health regulatory expenditures decreased between 1980 and 1990, but less dramatically.

The 1970–1990 period saw a 46 percent increase in the number of regulatory personnel, with all but 3 percent of this rise coming between 1970 and 1975. Between 1970 and 1975, there was a 50 percent jump in staffing for social regulatory activities. As the number of personnel employed by the regulatory bureaucracy grew greatly, so did its intrusion into the everyday decision-making processes of the private sector. Regulatory staffing patterns declined during the 1980–1985 period however, as there were 15 percent fewer personnel in 1985 than in 1980.[13]

In 1970, less than 70,000 employees staffed regulatory agencies for the federal government. In 1993, 126,501 employees are expected to act on regulatory matters. There are nearly 5,000 regulations in effect. About 65,000 of new and modified regulations are published each year in the *Federal Register*. Tables 12-2, 12-3, 12-4, and 12-5 illustrate spending and staffing priorities for the top ten economic and social regulatory agencies. Costs of staffing for private sector compliance with regulations notwithstanding, estimates for the 1993 federal budget call for fifty-three federal economic and social regulatory agencies to spend $25 billion—almost four times the amount spent in 1970. Public sector expenditures are a small proportion of the total cost of regulation by society.

Federal regulations cost the United States economy more than $400 billion in 1991. For example, the Clean Air Act, Americans with Disabilities Act, and Nutrition Labeling and Education Act, all enacted in 1990, are regulatory measures. The Clean Air Act costs business an estimated $25 billion a year in addition to the $32 billion companies spent annually prior to the 1990 amendments. The projected costs for the disabilities law is $20 billion a year over a five year period. The Nutrition Labeling and Education Act requires food industries to have labels listing specified nutrients and the amounts contained in each product. The costs of compliance to the new rules established by labeling law is between $4,000 and $6,000 per product. The benefits of having clean air, making accommodations to employ and serve the disabled, and educating consumers on nutrition are obviously not without tradeoffs.

According to Lawrence A. Hunter, vice president and chief economist for the U.S. Chamber of Commerce, "government regulation is a delicate balancing act between real costs and expected benefits. Unfortunately, the scale today has become tipped against business—particularly small business—and economic growth."[14]

There are three types of regulatory behaviors which fall into the categories of economic, social, and subsidiary regulations.

ECONOMIC REGULATIONS

What we will call *Regulation I,* or *economic regulation,* per Warren and Chilton (1989), focuses upon market aspects of industrial behavior, including rates, quality, and quantity of service, and competitive practices within a specific industry, or segment of the economy. Categories of economic regulation include finance and banking, industry-specific regulation, and general business regulation. The Comptroller of the Currency,

THE FTC AS THE FOURTH BRANCH OF GOVERNMENT

The Federal Trade Commission develops, evaluates, and implements consumer protection policies as the following Regulation I (economic) and Regulation II (social) decisions illustrate:

Payless Auto Sales, Inc., a used-car dealership in Virginia Beach, Virginia, has agreed to settle FTC charges that it failed to display the required "Buyers Guide" on the Commission's Used Car Rule. The dealership also violated the FTC's Warranty Disclosure Rule by not providing warranty information.

Davis Brothers Oil, Inc., a gasoline distributor headquartered in Clarksville, Indiana, and its president, Paul E. Davis, have agreed to settle FTC charges that they violated the Commission's Octane Rule by failing to certify the octane ratings of gasoline they transferred to retail service stations and by failing to keep delivery tickets or letters of certification on which the company based octane certifications. Under the proposed settlement, Davis Brothers would be required to pay a $25,000 civil penalty and be prohibited from violating the rule in the future.

The Right Start, Inc., of Thousand Oaks, California, and **The Sharper Image, Inc.,** of San Francisco, have agreed to settle FTC charges that they ran false and unsubstantiated advertising claims in their catalogs for certain products.

Macias Mortuary Services, of California, and its president and co-owner, Alex E. Macias, have agreed to pay a $60,000 civil penalty to settle charges that they violated the FTC's Funeral Rule by failing to provide consumers with pricing information.

Gracewood Fruit Company, of Vero Beach, Florida, has agreed to a proposed settlement with the FTC that would require the company to have reliable scientific evidence to back up future claims that eating normal quantities of grapefruit provides a variety of health benefits.

PerfectData Corporation, a California marketer of electronic office equipment care and maintenance products, has been charged by the FTC with making false and misleading environmental claims in the marketing of its "PerfectDuster II" aerosol cleaning product.

Channel Home Center, Inc., of Whippany, New Jersey, a retailer of home-improvement products, has agreed to settle FTC charges that it failed to make certain disclosures in its advertising for home-insulation products as required by the FTC's R-value Rule.

The FTC has charged **Solar Sales, Inc.,** of Fort Lauderdale, Florida, with misrepresenting that its "transient voltage surge suppressors" would save consumers 20 percent on their electric bills and extend the life of fluorescent light tubes by eight to ten times.

Precision Mailers, Inc., and its principals have agreed to pay $75,000 to settle FTC charges in connection with prize-promotion mailings they developed to help more than 200 businesses nationwide sell resort memberships and vacation timeshares. The FTC alleged that the mailings misrepresented the nature and value of prizes.

> **Michael L. Zabrin Fine Arts Ltd.** and its owner, of Northbrook, Illinois, have agreed to settle FTC charges of selling art works misrepresented to be creations of famous artists to art dealers who then sold them to customers. The settlement prohibits Zabrin and his firm from misrepresenting the authenticity of art works, the artist's signature, or any investment potential and requires them to pay $43,000 in redress.
>
> Source: **FTC News Notes** Vol. 93, Nos. 4 (January 25, 1993), 5 (February 1, 1993), 13 (March 29, 1993), and 14 (April 5, 1993) (Washington, DC: Office of Pubic Affairs, Federal Trade Commission, 1993).

Farm Credit Administration, Federal Deposit Insurance Corporation, Federal Reserve Banks, and National Credit Union Administration are regulators for finance and banking activities. The Commodity Futures Trading Commission, Federal Communications Commission, Federal Energy Regulatory Commission, Federal Maritime Commission, and Interstate Commerce Commission deal with industry-specific regulations. The Patent and Trademark Office in the Department of Commerce, Antitrust Division in the Department of Justice, Federal Election Commission, Federal Trade Commission, and Securities and Exchange Commission are general business regulators, dealing with agencies that are not directly related to finance and banking nor industry specific. Economic regulation is usually industry specific and focuses on market structure and firm conduct, regulating entry, exit, merger, and rates within markets.[15] For example, the ICC regulates railroads and trucking and the FCC regulates communications. The ICC and FCC each concentrate on a specific industry and each agency has no other responsibilities. Regulation I also concerns enforcement of congressionally mandated antitrust policies. The Justice Department and FTC regulate the frequency of mergers and combinations within particular industries. The goal of antitrust policies is maintaining and restoring competition within the market system. Competition and economic efficiency are objectives of Regulation I. One of the most criticized forms of economic regulation is the effort of the FTC to demand that businesses tell consumers the truth, the whole truth, and nothing but the truth. The disclosure of full and accurate information by business, however, should prove compatible for desired outcomes of sellers and buyers in the market system.

The top ten economic regulatory agencies for spending remained relatively stable over the 1970–1990 period. The Patent and Trademark Office, the Federal Deposit Insurance Corporation (FDIC), and the Comptroller of the Currency switched places in the two decades, but all remain in the top three. (See Table 12–2 for ranking of the top ten economic regulatory agencies, based on expenditures for the 1990 federal budget.)

TABLE 12-2 Top Ten Economic Regulatory Agencies,
Ranked Based on Costs in Real Terms, 1993
(Fiscal Years, Millions of Constant 1987 Dollars)

Agency	Rank	Costs
Patent and Trademark Office	1	$390
Comptroller of the Currency	2	278
Federal Deposit Insurance Corporation	3	222
Federal Reserve Banks	4	210
Securities and Exchange Commission	5	201
Federal Communications Commission	6	124
Federal Energy Regulatory Commission	7	119
Federal Trade Commission	8	70
National Credit Union Administration	9	52
Department of Justice Antitrust Division	10	51

Source: Melinda Warren and James Lis, *Regulatory Standstill: Analysis of the 1993 Regulatory Budget* (St. Louis, MO: Center for the Study of American Business, 1992).

SOCIAL REGULATIONS

Regulation II, or *social regulation*, controls the nature and types of goods and services and production processes.

Social regulations entail consumer safety and health, job safety and working conditions, environment, and energy. Consumer safety and health regulators include the Consumer Product Safety Commission, Departments of Agriculture, Health and Human Services, Housing and Urban Development, Justice, Transportation, and Treasury, and National Transportation Safety Board. Job safety and working conditions regulators include the Employment Standards Administration and Occupational Safety and Health Administration in the Department of Labor, Equal Employment Opportunity Commission, and National Labor Relations Board. Environmental regulators include Army Corps of Engineers in the Department of Defense, Fish and Wildlife Service and Office of Surface Mining Reclamation and Enforcement in the Department of Interior, and Environmental Protection Agency. Energy regulators include the Economic Regulatory Administration in the Department of Energy and Nuclear Regulatory Commission.[16]

Social regulation usually cuts across industries, regulating issues such as employment opportunity, environmental protection, and occupational safety.[17] Social regulation assumes control or elimination of socially harmful impacts occurring as by-products of the production process and protection of consumers and the public from unsafe or unhealthy products. If conservatives find Regulation I unpopular, they believe Regulation II an anathema. Regulation II focuses upon the subtle regulation of clean air, occupational safety, poison prevention, boat safety, lead-based paint elimination, product safety, political campaigns, pesticide control, water pollution, noise control, flood disaster, energy, commodity futures trading, hazardous materials transportation, and similar potential abuses.

Regulation II covers more industries and directly affects more consumers than Regulation I. For example, OSHA's regulations govern the activities of every employer whose business affects commerce. In other words, government is involved with detailed, sometimes minute, facets of the production process.

Two concerns are raised by Regulation II. The apparatus of the Presidency concentrates significant power and influence regulating health, safety, and environmental activities. Second, the accretion of new regulatory powers and controls could undermine citizens' faith in government—a negative reaction to overstrengthening of government and regulatory excesses of the mid-1970s. Social regulation is costly because many regulatory decisions are grounded in grossly inadequate information. Even if information is forthcoming, regulatory decisions may reflect the most extreme and unrealistic assumptions about the problem's potential social interference. There could be strong resistance to alternative and innovative problem solutions. The ranking of the top ten social regulatory agencies during the 1970s and 1980s illustrates interesting changes in federal regulatory priorities. (See Table 12–3 for ranking of the top ten social regulatory agencies, based on expenditures for the 1990 federal budget.[18]) The Environmental Protection Agency (EPA), reflecting the high level of public support for environmental regulation, has been ranked number one for the two decades indicated. The Nuclear Regulatory Commission ranked number seven in 1970, did not make the top ten ranking in 1980, but was ranked number five in 1990. The Three Mile Island disaster affected nuclear regulatory policies.

The Food Safety and Inspection Service, Occupational Safety and Health Administration, Office of Surface Mining Reclamation and Enforcement, and the Economic Regulatory Administration (energy price controls) moved to the top ten in 1980, as Americans demanded healthier foods, better working conditions, and appropriate ecological balance. Reflecting the deregulation of oil prices, the Economic Regulatory Administration did not make the top ten for the 1990 federal budget.

The EPA, Federal Aviation Administration, Animal and Plant Health Inspection Service, Coast Guard, Food and Drug Administration, and Bureau of Alcohol, Tobacco, and Firearms continue to dominate social regulatory spending, posting top ten rankings for the 1970, 1980, and 1990 budget periods, even though their relative positions in the top ten rankings have changed.

TABLE 12-3   Personnel Staffing for Top Ten Economic Regulatory
Agencies, 1993 (Fiscal Year, Full-time Equivalent
Employment)

Agency	Rank	# Employees
Federal Deposit Insurance Corporation	1	6,462
Patent and Trademark Office	2	4,863
Comptroller of the Currency	3	3,950
Securities and Exchange Commission	4	2,745
Federal Reserve Banks	5	2,477
Federal Communications Commission	6	1,782
Federal Energy Regulatory Commission	7	1,500
Federal Trade Commission	8	953
National Credit Union Administration	9	699
Department of Justice Antitrust Division	10	607

Source: Melinda Warren and James Lis, *Regulatory Standstill: Analysis of the 1993 Federal Regulatory Budget* (St. Louis, MO: Center for the Study of American Business, 1992).

SUBSIDIARY REGULATIONS

Regulation III, or *subsidiary regulation*, entails all regulatory activities accompanying Social Security, Medicare, Medicaid, Aid to Families with Dependent Children (AFDC), food stamps, veterans' benefits programs, Internal Revenue Service regulatory concerns, and categorical grant program regulations. Clientele of subsidiary regulations include individuals or state and local governments.

The general public has mixed feelings toward Regulation III. Americans would like to believe that there is no such thing as a free lunch. Freeloaders, welfare cheats, and food stamp chiselers bring on citizen suspicion, mistrust, and hostility. Most Americans do, however, consider Social Security, unemployment compensation, or veterans' benefits as legitimate. Unless there are clear and specific regulations for such benefit programs, the opportunities for cheating are virtually limitless, making the costs and benefits of Regulation III difficult to quantify. Programs range from deciding eligibility for benefit programs to providing equal sports opportunities for women in college and equal educational opportunities for the handicapped. Costs are largely intangible; the market value is not readily apparent.

Economic, social, and subsidiary regulations are diverse, contradictory, and value laden. The growth of administrative regulatory power changes responsibilities and relationships among branches and levels of government. Regulations control or restrict one's choices and/or behavior, and

TABLE 12–4   Top Ten Social Regulatory Agencies,
Ranked on Costs in Real Terms, 1993
(Fiscal Years, Millions of Constant 1987 Dollars)

Agency	Rank	Costs
Environmental Protection Agency	1	$3,643
Coast Guard	2	783
Food and Drug Administration	3	648
Federal Aviation Administration	4	504
Food and Safety Inspection Service	5	452
Nuclear Regulatory Commission	6	439
Animal and Plant Health Inspection Service	7	407
Bureau of Alcohol, Tobacco, and Firearms	8	300
Occupational Safety and Health Administration	9	236
Office of Surface Mining and Reclamation and Enforcement	10	217

Source: Melinda Warren and James Lis, *Regulatory Standstill: Analysis of the 1993 Federal Regulatory Budget* (St. Louis, MO: Center for the Study of American Business, 1992).

TABLE 12–5   Personnel Staffing for Top Ten Social Regulatory Agencies,
1993 (Fiscal Year, Full-time Equivalent Employment)

Agency	Rank	# Employees
Environmental Protection Agency	1	17,832
Coast Guard	2	13,261
Food and Safety Inspection Service	3	9,600
Food and Drug Administration	4	8,902
Federal Aviation Administration	5	6,552
Animal and Plant Health Inspection Service	6	6,000
Bureau of Alcohol, Tobacco, and Firearms	7	4,309
Agricultural Marketing Service	8	3,398
Nuclear Regulatory Commission	9	3,336
Equal Employment Opportunity Commission	10	3,071

Source: Melinda Warren and James Lis, *Regulatory Standstill: Analysis of the 1993 Federal Regulatory Budget* (St. Louis, MO: Center for the Study of American Business, 1992).

are blamed for all sorts of societal ills, including inflation, recession, the demise of the family, individual initiative, and the federal system. Despite criticisms, the societal conditions demanding counterbalance to the vast power that private corporations and industry exercise over the lives, health, safety, and happiness of Americans are still very much evident. In addition, nationwide polls indicate that the American public supports, generally, the concept of regulations.[19]

When the Reagan Administration came to power in 1981, one of its goals was to trim down the federal regulatory agencies. Attempts to "rein in the regulatory establishment," however, "virtually ceased in fiscal 1983."[20] In the first two years of the Administration, budgets and staffing were reduced across the board. But in the last six years of the Reagan Administration, expenditures for regulatory agencies (especially the Environmental Protection Agency) increased at a pace similar to the growth that took place under the Carter Administration. Staffing increased as well, but "has not yet returned to the previous growth rate."[21]

ADMINISTRATIVE RULES AND RULE-MAKING

Rule-making and adjudication are not the same process. Rule-making, in general, focuses on the future and is broad in scope. Adjudication is particular, focusing upon an instance in the present or the past. Prior to the adjudication of a person's rights, the individual is entitled to a hearing under the Due Process Clause of the Fifth Amendment for federal agencies and the Fourteenth Amendment for state agencies. The development of administrative rules follows the commercial development of the American west, tragedies of transportation accidents, development of the federal government as collector of revenues, government as benefit provider, and the populist rebuttal to the exploitation of the farmer by the rail trust.[22]

Regulatory law and administrative law, as we saw earlier, work in tandem, but are not the same thing. Congress does not like controversy; Congress is also a provincial political institution. In other words, members of Congress do not enjoy conflict-laden issues where they are likely to have constituents split over the solutions to a particular issue. Each member of Congress comes from a narrow, provincial, political base. Each member of Congress looks out for his or her district's narrow economic interests and not those of the entire nation. Partly because Congress is composed of politicians representing 535 political jurisdictions, they pass laws that do not speak very clearly. It is not difficult, therefore, to explain the presence of vague, ambiguous, and general laws that allow human discretion.

**FDA REQUIRES BEVERAGE INDUSTRY
TO LABEL THE REAL THING**

In order to implement provisions of the 1990 Nutrition Labeling Act requiring that the juice percentage be prominently displayed on the labels of beverages containing fruit or vegetable juice, the Food and Drug Administration (FDA) insists that the nation's beverage industry relabel thousands of juice products, ranging from sparkling ciders to wine coolers. The administrative rule is to clear up consumer confusion over how much juice they are getting in such products as juice cocktails and punches.

Beverage makers who sell pure juice benefit from the FDA rule as their products are on a more competitive footing with purveyors of heavily diluted juice look-alikes. The companies are required to list not only the total percentage of juice but also the juice percentages in blends. The juice-percentage rule forces some companies to rename brand products. Others have toned down the aggressiveness of their advertising and marketing strategies for certain juice blends and juice drinks with minimal juice contents.

Diluted beverages account for 40 percent of all juice products on the market. FDA estimated the costs of compliance at nearly $40 million, including $11 million for administrative expenses, $4 million for printing new labels, and $24 million for discarding old labels. The regulation affects at least 3,000 products. "Everyone is apprehensive of labeling becoming very specific," said Tom Berko, a beverage industry consultant. "The more restrictive the regulations, the harder it is to play marketing games."

Source: Bruce Ingersoll, "FDA to Propose Rules to Label Juice Products," *The Wall Street Journal,* July 1, 1991, pages B1, 6.

Administrative agencies serve to interpret the vagueness, ambiguity, and generality of these laws. For example, the FCC, by rule, restricts the number of commercial broadcasting stations a private corporation may operate. The IRS, by rule, determines which groups in society must pay or are exempted from paying taxes. The FCC creates communications law; the IRS makes tax law. Independent regulatory commissions, Cabinet agencies, independent agencies, public corporations, and the EOP have similar functions.

THE ADMINISTRATIVE PROCEDURE ACT

The Administrative Procedure Act, although not a comprehensive code of administrative procedure, provides a general framework of fundamental importance. The APA, in the minds of some authorities, serves as the "Magna Carta of Administrative Law." Regulatory law regulates citizen behaviors; administrative law oversees the administrative discretion of bureaucrats.

TYPES OF AGENCY RULES

There are four types of agency rules. Legislative or substantive rules, presuming they are authorized by statute, do not exceed or contradict the statute, and are applied according to correct procedure, having the force and effect of law. Interpretative rules advise clientele on what the agency interprets a statute or regulation to mean. Interpretative rules examine the construction of a law which an agency administers. Procedural rules regulate an agency's internal practices. All agencies establish rules governing their own procedures. General policy statements are philosophical commentary and are not accountable to the rule-making provisions of the APA. Procedural, interpretative, and general policy statements are published in the Federal Register.

Source: Stanley A. Reigel and P. John Owen, *Administrative Law: The Law of Government Agencies* (Ann Arbor, MI: Ann Arbor Science, The Butterworth Group, 1982), see Chapter 3: Rule-making, 39–59.

Judges interpret legal statements and prescribe the procedures that agencies, and their employees, follow. Judicial interpretation originates from Constitutions; primary, but not exclusive, origin for interpretation comes from due process clauses. Judges also interpret administrative procedure statutes, if applicable; some clauses within a statute require agencies to follow certain procedures, including conducting a full hearing of the concern. Administrative law, meanwhile, applies legal principles originating from statutes, common law, constitutions, and regulatory law.[23]

Public administrators, as implementors of regulatory law, implement rules. The terms rules and regulations are virtually synonymous. Unless rules are successfully undermined in a lawsuit as unconstitutional, rules have the force of law. What is a rule? The APA defines a rule as:

> *the whole or a part of an agency statement of general or particular applicability and future effect designed to implement, interpret, or prescribe law or policy or describing the organization, procedure, or practice requirements of an agency and includes the approval or prescription of the future of rates, wages, corporate or financial structures or reorganizations thereof, prices, facilities, appliances, services or allowances therefor or of valuations, costs, or practices bearing on any of the foregoing.[24]*

The first of the two types of rule-making delineated by the APA is informal or "notice and comment" rule-making. The characteristics of this procedure are advance notice and public participation. Notice of proposed rule-making gives the time, place, and nature of the rule-making proceeding, refers to the authority, or statute, under which the rule is proposed, and includes the terms or substance of the proposed rule or a description of the subjects and issues therein.

"On the record" formal rule-making occurs when a "trial-type" hearing precedes rules. The trial-type hearing is an adversarial process entailing production of evidence, testimony by witnesses, cross-examination, and representation by counsel. The more formal requirements apply when a statute determines that rules must be cited "on the record after opportunity for an agency hearing."

The *Federal Register* and the *Code of Federal Regulations* publish notices of proposed rule-making. The Federal Register Act of 1935 established a system of federal rules publication. The Act designated *the Federal Register* as the official publication of all federal rules, regulations, orders, and other documents of "general applicability and legal effect." On March 14, 1936, *the Federal Register* began publishing every day, Monday through Friday. In 1936, the Register published 2,619 pages of rules, orders, and other actions. In 1980, or more than 40 years later, the Register totaled more than 87,000 pages.[25] After each year passes, the issues of the Register are bound and indexed. The regulations published in *the Federal Register* for the preceding year are codified with regulations previously issued and still in effect. *The Code of Federal Regulations,* a collection of paperback books grouped together by agency, is divided into 50 titles, as each title more or less represents a particular agency or a broad subject area. Table 12–4 illustrates *the Federal Register* format.

RESTRAINT AND EXPANSION

Between 1970 and 1980, as measured in constant dollars, regulatory budgets nearly quadrupled. For example, during the decade of the 1970s, the FTC perceived its legislative mandate as a consumer policeman for the economy. For every six persons employed in federal regulatory activities in 1980 there were five employed in 1984. By 1988, the nation's federal regulatory agency will employ nine percent fewer persons than in 1980. The decline in regulatory staffing between 1980 and 1988 occurred in Consumer Safety and Health, Job Safety and Other Working Conditions, and Industry-Specific Regulation. With a 14 percent reduction in real terms from 1980 to 1984, regulatory budgets declined in the early 1980s.[26]

In the early 1980s President Reagan realized cuts in federal regulatory budgets, but these early reductions were more than countered by steady spending increases in the president's second term. In real dollars, the Federal Government spends 10 percent more on regulation in 1988 than was appropriated in 1980. The EPA, the largest of all regulatory agencies in terms of budgeting and staffing, experienced a 25 percent decline in spending on research and development in the 1981–1984 period, but Reagan was unable to convince members of Congress to keep EPA's regulatory budget at a low ebb. During the Reagan years, real spending for this agency

TABLE 12–6   Food and Drug Administration

Status of Certain Additional Over-the-Counter Drug Category II and III Active Ingredients 21 CFR Part 310 [Docket No. 9 1N-0505]

Agency: Food and Drug Administration, HHS.

Action: Notice of proposed rulemaking.

Summary: The Food and Drug Administration (FDA) is issuing a notice of proposed rulemaking stating that certain ingredients in over-the-counter (OTC) drug products are not generally recognized as safe and effective or are misbranded. FDA is issuing this notice of proposed rulemaking after considering the reports and recommendations of various OTC advisory review panels and public comments on the agency's proposed regulations, which were issued in the form of a tentative final monograph (proposed rule). Based on the absence of substantive comments in opposition to the agency's proposed nonmonograph status for these ingredients, as well as the failure of interested parties to submit new data or information to FDA pursuant to 21 CFR 330.10(a)(7)(iii), FDA has determined that the presence of these ingredients in an OTC drug product would result in that drug product not being generally recognized as safe and effective or would result in misbranding. This proposal is part of the ongoing review of OTC drug products conducted by FDA.

Dates: Written comments, objections, or requests for oral hearing on the proposal before the Commissioner of Food and Drugs by October 26, 1992. Written comments on the agency's economic impact determination by October 26, 1992.

Addresses: Written comments, objections, or requests for oral hearing to the Dockets Management Branch (HFA-305), Food and Drug Administration, rm. 1–23, 12420 Parklawn Dr., Rockville, MD 20857.

For Further Information, Contact: William E. Gilbertson, Center for Drug Evaluation and Research (HFD-810), Food and Drug Administration, 5600 Fishers Lane, Rockville, MD 20857, 301–295–8000.

Supplementary Information: In the Federal Register of November 7, 1990 (55 FR 46914), FDA published under §330.10(a)(7)(ii) (21 CFR 330.10(a)(7)(ii)), a final rule on the status of certain OTC drug Category II and III active ingredients.

Source: The Federal Register, Vol. 57, No. 165/Tuesday, August 25, 1992, page 38568.

increased by almost $1 billion, an increase of 63 percent. Growth in regulatory spending during the Reagan era increased by 62 percent in Finance and Banking, 34 percent in General Business, and 30 percent in Environment and Energy.

Therefore, the 1980s constitute an era of regulatory contradictions, restraint, and expansion in the financing of regulations and the work force committed to such activities. For example, in General Business, the Antitrust Division of the Department of Justice and the FTC had real spending

TABLE 12-7   Federal Preemption and Public Choices of Federal, State, or Local Regulation

| Issue Question[1] | Percent Selecting Government That Should Regulate | | | |
	Federal	State	Local	DK/NA
Should the federal government regulate the listing of health risks on the labels of food products sold throughout the country, or should each state government regulate the listing of health risks on the labels of food products sold in its state?	75	18	—	8
Should the federal government regulate banks so as to let them operate freely across state lines throughout the country, or should each state government regulate banks that operate in its state so as to be able to limit or keep out banks from other states if it wishes to do so?	50	38	—	12
Should the federal government regulate companies that sell life, fire, property, casualty, and automobile insurance throughout the country, or should each state government regulate the companies that sell these types of insurance in its state?	37	51	—	12

Should the federal government regulate the use of pesticides on home lawns and public grounds throughout the country, or should each local government regulate the use of pesticides on home lawns and public grounds in its community?	37	—	52	11
Should the federal government regulate the location and building of low-income housing in communities throughout the country, or should each local government regulate the location and building of low-income housing in its community?	21	—	72	7

[1]These questions were prefaced by the following statement: Now I would like to ask you about federal preemption. Preemption means that the federal government in Washington takes a power from state or local government in order to use that power itself. For example, the federal government has preempted the power of state and local governments to regulate prescription drugs, airlines, and atomic energy. Therefore, these things are regulated by the federal government. For each of the following, I would like to ask whether you think the federal government should take over the regulation of the activity in order to set uniform rules across the country, or whether you think state or local governments should continue to regulate the activity, each in its own way.

Source: U.S. Advisory Commission on Intergovernmental Relations, *Changing Public Attitudes on Governments and Taxes 1992* (Washington, DC, 1992).

ADMINISTRATIVE RESPONSIBILITY

Administrative responsibility incorporates accountability, competence, fairness, and responsiveness. Accountability is answerability, answering, in particular, to someone or something outside the organization itself. Accountability also refers to direction and control, for if things go wrong, someone is held liable. Competence implies expertise, prudence, and care for consequences rather than negligence. Recognizable objective standards guide the formulation and implementation of public policy. Fairness combines the individual concern for due process with the notion of justice and is designed to protect the individual from arbitrary and capricious decisions. Responsiveness acknowledges an organization's yielding to citizen demands for policy change and entails initiation of proposed solutions for problems.

Source: Paul N. Tramontozzi with Kenneth W. Chilton, *U.S. Regulatory Agencies Under Reagan, 1980–1988* (St. Louis, MO: Center for the Study of Business, 1987), 11–14.

---

cut by more than 25 percent since 1980, whereas the International Trade Administration and the International Trade Commission had a boost in real spending by 139 percent since 1980. The inconsistent efforts of the Reagan Administration to reduce the size and costs of the regulatory establishment placed additional emphasis upon improving the substantive aspects of the statutes themselves, which empower agencies to make regulations. In other words, the *quality* of regulations are as important as the *quantity* of them.[27]

ADMINISTRATIVE RESPONSIBILITY: PROFESSIONALISM, PARTICIPATION, AND PUBLICITY

In casting about for answers to the question of responsibility, we are at the outset likely to come across the phrase, "the public interest." Many see the entire solution to the question neatly encapsulated in this phrase, as though an administrator need only resolve to serve the public interest and his or her problems concerning responsibility will vanish.

This solution, like so many other easy solutions to difficult problems, only raises more questions than it answers. The most basic is this: Just what is the public interest? Walter Lippman once claimed that "The public interest may be what men would choose if they saw clearly, thought rationally, and acted disinterestedly and benevolently."[28] This leaves us with the task of defining "clear" vision and "rational" thought, concepts that, in practice, seem obviously susceptible to varying interpretations. Even deciding what course of action is truly "benevolent" and "disinterested" may produce more controversy than it settles.

TYPES OF ACCOUNTABILITY

There are four types of accountability. Bureaucratic accountability entails an organized and legitimate superior/subordinate relationship with close supervision or a surrogate system of standard operating procedures or clearly stated rules and regulations. Legal accountability, similar to bureaucratic accountability, is grounded upon relationships between a controlling party outside the agency, typically composed of lawmakers, and members of the organization. Bureaucratic accountability portrays a hierarchical relationship, grounded upon the ability of supervisors to reward or punish subordinates, while legal accountability presents a relationship of two relatively autonomous parties, involving a formal or implied trustee agreement between the public agency and its legal monitor. Professional accountability relies upon skilled and expert employees for providing appropriate solutions. Deference to expertise within the agency is the key to professional accountability. Political accountability asks: Whom does the public administrator represent? The general public, elected officials, agency heads, agency clientele, special interest groups, and future generations constitute potential constituencies. The key relationship is between the public administrator and his or her constituents.

Source: Barbara S. Romzek and Melvin J. Dubnick, "Accountability in the Public Sector: Lessons from the Challenger Tragedy," *Public Administration Review,* vol. 47, no. 3 (May/June, 1987), 227–238.

Political scientist Glendon Shubert grappled with the concept of public interest in a book bearing that title. After exhaustively examining the subject he wrote, "It may be somewhat difficult for some readers to accept the conclusion that there is no public interest theory worthy of the name."[29]

Another maxim that often presents itself is "following one's conscience." This, too, fails to furnish a usable guideline. The enforcers of the Inquisition who burned thousands of heretics at the stake felt they were following the most lofty appeals to conscience. The same can be said for so many other appalling actions that people have perpetrated on others. As Carl Friedrich has noted, "Autocratic and arbitrary abuse of power has characterized the officialdom of a government service bound only by the dictates of conscience."[30]

But while Friedrich rules out the use of conscience as a means of ensuring responsibility, he does have some positive ideas to offer in its place.

We have a right to call such a policy irresponsible if it can be shown that it was adopted without proper regard to the existing sum of human knowledge concerning the technical issues involved; we have also a right to call it irresponsible if it can be shown that it was adopted without proper regard for existing preference in the community and more particularly its prevailing majority.[31]

In keeping with this admonition, Friedrich sees the solution to the question of administrative responsibility lying in two areas: professionalism and participation. Professionals generally have been conditioned to uphold certain standards, and they usually subscribe to a code of ethics that governs the practice of their profession. As Friedrich sees it, professionalism constitutes something of an "inner check" on administrative irresponsibility. Participation, meanwhile, means that administrators must consult more and more interests and listen to more and more points of view. Allowing divergent parties to share in decision-making should make that process less arbitrary and subjective and more responsive and responsible.

To Friedrich's twin safeguards of *professionalism* and *participation* can be added a third protective device: *publicity*. Directing the public spotlight onto administrative decision-making should make such decision-making more responsible. Secrecy has rarely led to improved administrative decisions or better administrative behavior. Professionalism, participation, and publicity do not in themselves guarantee responsible administration. Professionals can act irresponsibly, and shared decision-making can produce irresponsible decisions. Publicity can, on occasion, distort an administrator's perspective, because what is immediate "good press" is not always most beneficial to the public. These caveats notwithstanding, these three "Ps" presented above—professionalism, participation, and publicity—provide a basis for better public management. As they become more and more a part of bureaucratic behavior, such behavior may move closer toward meeting the desires and demands of the American people.

Summary

- The fragmentation and personalism of our political system makes the typical administrative agency something of an isolated entity, continually developing and maintaining sources of support. Administrators must assume an activist role in developing that support. *Size, dispersion, degree of organization,* and *degree of ardor* contribute to the effectiveness of an agency's clientele.

- *Advisory committees, complaint handling,* and *public hearings* play roles in developing strategies for support by clientele. Advisory committees serve as a two-way transmission system for communication, bringing clients' concerns to the agency and bringing the agency's problems to the clients.

- Two current trends point towards increasing the amount of clientele capture of public organizations. The structure and orientation of public agencies based on *interest groups* and the *administrative decentralization* of program functions enhance the power of clientele.

- The full scope of regulatory power, in addition to the power to formulate rules, includes the authority for interpreting laws and regulations, enforcing rules and regulations, trying cases concerning violations of those rules, holding hearings for investigating and adjudicating such circumstances, and imposing sanctions on violators. *Administrative regulatory power* combines legislative, executive, and judicial powers.
- *The Federal Register* provides a uniform system for making available to the public regulations and legal notices issued by Federal departments and agencies. The *Register* includes Presidential proclamations and Executive Orders and Federal agency documents having general applicability and legal effect.
- *The Code of Federal Regulations* is a codification of the general and permanent rules published in *The Federal Register* by the Executive departments and agencies of the Federal Government. *The Federal Register* and *The Code of Federal Regulations* are used in tandem to determine the latest version of any given rule or regulation.
- Administrative power expands as the power and responsibilities of government expand. An industrialized, urbanized, interdependent society requires a more active role for government. The United States is a regulatory state where virtually all activities of organizations and individuals are part of administrative regulations and controls. There are three types of regulatory behaviors: *economic, social,* and *subsidiary.*
- *Rule-making* and *adjudication* are not the same. Rule-making is general and focuses upon the future. Adjudication is particular, focusing upon the present or the past. Administrative agencies interpret vagueness, ambiguity, and generality of laws; public administrators, as implementors of regulatory law, interpret rules. The terms "rules" and "regulations" are synonymous. There are four types of agency rules: legislative, or substantive, rules; interpretative rules; procedural rules; and general policy statements.
- *Administrative responsibility* entails the ideas of accountability, competence, fairness, and responsiveness. Executive control, pluralism, professionalism, and representative bureaucracy are especially important for achieving administrative responsibility. There are four types of accountability: bureaucratic, legal, professional, and political.
- *Professionalism, participation,* and *publicity* contribute significantly to administrative responsibility and provide a sound basis for better public management.

The following case portrays the social regulatory process in action. FDA's efforts to regulate the public's consumption of saccharin are diverse, perhaps contradictory, and certainly value laden. Do the regulators go too far?

CASE STUDY

FDA Tries to Ban Saccharin[32]

Some observers have noted that Americans are obsessed with the desire to be thin, as long as thinness can be gained without exercising or controlling the amount of food consumed. The annals of American regulatory history are replete with examples of the seemingly endless gullibility of the overweight and their willingness to purchase any product offered, no matter how absurd or occasionally dangerous it may be, when promised thinness and fitness with no effort. Private enterprise has not been hesitant in supplying the gullible with such products.

During the 1950s the weight conscious could consume soda pop, cookies, cakes, canned fruit, Kool Aid, gelatin, candy, and countless other food products, all sweetened with the original sugar replacement, cyclamates, and still reach the promised land of thinness. And consume they did. The diet food and drink industry became a billion-dollar industry and was rapidly growing when it ran afoul of the Delaney Amendment and the FDA.

The Delaney Amendment is one of the most controversial laws currently in existence at the federal level. It was added to the Food, Drug, and Cosmetic Act in 1958 at the insistence of former Representative James Delaney (D-NY). It specifies that "no additive shall be deemed safe . . . if it is found, after tests which are appropriate for the evaluation of the safety of food additives, to induce cancer in man or animal." The FDA, of course, is required to ensure that all food additives are safe and to ban those that are not. Usually there is considerable room for agency discretion as to whether an additive should be banned or not since "safety" is a relative term and subject to interpretation. The Delaney Amendment, however, seemingly leaves little room for such discretion: if a substance has been proven to induce cancer in man or animal, it is not safe, and the FDA must ban it.

There were already hundreds of these additives being used prior to 1958 when Congress finally required manufacturers to prove the safety of an additive before putting it in food. Since manufacturers were not required to test those additives and since the FDA had neither staff nor time to do so, the GRAS (Generally Recognized As Safe) list was developed. Additives in long use were automatically put on it and could be used in food. The presence of an additive on the GRAS list did not mean that it was safe; it meant that nobody had proved that it was not. Both cyclamates and saccharin were on the GRAS list.

The first disturbing research results concerning cyclamates had reached the FDA as early as 1954 when a study by the Food Nutrition Board of the National Academy of Sciences (NAS) reported that test results indicated a highly suspicious frequency of lung, kidney, and skin cancers among laboratory animals tested with cyclamates. Sporadically, until 1968, NAS continued to report research results that raised questions concerning cyclamates' safety. In 1968, FDA chemists tested cyclamates on chicken embryos and reported a direct correlation between cyclamates and birth defects, deformities, and chromosome change. Convinced by mounting evidence, the FDA proposed to ban cyclamates as additives.

The reaction to the proposed ban ranged from approval to outright dismay. The most disbelieving and dismayed were the major producers of diet soft drinks and the consumers of those beverages. Demands for a Congressional investigation or for presidential intervention and accusations that the FDA was un-American reverberated throughout Washington and the country. The FDA persisted and cyclamates were banned as a food additive in October, 1969. The controversy surrounding that decision has not yet been settled. There were, however, three factors present at that time which made the decision to ban cyclamates more feasible than the current controversy surrounding the saccharin ban: First, there was the ready availability of saccharin as a cheap and effective substitute; second, the sugar industry, more powerful and well organized than at present, rallied to the cause; and third, the general attitude toward government regulation, both in Congress and among the public, was far more supportive and favorable than at present.

Exit Cyclamates, Enter Saccharin

Cyclamates are banned. Long live saccharin! Food producers quickly switched to the use of saccharin and soon it was found in the same vast number of products as cyclamates had been: sugarless gum, toothpaste, lip balm, mouthwash, soda pop, cookies, cake mixes, and countless other food products. As later research was to indicate, an age group that is one of the heaviest consumers of saccharin consists of children under the age of ten. It is estimated that one-third of the children in this age group consume saccharin, and their consumption of it has increased by 160 percent since 1972. Furthermore, the highest percentage of saccharin users by sex is scored by males under the age of 10. Saccharin, as anyone's grandmother will tell you, has been around and used for a long time. Doubts about its safety, which grandmother may not tell you, have been around nearly as long.

By the early 1970s, research interest in saccharin was revived, and the FDA began receiving research reports from independent, scientific studies that raised questions about saccharin's safety. In 1971, tests by the Wisconsin Alumni Research Foundation indicated that seven out of 14 male rats fed saccharin as five percent of their diets for two years developed bladder tumors. The FDA's initial response was to remove saccharin from the GRAS list and to require that all products containing saccharin carry a warning label, cautioning that the product should be used only by those who must restrict their intake of sugar.

On the basis of a 1973 FDA study which indicated that saccharin could cause cancer in rats, the FDA requested the National Academy of Sciences' National Research Council to review the evidence. In 1974, the Academy reported back that it could not conclusively state that saccharin caused cancer in laboratory tests on rats and raised the possibility that the carcinogenic agent might be OTS (orthotoluene sufonamide), an impurity found in saccharin. The groundwork for the controversial Canadian research study was laid.

FDA scientists received and began studying the Canadian report in early 1977. That study began in 1974 and ran for two and one-half years. It indicated that of 200 animals fed OTS-free saccharin, 21 developed bladder tumors; none of the animals fed OTS developed such tumors. The study further indicated that second generation rats whose mothers had been exposed to saccharin during pregnancy showed a similar high rate of cancer. The Canadian study was the third, two-generation study to produce evidence that saccharin is carcinogenic in rats. Despite considerable debate and misgivings over the results, methods, and conclusions of the study, a panel of FDA scientists recommended that saccharin be removed from the GRAS list and banned as a food additive.

On March 9, 1977, former FDA commissioner, Sherwin Gardner, announced that the FDA proposed to ban saccharin as a food additive, effective in mid-July, 1977. The proposed ban would have eliminated the use of saccharin in foods, beverages, and cosmetics likely to be ingested and in drugs where it was used only to improve taste. It would have permitted continued marketing of saccharin as a single-ingredient drug available without prescription, provided that manufacturers proved it was medically effective in controlling diabetes or obesity.

The FDA announcement of the proposed ban immediately generated a storm of resentment and resistance which made the reactions to the cyclamate ban appear mild in comparison. The diet soda and food industry created the Calorie Control Council to act as the spearhead of a concerted lobbying effort to forestall the ban. The CCC ran two-page advertisements in major U.S. newspapers urging concerned readers to write their Congressmen. Members of Congress were flooded with constituent mail and phone calls protesting the ban. The first official congressional response took the form of "routine" oversight hearings by the Health Committee of the House Committee on Foreign and Interstate Commerce.

Regulatory Issues

The issues raised at those hearings were the ones that were to dominate the continuing debate over the FDA ban, and, in a broader sense, are recurrent themes in many conflicts involving government regulation. The first major issue concerned the validity of the scientific evidence on which the ban was to be based and, particularly, the experimental methods used to test saccharin. To nonscientists, the contention raised by industry groups that "a human being would have to drink 500 cans of diet pop a day to consume the equivalent of what those unfortunate Canadian rats did," had at least superficial validity. FDA scientists and other researchers defended the method, but the procedure was clearly baffling to many members of the public, the press, and Congress, in particular.

The second issue involved the lack of agreement among scientists and health professionals on the interpretation of the data, even if it were valid. FDA scientist, Dr. Richard Bates, contended that if the Canadian data were applied to humans, the " 'maximum level of risk' to humans in developing bladder cancer would be four cases [of cancer] per 1000 population if 10 cans of diet soda a day were drunk over a lifetime, and four cases [of cancer] per 10,000 population if only one can a day were drunk." Other scientists were equally adamant that banning saccharin would cause greater damage to the public health since diabetics would turn to sugar, with far more certain damage to their lives and health.

The final issue was public resentment at one more unnecessary violation of freedom and individual rights. Undeterred, the FDA held public hearings, as required by the Federal Administrative Procedure Act, on May 18 and 19, 1977. The hearings, as is frequently the case, turned up little new evidence, but permitted a thorough airing of the issues. The report from OTA was equally inconclusive. The OTA panel of scientists agreed that saccharin was a potential carcinogen, but disagreed as to how serious a risk was involved in its continued use. Public opposition, however, had not abated, and Congressional intervention appeared increasingly likely.

Specialists versus Generalists

Various bills were introduced in the Senate to postpone the ban. Congress intervened, however, and the FDA did not impose the ban. On November 4, 1977, Congress passed legislation which delayed the ban for 18 months and required that in the interim, new studies be performed by the National Academy of Sciences on both saccharin, specifically, and food additives in general. The FDA and the National Cancer Institute were also instructed to study the actual human impact of saccharin use. The only consolation that public health interest groups received from the legislation was a requirement that during the moratorium, all products containing saccharin carry a warning label and all retail stores selling such products post clearly visible and readable warning signs.

In November, 1978, the NAS released its first report on saccharin and more or less affirmed the previous research findings. It agreed that saccharin was a weak carcinogen and that it promoted the development of cancer initiated by other substances. The NAS report also pointed out that there was no scientific evidence for the claimed medical benefits of saccharin for diabetics or the obese. Beyond that, however, the NAS would not go. It made no recommendations for FDA action and concluded that the ultimate judgment must be made through the socio-political process.

If the administrative process is frequently slow, the political or, more aptly, the legislative process can be even more so. The moratorium expired on May 23, 1979; Congress was still trying to decide if the entire catalog of federal food regulation law should be revised. The FDA chose the path of least congressional resistance. Although technically in violation of the law, the FDA put a hold on the saccharin action until Congress could decide its preference.

In early 1980, three new scientific studies on saccharin were released. Despite claims by the diet food industry, the studies failed to give saccharin a clean bill of health, and were able to ascertain only that while overall there seemed to be a lack of significant relationship between saccharin consumption and urinary tract cancer, for some groups of the population—children, young women, and pregnant women—danger was more pronounced. Finally, in June, 1980, Congress voted to extend the moratorium until June 30, 1981. In July, 1981, Congress extended the moratorium for two more years.

The attempt by the FDA to ban saccharin illustrates many of the major aspects of the contemporary regulatory process and the circumstances in which regulatory agencies must operate. Although Congress creates the agencies and passes the legislation which they must enforce, agencies cannot always rely on Congressional support in enforcing the legislation if the rules they promulgate antagonize powerful interest groups or run counter to public opinion.

Many regulatory decisions also involve complex technical and scientific questions on which there may be little or no agreement among the experts. In such cases, the agency must make decisions on less than totally complete evidence, based on its expert assessment of that evidence. Regulatory decisions frequently involve more than one administrative agency, and although in the saccharin ban the agencies were in basic agreement, just as frequently disagreements occur and jurisdictional battles result.

The saccharin ban illustrates the ways in which the much criticized slowness of the regulatory process results from two major causes: procedural requirements such as notice, required hearings, and weighing the evidence; and political reality—opposition and resistance that delay regulatory action. In the end and regardless of the ultimate decision made on saccharin, the case study indicates the impact that regulatory action or inaction can have on the lives and health of individuals and on the business community.

QUESTIONS AND INSTRUCTIONS

1. To whom are the FDA regulators accountable?
2. Administrative power expands as the power and responsibilities of government expand. In cases like this one, how much power should FDA regulators possess?
3. Clientele groups were an omnipresent factor in the FDA's decision-making processes concerning the saccharin ban. What rights should clientele have in the regulatory process?
4. What roles, if any, do partisan, policy, and systems politics play in the saccharin ban controversy?
5. In a regulatory case such as this one, do the "specialists," or scientists, possess too much influence? Why or why not?
6. Do you believe freedom and individual rights were jeopardized in the FDA's attempt to ban saccharin?
7. If regulatory agencies do not protect consumers and the public from unsafe or unhealthy products, who will?

8. Regulatory decisions may reflect the most extreme and unrealistic assumptions about the problem's potential social significance. Was this assertion a reality in the FDA's deliberations over banning saccharin? Why or why not?

9. Having read this case study, do you believe regulations are a positive or negative feature of modern society? Why or why not?

ENDNOTES

1. Morton Grodzins, "The Federal System," in *Goals for Americans: The Report of the President's Commission on National Goals* (Englewood Cliffs, NJ: Prentice-Hall, 1960), 274.

2. Francis E. Rourke, *Bureaucracy, Politics, and Public Policy* (Boston: Little, Brown, 1969), 12.

3. Rourke, *Bureaucracy, Politics, and Public Policy*, 103.

4. *New York Times*, 3 December 1970.

5. *New York Times*, 4 March 1972.

6. Leonard Sloane, "Corporate Ombudsmen Respond to Consumers," *New York Times*, 21 March 1971, Business and Finance Section.

7. Diogenes [pseud.], *The April Game* (Chicago: Playboy Press, 1973), 6–7.

8. Philip Selznick, *TVA and the Grass Roots* (Berkeley, CA: University of California Press, 1949).

9. David Truman, *Administrative Decentralization: A Study of the United States Department of Agriculture* (Chicago: University of Chicago Press, 1940).

10. Florence Heffron with Neil McFeeley, *The Administrative Regulatory Process* (New York: Longmans, 1983), Chapter 1: Scope and Impact of Administrative Regulation, 1–23.

11. Douglas Costle, "In Defense of the Public Service," *Public Administration Times*, May 1, 1980, 3.

12. Heffron with McFeeley, *The Administrative Regulatory Process*, 6.

13. Melinda Warren and Kenneth Chilton, *The Regulatory Legacy of the Reagan Revolution: An Analysis of 1990 Federal Regulatory Budgets and Staffing* (St. Louis, MO: Center for the Study of Business, 1989), 9–12.

14. David Warner, "Regulations' Staggering Costs," *Nation's Business*, Vol. 80, No. 6 (June 1992), 50–53.

15. Douglas R. Wholey and Susan M. Sanchez, "The Effects of Regulatory Tools on Organizational Populations," *Academy of Management Review*, Vol. 16, No. 4 (October 1991), 743–767.

16. Melinda Warren and James Lis, *Regulatory Standstill: Analysis of the 1993 Federal Regulatory Budget* (St. Louis, MO: Center for the Study of American Business, 1992), 1–2, 5, 7–9.

17. Wholey and Sanchez, *op. cit.*

18. *Ibid.*, 13–16.

19. Heffron with McFeeley, *The Administrative Regulatory Process*, see Chapter 13: The Consequences of Regulation, 347–371.

20. Warren and Chilton, *1989 Federal Regulatory Budgets and Staffing: Effects of the Reagan Presidency* (St. Louis, MO: Center for the Study of Business, 1988), 4.
21. *Ibid.*
22. James T. O'Reilly, *Administrative Rule Making: Structuring, Opposing, and Defending Federal Agency Regulations* (New York: McGraw–Hill), 4–6.
23. Lief H. Carter, *Administrative Law and Politics: Cases and Comments* (Boston: Little, Brown, and Company, 1983), 14–39.
24. Administrative Procedure Act, P.L. 404, 60 Stat. 237(1946), 5 U.S.C.A. 551.
25. William F. West, *Administrative Rule-making: Politics and Processes* (Westport, CT: Greenwood Press, 1985), 17.
26. Murray L. Weidenbaum and Ronald J. Penoyer, *The Next Step in Regulatory Reform: Updating the Statutes* (St. Louis, MO: Center for the Study of Business, 1983), 24–32.
27. Paul N. Tramontozzi with Kenneth W. Chilton, *U.S. Regulatory Agencies Under Reagan, 1980–1988* (St. Louis, MO: Center for the Study of Business, 1987), 11–14.
28. Walter Lippman, *The Public Philosophy* (Boston: Little, Brown, 1955), 42.
29. Glendon A. Shubert, Jr., *The Public Interest* (New York: Free Press, 1952), 223.
30. Carl Friedrich, "Public Policy and the Nature of Administrative Responsibility" in *The Politics of the Federal Bureaucracy*, edited by Alan A. Altshuler. (New York: Dodd, Mead, 1968), 417.
31. *Ibid.*
32. Florence Heffron with Neil McFeeley, *The Administrative Regulatory Process* (New York: Longmans, 1983), Chapter 1: Scope and Impact of Administrative Regulation, pages 12–16. Reprinted with permission of Longman, Inc. See also Mark Link, "Proposed Saccharin Ban Causes Controversy," *Congressional Quarterly*, March 26, 1977, 540–541; R. Jeffrey Smith, "NAS Saccharin Report Sweetens FDA Position, But Not by Much," *Science*, November 24, 1978, 852; Elizabeth Wehr, "Congress Plans Major Review of Food Laws," *Congressional Quarterly*, February 10, 1979, 233–234; "Saccharin: Where Do We Go From Here?," *FDA Consumer*, April, 1978, 18; "Saccharin Ban Delay?," *Congressional Quarterly*, June 11, 1977, 1164.

$\star\ \star\ \star$

INDEX